DATE DUE			

The Right Time

By Harry Golden

Only in America

For 2¢ Plain

Enjoy, Enjoy!

Five Boyhoods, *with Howard Lindsay, Walt Kelly, John Updike,*
   William Zinsser, and Harry Golden

Carl Sandburg

Forgotten Pioneer

You're Entitle'

Mr. Kennedy and the Negroes

So What Else Is New?

The Spirit of the Ghetto, *with Hutchins Hapgood*

Ess, Ess, Mein Kindt

A Little Girl Is Dead

The Best of Harry Golden

   and

The Right Time

The Right Time

An Autobiography
by Harry Golden

G. P. Putnam's Sons

NEW YORK

PRINTED IN THE UNITED STATES OF AMERICA

This book would have been impossible except for the work of my eldest son, Richard Goldhurst, who arranged my material chronologically and edited all my writings.

This book is dedicated to the people who eased my way in Charlotte, North Carolina. I am fortunate that they are so numerous:

Dr. George Abernathy, Fred Alexander, Kelly Alexander, Father Cuthbert Allen, Mayor Herbert Baxter, Judge J. Spencer Bell, Mack Bell, Dr. Thom Blair, I. D. Blumenthal, Legette Blythe, Ty Boyd, Elizabeth Brice, Dr. Claude Broach, Mayor Stan Brookshire, Anita Stewart Brown, Cyrus B. Campbell, Marion Cannon, Hermann E. Cohen, Charles Crutchfield, Jonathan Daniels, Burke Davis, Harriet Doar, Mayor Ben Douglas, Tom Fesperman, Leo Finman, Dr. Jack Freedland, William Friday, Hilbert Fuerstman, Hoyt Galvin, Kays Gary, Rabbi Israel J. Gerber, Dr. Billy Graham, Dr. Frank P. Graham, Brodie Griffith, Arthur Goodman, Dr. Warner Hall, Dr. Reginald Hawkins, Rabbi Michael Hecht, Judge Fred Helms, Rabbi Nathan Hershfield, George P. Houston, Martha Williamson Huntley, George M. Ivey, Jay Jenkins, Ambassador Herschel V. Johnson, Charles Raper Jonas, Reverend Joseph Kellerman, Jimmy Kilgo, Walter Klein, Sol Levine, John "Red" Lisk, Police Chief Frank Littlejohn, David M. McConnell,

Elizabeth McGriff, Katherine McIntyre, Judge James B. McMillan, Joseph and Pearl Morrison, Allen Newcomb, Judge John J. Parker, Dr. Ernest F. Patterson, Bert and Billie Raff, Moses Richter, Ken Robertson, Sanford and Elizabeth Rosenthal, Dr. Otho Ross, Carl and Paula Sandburg, Governor Terry Sanford, Dr. Paul Sanger, Julian Scheer, Governor W. Kerr Scott, Hal Sieber, Al Smith, A. E. Spears, Morris Speizman, Maureen Titlow, Hal Tribble, David and Bea Wallas, Dr. Raymond M. and Julie Wheeler.

Illustrations follow page 226.

PART I

Yesterday is for regret
Tomorrow is for grief.
The time for laughter,
The time for laughter,
The right time, is now.

—Ballad from the Yiddish theater

Chapter 1

In February, 1968, I decided to close down the *Carolina Israelite,* the personal journal which I had published for the last twenty-six years in Charlotte, North Carolina. Carey McWilliams and James Storrow of the *Nation* undertook to fulfill the obligation to my subscribers as well as to furnish me with a page in their magazine from time to time. It was the easiest and quickest, if saddest, business transaction I ever completed. The lawyers never had a chance to raise their voices.

I readied my last issue, and I suppose the word got around. It was gratifying to know that my closing down disappointed some. On February 25, Douglas Robinson of the New York *Times* came to Charlotte for an interview, which was published the next day. It was the first public announcement that the *Carolina Israelite* was defunct, down-and-out.

People called and wrote to ask if it was really true, and I answered, yes, it was true. One of the letters was from then Vice President Hubert Humphrey:

DEAR HARRY:
   What's this I hear about you closing down THE CAROLINA ISRAELITE? This whole world of ours will never be the same if you do that, but I can well understand that there comes a time when a fellow wants to take it a little easier; in fact, I am beginning to feel that way myself. These are the most difficult and trying of days.
   I have just finished reading your interview in the New York

11

Times today. As always, you seem to get right to the point and your comments are filled with provocative thought and revealing insights.

Best of all, however, is your good cheer, your sense of humor, and your deep and abiding faith in our country. You are like spring tonic to me. I always feel better when I think of you and read what you have to say. God bless you.

Sincerely,
HUBERT H. HUMPHREY

The Vice President's message made me smile, not so much from his sentiments, which touched me, of course, but from the memory of the first letter he sent me.

In the July–August, 1959, issue of the *Israelite*, I devoted a front-page editorial to the names of Presidential candidates. I discoursed on how I thought Paul V. McNutt would have been Franklin D. Roosevelt's running mate in 1944 but for his name:

> People just won't vote for a man named McNutt. Names like this upset the taxi driver and the barber and the suburban housewife, those paragons of wisdom. But Adlai Stevenson can count himself a little more secure as a possible candidate. "Adlai" though an uncommon name, is still in the Bible. The fellow who is in real bad trouble is Hubert *Humphries*. His name is not in the Bible and the taxi driver usually makes jokes about the name "Hubert." Humphries would do well to change his name to "Joe." But as far as names go, Jack Kennedy is in the best shape, but he'd be in even better shape if he anglicized his name to Goldberg.

After the issue reached its subscribers, I received a letter from the United States Senate Committee on Government Operations:

DEAR MR. GOLDEN:

I read with enjoyment your editorial on the names of presidential candidates. I do not know who Hubert or Joe Humphries is, but I do know a Humphrey who will give them a real run for their money.

Sincerely yours,
HUBERT H. HUMPHREY

Thus the joy of a personal journal. I could always accommodate my own mistakes, for they all became grist for my mill.

I had many reasons for suspending publication. Chief of these reasons was the expense. It is cheaper to open a Cadillac franchise these days than to publish a magazine. We can send astronauts through space, pave highways over which cars six abreast can traverse at 70 miles an hour, build skyscrapers which become soaring towers of glass, but no one has managed to invent a cheap aluminum printing press on which a cranky editor can grind out his opinions.

Roughly, I spent $62,000 of my own money to keep the paper alive in the last three years, and I was approaching an age where this expenditure was foolish. I was trying to swim against the tide. Newspapers, big-city newspapers, have been folding right and left for the last decade, unwept, unmourned, and never missed.

Nor was I sure the *Carolina Israelite* had a role in the crucial decade ahead of us. The romance has gone from the civil rights movement. It went out the day the black militant came in, the day the nice suburban neighbor began to complain, "What in the world do *they* want now?" There is nothing funny or amusing about the struggle of Negroes for equality. No doubt the struggle is more heroic, no doubt the struggle demands greater devotion because it is more wearying, but I am not sure there is any humor left in it. Frankly, there is nothing funny about the Ku Klux Klan, which now dresses in suntans and helmet liners and, shoulder patches displayed, marches through the streets of Belmont, North Carolina, the home of a Roman Catholic College and monastery.

Yes, the struggle changed since I authored the Golden Vertical Negro Plan. The high-water mark of that struggle was the March on Washington in 1963. Since then even liberal suburbanites up North have come to see the school bus as the vanguard of desperate invaders.

The struggle is now infinitely more tedious, infinitely more in the balance, and will be infinitely longer because of the successive assassinations of Martin Luther King and Robert Kennedy.

I did not know Martin Luther King well. I met him several times, usually at meetings where we spoke to raise money for the Freedom Riders or the NAACP Legal Defense Fund, and I talked with him on the occasion of the March on Washington in 1963. When he was assassinated, I thought another accidental maniac had murdered a courageous leader.

When Bobby Kennedy, who *was* my friend and on whose behalf I had traversed all the B'nai B'riths in California, was murdered two months later, I realized the maniacs may have been accidental, but their purpose was not. The deaths of King and Kennedy changed the terrains where the armies contended.

Martin Luther King and Robert Kennedy were equally important heroes. They were heroes because they were leaders to whom all of us, white and black, could relate.

King's singular contribution was to prove that Christianity still had its uses. He was able to portray the civil rights movement as a moral drama. Americans always have trouble with moral difficulties. King had defined the struggle so that all could understand its moral implications. We want all moral issues to have two sides. Unfortunately for our ease of mind, the Bible says they do not. In short, Martin Luther King thought "white." He was the kind of colored hero white men could understand, and though white men understand Philip Randolph and Roy Wilkins and Whitney Young, these Negroes no longer control the colored constituency: Charlie Kenyatta and Eldridge Cleaver and Stokley Carmichael control it. Martin Luther King had a constituency, a constituency dispersed by his death. The difficulty in maintaining a dialogue with Stokley, Eldridge, and Charlie is, first, that we insist they speak our language, which they often choose not or cannot do, and, second, that they cease and desist telling us we are not nice people, which we indeed are not, though we want to hear we are. These Negro leaders—and almost all Negro leaders are in the mold of Malcolm X—have no intention of calling the mayor Mister Mayor; they have had to call too many unworthy whites Massah for too long to concern themselves with amenities.

The white man who could speak their language was Robert Kennedy, one of the few white men I ever met who could think "black." Kennedy and John Lindsay, mayor of New York, were the only two white men capable of telling a Negro ghetto to "cool it." Kennedy shared much with Martin Luther King. He, too, saw the issue as a moral issue. He once exclaimed to Governor Ross Barnett of Mississippi, who sent state troopers to deny James Meredith entry to the university, "But it's wrong!"

Where Martin Luther King chose religion as the vehicle which would unify black and white, Kennedy chose politics, elective office, pressure groups, lobbies. He won the California primary, in one instance, because he was able to recruit hundreds of Mexican farmworkers and weld them into political cells, telephoning

14

Mexican friends and neighbors, ringing doorbells, handing out foreign-language pamphlets. They worked for him because they knew he would deliver as he promised. In California, Kennedy set up the nucleus of a powerful minority bloc. Had he lived to become President, perhaps he would have so organized the country with nuclei intent on achieving law and justice in order to secure law and order.

With Martin Luther King gone, equity for all will not come through a religious crusade; with Kennedy gone, it will not come through political innovation. It will not happen that way now.

If the Second March on Washington, led by Dr. King's successor, Ralph Abernathy, could not prompt sympathy, let alone dictate legislation, then the *Carolina Israelite* was bound to be even less effective. I would have to recruit a new kind of subscriber, invent a new polemic in a new format. And then I would probably fail.

The struggle was lonelier for me. My friends and allies have gone. Adlai Stevenson died in London, and we had been good friends since I rode his campaign train through North Carolina. I myself underwent three serious operations which weakened me. I had no sooner recovered when the best friend any man ever had, Carl Sandburg, died at Connemara.

The last thing I did before I went to the hospital was dispatch all the letters Adlai had written me over the years to the authorized editors of the Stevenson correspondence in Chicago; one of the first things I did when I came back from Memorial Hospital was to agree to serve as one of Sandburg's literary executors.

I dwell on these matters because my publishing the *Carolina Israelite* is the only reason anyone would want to read my autobiography. As the reader gathers, I am proud of having published this paper, one of only two journals below the Mason-Dixon Line to applaud the 1954 decision of the United States Supreme Court outlawing school segregation (the other paper was the Louisville *Courier-Journal*). I gave up the *Israelite* not because the country was going to the dogs but because I was old and going broke and my old pals weren't there to cheer me on.

Publishing the *Carolina Israelite* made me a celebrity. The difference between fame and celebrity is the difference between fact and idea. Einstein, say, represents an idea about the universe. Harry Golden represents a fact about the way we live now.

I travel all over America lecturing. The bellhops, the airline ticketing agents, the cabdrivers say, "You're Harry Golden, aren't you? I saw you on the *Johnny Carson Show.*" Or they tell me the local newspaper carries my column. Or that their brother subscribed to my paper.

Most of the folks who are celebrities don't set out with that end in mind. After all, a celebrity has to have done *something.* Porfirio Rubirosa married rich women; Greta Garbo wanted to be alone. I became a celebrity after writing a book of editorials. We become celebrities—major or minor league celebrities—by virtue of the fact that life for all of us, the famous, the celebrated, and the anonymous, is prosaic. We transcribe erratic orbits like tramp stars. But the celebrity commands a focus because he or she appears to have invested life with purpose and invested it with the sweetest of all purposes—a certain intense devotion to the self as self and not as social integer. A celebrity is a person who willy-nilly affects people.

The *Carolina Israelite* consisted of two old houses, sitting side by side on Elizabeth Avenue near downtown Charlotte, North Carolina. The first house, which I always called the manse because of its white-pillared porch which was half as big as the house itself, contained the offices for my staff, editorial and administrative. I had a bedroom, a sitting room, a desk, a downstairs shower, and a cramped corner for my secretary. Upstairs I put our bookkeeper and the two advertising salesmen who sold space over the telephone. Next door, in the house I call the cottage because it has no veranda, was my machinery—the graphotype which made the plates, the speedomat which printed them, and the sealer which wrapped the paper for mailing.

While this describes the ordinary complex of any small publishing venture, still it was a tourist attraction. Charlotte is one of the convention centers of the South, entertaining delegates as varied as the textile manufacturers and American Legionnaires. Some of the folks liked to see the town. They hired a cab out to the Coliseum, which resembles a geodesic ice-cream cone; proceeded to Douglas Airport, where the bulldozers and backhoes forever plow to make more runways to accommodate more jets; and then the cabdriver returning his fares to the Barringer, or the Manger, or the Downtowner turned down Elizabeth Avenue and pointed to my place and introduced me as the "immigrunt feller who was on the *Person to Person* show and the best-seller list."

The place is empty now, a "for sale" sign on the front lawn signaling buyers. The machines are shipped away. My secretary rambles about the place alone, wondering what work is there for her to do.

There's this, I tell her, the autobiography.

I like to say I don't take myself seriously. In fact, I often say I would be in a hell of a lot of trouble if I ever did take myself seriously. These remarks win me indulgent smiles from the people I know and love. Of course, I take myself seriously.

Socrates argued that the unexamined life was not worth living, and I argue that the man who never thinks about himself seriously is not examining. But I never argue that I am a self-made man. Nobody is ever a self-made man, no matter how many disappointments he overcomes, no matter how many obstacles he climbs alone. Anyone who argues he is a self-made man is not taking himself or his fellows seriously.

A great many serious things happened to me. I want to detail as accurately as my memory serves what these events were. I want to describe the people who helped me and the people who hurt me, introduce you to the people who gave me my first ideas about the possibility of America and the people who put me in jail. My autobiography is about mothers and fathers and wives and sons and about the men who made these perilous times in which we live—the single taxers, the Jews, the civil rights leaders, the editors, and the publishers.

This book is about a certain time, too, about the time when New York was a city of foreigners, where a man could make $1,000,000 and a decade later have to grub for a little stake.

Perhaps one of the reasons for the phenomenon of the celebrity is that it is hard to be an American and have roots, roots in the sense of place and recognizable environment. The sales manager who grew up in Bangor lives today in Dubuque, and though he remembers Maine, those meadows now are filled with housing developments. The postbellum homes which lined Elizabeth Avenue in Charlotte when I first settled here—the homes with their pillars, wide porches, their dormer windows standing like sentinels over the street—are gone, their places filled by the new concrete that is Central Piedmont Community College.

As often as place changes, so is the self altered, an alteration not always of our own making. The Harry Golden who enjoyed an Orthodox Jewish boyhood on the Lower East Side of New York married an Irish Catholic girl when he went to Wall Street. The Harry Golden who corresponded with Presidential candidates was, before that, the broker from Larchmont, New York, who heard a judge sentence him to prison for mail fraud.

Chapter 2

My father was Leib Goldhirsch, a Hebrew teacher and the son of a Hebrew teacher. Leib was born in Mikulintsy, a village in eastern Galicia, then part of the Austro-Hungarian Empire, now in the USSR. His birthday was October 20, 1860, and I remember as a boy how proud I was to bring his birth certificate into the classroom and tell the teacher and my classmates my father was five years old when Lincoln was shot.

My father spent his youth and early adulthood in a *shtetl*, which was no more than a restricted ghetto for the Jews. He had a thorough education in Hebrew, which made him an important man in this little enclave, for his education automatically qualified him as an intellectual. He could teach in the *shtetl* school as long as he lived and never want. The Jews in this quasi suburb would always defer to him.

But as soon as he had a family, my father left Mikulintsy. Though there were no bars on the *shtetl,* still it was a cage. Austria-Hungary literally offered no opportunity for his children. They could not work as civil servants. They could not serve in any military rank higher than sergeant. They could not go into business. At best, they could become apothecaries and then only after expending considerable sums in bribery. In 1904 my father and my oldest brother, Jacob, who was then in his teens, left Mikulintsy for Winnipeg, Canada.

Landsleit made them choose Canada; *landsleit* is the reason most immigrants got anywhere. *Landsleit* is the collection of

19

friends, relatives, neighbors, who had arrived at someplace earlier. In our case, it was the Watermans who had emigrated in the previous decade and who helped finance my father's trip. Noah Waterman was an insurance man with Montreal's Sun Life Company. Other Watermans started a chain of five-and-ten-cent stores in Edmonton, Calgary, Moose Jaw, and Medicine Hat. My father might have made his home in Canada, but the intense cold brought on a serious eye affliction, and a doctor advised him to move farther south. My father and Jacob went to Minneapolis, then to Chicago, and when a job at the Educational Alliance opened up, both my father and brother went to New York City.

Jacob got a license and a pushcart and started peddling, and Leib taught Hebrew, and between them they saved enough money to pay the passage for my mother, my two sisters, and me. We traveled from Mikulintsy to Hamburg, where we spent three nights on cots in a huge barrackslike wharf. Though I was only two, I still have a vague recollection of the trip over on steerage. I can recall my sister Clara combing her hair with a fine-tooth comb to clean it of lice.

The *Graf Waldersee* of the North German Lloyd Line left Hamburg on April 1, 1905, and beat the *Mayflower* to America. It took only eleven days for the *Waldersee* to get to the New World compared to the three months for the *Mayflower*. When America declared war in 1917, the *Graf Waldersee* was in New York Harbor, but before we could intern the ship, the lousy Germans scuttled it.

On Ellis Island my mother wore a big red tag which spelled our name. She carried me, and Clara and Matilda tugged at her skirt. For their own convenience and probably through their own ignorance, the immigration officials changed the spelling of our name from Goldhirsch to Goldhurst. More than fifty years later I stayed at a hotel in London which bordered a street named Goldhurst Terrace, and on April 17, 1959, my son Billy informed me that Goldhurst ran second at Jefferson Park, New Orleans, paying $14.40. It was the only money Goldhurst ever paid. "That horse is still running," wrote Billy of Goldhurst's last race. "He is going to run right into the glue factory."

From Ellis Island my father took us to the home of cousins, where we stayed until we moved into a tenement apartment at 171 Eldridge Street. We had a railroad flat, four rooms lined up one after another, for which my father paid $14 a month. These tenements were called dumbbell apartments because the floor plans for each resembled a dumbbell: two rooms in the front, two rooms in the back, connected, two to two, by a narrow hallway. The hallway, with one slit window, let upon a shaft, the bottom of which was always filled with refuse.

All my life I have heard gossip about the ownership of these tenements. I have heard that a star of stage, screen, and radio owned them and that a manufacturer of a gigantic flying company was his partner. I know our landlord lived in a tenement the exact duplicate of ours except that he had three more kids.

The apartment admitted sunlight only through the two windows in the front which faced the street. This room was invariably let to boarders or to relatives newly arrived from the old country or occupied by my father who entertained neighbors there once a week with a spirited discussion of Talmudic law or an even more spirited discussion about Socialism. They drank hot tea as they argued, as they bellowed, their opinions. Tea and anarchy I thought filled their whole lives.

I learned a great many forensic tricks watching these men, especially Dudja Silverberg, my father's dearest friend and most combative opponent. When my father pinned Dudja logically, when he proved Dudja did not know his facts, had not read his Talmud, then Dudja would suddenly reach across the table, pick up a quartered lemon, put it between his teeth, bite hard, suck deeply, quickly sip the hot tea from the water glass, and sigh, "A glazl varms, Leib. A glazl varms." All the time, while the others watched this acidic test, Dudja's mind was clicking, and invariably he left my father frustrated.

I slept in the room behind this, a windowless space, small, sharing a bed with my brother Max, another bed opposite for Jake. My job for the few years Max was an infant was to put the rag in his mouth which served as a pacifier in those days. This was the only room in the tenement covered by linoleum which the last tenants had left.

The hall was covered by a rug which my mother had hooked in the old country and which she preserved all her life. She would not let me beat it when she hung it across the wire in our backyard. She cleaned it with a brush liberally dipped in naphtha. The kitchen, which contained a big black cookstove, was where we ate. During the winter the stove heated the tenement. We provided additional heat with a kerosene heater. Twice a week a begrimed Italian carried a five-gallon can of kerosene up five flights of tenement stairs while balancing a cake of ice on a strip of burlap flung over his shoulder.

In the kitchen, too, was our dining-room table with chairs and stools around it, always enough to accommodate everyone. In one corner was the icebox, a drip pan beneath, which my mother emptied once a day every day of her life. In the other corner was the bed on which Matilda and Clara slept. The back room, sunlight filtering through the braces of the fire escape, belonged to my mother and father, and on the dresser was every memento they held dear.

These four rooms at 171 Eldridge Street were my father's domain. He was a short man, though very well proportioned, and until he grew stout in late life, he was considered handsome. He had little vanity but an abundance of self-assurance. He was an estimable man in all ways except one: He refused to enter the American mainstream on its terms, which is to say he could not understand why money was at all important. I doubt whether he ever handled as much as $50 at any time in his life. Once when he was off to Montreal to deliver a lecture, I said, "Papa, you only have a dollar in your billfold. You're going to a strange country. You'll need more than that."

"The committee has sent me the ticket," he said. "They will meet the train and take me to where I am to speak. They will provide me with dinner and return me to the train."

When he came home, he still had the same dollar.

In the Galician *shtetl*, of course, money *wasn't* important since there was none. Status descended on the learned man, and that my father was. In Europe he had all the status he wanted. In America, he became a status wanderer. He never comprehended why a tailor could become the president of the shul. Leib conveniently chose not to count in the equation that the tailor had a chain of stores selling ready-made suits and that perhaps it was the tailor's generosity which furnished the shul with its religious ornaments. A tailor was a tailor to him. No tailor should expect status or prestige. My father insisted that no matter how much money a tailor made, he would never be able to wear a high silk hat. Most tailors would have to stick with caps, moving up at best to a derby or a fedora. Only learned men wore silk hats, men like Leib.

But if the tailors didn't take my father on his own terms, the old-timers did. They called him Reb Lebche, a salutation of singular respect. Nothing is dearer to the heart of the learned Jew than a nickname. Maimonides, the Renaissance philosopher, is called by Talmudists simply the Rambam. During World War I, the old-timers also called my father Hindenburg because he was the supreme authority on the displacement of all the army divisions of both the Allies and the Central Powers. Do not think, therefore, my father wandered in a never-never land of his own imagining. He was part of his own time, just not part of the future.

Whenever he spoke, Reb Lebche commanded attention. I remember him telling the old-timers a story of the *shtetl*, of the Gentile peasant who went to the Jewish apothecary one Passover to buy cough medicine for a sick boy. "But they wouldn't open the door for me," said the peasant. "They stayed in the back room with their celebration. But you, Reb Lebche, you asked me to drive you to Mihalin on Christmas Day, which was my holiday. And I came out of church and drove you. Why?"

My father would look the Mikulintsyers in the eye, pause dramatically, and answer his own question: "I told the peasant the apothecary was wrong."

He was a free-lance man all his life, a free-lance teacher, a free-lance philosopher, and a free-lance writer. Leib Goldhurst, in fact, wrote the first sports story published in any of the American foreign-language newspapers. He described the Jim Jeffries-Jack Johnson fight which took place in Reno, Nevada, in 1910 for the *Jewish Daily Forward*. In the story he never called Johnson Johnson but always the *schwartzer* (the black man). He meant no disrespect to Jack Johnson; he was only trying to explain the democratization of sports in America.

He wrote a subsequent article for the *Forward* in which he argued that America is a civilization different from all others. "I pass along the street," he wrote, "and stop at a Catholic church and examine the architecture. A priest comes out and smiles and says, 'Good morning,' to a bearded Jew. America is good for him. And good for me. It has made us both more understanding."

On the High Holidays, my father earned money by chanting the prayers before the congregation. He was a Bal T'vilah, an auxiliary cantor.

He performed at least 2,000 marriages as a free-lance justice of the peace. When the couples appeared at our tenement, he summoned my sister Matilda to play "Here Comes the Bride," and I filled out the marriage certificates for the county clerk. My father performed many a marriage for couples whose children were in attendance. These were people who had been married in Europe by a rabbi and realized it was only by a civil service in America they could obtain a legal certificate. My father and mother as well contracted a second marriage in America. Leib charged a flat fee of $5 for a wedding.

There was every reason then for the Jewish congregation in our neighborhood to defer to him. Indeed, they asked his advice many times. A Rabbi Shmelner had come from Rumania to collect funds to help the victims of a pogrom. Though Shmelner was a rabbi, he was also more unfortunately an embezzler. He had defrauded these Lower East Side Jews and they caught him at it. He was tried and convicted. This was a painful scandal, and my father was covering this story for the *Forward* the morning the jury rendered its verdict. Though a Jewish prosecutor had argued the state's case and a Jewish jury returned the verdict, the judge summoned my father to his chambers, where he confessed to Leib the whole affair was deplorable. He wanted to know what the neighborhood Jews thought was fit punishment.

"Send him to Mattewan," said my father. "It is a hospital for the criminally insane. But there he will be able to keep his beard, and there he will still keep the dietary laws because someone can bring his food to him. In a few years he can get out, and it won't be such a disgrace." Which is precisely what the judge did.

In religion, my father tended toward rationalism. He was conversant with Spinoza, Darwin, and Kant, yet he never failed to observe every Sabbath and to observe every holiday. He displayed a surprising equanimity when I married Genevieve Gallagher. He confided his regret that his English was so imperfect he could not talk facilely with my wife's mother, Emma Nolan Gallagher.

When I was young and precocious, I chided him about his piety. My father answered, "A Jew is a Jew like a Frenchman is a Frenchman. No race of people can survive long without a ritual and some degree of discipline. These are my people—the people I live with, the people with whom I came to America. My beloved friend Dudja Silverberg goes to the shul to talk to God, and I go to the shul to talk to Dudja."

Like every father, he held part of himself inviolate. He was inviolate, I suspect, to antagonize me. He bought every morning newspaper and every afternoon newspaper. In those days that was roughly fourteen newspapers. I was the only inveterate newspaper reader in the house. Yet I could not read one of these papers until he had discarded it. When I asked could I read the bottom edition, he shifted in his chair as though sitting on glowing coals. I put it back. He concentrated. I picked up only the papers he discarded on the floor.

No matter how carefully I sneaked reading a newspaper when he was out of the room or busy elsewhere, he knew. He would throw the paper away no matter how professionally I had refolded it. I never understood this attitude until a half century later when I was publishing the *Israelite*. I would return from a lecture trip late at night, repair immediately to the printing shop, where I found my son and my advertising manager had copy-edited, proofread, dummied, reedited, and put the *Israelite* to bed. They were awaiting the first press proof which I took from their eager hands to read by myself. When they looked at me like two injured puppies, I said, "To hell with you both. This is my house."

My father was the president of the Mikulintsyer Verein, a fraternity populated by those who came from Mikulintsy. He never missed a meeting, and year after year he won reelection. I accompanied him to a funeral one day. Our limousine stopped first at the tenement of my cousin Joe Goldhirsch, a poor man who owned a candy store. Joe wasn't ready, and after a one-minute wait our limousine started to pull away from the curb. Just then Joe appeared and chased after us, holding his sweater and cap in one hand and a paper-wrapped sandwich in the other.

Next, the limousine stopped at the home of Barney Silverman, a wealthy contractor. Barney Silverman was not on the stoop. But this time the Mikulintsyers dispatched the chauffeur, who returned with the news, "Mr. Silverman is having breakfast." We waited for Mr. Silverman a good half hour.

When I asked my father about this, he answered me with a

sentence I have used in all my writing ever since. He said, "We Jews are just like everybody else—only more so."

I went often to that cemetery in which the Mikulintsyers owned a large plot. On the stone markers over each grave were tintype portraits of the deceased, oval in shape and often badly faded from the wear of the elements. English and Hebrew lettering was engraved on all the markers. Passing through the cemetery from the oldest portion to the new, I noticed the rusting nails which once held tintypes, but in the newer sections no tintypes had ever been affixed at all. I realized sadly these people in the old section were dead and all the people who knew them were dead. After a while the Hebrew characters disappeared from the markers, too.

Because he was president, the Mikulintsyer Verein had bought a plot for him. Seeing this grave made me realize with a visceral ache that this would happen to my father, too. He saw my consternation and said, "If it were to happen only to me, I would write a letter to the Congressman. But it happened to Thomas Jefferson, Henry George, Lincoln, and George Washington, too."

Once my father stopped to chat with a professional mourner, a man who earned a small living praying over the dead. My father asked me, "Please lend me ten dollars," which I did. He gave it to the mourner and later explained, "When I came to America, I stayed in that man's home. When I left, he took me to the street car and gave me a five-dollar bill. Now it's my turn."

Next to *Verein* electioneering, Leib loved American politics. He knew all the ins and outs of Tammany Hall and was ready to surmise accurately what the latest stratagem of either Democratic boss Charlie Murphy or Republican Sam Koenig portended. He knew the names of all the New York mayors from McClellan through Jimmy Walker. Over and over he predicted that a Rockefeller or a Frick or a Morgan would become President of the United States. "These rich men will enter politics," he said, "and they will perform a good service for America."

The two presidents he particularly revered were Theodore Roosevelt and William Howard Taft. All the Jews on the Lower East Side revered "Tudder" Roosevelt because his signature was on their certificate of immigration. "Tudder Roosevelt—he brought me to America," my father said.

During William Howard Taft's administration, Congress passed a bill extending to ordained ministers half-fare railroad privileges. My father wrote President Taft asking why the same privileges could not be extended to rabbis. Taft wrote him back and said it was indeed a fair request and the bill would be amended to include rabbis.

While my father never liked Warren G. Harding, he did like Herbert Hoover "because Hoover fed the poor people of the world," and he adored Franklin D. Roosevelt for the New Deal and its social legislation. "When the Gentiles are in trouble, we Jews catch hell, and Franklin D. Roosevelt has removed the Gentiles from trouble with the CCC and the subsidies."

Leib and I had a continuing argument over William Randolph Hearst. My father always remembered Hearst's Socialist days when the publisher ran for office boosting the Municipal Ownership League. I always despised Hearst for his anti-British prejudice.

In 1928, in the waning days of that gorgeous early-century optimism, Jacob and I sent Leib to Europe with $4,000. He used some of this money to hand out small dowries to Jewish girls. He toured Mikulintsy, wearing his high silk hat and cutaway. He was an impressive dignitary to these Jews, and as he toured the streets, tipping his hat, some of the people threw messages into the car addressed to relatives in the United States which they hoped Leib would deliver.

My father died in 1942, a few months after America had entered the war. One of the last conversations I had with him was in reminiscing over this trip. He and I wondered how many of those Austrian Jews Hitler had already killed. We guessed all of them.

Chapter 3

Aₙₙₐ Klein was my mother. She was a tall woman, thin, with a pleasant face and hair pulled back into a bun. She was born in the small town of Mihalin in Rumania in 1867. She loved Rumania. She always kept a portrait of Carmen Sylva, the queen, in her bedroom. Mihalin was on the *granetz*—the border of Galicia—and the young Galicianers used to go over to the Rumanian side to look up girls, as young boys do throughout history in all times and all places. Anna was the daughter of a grain merchant and she met my father when she was nineteen years old. She married him within the year.

When she died in 1924, she had never ridden in a car, never been to a movie, never, for that matter, seen Grand Central Station. But she had come from one world to another, borne seven children, seen two of them die, and had worked hard every day of her life.

Emil and Joseph, my brothers, died in Europe during a typhus epidemic. Emil died first, on a Friday morning. In accord with Orthodox principles, Emil had to be buried that day since he could not be buried on the Sabbath, Saturday. My father had to dispatch Jacob for the coffin, but before he left the house, the doctor told my mother and father, "You had better order the second one at the same time. Joseph will die today, too."

My mother usually took me with her when she went shopping under the Williamsburg Bridge about eight blocks away. I carried one of the baskets as we zigzagged back and forth from store to store, stall to stall, the span of the bridge arching above us. She stocked up for the week, buying butter, eggs, cheese, meat, fruit, and vegetables. My specific duty was to present the butcher with old newspapers, into which he dropped a piece of liver for the cat, and present more newspapers to the grocer, who used them to wrap the soup greens. No one can buy a plate of soup like the soup my mother made from those greens. A restaurateur is unashamed to charge 35 cents for a bowl of turkey broth. My mother used that stuff to rinse out the pot.

We left for the market early because she wanted to give a peddler or a merchant a first. A first was the first sale in the morning when the merchant opened his stall or when the peddler set his cart down at a corner and began to bawl his wares.

A first meant good luck to both parties, to the buyer and to the seller. For the seller, it meant a good day; for the buyer, it meant a special merit in the book to be opened on the Day of Judgment because there is nothing more important in the eyes of God than earning a livelihood, which we Jews call *parnosseh*.

As the morning wore on, there was always one merchant or peddler who had not yet made his first sale, and he would announce: *"Balabusten, balabusten* [Housewives, housewives], I haven't had a beginning." Someone hurried to make a purchase. A first was always a bargain.

Coming back from the market with the heavy basket was a tiresome chore. Sometimes as we crossed toward Eldridge Street my mother would look up to our fifth-floor tenement, and the prospect of climbing those stairs was anything but pleasant. She would say to me, "Oh, for Rumania. What a beautiful time it was in the morning with the dew sparkling in the fields. But this is better, better for the children." And with that determination, she would trudge up the stairs.

My mother was an excellent cook. Her *holishkes*—stuffed cabbage—was superb. Nor have I ever tasted such borscht. Bread was a holy object to her. She revered it. We never cut the piece of paper which identified the union seal from the crust but ate it rather than waste even a minute portion of this blessed food. My lunch was often a bowl of potato soup, to which my mother added browned onions and two slices of pumpernickel bread spread with *schmaltz* (chicken fat). My dessert was a penny. At Cheap Haber's on Rivington Street, I could buy many things with a penny. The owners of these penny stores always used the prefix "Cheap"—Cheap Abe's or Cheap Max's. A second penny took me into the movies. I remember the news leaked out that our movie idol, Bronco Billy Anderson, was a Jewish boy whose real name was Max Aronson. My mother and other Orthodox Jews spat three times to show they were not impressed. "A Jewish cowboy yet?" she asked. "What else will happen to us in America?"

She spent a good part of her life in the kitchen. As soon as one meal was finished, she immediately busied herself setting the table for the next. There was never a moment the dining table did not await my father and her children.

A supreme seamstress, she made hundreds of dresses for our neighbors. She was speedy and dexterous. She noticed my jumper was soiled one morning before I left for school. While I finished my breakfast, she cut the muslin, sewed it, finished off the buttonholes, all before I left for Public School 20.

Two of the household items I see clearly to this day were the dressmaker's dummy my mother kept in the corner of our living room and the pewter sugar bowl into which she faithfully put the weekly 50 cents' premium for her sewing machine. She used to say she and the Singer Sewing Machine man were growing old together.

Faithfully she saved Octagon Soap wrappers. She redeemed these premiums only for cut-glass china. She would collect forty or fifty wrappers and send me to the store with the instructions: "Get some saucers. We have dishes and pitchers and cups. Now we need some saucers."

We bathed in washtubs. When the bathtub was introduced into 171 Eldridge Street, my mother used it to store the coal for the stove. On top of the stove was a shelf where she kept the baby, Max.

She was forever keeping track of my reading. I've always had trouble with women and books. All of them have offered the same complaint: "You're always reading. You always have your nose in a book." My wife has said this, my sisters and my mother. She would say, "You're always reading," and come into the bedroom and turn off the gaslight, the flame protected by a shade we called a mantle which sizzled when you lit the jet. It gave off a pretty light, and the room was indeed dark when it was off. The only woman I ever closed the book for, however, was my mother.

She went to the public library on Rivington Street and held up three fingers to indicate the number of cards she wanted. She handed these to us with the instructions: "Here, go, become an American. Learn, study, read." On my first Talmud, she put a drop of honey, so I would always associate learning with sweetness.

A pious woman, she went punctually to the shul, where her prayers fell in torrents. She prayed every night, blessing everyone she met during the day. She could neither read nor write, she only repeated the prayers by rote, but they were fervent.

Her piety demanded great expenditures of energy. If a rabbi was going to visit us, or the Hebrew teacher—the melamed—or even a member of the priestly caste—the Cohanim—my mother forthwith washed all the floors.

When I came in, she cautioned me, "Herschele, don't walk on the floor; the rabbi is coming."

"On what will I walk, Mama?"

"Not on the floor, Herschele," she commanded sternly. She spread a trail of papers from the front door to my room, and there I stayed until it was my turn to come out and say hello to the rabbi.

I have not met any woman who ever washed the floor with the fervor my mother did, but then I haven't met many rabbis who visited as punctually as the old ones did.

Next to God, and my father, a rabbi was the most important man in her life, any rabbi. There were no qualitative degrees to rabbis. They were all men of the Book, devoted to God. I showed my mother a newspaper photograph once of Rabbi Stephen S. Wise and told her this was the most influential rabbi in America. She studied the photograph and asked, "This you call a rabbi? How can he be a rabbi without a beard?"

When she went to the shul, she had to pass a Roman Catholic church on Second Avenue. She never failed to spit three times, *poof! poof! poof!* "Oh, what memories!" she would say. On one occasion, a casual passerby approached us. She held me by the hand and waited until he passed. She would never spit in front of a stranger. Once gone, she went *poof! poof! poof!* "Oh, what memories." There were occasional Jews along the Lower East Side who got drunk. Whenever my mother saw one, she would say scornfully, "Just like a Christian."

31

My mother was so pious that I remember when I was ten years old, she had me turn my face to the wall as she rearranged her petticoats. Yet there were no sexual inhibitions along the Lower East Side. When the women came from the mikvah—the ritual bath after menstruation—they would walk home through the streets with towels around their necks and smile when neighbors cried, "I hope it's a boy." For the mikvah means she will make love with her husband that night. These Orthodox Jews used to say of wives, "Two weeks she belongs to God; two weeks she belongs to you."

Like many pious Jews, she was sure she had a personal relationship with God. As often as she sent me on an errand, she would turn her face toward heaven and say to Him, "Now watch mine Harry as he crosses the street." It was a clear-cut proposition for her. She did everything according to the Covenant, and she expected God to do His share. No matter what my father or my brothers or my sisters proposed doing, she amended their statements immediately with, "With God's help, you'll go to the movies. Repeat after me, with God's help."

Once a week she sat at the table with a silk kerchief over her head in her one good dress with the little fleur-de-lis print and knew supreme joy as she watched her family eat the Sabbath meal. The Sabbath is the most important part of the Jewish religion. Irish and Italian boys had Christmas once a year. Jewish boys had the Sabbath which came once a week. When the Temple was destroyed by the Romans, the Jews took their temple with them into their homes. The Sabbath lifts the Jew above his drab everyday existence, above the harrowing seriousness of reality and makes the mother of the home a queen.

My mother did not cook on the Sabbath, which is forbidden. She kept the food, the dish called *cholent,* warm in the oven, where she stored it Friday afternoon. My mother ushered in the Sabbath as all Jewish women usher it in, by kindling special lights to do honor to this day. She spread her hands over the candles and recited the blessing: "Praised be Thou, O Lord, our God, King of the universe, who has sanctified us by Thy commandments and commanded us to kindle the Sabbath lights."

Historically anyone born of a Jewish mother is a Jew whether the father is Jewish or not. The mother is a Jew because it is she who maintains the Sabbath so the men can worship. God told

Moses, "There is a magnificent gift in my treasure chamber and its name is Sabbath and I shall give it to Israel." The Sabbath is a time of joy, the streets and the workshops still, the home filled with celebration and reverence. The Sabbath is probably the secret of the Jew's survival. My mother, in her one dress and her silk kerchief, was the Queen of the Sabbath.

Orthodox Jews are prohibited from lighting fires on the Sabbath. To heat the food, they must employ the *Shabbas* goy, a Gentile paid to come and get the ovens started. Our *Shabbas* goy was an Italian named Angelo who served the entire tenement. To light the stove on Friday night, he charged three cents and to rekindle it Saturday morning, one cent.

My mother got to like Angelo, which proves that stereotypes, no matter who holds them, are often wrong. She had many preconceived ideas about Christians, but Angelo fitted none of these preconceptions. She developed a great fondness for him and always stuffed his pockets with cookies and sweets for his children.

My father was above commenting on Angelo. Angelo worked with his hands; my father worked with his head, to him a more profound difference from that of being a Christian and being a Jew.

My father, impressive in his silk hat and Prince Albert coat, left our home every morning. He put his foot on the chair by the front door, and my mother rushed with a cloth to polish his shoes. She no sooner bent to her task than he moaned, *"Oy, der krizhes,"* which roughly translates as "Oh, my aching back."

She was polishing, but his back ached. "You'll outlive me by twenty-five years," she said, straightening. This same ritual was consummated every morning for as long as I lived in the house.

Though our tenement was crowded, I never saw my father put his arms around her or kiss her. This was nothing unusual for an Orthodox home. In 1909, when my mother gave birth to my youngest brother, Max, a midwife attended her. She was too pious to admit a doctor's examination.

Mother and Father did argue occasionally. He was strict and severe with us, and often my mother would snap, "Leave the boy alone." One of the strict provisions he laid down was that we all had to be present at the dinner table when he sat down. There were times when I had to prowl through three different movie houses to find Max. I knew the kid could take care of himself and I was hungry, but I also knew we couldn't have dinner until all of us were there. One of us had to be in the hallway to take Papa's coat, another to remove his rubbers, and all of us had to welcome him. We ate in quiet, Leib initiating all conversation. If one of us talked to the other, he always raised his eyes and said sternly, "Jewish boys don't make noise."

My mother had to remind him once in a while that after all, she had spent the day in sewing, cooking, and cleaning and maybe a little laughter at the evening meal wasn't as offensive as he made out.

These arguments were rare. She seemed to me for the most part a contented wife and mother. On Saturday afternoons, when my father collected his intellectuals for debate in the living room, Anna laid out boiled potatoes and chick-peas and withdrew to the kitchen. She could hear the men arguing about the relative merits of the cantors Kwartin and Rosenblatt, hear the men insist all the others were peddlers, nothing more than *schleppers*. She could hear them argue, too, about Socialism, about Eugene V. Debs and Morris Hillquit, and one man always spoke up for Karl Marx. My mother would retreat to the kitchen and sigh, "What is this all about? What does a man need but God?"

Her world was a clearly defined world. It consisted of children, work, and prayer. A bad Christian was an anti-Semite and a good Christian was not. She was proud of her husband because people sought his advice and called him a philosopher.

Anna Klein Goldhurst's English vocabulary consisted of the words "Enjoy! Enjoy!" and the old East Side reliable "Likewise." As she served our dinner, placing before us the dishes over which she had labored, she kept saying to each of us, "Enjoy! Enjoy!" When we went off to a school outing, her last instructions were, "Enjoy! Enjoy!"

"Likewise" took care of a multitude of similar situations. My schoolteacher, Miss O'Day, met her and said, "How do you do? You have such a smart boy in Harry." My mother replied, "Likewise." When I told her, "This is Nate Zuppert, a friend in my class," she said, "Likewise, likewise."

Her English improved after the telephone was installed in our home. It was pretty difficult to persuade her to take a message, however.

"Mama, this is Harry," I said.

"Harry ain't home," she said.

"But, Mama, this *is* Harry."

"Harry ain't home."

The purpose in calling was to tell her I was going to be late, and after the experience I decided to get home that night at the usual time, so maybe she knew what she was up to.

My mother died in 1924 of cancer of the spine. Only my brother Jake and Clara knew this. They told no one she had cancer. Cancer was a taboo subject then. No one mentioned cancer any more than they mentioned syphilis. She was semiconscious the last time I saw her in the hospital. Yet she reached for my shirt cuffs and pulled them down to see if they were clean. She was always inspecting to see if we were presentable, and she did this on the last day of her life.

A man thinks of many things as his mother is dying. I thought of her kindness and generosity. One day she had given me a $5 bill to buy groceries. Fooling around in the park, I lost the money. I was frantic. I looked all over. I lit matches in the dark and looked along the gutters. Finally, I gave up and sat down on a bench in the park, afraid to go home. Five dollars was a big item at the Goldhursts'. At last I had to return to the tenement. I came in the house crying. I explained to my mother that I sat in the park for hours wondering what to do because I lost that $5. I thought of the situation at this moment when she was dead. I remembered her putting her arms around me and holding me close to her breast, saying, "It's better than giving it to a doctor."

Chapter 4

M~Y~ brother Jacob was almost fifteen years old when he came to America with my father. Since he was born in Europe, automatically we called him Jake or, interchangeably, Jack. To keep my readers oriented, throughout I shall call him Jake. Had he been born in America and named Jacob, we would have called him Yonkele, a Yiddish endearment meaning "little Jacob"—the first attempt of the ghetto to become Americanized, the second the attempt to recapture the flavor of the old country.

Jake sold soft goods, *shmatas* as he called them—rags—which he measured off with a yardstick and snipped adeptly. He tolerated with a seething frustration the policemen who always arrested peddlers for a minor offense and then ransacked his cart while he waited helplessly to pay a magistrate a fine. Later on, William J. Gaynor, the mayor, instructed the cops not to arrest peddlers for minor infractions but to serve them with a summons instead.

Jake led a hard life. He learned the English he needed at night school. There were a few immigrant Jews who became merchant princes up on Fifth Avenue, but there were thousands of others who started off and stayed with their pushcarts, trudging the neighborhood streets from sunup to sundown, haggling forever with housewives, barely making a meager living to support their families.

Things looked up for Jake when he got a job in a pocketbook factory operating the press which clamped the metal frame onto the leather. One day a fellow worker ran all the way to our house to tell us the stamping press had cut off three of Jake's fingers. I believe the employer paid Jake's hospital bill, but in those days there were no unemployment compensations or liability insurance.

Jake was in the hospital several weeks, but when he was discharged, he found a job the same day as a night clerk in the Jefferson Hotel. He worked seven days a week, although he had every other Sunday off. He worked ten hours a day and made $17 a week. My mother was always trying to keep us quiet so Jake could sleep.

Every Friday night my mother prepared a "Jewish" meal for Jake. She made gefilte fish, chicken soup, chicken, and *tzimmes,* a hot dish of carrots and plums. After school I took the Sixth Avenue streetcar to Thirty-eighth Street carrying two brown enamel pots with Jake's dinner. Beside the Jefferson was Offer's Restaurant whose sign proclaimed NO ONE OFFERS WHAT OFFER'S OFFERS. The chef there put the pots on the steam table to keep them warm until Jake could find time to eat.

My reward for this chore was to spend the night in the hotel, which was a small theatrical rooming house. I saw Bert Lahr, Lightning Weston, and Doc Rockwell. One night Jake gave me the key to Room 4C, which had been let to Bella Cohen, a famous Yiddish actress. Miss Cohen was playing Coney Island and was not expected back that weekend.

No sooner had I fallen asleep, however, than the light in the front room of the suite snapped on and into the bedroom came Miss Cohen. She stood studying me while I stammered that if she gave me a few minutes, I would get dressed, and my brother downstairs would find another room for me.

Miss Cohen said, "Turn your face to the wall and go to sleep." Which I did. I turned my face to the wall and she put out the light. But I could hear her unsnapping her dress, and it was the first time I heard that marvelously mysterious rustling of a woman.

Because of his disability, Jake did not go to World War I. Through a marriage broker, which we Jews called a *shadchen,* Jake met Lillian Temel and married her. With her dowry, he bought a partnership in the leasehold on the Jefferson. Lillian Temel's mother worked as a seamstress all her life, frugally collecting every spare penny to give her daughter a start. I remember asking

Jake, "What is the dowry?" and he replied, "A couple of thousand dollars."

Jake did well at the Jefferson. By 1924 he was able to acquire the Hotel Union Square, on Fourteenth Street. All the Yiddish actors, actresses, playwrights, and producers frequented the Union Square. Dozens of them used it as a mailing address. Paul Muni's mother lived at the Union Square for quite a while, and strange as it may seem, the Boston Symphony kept coming to this old hotel, out of habit from the days when the Union Square was one of the leading hotels in America. President Theodore Roosevelt had his campaign headquarters there in the race to succeed himself. Henry George, the single taxer, died in one of its rooms on the eve of the 1897 mayority campaign, in which he was the favorite, and Bob Fitzsimmons, the fighter, had tended bar in the café. Testimony in the famous Becker case revealed that the four gunmen had met in one of the Union Square's rooms to make the final arrangements for the murder of Herman Rosenthal, the gambler.

Next, Jake took on the Hotel Markwell on West Forty-ninth Street, near Broadway, where I was the night manager until 1937. Just before the New York World's Fair of 1939 Jake added the Hotel Cadillac to what we were sure was his growing empire. The Cadillac was at Broadway and Forty-third Street opposite the New York Times Building. But nobody came to the fair, and the Cadillac went bust. Each of Jake's hotels was a separate corporation, so he could have let the Cadillac go into bankruptcy and paid off its creditors a few cents on the dollar.

Not Jake. "After all," he said, "I did business with my friends, the laundryman, the caterer, and the fellow who supplied cleaning equipment, and I do not want them to lose." He turned his other properties over to a receiver, and I am sure each of the Cadillac creditors received 100 cents on the dollar. Afterward Jake went to Springfield, Massachusetts, and took over the Hotel Worthy.

Jake had a specific reason for selecting Springfield. He had three daughters, and any Jew with three daughters is in bad shape if he wants to marry them all off. So Jake made a study of all the towns in the Northeast with a population of more than 10,000 Jews, figuring if he settled in one of those, the daughters of the hotelkeeper would have a certain attraction for eligible Jewish boys. With luck, he hoped he would have a lawyer, a doctor, and a dentist for sons-in-law. Springfield had the 10,000 Jews and the hotel for sale. The strategy worked. For sons-in-law, Jake has a lawyer, a dentist, and a merchant.

Clara and Matilda, my sisters, went to the working world early. Everybody did. Before they reached their teens, they were working in a necktie factory making $5 a week. They held a succession of these jobs. Once, after a sudden rainstorm, my mother dispatched me with an umbrella and rubbers to Clara's factory. I saw hundreds of girls at sewing machines. How foolish those employers were! It took them years to realize these girls who stitched up blouses and skirts were the best customers in the world and that one day these customers would spend more on their clothes in a year than ladies then spent in a lifetime.

On another occasion I came home from school to find all the mothers in anguished groups along the street.

"Run to Clara's factory," cried my mother. "See if everything is all right."

I ran to Greene Street. Everything was all right. On the way back I learned of the terrible Triangle Shirtwaist Factory fire, which took the lives of 146 working girls, who were burned to death or died leaping from the windows.

One hundred thousand people followed their cortege through the Lower East Side. All the girls were buried in a mass grave at the Workmen's Circle Cemetery.

These were sad days on the Lower East Side. First came the sinking of the *Titanic,* which took the lives of Mr. and Mrs. Isidor Straus, great friends of the immigrants. The Triangle fire was followed by the Mendel Beiliss case in Russia, where a Jew was charged with the ritual murder of a Gentile schoolboy. Then Leo Frank, a twenty-nine-year-old Jewish factory superintendent, was lynched in Georgia. Frank was innocent of the murder of fourteen-year-old Mary Phagan, but a violent upsurge of anti-Semitism afflicted Georgia, and mob rule invaded the courtroom. The *Jewish Daily Forward* ran the headline of Frank's death in red ink, and I ran through the Lower East Side shouting, "Leo Frank murdered," because I knew the word "lynched" would have little

39

meaning for Jewish immigrants. When the *Titanic* went down, my mother pinned black cloth to our windowsill, and it seemed the cloth never came inside.

Both Clara and Matilda went to night school. They learned English, typing, and stenography—"all three," as Lower East Side parents put it. Clara got a job as a bookkeeper for the White Studios, and my mother used to say proudly, "Clara is working *up*-town." In 1920, Clara became the first woman broker on Wall Street. She sold stock options, about which more later. The Crash wiped her out, and she turned to public stenography and later to realty, renting apartments. She still carries on her business, working out of 1776 Broadway, the Liberty Building.

Matilda had my mother's talent for sewing. She was good enough to find a job with a small dress firm as a designer. She carried a pad and pencil in her raincoat, and on Sundays she would go to the services at St. Thomas' or St. Bartholomew's or St. Patrick's, all the fancy churches on Fifth or Park Avenue, to copy the dresses the ladies wore. From these sketches she made a pattern, and the cutters and the seamstresses went to work, and in a few weeks the most expensively tailored gown was selling at a tenth the price off the rack.

Matilda was pretty, with brown hair and what we called a Polack nose, short and stubby. The rest of us were aquiline. Matilda played the piano and sang with a natural sweetness. A neighbor of ours, who taught violin, suggested she might profitably plan on a concert career, but the course of study was protracted, the expense prohibitive, and Matilda herself too much in a hurry.

She fell in love with a first cousin of ours, Alex Goldhirsch. They wanted to marry. My mother, so pious she distrusted kosher butchers, wouldn't hear of it. My father sided with her. Matilda, who complained of my father's atheism, could not win them over, nor could she put aside her own religious compunctions. Embittered, she left our home, setting up her own dress design studio first in New York and later in Hollywood, where she made gowns for movie stars.

A few years later I was able to resolve this difficulty which beset parents who grew up in the old world and children who grew up in the new when I married an Irish Catholic. No one in the family liked it; Genevieve and I heard some cruel objections, but nobody, as was threatened, died over the marriage.

I never saw Matilda after she left home, but I was reminded of her sadness when I was autographing books in a Los Angeles department store forty years later. A reporter handed me a penciled note which read, "Herschele, always thinking of you, Matty." Try as we might, that reporter and I with a phalanx of clerks and even the store detective could not track down Matilda.

Neither of my sisters ever got in my hair. I ran errands for them once in a while, but they were undemanding, hardworking girls tied closely to an integrated family unit. When I was young, I read all the time, and they always asked me to describe the books. I told them about Jules Verne, about Plutarch, about Malory's *Morte d'Arthur*, always translating into Yiddish for the benefit of my mother and father.

Who got into my hair was Max, the baby. He could not have been seven years old when he began to tag along after me. Tagging along was his *raison d'être*.

I went. I looked around. There was Max. I complained to my mother. It did no good. Max followed me everywhere. I brought him home and sternly told him to stay put. Before I left the front stoop, I could hear him on the tenement stairs, coming on down to follow me.

My mother called him *mein Columbusl* (my little Columbus) because he was born in the new country. She said he looked like an Irishman, the race we immigrant Jews most admired. He was the athlete of the family, a little taller than the rest of us, certainly a shade more graceful. Could he dribble a basketball! My father went to see him play, and though the old man didn't understand the game, it thrilled him to see Max feint and drop the ball through the hoop. Max, in fact, tried out for one of the Olympic swimming teams. He didn't make it, but we always thought it was because the other fellow had a longer reach.

Max was not only the first native-born of our family but the first to grow up outside the ghetto, for we moved to the Bronx in 1918. He married an exceptionally pretty girl named Ann Marshall and spent thirty-five years with the Metropolitan Life Insurance Company, first as a salesman, then as a general agent. Recently he went back to selling. He had grown up and lived in one area of the Bronx all his life. In the last decade this area has become almost wholly populated by Puerto Ricans. The Puerto Ricans buy as much insurance as the Jews, but Max confessed it took different techniques, and he was too old a dog to learn new tricks.

Chapter 5

My brother Jacob registered me in Public School 20 on the corner of Rivington and Eldridge streets in 1908. Public School 20 was all boys. My sisters went to Public School 91, a few blocks away, which was all girls.

Jake also took me to the De Milt Dispensary on Twenty-third Street and Second Avenue. There the doctor vaccinated me, and later I brought a note to the dispensary signed by my teacher, Miss Marjorie Tibbitts, which said I needed eyeglasses. The doctor fitted me with a pair of steel-rimmed spectacles, and I have worn glasses ever since.

Public School 20 smelled just like the De Milt Dispensary. Ammonia and Lysol were as much a part of the educational process in those days as blackboards and erasers. A janitor was forever swabbing the halls, dragging a steaming pail of water behind him as he moved down corridors.

The school resembled a bastion. It was surrounded by a steel picket fence, and its two main doors looked like a gigantic Renaissance diptych. We went out those doors only during fire drills, and I used to wonder who did use them. Public School 20 was several stories high with four decorative turrets. The halls were dark, but the rooms had big windows, which we boys had to open and shut with a long pole on the end of which was a brass hook.

The stairs were steel, but the banisters were wooden, shiny from years of handling by boys trooping up and down. It took a boy about three days to learn to slide down these banisters sidesaddle, leaping off like a track star as he approached the landing. Sometimes a boy zipped right off the banister into the wall, which led to injunctions and prohibitions from the school hierarchy.

My first principal at P.S. 20 was Robert Smith, a tall man, with a russet beard. Smith had lost an eye at the Battle of Shiloh during the Civil War. Having Mr. Smith as a principal therefore made us immigrant boys feel close to the course of American history.

Mr. Smith was succeeded by Dr. I. Edwin Goldwasser, who later became the first director of the Federation of Jewish Philanthropies. Still later Dr. Goldwasser became a successful commercial banker, and today he is in his nineties and I hear from him from time to time. Fifty years after Dr. Goldwasser took over at P.S. 20, his daughter, Mrs. Joan Schine, became the second Democrat in more than a decade to win election to the Board of Education in Westport, Connecticut. One of the town committeemen who nominated her was my son, Richard Goldhurst. As I say, we all are on the same ball of twine.

When the great waves of Jewish immigration came, the newcomers knew nothing about baseball, football, or straight pool. For a whole generation their sport was talk. So Dr. Goldwasser kept his classrooms open until midnight to give immigrants a place to argue. These nighttime music and drama critics, Talmudists, Zionists, single taxers, Socialists, Democrats, Republicans, and Tammany Hallniks lent the school an air of intellectual ferment and vitality that carried over into the classes I attended next day.

Built in the 1880's, P.S. 20 has been closed down. But because it represented something more than a physical plant, a new P.S. 20, named in honor of the old one and for Anna Silver, mother of alumnus Charles H. Silver, former head of the New York City Board of Education, opened its double doors a few blocks east on Essex Street in 1965.

In this brand-new P.S. 20 is a 20-foot mosaic called the "Wall of Our Forebears." In it stand likenesses of such P.S. 20 alumni as Paul Muni, George Gershwin, Edward G. Robinson, Senator Jacob J. Javits, Irving Caesar (the lyricist who wrote "Swanee" and "Tea for Two"), and me.

In those days Jake Javits, like me, was a lonely fellow, a bookworm. Robinson was a good student, more talky than Javits. It was

44

Robinson, not Javits, who was the politician. He was on the debating team; he organized theatricals, collecting pennies for shows that cost a dollar or two to put on—a real Chamber of Commerce type.

The first words the immigrant schoolboy learned were "son of a bitch" and "fuck." The kids who had been here longer took foul advantage of the greenhorn. They would tell him in Yiddish, "When teacher says, 'Good Morning,' you say, 'Fuck you.' That's what you say in America." Sometimes they varied this with "son of a bitch." Sure enough the greenie parroted these instructions to the merriment of the classroom.

The teachers tolerated this mischief with good grace. They were compassionate. They took the greenhorn aside and explained the whole situation as best they could, and afterward the greenhorn was less naïve. In six months, the greenie couldn't wait for his chance to take advantage of another innocent. After a while the teachers even anticipated the situation and warned the greenie ahead of time.

I fell for the trick the second or third day in school, and I remember my mother telling a neighbor later that the word "fuck" meant "fire" in Rumania. I hoped so at the time.

How long does it take a greenhorn to become an American?

Not as long as one would think. I arrived from Mikulintsy in 1905, and four years later I was the "king" in a school pageant parading down Fifth Avenue, a participant in the Hudson-Fulton Celebration of 1909. My "queen" was Sheila, whose parents ran the hand laundry in the basement of 171 Eldridge. Their name was Cohen, and Sheila's sister had a big red birthmark on her face. Her parents kept her indoors all the time, and whenever she did venture into the streets, she held her hand over this blemish, hiding it because the rest of us always called her Red Nose. It gives me shivers to remember this cruelty, just as it does when I remember we called a teacher with a withered stump Crooked Arm.

I loved school. I loved reading. I read everything I could about American and English history. I was as deeply interested in the War of the Roses as I was in the American Revolutionary War. Before I was fifteen, I had read Malory's *Morte d'Arthur* three times. I was taken with King Arthur and his knights. I have never stopped reading Malory and I think my affection for the *Morte d'Arthur* has had a genetic influence on my youngest son, Billy, a professor at the University of Florida, whose book *Confrontations* includes a systematic interpretation of the *Morte d'Arthur*.

Every Saturday morning I went to the Settlement House Library, where I read Jules Verne, Victor Hugo, Bulwer-Lytton, Dumas, and the Dick Hazzard series. There were books I could not give up even though I had read them several times. I carried *Enoch Arden* in my back pocket all one summer and learned how to read a book walking along the street as soldiers learn how to sleep when they march.

Ralph Waldo Emerson impressed me in my teens, and I will bet I have read *Miscellanies* twenty times since then. When a critic who reviewed my book *Only in America* said I was no Emerson, I was forced to write that the critic was no Edmund Wilson. I never set up as Emerson. Emerson is that American writer who means to me what Melville means to others and Mark Twain to still others. I venerated Emerson. I always wanted his picture up there on the classroom wall between Lincoln and Washington.

I did well in school. My first report card read A, A, A, and it always read A, A, A, until I was graduated in 1917. As soon as I brought my report card home, my mother took it and proudly displayed it for days on end to the whole neighborhood.

The teachers at Public School 20 always gave the smartest kid in the class a medal at the end of the year. I won several of these. One of them I received for inventing a sentence by which a man can easily remember the names of the first eleven Presidents of the United States. "When a just man makes a just bill he takes pay," which, using the first letter of every word, is Washington, Adams, Jefferson, Madison, Monroe, Adams, Jackson, Van Buren, Harrison, Tyler, Polk." Regretfully, I have never invented the phrase which makes sense to continue this memory crutch through Lincoln.

When I brought these medals home, Clara always expropriated them and wore them as pendants. My medal-winning ability came to an end in 7B. Miss O'Day had chosen me to recite Henry Wadsworth Longfellow's "The Building of the Ship" in the year-end assembly.

> Sail on, O Ship of State!
> Sail on, O Union, strong and great!

Humanity with all its fears,
With all the hopes of future years,
Is hanging breathless on thy fate!

The poem which much more fascinated me was "The Sinking of the Titanic," whose author I no longer remember. Unfortunately I did remember the poem and proceeded to substitute it to the clamor of the assembly:

Unsinkable monster, diminish your pace
Give heed to the dangers surrounding Cape Race!

My recitation enthralled everyone except the teachers. The next day Mr. Rosenthal, one of the teachers who disciplined boys, called me from the classroom to his office. Mr. Rosenthal wore thick eyeglasses. The sunlight glinted from them as his eyes bored into me. I was supposed to do as I was told. Yes, sir. Did I know I had disappointed Miss O'Day? I'm sorry. There wasn't enough time remaining for me to serve my detentions. I'd serve them next year. "No," said Mr. Rosenthal, "you won't get your medal this year." So poor Clara went pendantless.

One way or another the trauma ended my prizewinning ways. At graduation a year later, another boy proved smarter, and I have never won another prize or medal, not even the Mayflower Prize awarded annually to a North Carolina author by the Daughters of the American Revolution. In my late middle age I have decided I am against all prizes and medals unless they are given to me.

What made Public School 20 a significant experience for me were the teachers, the first Christians with whom we immigrant Jews had contact. They were unlike the Christians of whom our parents talked, the European peasants who used every Easter as an occasion to assault the ghetto, to clip the beards off pious Jews, and rape the young Jewish girls. These Christians were different; they were kind, gentle, and generous. They thought of Jews only as students and knew they were poor students.

One of the chores they assigned the boys was to clean up the teacher's room. The teachers always left chocolate cake and coffee, Armstrong's Coffee, for the several monitors who performed this duty.

My favorite teacher was Miss Tibbitts, who taught the sixth grade. She had green eyes, long, graceful hands, and she always smiled. One Christmastime, for my syndicated column, I wrote a piece about this wonderful lady. Another of my teachers, Miss Schloss, saw it, and I had the exquisite pleasure of hearing from both these ladies.

It is a remarkable thing to sit and ponder the first names of these teachers. I suspected then these schoolteachers were so extraordinary they did not need first names. But forty-five years later I learned Miss Tibbitts had the first name Marjorie and Miss Schloss the first name Linda. In truth, these teachers were inspired. They turned an immigrant population into a citizen population and did it within a single generation. It took Rome 200 years to accomplish the same goal, and the Romans were not fully successful in transforming all the races into *cives Romani*.

Mr. Ryan, whom we all called Our Irishman, was the teacher of 8B, the graduating class of Public School 20. Near the end of the term, we filled out our slips determining the high school each of us would attend. Mr. Ryan, solemn and judicious, said, "This is your last chance. Those of you who are Itzak and want to be Irving, put that down. Those who are Moishe and want to be Maurice, this is your moment. Those who are Yussell and want to be Yale, dare it now!" On this day I went from Herschel to Harry.

Years later I became good friends with Herschel Johnson, the first United States Ambassador to the United Nations. Herschel Johnson was a longtime Charlottean. I said to him, "Your name was Herschel, and you remained Herschel because you're a white Anglo-Saxon Protestant. My name was Herschel, and I became Harry so I could become a white Anglo-Saxon Protestant, too."

I do not mean we never encountered anti-Semitism on the Lower East Side. As the cortege following the coffin of Rabbi Benjamin Joseph crossed the Williamsburg Bridge, employees in the windows of the R. Hoe Company began hurling nuts and bolts and then directed a stream of hot water at these Jews, shouting "Christ killers." Many of the mourners lay on the ground, writhing, holding their heads in pain until the police came to restore order. No one in the R. Hoe factory was ever arrested for the assault, but the company and its officers published an apology in the press. The next night a posse of tough Jewish kids from

Clinton Street broke every one of the windows in the R. Hoe building.

My first brush with anti-Semitism came when I was ten years old. I ventured a block or two beyond our slum into the Irish slum. Some Irish kids chased me.

A year later, three of these Irish buckoes caught me when I dared a similar venture. They "cockalized" me. There are hundreds of men in their sixties who know what it is to be cockalized. Indeed, cockalization was universal. My father once told me there were specific Polish and Russian words for the process. The enemy kids threw the Jew to the ground, opened his pants, and spat and urinated on his circumcised penis while they shouted, "Christ killer."

The ritual of cockalization has disappeared in recent years. One reason is that so many Christian fathers consent to having male offspring circumcised. The more important reason is that anti-Semitism has had a separate secular career aside from its religious one.

Do not suppose I was any Goody Two-shoes. I was a smart kid but precocious only in mischief and villainy. I played hooky and went to the movies. The Gem and the Odeon were my favorites. I was unconscionably capable of forging a note the next day to explain my absence. "My son Herschele was sick yesterday. (Mrs.) Anna Goldhurst." Instinctively I knew "Herschele" and the parentheses would lend absolute verisimilitude to my forgery. The teachers called me Harry, but they knew my mother would call me Herschele.

Moe Yasser was my friend and accomplice. Moe is a manufacturing furrier today who has himself raised and educated a family of his own. I was a roly-poly fat kid, while Moe was strong, well coordinated, intrepid. Moe convinced me when I was six or seven that it was perfectly possible for a boy to walk across the Brooklyn Bridge alone. I went along because I was sure they wouldn't let a boy near the bridge unless he was with his mother or his brother Jake. But Moe was right. We walked across. I was frightened, but Moe wasn't. At least he said he wasn't.

One afternoon, Moe led me behind the alley of Katz's Turkish Baths on First Avenue and Second Street. It was Wednesday—ladies' day. Moe had discovered a peephole. We took turns. After

49

a half hour, Moe turned to me and in deep disappointment said, "Aw, you can't see nothing but the hair."

I took Moe into St. Patrick's Cathedral on Fifth Avenue. It was a Sunday afternoon, and we had come uptown on the Fifth Avenue bus to see the sights. After we spent an hour in one of the pews, I said, "Moe, now you are a Christian. I guess I am a Christian, too."

We walked back to the Lower East Side worrying about our conversion. Neither of us went home. We sat dejectedly on the steps of the Settlement House. Finally, past dark, we decided to ask my father.

As we told him, he was serious. He kept stroking his beard, which meant he was thinking furiously. We finished. He laughed. He said, "Moe, Harry. You are still good Jews. You have my word on the matter and I am sure the Pope's."

In the corner of the living room was my mother's dressmaking dummy: The torso was muslin tightly stitched over batting, the hips and legs wired steel hoops. One afternoon Moe and I found it dressed. We clamped one of Clara's discarded hats on its neck and carried it to the roof. We wrapped a length of clothesline around its waist and gently tipped the dummy off the precipice for a minute. We pulled it back. We peered below. A crowd was gathering.

We tipped the dummy again.

"Don't jump!" someone yelled below.

We waited. Another tilt. A collective moan of anguish. Now we were giggling. Again.

The roof door blew open, and three Irish policemen panted toward us, drawing up in absolute surprise. Moe and I dodged around the skylight once, but they cornered us.

Only my mother reacted sensibly to the situation. One of the policemen delivered me to my father by my ear. My father shamed and spanked me. My brothers and sisters avoided me as though I were contaminated. I couldn't bear myself. But my mother that evening took me in her arms and sighed, "Herschele, Herschele, as long as you're healthy."

Moe and I were what parents call a bad team, but every prince has his Falstaff and every Captain Boyle his Joxer.

Another pal was David Itzkowitz, today a salesman for a silk house. David was the philosopher, forever worried about the future. Would we become big-leaguers, playing for John McGraw in the Polo Grounds, or would we be better off as cops, provided the police accepted Jews? Hyman Reinstein always answered he was going into business for himself. We called Hyman Servo because he immediately favored Servia (Serbia) when Austria-Hungaria declared war in 1914. The Lower East Side Jews worshiped Emperor Franz Josef. One of the ways to sell newspapers on a day there was no news was to race through the streets shouting, "Extra! Extra! Franz Josef ill!" The Jews also detested the czar. But America decidedly favored England. Hyman, therefore, always qualified his partisanship with the proviso that somehow he hoped Serbia could win while Russia, England's ally, lost. Damned if it didn't happen after the Bolsheviks stormed the Winter Palace.

One of my classmates was Vincent Pareli, an Italian whose father operated a shoeshine parlor outside the Flatiron Building on Fifth Avenue and Twenty-third Street. Vincent also shined shoes in the afternoon and on the weekend. He told me about the men who climbed on the chair and sat there for three or four shines so they could watch the pretty girls betray an ankle as they boarded the trolley car. The Italians began to move eastward, across the Bowery, around 1910. Within a year all the tenements on Chrystie Street were filled with Italian families, and their children began to invade the classrooms of Public School 20, which up to now we thought of as "our" school. But of course it was not our school; it was a public school.

Our street games were puss-n-cat, Johnny on the Pony, and box ball. Puss was a four-inch length of broom handle; cat was the remaining length of a broomstick. We teed off from a manhole cover, and the regular rules of baseball applied. In Johnny on the Pony one team was "it." Its members bent over against a wall and braced themselves as the others leaped on their backs and tried to shout, "Johnny on the Pony," three times before falling off. If the "it" team caved in under the weight, they remained "it" forever. In choosing up sides, I was always the prime choice because of my weight. Box ball was played with a small rubber ball, using the cement squares of the sidewalk as a court. A player was allowed one bounce before returning the ball. The game ended if the ball bounced into the sewer.

In Public School 20 every boy played basketball. We went at

it on the asphalt playground, shooting through a hoop whose net had long ago deteriorated. We revered the Settlement House because it had a real basketball court, just like the one in the YMCA we heard about. We produced some great basketball players. There was Sam Strom, who later became the captain of the Columbia varsity, and Arnie Moskowitz, who joined a professional team.

Jewish boys were adept at basketball because it was an indoor game. The Irish on the West Side held the Hudson River, and the Italians held the East River and the public parks. We were landlocked, so we never became football or baseball players or great swimmers. But basketball was our game. Mr. Herman Brown was our basketball coach and our physical training teacher. He is still in the public school system. He must have been the eternal optimist because he once entered me in a 70-yard dash at the Seventy-first Regiment Armory during an interscholastic meet. I shot from the couch like Jesse Owens and finished fourth in a four-man race. The cheering had already subsided when I panted across the finish line. No medal for that!

The East Side Jews loved Italian opera. The phonograph set was the supreme luxury. Why Jews preferred the "Sextet" from *Lucia di Lammermoor* by Donizetti and the "Intermezzo" from *Cavalleria Rusticana* by Mascagni still escapes me. There is no doubt these were the favorites. When I first opened an office in Charlotte in an old office building downtown on Tryon Street, I played these two selections twice a day. A native-born Tarheel down the hall, a textile broker, stopped me by the stairs and asked me the name of the Jew music I was playing; he thought it was right smart catchy.

Early on I began to go up to the Metropolitan Opera House at Forty-first Street and Broadway. For $1 I could buy standing room in the top balcony. The line for standing room began to form at half past four, just when school let out. By seven o'clock it wound around the block. At seven thirty every Monday night a little, well-dressed old lady who always carried a woven shopping bag paid me 50 cents for my place. I went to the rear of the line, and she bought standing room in the orchestra, which was, of course, the premium ticket. This lady asked me once, "You weren't here last week?" and I replied, "It was a Jewish holiday, Chanukah," and she said, "Oh."

I took my father to hear Caruso sing the role of the Jew Eléazar in the opera *La Juive*. Not long afterward Caruso died, and my father reminded me, "The Jews have no luck."

In June, 1917, I was graduated from Public School 20. I enrolled immediately in the East Side Evening High School, whose classes were conducted in the same building, and completed the high school course in three years. From there I went to the City College of New York at Twenty-third Street and spent three more years studying five nights a week.

Chapter 6

My first job was selling newspapers. I hawked papers from the corner of Delancey and Norfolk streets from 4 P.M. to 6:30 P.M. every afternoon after school. My customers were the men exiting from the sweatshops who were making their way to the Brooklyn Bridge local stop of the subway, which took them over the bridge into Brooklyn. I remember the faces of many of these men, and out of nowhere I can remember what some of them said. One fellow bought a paper the day William Randolph Hearst announced his candidacy for the mayoralty nomination. "Hearst, Hearst," this fellow said seriously to me, "Hearst ain't the worst."

I sold the *Journal, World, Mail, Telegram, Sun, Globe,* the *Jewish Daily Forward,* and the *Post.* Each of them was deposited on the corner in a bundle of 20, and I opened them, spread them out, and started off with the one with the most lurid headline. Another Balkan incident was what we newsboys thought of World War I.

A little after six in the evening the distributor would come around to collect. First he had a horse-drawn cart, but before I moved on, he was driving an electric truck. I paid a penny for every paper and sold them for two cents. I could sell 100 papers a day; with a good headline, 150. Once a week I sold a Chinese newspaper named *Mong Gee.* It was a profitable sideline. *Mong Gee* cost a nickel, and I kept three cents. And I traversed Chinatown, for we fantasized this was the wicked and exotic East, not knowing it was the most law-abiding and decent neighborhood in all New York.

Near Norfolk and Delancey was Allen Street, which was lined with brothels. I ran occasional errands for the whores who lived there. They always gave me an extra nickel for delivering the paper and another nickel for running to the grocery store or the soft-drink stand. These brothels were $1 whorehouses, and on my way home in the evening I often saw the girls standing on the stoop, opening their robes to induce the passersby upstairs. There was a strip of oilcloth at the bottom of every bed so that the customer didn't have to take his shoes off.

In the summer I had another job. I delivered pretzels to the Polo Grounds for Bock and Company. Mr. Bock gave me two big baskets of pretzels, two nickels for carfare, and a dime for myself. I took the pretzels to the Stevens concession on the mezzanine and had to be there by 10 A.M. Then I could hang around the ball park until the game started that afternoon.

After delivering the pretzels, I made a beeline for the center field bleachers, where I could talk to the players going in and out of the clubhouse. I got to know some of them pretty well. Larry Doyle, the captain, a happy-go-lucky Irishman, no doubt the best second baseman in the league, asked me to get him a pack of Sweet Caporel cigarettes once, and Hooks Wiltse gave me a quarter and asked if I would find him a bunch of bananas.

In the clubhouse I met Christy Mathewson. I called him Mr. Mathewson, as did most of the younger players. He was the first college man to become a baseball star. He was graduated from Bucknell and also distinguished himself by becoming the first baseball player to go into uniform in 1917. He won 373 games in his lifetime.

The Jews of New York were hungry for a Jewish ballplayer, so they cheered Benny Kauff. But in the clubhouse intimacy I found out Benny Kauff was a Slav from the Pennsylvania coal mines. Some years later, John McGraw did start a Jew named Andy Cohen at second base, but Andy didn't cut the mustard.

At game time, everybody stared at the box behind third base occupied by a pretty woman in a big picture hat. As the Giants took the field, she stood up and bawled, "Come on, Artie! Give it to 'em!" and Artie Fletcher always tipped his hat to her and the umpire said, "Play ball."

My favorite ballplayer was Jeff Tesreau, another pitcher, called by his teammates Old Doc. We became friends because he was deeply interested in the Lower East Side Jews. I took him to my home one Friday night, and after the Sabbath dinner he stood around the piano singing with my sisters. He was a big blond man with curly hair and his right arm was twice as big around as his left.

Fifty years later I recalled these men to a fellow passenger on an airplane going to Chicago. In my companion's lapel I saw a Hall of Fame button, and we got to talking. He was Ray Schalk, the same "Cracker" Schalk who was a catcher for the Chicago Black Sox in 1919, when eight of his teammates threw the World Series to the Cincinnati Reds. Still a thin, wiry man, Schalk is the baseball coach at Purdue University. "I knew something was wrong," he said. "I could feel it. It just never occurred to me that a ballplayer would really throw a World Series game. It's a great honor to be a big-leaguer. It's a great honor to play in the World Series. The game is an honest game. That they didn't care about this was something no other ballplayer would suspect. I never suspected until the last game."

At eleven, I got my first regular job with the Postal Telegraph Company as a messenger. I worked in the Times Square Station on West Forty-fourth Street. My boss was Sam Roth, a young fellow whom we Jewish boys described as a "leaning Jew." We said he was a leaning Jew because he leaned backward to give all the good "books" to the Irish and Italian messengers. A book was a single telegram addressed to several people. Since we were paid two cents for every addressee, a big book was a much-desired assignment. During World War I, I carried a book from the Red Cross offices which was sent to at least 100 different addresses. It was a good day for me.

Another good assignment was delivering a telegram to Mr. Nathan Straus, the great philanthropist, the owner of R. H. Macy's. Mr. Straus had an office in Aeolian Hall on Forty-second Street. There were no red-tape secretaries or straw bosses to impede the Postal Telegraph messenger. I went in to Mr. Straus himself, handed him the telegram, and he gave me a $1 bill for a tip. I delivered only five or six telegrams to this magnificent gentleman. Perhaps some of the other boys got a chance for the dollar, too. It is perfectly possible the manager, Sam Roth, went over there with telegrams when he learned Mr. Straus believed philanthropy began at home.

I took a telegram to Mr. Job Hedges at Churchill's Restaurant at Broadway and Forty-ninth Street. The headwaiter pointed out the table, and when I approached, I was rooted to the spot. There beside Mr. Hedges was Lillian Russell, the one and only Lillian Russell. The event gave me a profound insight into the mystical experience. I know exactly how St. Thomas felt when God talked to him. St. Thomas dropped the basin in which he was shaving, and I dropped the telegram. Mr. Hedges tipped me $1 when I retrieved it. I suppose I should have disliked Mr. Hedges. The Socialist magazines I was reading called him a "traction magnate."

One summer I delivered pants for a tailor on Houston Street. In those days, when a man ordered a custom-tailored suit on Fifth Avenue, the fancy tailor cut only the jacket and jobbed out the trousers. Sam Lazarus was one of these jobbers. He paid me fairly, but he always insisted I hang around the shop when my deliveries were finished.

On a blistering hot day Sam would instruct me, "Sweep me the store; set me no fires; watch me the pants." Off he'd go to Coney Island, leaving behind the promise that he would return by five-thirty. I noticed he never made it. After I got on to his trick, as soon as he left, I closed up shop, too.

At this time I thought of an idea to make $5 and more on Saturday nights. David Itzkowitz and I hired a horse and wagon and rented a piano. We took our place on a good corner, Avenue A and Fourteenth Street, and plugged the latest songs. Dave played and I sang through a megaphone, and we sold the sheet music at 10 cents each, for which we paid a nickel at Feist & Feist and other music publishers.

I still remember all the songs we plugged, and the biggest seller was "Till We Meet Again," followed by "Just a Baby's Prayer at Twilight." There were others, of course, and I remember them all. At a "then-I-wrote" party at Wolfie Gilbert's home in Beverly Hills I was able to remind Wolfie of a song he had written but had forgotten: "Adair, My Sweet Adair."

The bar mitzvahs which took place on the Lower East Side of New York City years ago made a thirteen-year-old boy not only a member of the congregation, but a male adult with all the consequent responsibilities. It could not help doing this, since the children on the Lower East Side were surrounded by adults. Children today are surrounded by adults, but there is this difference: There was no special or unique world for the East Side boy, only one world—the adult world with all its pain and happiness. If the child wanted social contact and love, that was the world in which he achieved it.

I think this made it a better world for children.

It did not necessarily make better humans out of them, but all children must enter the adult world sooner or later, the world where you don't get everything you want—where there are such things as vain toil, crushing disappointments, stern and fierce competition, praise and blame. The earlier a child partakes in that world, the better adapted he is to survive its defeats and challenges and make a place that is his own.

It is no coincidence that the Anglo-Calvinist world, inheritors of the Judaic ethic, once shared the tradition of early adulthood. Englishmen put a topper and tails on a thirteen-year-old when they sent him off to prep school.

Thus it was that the East Side boy wanted working papers as soon as he could pronounce the words. He had to be fourteen years of age.

Thus, after leaving Public School 20, I got a job as a sizer in a straw hat factory on Twenty-third Street. Arnold Rosenbaum and Company occupied a whole story in a gloomy loft. There were a battery of thirty women at sewing machines stitching the hemp into shapeless hats. These hats were wheeled by the dozen to my station. I took each of them, dipped it into the boiling glue, spun it once so there was no Achilles' heel on the brim, and planted the hat firmly on several wooden blocks, approximating the sizes and shapes of different heads.

The vats of glue bubbled constantly at 100 degrees. The workingman adjusts. To this day I can dip my hand in boiling water with no ill effects. From these wooden blocks, Yonkel, the blocker, put them through their final process, a hydraulic steam press. Yonkel had only recently emigrated from Russia and spoke little English, but he had already devised a system to time how long he should keep the hat under the press without burning it. He sang a song with each hat:

Es vet kommen a tzeit

*Vet nicht zein vos
tzu essen.*

Translated, the song went, "There will come a time when there won't be anything to eat." Over the next year and a half I heard that song 100 times a day and never learned the subsequent lyrics. As soon as he finished, Yonkel released the press, and the hat went to the trimmers who decorated it with a ribbon and a hatband.

I was working at Rosenbaum and Company the day World War I ended. Mr. Rosenbaum ran into the factory, yelling, "They've signed the Armistice."

"The war is over!" we yelled, delirious.

"Go home and bury the Kaiser," said Arnold Rosenbaum, giving us the day off, and forthwith we all joined the people in the streets, as sure in our hearts that the world was safe for democracy as Neville Chamberlain was sure twenty years later that because Hitler signed a piece of paper, there would be peace in our time.

The war's end introduced a continuing argument between my father and me. My father disliked Woodrow Wilson and exhibited no sympathy for the League of Nations. "The Austro-Hungarian Empire was already a League of Nations, and Wilson helped smash it up. The Hungarians had their own schools and their own newspapers. The Czechs had their own schools and their own newspapers. The Slovaks the same. Wilson should not go to Europe; he does not understand Europe; he wants simply to Balkanize Europe. The reparations we demand from the Germans cannot be paid. Nor will the Germans try. That for Woodrow Wilson."

Rosenbaum and Company paid me $12 a week. The Cap and Hat Makers Union began organizing the shop. I signed up with the other workmen. We went on strike. I carried a picket sign which read, in Yiddish, UNFAIR TO LABOR. Mr. Rosenbaum came, saw us, and began crying, "Wasn't I good to you men? What are you trying to do to me?" Stonily we marched past him. "My God, I can't make a living myself," he wailed. Two days later, having exhausted all his dramatic ploys, Mr. Rosenbaum gave in and signed a contract. He gave us all union wages and back pay for the past two months. I went home with $70 extra that Saturday noon.

A week later Mr. Rosenbaum fired me. If he had to pay a sizer $17 a week, he told me, he was going to pay a family man, not some fresh kid who spent his noontime talking to the shop steward. I had unionized myself out of a job. I complained to the Cap and Hat Makers about the situation. Mr. Sy Goldberg sighed and said, "I'll give you a job. Sit at that desk. This union is going places, and you'll be a big labor official one day."

Every member of my family urged me to accept this offer. But I had the vague idea I wanted to become a teacher. Working for the union meant giving up night school, and it meant only $5 a week. I turned the offer down. Nor have I ever regretted it. Within the week I found a job as stock clerk with Oscar H. Geiger and Company, Furriers. Mr. Geiger was soon to change me completely. After my father and Public School 20, Oscar Geiger exercised the most profound influence over my life.

My cousin Phil Goldhirsch told me, "There's a job over at the place where I work. My boss is a nice fellow. Maybe he'll take you on."

Oscar H. Geiger was a furrier whose company was at 6 West Thirty-seventh Street, catercorner from the fashionable Brick Presbyterian Church on Fifth Avenue. One morning, still in knickers, cap, and sweater, I got on the freight elevator with Phil Goldhirsch, went up to the modest loft on the fourth floor, and told Mr. Geiger if he had a job open, I wanted it.

"Why is a young man like you out of work?" he asked.

I told him I had just unionized myself out of a job with Arnold Rosenbaum and Company.

"I know Arnold," Mr. Geiger said. It was an encouraging start. "How old are you?" he pursued.

"Fourteen."

"I can pay eight dollars a week," he said.

I started that morning. I was a floor boy. Mr. Geiger manufactured fur coats and stoles. The company contained first a showroom with gilt-edged mirrors, chairs, an efficient bookkeeper in the person of Phil Goldhirsch, and one light rack of furs. Behind the showroom was the factory. Lined along the windowless wall were bins where the various fur pelts were graded by size and quality. One of my jobs was to move the furs from the street once Mr. Geiger had bought them, up the elevator, and deliver them to Mr. Kicke, who sorted them in their appropriate bins. Mr.

Kicke was a German with a heavy accent who not only sorted the furs, but matched them for the coats and cut them as well. Laying the fur out on a long wooden table which resembled a butcher's block, Mr. Kicke gave each pelt three swift diagonal slices with a special knife to make the piece resilient. But before he slashed, he studied each fur with the solemn attention a diamond cutter gave each stone.

Another of my jobs was to pull the furs from the bin, stretch them, and hold them up for Mr. Kicke's inspection. When he didn't think one pelt would match another, he would shake his finger and scream, *"Nein, nein, nein."* There were afternoons when a woeful guilt washed over my whole being. Mr. Kicke just couldn't match the pelts, and the more I tried, the angrier he got. He could toss his cutter into the table with the skill of a schoolboy playing mumbly-peg with a penknife.

Once Mr. Kicke had matched and sliced the furs, another German named Franz stitched them together. He used a special sewing machine. The threads never showed. It was also one of my jobs to claim these coats and deliver them to the two women at the rear of the factory who did the finishing work, the lining, the collar, and the buttons.

Then I would deliver the finished fur. Among his customers, Mr. Geiger numbered some of the aristocratic elite. There was Mrs. Frank Vanderlip, wife of the wealthy banker; Mrs. Herbert Lehman, the wife of the man who would one day become governor of New York; and Mrs. Stanton Van Wee, who was married to a famous golfer of the era.

Oscar H. Geiger specialized in mink and Hudson seal. Hudson seal was popular in those days. The coat was muskrat, dyed black, a process invented by the Newark, New Jersey, firm of Mike Hollander. Hudson seal was appreciably cheaper than authentic seal, and it wore and looked better because seal turned red with wear while Hudson seal stayed black.

My boss was forty-five years old when I first met him, six feet tall, trim and wiry, with black hair and a neatly trimmed mustache. His eyes were slightly protuberant, and he wore rimless glasses, but they were still a mysterious liquid brown. He was meticulous. His shoes were always shined, his suits neatly pressed, his shirt always white and starched. On the hottest July days he never removed his coat to roll up his sleeves. Women found him

61

attractive, and Oscar had an undeniable way with them. Show him a woman and he could sell her a fur coat, he always said. He had wit, charm, a certain business sense—everything which should have made him a millionaire furrier with a string of mistresses from Lenox Avenue to Miami Beach. But he was not and had none of these. The single tax was his undoing.

When he was a young man, Oscar Geiger met Henry George, the economic radical who wrote *Progress and Poverty*. Oscar Geiger was transformed by this meeting in the way a man struck by lightning is transformed. Nor was Oscar Geiger the only man so transformed. George Bernard Shaw thought Henry George opened the gates of heaven and not only that; Shaw tried emulating Henry George's style, an act of love which Shaw fortunately turned to his own advantage.

Henry George, born in Philadelphia in 1839, buried in New York fifty-eight years later, saw that progress is always attended by poverty. One of the reasons for this absurd paradox, George noted, was that while population increases, land does not. Land simply appreciates. As soon as the population grows, realty prices go up. It is possible, therefore, for the landowner to grow rich doing nothing. Land, labor, and capital are the sources of all wealth, George argued, yet labor is constantly in debt. That was because spiraling costs separate people from the land. To abolish poverty, Henry George proposed the single tax. It is the government's duty to confiscate the unearned increment of land values. For it is the burgeoning population, not the landowner, who pays for the schools, policemen, firemen, the burgeoning population who becomes the consumers by virtue of which land becomes more and more valuable.

Mr. Geiger always gave as an example the people of a town who want to get rid of dogs. They tax the dogs. The higher the tax, the sooner the dogs disappear. The government could tax improvements on property until at last private property disappeared.

The single tax was not Henry George's only contribution to economic philosophy. He also advocated rent control, public housing, a minimum wage, the abolition of child labor, a graduated income tax, government control of railroad and utility rates, a forty-hour workweek, unemployment insurance, and public ownership of public utilities. Naturally Henry George was considered a lunatic. So were his disciples, men like Oscar Geiger. But

Oscar was in good company. Senator Robert M. La Follette of Wisconsin was a single taxer; so was Newton D. Baker, Woodrow Wilson's Secretary of War, as well as Tom Johnson, the mayor of Cleveland; even Woodrow Wilson subscribed in part to the Georgian thesis.

It is true, Henry George overestimated the role of land and rent in economic development. But Henry George was the first systematic philosopher to argue that poverty was not a natural condition, a state produced by immutable laws. Poverty was the result of bad planning. One kind of planning will result in one kind of economic structure, another kind of planning in a different one. To this day I say amen to that.

Oscar Geiger gave up a job as the director of the Hebrew Orphanage to help Henry George campaign for mayor of New York in 1886. On a reform ticket, George ran against Democrat Abram S. Hewitt and Republican Theodore Roosevelt. Hewitt had 90,-000 votes; George, 68,000; and Roosevelt, 60,000. As Oscar Geiger never tired of repeating, Tammany fixed 12,000 votes. Henry George should have been mayor of New York. In 1897 George ran again. He was a shoo-in when apoplexy killed him two nights before election in his campaign headquarters. The single taxers put the name of Henry George, Jr., on the ballot. But it was no use. The man had died. But Oscar Geiger saw to it the work went on. Oscar Geiger wrote the slogan of the Single Tax Party: "The Earth Is the Birthright of All Mankind—and All Have an Equal Right to Its Use."

He was, to say the least, a different kind of furrier. Oscar was the son of a Jewish emigrant from Germany. He was as well a descendant of the famous Rabbi Abraham Geiger who started the Jewish reform movement in the nineteenth century. He had studied for the rabbinate himself, but before his ordination he left the shul. A little later he began to take instruction with one of the Paulist Fathers at the church at Fifty-ninth Street and Columbus Avenue. Geiger's searching questions discouraged his instructor, and he left unconverted, but let us hope not unblessed.

Working for Oscar Geiger, I saw that he spent an inordinate amount of time discussing political theory and a dismaying amount of time selling furs. The furs interested him not at all. The theories set him on fire. I didn't know it, but most of his time was spent with either Joseph Dana Miller, the head of the

Single Tax Party, or with party stalwarts Morris Van Veen or William Pleydell.

On my first payday, Oscar Geiger gave me Henry George's *Progress and Poverty, Social Problems,* and *A Perplexed Philosopher.* I thanked him. Anyone who has read Henry George knows his style is cramped. Although he strikes some telling phrases, his paragraphs are fatiguing. *Progress and Poverty* was a tall order for a floor boy. But I was game.

Oscar Geiger cross-examined me Monday. I said Henry George was a lot harder than Shakespeare.

"You read Shakespeare?" he asked.

"I'm more interested in history than in economics," I said.

"But Shakespeare is the proper preparation," he said. "I doubt very seriously if a man can understand Henry George who cannot understand *Julius Caesar, Hamlet,* or *Macbeth.*"

I allowed then as I might like Henry George sooner rather than later. What I didn't realize was that every classic, every author was preparation for Henry George. As I say, not only was Henry George gravity, but he was $E = mc^2$.

"In fact," Geiger went on, "I have a club, a boys' club, which meets every week at my house. I think you'd like to join."

The single tax ruled not only Oscar Geiger's working life and his leisure hours but his family relationships. Several years before, Oscar had recruited his son, George, named after the philosopher, of course, and George's pal Elliott Barrett, and established the Round Table Literary Club, to which members were added from year to year.

The patience of the man! Twice a week he was able to focus the attention of teen-age boys on the social problems of the day and on the treasures of the past. Each meeting opened with Oscar Geiger depositing on the round living-room table before him an octagonal gold watch, a pad, and a pencil. He read the convocation, which was a passage from *Progress and Poverty,* and he closed the meeting with a benediction from *Social Problems.* The Round Table was dedicated to truth, exactitude, and friendship. We were given turns at opening the meeting. I always chose the passage from *Progress and Poverty* in which Henry George charged that poverty is a crime. Murder is a crime, he added, but it is not a crime to be murdered.

The Sunday after the invitation I went up to Harlem to 212

West 118th Street. It was white Harlem then, a prosperous middle-class neighborhood with wide streets and the brownstones set far back on the sidewalks. The stoops were guarded by iron banisters painted either white or black, in the foyers the mailboxes gleamed like mirrors, and a rug or mat covered the white hexagonal tiles. All these buildings had been designed some decades before by the architect Stanford White. Though the very rich had left them and they had been converted from homes into multiple dwelling structures, they still reflected opulence. Halls were clean and carpeted. The ceilings were high. The floors were burnished with wax.

The Geigers lived on the third floor. When I rang, Mr. Geiger welcomed me and led me into a spacious apartment, seven rooms in all, each of the rooms with a door. Where I lived, the rooms were laid out one after the other. Here they were adjacent to each other, like spokes spreading from the living room, which was the hub.

I passed through a small hall, and there I saw it, the round table covered with a lace tablecloth. A hanging Tiffany lamp illuminated it; its shade was composed of varicolored glass. Curtains shielded the room from the sun. The windows were clean, not begrimed. In each corner of the room were easy chairs. A bathroom, complete with tub and sink, was inside the apartment. Where I lived, we stacked the garbage in the hall and all the tenants used a common toilet. Through the glass-doored cabinets of the kitchen I could see tureens, plates, cups, and saucers. My mother went through her stack of cheap pottery at dinnertime like a gambler through a deck of cards looking for an ace.

I stared now at boys in suits and neckties. For the first time I was looking at the middle class. From the moment I entered that brownstone, I resolved that this was what I wanted. I felt just like Pip in Dickens' *Great Expectations* when he met Miss Havisham. I have gone bankrupt, been imprisoned, cursed employers, and had employees curse me in pursuing these values, yet for the life of me I cannot take back the splendor I thought I saw that Sunday morning. We are a middle-class society, and that first vision is almost apocalyptic. I know the middle class inculcates a selfishness and a carelessness in us, a wish that it all be for us and us alone, I know the middle class victimizes the best and encourages the worst, yet to this day I want it.

65

There were nine boys around the table staring just as curiously at me. They all had attended Public School 10 in Harlem and were now at De Witt Clinton High School. All of us have played into and out of our lives since then. These nine were: George Geiger, called Gigs, my good friend; John Duff, perhaps my closest friend; Murray DeLeeuw, called Mush; Milton Bergerman; Sidney Davidson; Robert Gomperts; Chester Edelman; Henry Lowenberg; Elliott Barrett; and Milton Norwalk.

Gigs had his own room, which surprised me. My surprise was compounded by the knowledge each of these boys at home had his own room. It surprised me to see them rise when a lady entered a room. It surprised me that their table manners glittered like diamonds. It surprised me that they had read all the books I had and more. It surprised me when they wanted to know what a hat factory looked like.

Mr. Geiger introduced me to each of them. He called them "his boys" and insisted all his life he was their second father. The Round Table Literary Club conducted itself according to parliamentary rules. It had a president, a secretary, and a treasurer, though for the life of me I cannot remember ever having paid any dues. Once a year we elected officers, and though the post of treasurer circulated among all of us, no one but Gigs ever opened a meeting and no one but Milton Norwalk ever took notes.

"New business," said Oscar Geiger, watch, pencil, pad at the ready, "is Milton's *Paradise Lost*.

" 'Of Man's first disobedience, and the fruit/ Of that forbidden tree . . .' " began Gigs. We took turns reading, Oscar always explaining, questioning, wondering, demanding of us what made the poem great. We finished *Paradise Lost* in three months and went on to Dante's *Divine Comedy* and *Don Juan* by Lord Byron.

This wasn't all we did in our sessions. Mr. Geiger was known as an intellectual in the city, and he was able to invite to our meetings people like Samuel Seabury, Louis F. Post, Assistant Secretary of Labor in Woodrow Wilson's administration, Henry George, Jr., and Mr. and Mrs. William C. De Mille (Mrs. De Mille was Anna George).

Sideline reading was *Far from the Madding Crowd* and *Return of the Native* by Thomas Hardy; *Don Quixote* by Cervantes; *The Way of All Flesh* by Samuel Butler. We read Ibsen and

Shaw, and each summer before we adjourned until the fall, we acted out one Shakespearian tragedy.

During these years of Georgian instruction, I still read voraciously on my own. I read Lincoln Steffens' *The Shame of the Cities* and Jane Addams' *Twenty Years at Hull House,* and *The Spirit of Youth and the City Streets.* I knew Booker T. Washington's *The Future of the American Negro* and *Life of Frederick Douglass.*

Douglass was a great man severely criticized for marrying a white woman. He was a fugitive slave from Baltimore who saved his wages to purchase the freedom of his childhood sweetheart. When she died years later, Douglass remarried. Whites heaped scorn and contempt on him; Negroes called him a traitor. To all this Douglass replied, "I do not see what they are troubled about. My first wife was the color of my mother. My second wife is the color of my father." Douglass was welcomed by Lincoln in the White House, an event about which he wrote an essay saying that in Lincoln's presence, he, Douglass, was color-blind.

Good going, I thought.

I read W. E. B. Du Bois' *The Souls of Black Folk* and *Color and Democracy.* George Geiger told me about Thorstein Veblen and John Dewey, and I told him all about the great Socialist tracts —Ray Stannard Baker's *The Tragedy of the Mulatto* and *The Black Man's Silent Power,* as well as his epochal *What Is A Lynching?,* written in 1906 and still a definitive study.

There was H. L. Mencken and George Jean Nathan in the *Smart Set* and later in the *American Mercury.* There was the *Nation* with Oswald Garrison Villard, and little did I dream I would one day be a steady contributor to the magazine Godkin founded, the oldest liberal publication in the world. There were also the *New Republic* with editorials every week by Herbert Croly, whose book *Progressive Democracy* I reread every five years. Croly's father invented the word "miscegenation." I read Oscar Ameringer's personal journal, *The American Guardian,* in which he said, "Cannibalism gave way to capitalism when it was discovered it was much better to exploit man than eat him."

I read the *Appeal to Reason,* the periodical later taken over by my friend E. Haldeman-Julius, for whom I wrote many of his *Little Blue Books* in the 1940's. Haldeman-Julius always wrapped up two $20 bills in tissue paper and mailed them to me for each article.

Walter Lippmann was beginning his career in those years, he of whom Carl Sandburg said, "He was born smart." And there was Carl Sandburg himself. Out of curiosity I read the *Chicago Poems* in 1918 because Herbert Croly said they were a new language. I cannot recall the date of issue of that *New Republic*, but I can remember it contained on one page Thomas Hardy's last poems and on the facing page one of John Crowe Ransom's first. My sons Richard and William both studied modern poetry with John Crowe Ransom at Kenyon. Both of them respectively were surprised when I said, "I know his work."

Every two months the Round Table convened at the nearby Wadleigh High School and met in debate with another club. We debated such issues as "Resolved: Immigration Should Be Restricted" and "Resolved: Capital Punishment Should Be Abolished." Geiger made these arrangements for us through the Board of Education, prescribed the books for the research, heard us out in practice, and judged us in competition. We were often our own audience except for the vagrants who would straggle in out of the cold to hear whether or not the United States should join the League of Nations.

We also gave our own talks on topics which specifically interested us. Once Milton Norwalk, describing prehistoric man, stated that *Pithecantropus erectus,* or the Java Man, lived 500,000 years ago.

"Five hundred thousand years ago?" asked Geiger suddenly, "or five hundred thousand B.C." He and Norwalk got so wrapped up in the subject that we all quite lost our bearings until Gigs asked, "What difference does nineteen hundred years make?"

"Exactitude, exactitude," snapped the father. "Now which is it, Norwalk? Five hundred thousand years ago or five hundred thousand B.C.?"

Don't think he was without his humor. He had a quick wit. We watched him teach a class of young toughs one night at a settlement house. As soon as he turned his back, one of these boys let fly with a wad of tobacco, which fortunately missed Geiger but slapped hard against the blackboard. Geiger picked up a piece of chalk and drew a pyramid under the plug. "Now watch," he told the class, "let's see if it will fall off." He won them.

Geiger's personality secured the club. He was a positive man. He assured us he was the final word on many subjects. There was no reason to doubt him. He taught us subjects on which our schoolteachers never touched. He nurtured a camaraderie which lasted through all our lives. And he never allowed our meetings to become competitive.

When I, a father myself, tried to start a similar society in Shrewsbury, New Jersey, years later, all I did was reduce a patent attorney named Sam Ostrolenck and myself to dewy eyes by reading Myra Kelly's *Little Citizens* aloud while our several sons fidgeted restlessly and impatiently for the first and last meeting of the Round Table Literary Club II to adjourn.

The boys who congregated at Oscar Geiger's were the first assimilated Jews I had ever met. I grew up with Jews who revered ritual and the Talmud as Oscar Geiger revered the single tax and Henry George. My father always wore a *yarmulke,* the cap worn by Orthodox Jews. I *davened* (prayed) every morning. My mother kept a kosher kitchen. On the Lower East Side we had heard of the fancy uptown Jews who sat in temples and listened to organ music just like the Christians, but we didn't think we would ever be subjected to their impiety. Oscar Geiger and the boys who attended the Round Table Literary Club were relaxed about their Judaism. They mixed freely and unself-consciously with Gentiles.

In fact, Oscar Geiger was married to a Gentile, Nina Daly, a handsome, petite woman with brown hair and blue eyes. While she treated each of us politely, she was obviously our equal. She joked with us, advised us sometimes, gave us her own views on important matters. She wore stylish dresses, like the ladies in the rotogravure. My mother still wore a babushka and a long home-spun dress. Nina Daly Geiger had been born in America, too, like her husband and the other boys. She was far from my idea of what an Irishwoman was like. She told me once, "Jesus is a back number." I think one of the reasons I married Genevieve Gallagher was that I knew and admired Nina Daly and the home she made for Oscar Geiger. There was an equality between them, an atmosphere of give-and-take which was different from the atmosphere in my home where my father reigned as the paterfamilias, right or wrong. The Geigers could divide responsibilities and still share them.

Mrs. Geiger's mother, Kitty Daly, also lived in the apartment. She had emigrated from Ireland to America right after Lincoln's assassination. She was, at the time that I knew her, a frail old lady. Bob Gomperts always called her his century plant, and she shook her cane at him as often as he said it. She died at ninety, and toward the end she lost her sight. Her health was too bad to risk her traveling up and down the stairs and streets. Every week a young priest from the neighborhood Roman Catholic church visited her. Once Gigs, John Duff and Milton Norwalk decked me out to resemble the priest, and I went into Kitty Daly's room to fulfill the masquerade. When she told me she wanted to make her confession, I lost my nerve and bolted. Thereafter she shook the cane in my direction, too.

Murray DeLeeuw's family had come to America from Holland over a century before. I told my mother Mrs. DeLeeuw could not speak Yiddish, only English. My mother shrugged and said, "She can't be a real Jewish mother, Herschele."

The boys of the club gave me lots of new ideas. My father angrily declaimed, "That a boy should study to become a good Jew, fine. That he should study to become a bad Jew is foolish. You come from the homes of goyim and ask your mother for to-mah-to juice with a white napkin. Is your mother a German Jew who should squeeze with her hands the to-mah-to from New Jersey?"

"It isn't to-mah-to," I said arrogantly. "It's tomato. It makes us healthy. It has vitamins."

"And the white napkin? That has vitamins?"

"The white napkin is to make us Americans."

After Oscar Geiger came down to our tenement for dinner, my father no longer deplored the Round Table Literary Club. I am not sure my father accepted the single tax as the motivating force of the universe, but he did agree with Oscar Geiger that the election of Warren G. Harding as President was a disaster of unprecedented proportions.

I was an anomaly to my friends. Moe Yasser did not believe there were Jewish boys who had never been bar mitzvahed. "What kind of life can there be without the shul?" he asked. But indeed there was a life outside and without the shul, as many of these Lower East Side boys soon learned.

John Duff became my closest friend. I never met a smarter Irishman, save my wife's brother, Hubert D. Gallagher. John was the son of a fireman. He was already a big bluff boy, with a leg crippled by polio in infancy. Mrs. Duff, his mother, always insisted on renting the top floor of the apartment in which they lived so that John would have to climb several flights every day. John's limp was noticeable but not pronounced.

We used to tease John about the size of his mouth. Physically it was the biggest mouth I have ever seen. He could insert a whole sausage and smile and talk while he chewed it. Years later, when we were all grown men, I invited the Round Table up to Larchmont to celebrate the arrival of my first son. John won a bet he could drink a schooner of beer at one draft.

His leg kept him from playing sports, but John loved baseball, football, and basketball. At the High School of Commerce he was the manager of the baseball team, the first baseman of which was Lou Gehrig. The baseball coach once confided in John that Lou was in a little trouble over an upcoming Regents examination. The coach was right. John said, "Lou had a blank face and a blank paper." He did what every dedicated baseball manager would do—he helped out.

John wanted to become a sportswriter, but his family prevailed upon him, and he entered Fordham University and prepared for law. But a lot of his practice was always with ballplayers, prizefighters, and sport promoters. He was the first man I ever knew who went to a professional football game. "On a Sunday?" I asked him incredulously.

He was not as far as I could determine a "punctual" Catholic. If he was anything, he was a rationalist. He had no curiosity about other religions. What did matter to him, even in his early youth, was civil liberties. The day he hung out his shingle he started taking cases from indigent Negroes, and he took them on all his life. In 1960 he published *A. Lincoln: Prairie Lawyer*. The book satisfied a lifelong ambition.

It is true John had talents which he wasted, that he was gruff and hard-boiled. I think I was one of the few people who ever saw him cry. I was in the room with him when his father died. Duff senior's last words were, "O, believe me if all those endearing young charms . . ." I heard John's sobs. One of the regrets I must accommodate is that I was away on an extensive lecture trip when John fell ill and died. I did not learn for a month that he was gone. When his wife told me, I thought, *I meant to call that man last week.*

John and I were the sophisticates of the Round Table, by which I mean we knew a woman before any of the others. When we described this delicious adventure, Murray DeLeeuw begged us to take him. We even made a date with little Annie O'Donnell, one of John's special pals, who decorated the wall of her room with a picture of the Sacred Heart.

I do Murray no disservice when I say he was devoted to his mother and she to him. When he worried that his mother might question his activities for the evening, we advised that we would call and leave shortly thereafter on the pretense we were going to the club.

We arrived that Saturday. We found the DeLeeuws, mother and son, sitting together on the living-room couch. Conversation was desultory. At last, John, slapping his thigh, said, "Murray, I have a good idea. Let's go over to the club."

"John," said Murray quietly, "I've told Mother everything."

"Well, you goddamned fool," said Duff. "Good night."

On election night in 1928, John Duff and I were in Joe Mc-Cormack's Tammany Club on the West Side. Joe McCormack was the marriage clerk of the city of New York and a powerful Tammany leader, although he lost his grip on the West Side when the United States government sent him to jail for income-tax evasion. Duff and I were enchanted as the Tammany men kept listing the election returns on a slate blackboard with a rasping piece of chalk.

"Eighth Assembly District—Smith, 1,022; Hoover, 9. Ninth Assembly District—Alfred E. Smith, 2,687; Hoover, 901." These districts were Joe McCormack's duchies. Joe looked happy about the whole thing. It was a big night for the Democrats. John and I decided to go down to Times Square and lend our presence to the celebration. The first thing that met our eyes as we exited from the subway was the lighted ribbon of the New York *Times'* bulletin board. It kept flickering and the sentences kept chasing: "Hoover by a landslide."

"Son of a bitch," said Duff. "If we had stayed at McCormack's club, Smith would have won."

Lou Gehrig also affected the destiny of Gigs Geiger. Oscar

72

Geiger believed in athletics. Not only was the whole man a single taxer, but he was also physically fit. All the Round Table Literary Club members were proficient sportsmen, save me. After a series of downs in football, I was invariably found on my back panting like a ferry unable to leave its wharf. George Geiger was an exceptional first baseman. He would have led Columbia to the Ivy League championship. Except that Lou Gehrig led them to the championship.

Gigs instead became a philosopher, one of the most profound students of Dewey and pragmatism the academy has ever known. John Dewey wrote the introduction to George Geiger's published doctorate, *The Philosophy of Henry George*. Since then George has published a series of important philosophical works, among which are *Theory of the Land Question*. *Toward an Objective Ethic, Philosophy and the Social Order*, and his book *John Dewey in Perspective* remains to this day a final assessment of this great American thinker. If George were the only philosopher you ever met, you would think they were a race of men kind, polite, courteous, fair, a little sentimental, and all good listeners, a series of virtues I submit is far from the truth. Most philosophers I've met are at pains to tell you they have found the truth, the whole truth, they found it years ago and goddamn it, will you shut up and listen?

Baseball's loss was philosophy's gain. I suspect if the single tax hadn't entered George's life as early as it did, he would have become an actor. He was an extraordinarily handsome man and a superb dancer. He and my wife, Genevieve, just taking a turn around the floor, came in second in a mammoth dance contest in Coney Island. George has always taken part in amateur and college productions.

He is also able to turn a felicitous phrase. I have swiped as many as he has ever confided in a letter.

Having earned his doctorate, he went off to teach in North Dakota. I wrote him, "What can Fargo, North Dakota, offer that New York can't?"

"Among other advantages," he replied, "Fargo has a movie theater which plays Clark Gable pictures, it has an air-cooled five-and-ten, and I earn my living here. Little wonder that I love it."

George was always the first to congratulate me: He was happy when I married; he sent me a wire when I was paroled, when I published the first edition of the *Carolina Israelite,* when *Only in America* came out, and when I told him I was writing this autobiography. For the last three decades he has been a professor of philosophy at Antioch College in Yellow Springs, Ohio, where he has made his home with Louise, once a Spanish teacher at the same school.

Bob Gomperts was our track star, the fastest single taxer who ever ran the 100-yard dash. He was always good company, but he never had a clear idea of what he wanted to be. At one point Oscar convinced him chiropracty was the coming thing. Oscar wanted each one of his boys to fill one of life's many departments, and there was a vacancy at the moment in chiropractic. Gomperts tried it, gave it up, and became instead a successful lawyer.

Milton Bergerman was slow but persistent, steady, and sure to succeed. He was essentially a farm boy, whose parents had moved from New Jersey to New York when his father became head buyer for Hearn's Department Store. Before he entered college, Milton broached the idea of changing his name.

"What name?" asked Oscar.

"Gainsborough," said Milton.

"Milton Gainsborough?" asked Oscar.

"Yes."

"Not Thomas Gainsborough?"

"I don't want to be confused with the painter," Milton answered.

The name Milton Bergerman should be familiar to New Yorkers. For many years he was the head of the Citizens Union, a dogged watchdog of the city's treasury.

Chester Edelman was cool and calculating. He could punt a football 60 yards. He was also the catcher for the City College baseball team. Oscar never had to give a second thought to what department in life Chester would populate. Edelman said he was going to be the millionaire, and Edelman was right. Whether he is still a single taxer or not I don't know. He didn't sound like one the last time we met in the 1960's.

Mush DeLeeuw's mother was a widow who supported herself and Murray by giving piano lessons. Murray may not have been concert caliber, but to this day it is a delight to hear him play. He was a compulsive gambler, yet possessed the best card sense I have ever seen. He could play bridge with the best of them. After he was graduated from Columbia, in fact, he remarked casually to Ely Culbertson that a bridge dictionary might not be a bad idea, a suggestion which, to Murray's distress, Ely Culbertson took to heart. Murray was the only one who could beat Oscar consistently at chess.

Not long ago when I spoke to a Jewish audience in Rochester there in the front row sat Murray DeLeeuw, one of the ablest lawyers in the city. I told the folks how Murray had introduced me to the joys of tomato juice.

It was the boyhood friendship between Gigs and Elliott Barrett that inspired Oscar to found the Round Table. Elliott Barrett was perhaps the most interesting of us and the most alarming. George Geiger told me he spent happy years playing cowboys and Indians with Elliott except George was always the Indian. Elliott was incredibly brilliant, violent, irascible, anti-Semitic. In short, a *meshuganah*.

He disappointed me bitterly during one of the club debates when he argued dogmatically that the Jews had all the money. When I pointed out that I was working for $8 a week for a furrier who was far from rich, Elliott insisted neither Oscar nor I was a representative Jew. At Columbia, Elliott was the intercollegiate fencing champion. He was the strong boy of the group, tall with big shoulders and strong hands.

Elliott was a chemist for Du Pont and spent most of his life in Baltimore. One of his great friends was Warren McCulloch, the world's leading expert on cybernetics and brain psychology. A Civil War buff, Elliott's grandfather had taken a minié ball in the face at the Battle of Shiloh. An earlier ancestor fought at Bunker Hill. Elliott was our only "old American."

He subscribed wholeheartedly to the Vedic philosophy, and at one of our meetings he told Oscar he had discovered he could separate his spirit from his body. When we scoffed, Elliott reddened. He began his trance.

Oscar interrupted him. "Elliott, it could have fatal results, fatal. We need to separate the land from the landlords before we go on to soul and body."

Long before I met him, Henry Lowenberg had resolved to become a lawyer. And a lawyer he is, a cagey, tough criminal lawyer. Henry revered Oscar Geiger and named his first son Oscar. He married early, and we all envied him the beautiful blonde he captured.

Milton Norwalk, whose devotion to the club is as strong today as it was in 1918, is still the recording secretary, keeping everyone posted on everyone else's activities. The Round Table Literary Club kept him from joining a fraternity at Columbia. He told the boys who wanted to pledge him that he was afraid the fraternity would interfere with the schedule of the Round Table, which, after all, was the only club in the world which convened solely to discover the truth.

Milton spoke haltingly. Oscar once advised him to go to the Sheep Meadow in Central Park and orate to the rocks as Demosthenes once orated to the sea. It didn't work appreciable wonders, however.

He was an honors graduate at Columbia and went on for an advanced degree in history but has made his living in the spice business. Norwalk had an unbounded intellectual curiosity. One of our amusements was to hike along the New Jersey Palisades. We took the ferry over and spent the day along the paths and trails. On one of these expeditions, Milton tripped and plunged off a precipice. Mush DeLeeuw lowered himself, expecting bleeding flesh and a crumpled corpse. He came upon a meditative Milton, who, despite his torn knickers and scraped knees, was studying the flower in the crannied wall. "Isn't this a wonderful example of cross-pollinization by wind action?" he asked DeLeeuw. Last year, when Milton visited Gigs in Yellow Springs, he insisted on knowing the names of all the Ohio flora and fauna, a pursuit in which Gigs confessed he was less interested than proficient.

Sidney Davidson was kind and affable. His parents were divorced, and Sidney lived with his mother. When we played poker at Sidney's house, she couldn't do enough for us. Sidney became an eminent doctor, the chief surgeon at a hospital in Long Island. He is also a painter of considerable skill and has several times had galleries stage one-man shows of his work.

Sidney and I met at the Algonquin not long ago and reminisced about the club and Oscar. Sidney said, "Oscar knew everything. He never doubted. He insisted it was indigestion that night when it was a heart attack. More men who know everything die in the bathroom of a heart attack because they are positive it is indigestion."

In 1924 the Single Tax Party, later to become the Land and Liberty Party, nominated Oscar Geiger for Senator. At the convention, which I believe was held in a rented theater, one of the executive committee members said, "Oscar, it's your turn to run for something. I ran last time." Oscar said he'd put his name up wherever they needed it most. After the delegates nominated Oscar for the Senate, the band struck up, which led one of the reporters to comment that it was the first funeral he'd ever attended where the deceased provided his own music.

The platform? Single tax. Votes? Never counted. But the club trooped after Oscar, and all of us learned to be soapboxers. We opened our meetings either in Lincoln Square or on one of the street corners in the West Seventies on Amsterdam Avenue. Mr. Geiger or Morris Van Veen or Joseph Dana Miller mounted the box and started spieling. The rest of us took our turns. It was no simple thing to contend against Tammany Hall with the explanation of the unearned increment of land values. Often, when one of us finished, and looked down, there was no one left except Morris Van Veen holding the flag and someone else holding the soapbox.

Haranguing one crowd, I wanted a dramatic example of unearned increments. "Look at Ward's Shoe Store," I shouted. Everyone turned to look. There, in front of Ward's Shoe Store were two exceptionally pretty girls, chatting as they twirled their parasols. That was that for the audience. I never got them back.

One night as Oscar was holding forth from the soapbox, a policeman approached and asked, "Do you have a permit for this speech?" Oscar paid no attention to the question.

More sternly, the policeman persisted, "Let me see your permit."

In aggravation over the interruption, Oscar turned and said, "My permit was given to me in the city of Philadelphia on July fourth, seventeen seventy-six."

The cop ran to the call box to ask his precinct captain how to proceed.

The Socialists also made harangues from street corners. Morris Hillquit was a brilliant speaker; so, too, were Louis Waldman and Congressman Meyer London. My special favorites were Scott Nearing, Algernon Lee, Norman Thomas, and August Claessens. Claessens was a Roman Catholic. He pleased and flattered Jewish audiences by including several Yiddish words in his oration. He insisted he wanted to be buried in the cemetery of the *Arbeiter Ring*, the Workmen's Circle. He wrote, "The last place the devil will look for a goy will be in a Jewish cemetery."

Tammany Hall did everything to harass these Socialists. Tammany Hall would set up on a nearby corner and when the Socialist began to speak, the Tammany men would sing:

> Tammany, Tammany!
> Heap big chief in his tepee
> Cheering braves to victory!
> Swamp um, swamp um, get the wampum
> Tammani-eee!

Oscar knew everything. Spiritualism always interested him. I remember him delivering a eulogy over a dead man in which he spoke to the deceased as though he were actually present. At the end of his life, he was the pastor of the First Spiritualist Church.

He talked often to the dead and arranged for the club to attend séances, where we, too, communicated with the dead.

One of these expeditions was conducted in the home of a medium named St. Ives. The heavily draped room was completely dark and there was no sound except for three muted trumpets which lay in a phosphorus circle on the floor. For some unexplained reason, mediums always found I was "clairvoyant" with the shade of an Indian maiden who had died 400 years ago. She guided me, and I guided the Round Table.

We held hands and sang, usually the hymn "In the Sweet Bye and Bye," and then I spoke, first to Henry James and then to the Polish general who fought for the Continental Army, Thaddeus Kosciusko.

There were other mediums we met—Mrs. Cook, a handsome flaxen-haired woman from Chicago, and Frank Montsko, who had a harelip, but the voices he summoned never betrayed this affliction.

Oscar remained persuaded, but the rest of us walked away. Why, I wondered, could the dead not bring themselves to talk to Woodrow Wilson or David Lloyd George, Prime Minister of England, or the Tiger of France, Georges Clemenceau? The dead remain curiously content to talk to a housewife in Kalispell, Montana, or to two adolescent girls in Boston, Massachusetts (so many of these things originate in Boston!).

Last, though I was clairvoyant, none of the dead ever spoke Yiddish. I have had thousands of relatives pass in the great beyond, I told Oscar, none of whom could speak anything but Yiddish. Why should Henry James of Harvard come through to me and not one single relative from Galicia?

I worked for Oscar Geiger until 1923. I was raised from $8 to $23 a week. I left because I had a chance for a job in Wall Street, but my relationship with the members of the Round Table continued.

In 1924 later some thieves broke into Oscar Geiger's loft and stole all his valuable furs. These furs were uninsured, and shortly thereafter, Oscar Geiger went into bankruptcy. Oscar went to work then for Arnold Constable as a fur buyer. Later he worked for Thorne furs.

The last years of his life Oscar Geiger spent in founding the Henry George School. He had come to believe education took precedence over politics. Oscar got some needed help from John Dewey and Harry Carman, the dean of Columbia College, and persuaded the New York Board of Regents to certify the school for adult education, which meant teachers could take courses there for credit. His first class was held in the corner of Joseph Dana Miller's editorial offices, but a year later the single taxers raised the money to rent a brownstone building at 211 West Seventy-ninth Street. The New York Board of Regents at John Dewey's prodding, chartered the school in 1932. Today the Henry George School occupies all of its own building on East Sixty-ninth Street and has branches all over the world.

One of the reasons which convinced Oscar Geiger the single tax needed a school of its own was the election of Franklin D. Roosevelt in 1932. When Roosevelt ushered in the New Deal, Oscar said, "You cannot divide the country into two classes, the rich and the poor. You cannot really reform an economic system by taking from the rich and giving to the poor. The reform must be total, not *ad hoc*. Therefore, I am against Roosevelt."

Thus the single tax. I was fifteen when I joined the Young People's Socialist League. Algernon Lee of the Rand School inducted me. There were about eight of us that night. I was familiar with the pamphlets of Sandburg and Eugene V. Debs, and I believed in them. Those were the days of the Molly Maguires and the Pinkertons and the Homestead Strike and Morris Hillquit, the number one Socialist of New York, who, when he rose to speak, had but to shout the name Rockefeller to capture his audience.

The Socialist Party lost its steam with Franklin D. Roosevelt, whose legislation during the famous 100 Days duplicated the Socialist Party platform of 1908.

The American people took from a senior warden of the Hyde Park Episcopal Church, who wore a Navy cape, what they would never have taken from the Socialists who wore beards and spoke in German, Swedish, and Jewish accents.

Mr. Geiger was put-out with me when he heard that I had joined the YPSL's. He thought this would water down my enthusiasm for the single tax. I saw no conflict between the YPSL's and Henry George. Both spoke for humanity for the dignity of man, for the working class.

In this matter I was closer to my father than to Mr. Geiger. My father, too, was a Socialist, and when ignorant editors talk about Communism and Socialism as one, they do not know we young Socialists heckled Communist speakers of the Third International when the superpatriots couldn't put their finger on Russia on the map. Capitalism was an enemy we could correct through legislation. Communism was the real enemy and we understood this early in the game. In 1934 my father wrote, "The Nazis burn our books and the smoke reaches to the sky for everyone to see, but the Communists bury us in a dungeon. When you write the Russian ambassador asking about the whereabouts of a certain missing poet their answer is that they never heard of him."

Still, Oscar Geiger knew there would be a day when there were no more poorhouses, and indeed we glimpse that day now. He knew electric light would become universal because someone would string power lines across the country. He prophesied that that someone would be the federal government. He knew our ever-increasing longevity would force the enactment of Medicare. Oscar Geiger didn't live to see all this. In 1934 he awoke in the middle of the night sure that he had an attack of indigestion.

Before his funeral, I asked Nina Geiger if my father, a Jewish writer, could say a few words at Oscar's funeral. She said she preferred a secular burial. I realized I had made a presumptuous request. Oscar Geiger had devoted his entire life to a social ideal. My father's dedication was to some ideal of personalized Judaism not viable for this time and place. There was something selfish and conceited in my father, just as there was something zany and illusory in Oscar Geiger, but knowing Oscar Geiger meant realizing a certain quality of life.

When I went to jail, my father said, "My son, my son."

Oscar Geiger wrote me a letter in which he said, "In the great game of life you have stubbed your toe. You will survive it."

Chapter 7

O<small>F</small> all the brothers and sisters, Clara and I were the closest. She was the surrogate mother when I was an infant. On the way over from Europe, Clara made sure I was fed when my mother and Matilda lay groaning with seasickness, writhing with other emigrants, all sure they were going to die. As I grew older and rebelled against her commands, she always reminded me, "Mama told me on the boat, 'Save the baby.'" There was eight years' difference between us, yet we have always enjoyed a natural sympathy. Jake was the older brother whom she respected; I was the younger one with whom she played.

Clara is an affectionate woman, filled with laughter. When my brother Max was born in 1909, Clara at fourteen was already working in a necktie factory. In 1968, Max estimated he received at least three calls a day from Clara. She wants only to know about his health. "Clara's phone calls," says Max, "are like arthritis. You can only take aspirin." She calls Max because he lives in Rego Park and handles her insurance. I live in Charlotte which is long distance. Clara has never felt kindly toward American Tel and Tel since they took away her telephone in 1929, when they were closing off the service of virtually every other broker on the street.

All her life she has found work. For a couple of years, every election day she was a Tammany counter. The night before an election a mysterious hand always threw a $100 bill over the transom with Clara's name written on it. Tammany sachems also gave her a ring which had a setting but no stone, just a piece of charcoal. Clara used the ring to void Republican and Socialist ballots. If the X for any opposing candidate was one-millionth of an inch below the square—mark it void.

Clara learned bookkeeping at night school. She was keeping the accounts for the White Photograph Studios in 1920, earning $22 a week when she spotted an ad in the New York *Times*. A man in Wall Street offered a salary of $250 a month, unheard-of money for a bookkeeper.

The next morning Clara went down to 50 Broad Street and presented herself to the prospective employer, Randolph Rose. Rose interviewed her, approved her credentials, sighed, and said, "I really must have a bookkeeper who understands the business."

Clara answered, "I understand stocks and bonds in Wall Street."

"This is puts and calls," Rose said.

The interview was over. The truth was that Clara didn't understand puts and calls any more than she understood stocks and bonds. But Rose was so courteous, the job so attractive, she brooded all day that she hadn't landed it.

The next morning she took the subway again to 50 Broad Street and walked into Randolph Rose's office. "If you want someone to learn a business," she argued, "you've got to give them a chance at it. Give me that chance and I will learn in no time the puts and the calls."

Randolph Rose smiled. The applicant before him was a young woman, twenty-five years old, with fuzzy hair, brown eyes, a smooth complexion, and a smile beaming from a round face. She was 5 feet 4 and weighed 130 pounds. Perhaps he knew then he and Clara Goldhurst were going to become good friends.

"All right," he said, "if you want the chance, you're on." It was a lucky moment for the two of them.

This new employer and patron, Randolph Rose, was a tall, handsome Southerner with impeccable manners. He came from a plantation family in Georgia, an aristocrat with a flair for taking a chance. The precision of his speech barely betrayed a slight drawl. There was a cleft in his forehead, which was the result of an accident ranging from the Apaches to the Argonne, depending on his mood; some years later Clara learned he had been sapped by a thug and robbed one night when he was "drunk and silly" in Richmond, Virginia.

In 1920, Rose was forty-three years old. He had been a successful distiller in Atlanta until Fulton County, under local option, voted itself dry in 1914. Prohibition put Rose Whiskey down the drain, so to speak.

Rose sold off his vats and drays and came to New York, where he started trading in the Cotton Exchange. He made money, and branched out as a stockbroker. At 50 Broad Street, he had a small suite of four rooms, and he employed twenty people. On the wall was a blown-up photograph of the building with the legend below: "Fifty Broad Street—the Home of Randolph Rose." He sent this picture to every cotton broker and customer below the Mason-Dixon Line.

There was nothing shady about him—50 Broad Street *was* his home—but there was a great deal that was innovative. He had learned in his youth how to sell whiskey, and with these techniques he learned how to sell Randolph Rose Enterprises.

As soon as he made money up North, he took a trip back through the South hiring the most popular boy of the graduating class in each small town. He set that boy up in an office as the local representative of Randolph Rose Enterprises. The most popular boy who becomes an instant success always pays dividends, and Randolph Rose reaped them to the despair of the Cotton Exchange, which considered him an adventurer.

Once, when one of his customers came to the office in a frenzy because he would have made a killing but for the fact Randolph had not endorsed the purchase, Rose paid him off immediately. The customer had laid out $40 on margin after the close of business. Overnight the stock he bought jumped fifty points. Rose paid $3,000 without an argument, paid, in fact, with sheer delight. When Clara congratulated him on his honesty, Rose said, "I'm going to get a photostat of that unendorsed order. I'm going to get that three thousand dollars back many, many times."

He was, I believe, the first man on the Street to sell stocks with slogans. One of them I particularly remember concerned a venture which to call speculative was to do it honor. But Rose sold thousands of shares by advertising "No Widow Should Buy Mexican Petroleum."

Everyone who came into the Rose Enterprises always walked out with a pound of Hicks' Coffee, a gift from Randolph. There was nothing special about Hicks' Coffee; it cost no more than other coffees; it was no better. Randolph Rose, however, owned some of its stock. By the time Rose got through touting the coffee, his visitor believed Hicks' was sold only at Tiffany's.

A little while after Clara went to work for him, Rose hit upon the idea of partial payment, a way of selling stocks on the installment plan. "The Road to Financial Independence Is Yours," he advertised. The idea was a bonanza. It was all that Randolph Rose could do to handle the volume. It was then that Rose suggested to Clara, who had been with him almost two years, that she handle the puts and calls in a separate company.

Thus, my sister became the first woman broker on the Street, heading C. Goldhurst Company, which sold puts and calls options. She had, to say the least, learned the business. Her first day of business provided all the New York papers with a news story. There was Clara's picture under a bold headline, her quotes flashing out the story.

There was even a cartoon to illustrate Clara's advent on Wall Street in the New York *World* of May 1, 1921. It showed a lady holding an umbrella traversing a stock-ticker tightrope stretched between two skyscrapers. Underneath, the legend read: "A Line a Lot of Women Should Try."

Your picture in the paper was an unusual experience for Lower East Side Jews. At a conservative estimate, I would say Jake, Matilda, my father and mother, and I bought 200 copies of each paper. Clara still has a folder stored in her desk drawer with those yellowing clippings. My mother was breathless at the honor. "Your picture in the paper," she said, *"a lab'n zul* Columbus [God bless Columbus for discovering America]."

English brokers, a century ago, devised puts and calls as a form of insurance to preserve profits. The buyer of a put owns the right to sell a certain number of shares of a specific stock at a stated price on or before a future date. The buyer of a call owns the right to purchase a certain number of shares of a specific stock at a stated price on or before a future date.

If an investor, say, buys 100 shares of stock at $100 a share, the purchase costs him $10,000. If the stock rises to $200 a share, he has made a paper profit of $10,000. Though the investor thinks the stock will still continue to rise, he may want to protect that profit. He pays a broker a premium to buy a put which enables him to sell that stock at any time in the next six months at $200 a share. If the stock continues to rise, he sacrifices his premium. If the stock drops, he sells and takes his profit.

If an investor wants to buy 100 shares of a stock selling at $100 a share but does not want to risk the initial investment of $10,-000 he buys a call enabling him at any time in the next six months to buy this stock at the stated price. If the stock drops, he sacrifices his premium. If the stock rises, he buys at the price he offered.

A puts and calls broker guarantees, or endorses, this contract. The broker promises to sell or produce this stock when an investor exercises his option. There are many variations. An investor can sell a put and he can buy a call. He can straddle, his premium giving him the option on both a put and a call at the same price. He can spread, his premium giving him an option on a put and a call on the same stock at difference prices. An investor can strip and strap, the first buying an additional put, the second an additional call. There is an infinite variety of buying puts and calls, and I wish I'd never heard of any of them.

The puts and calls broker, of course, sets the prices at which his or her firm will either sell or buy the stock. The broker also sets the premium for these options. Clara, like all puts and calls brokers, had to understand the market and gauge its fluctuations accurately, or she would have gone broke within the hour.

Since the establishment of the Securities and Exchange Commission in the early days of Roosevelt's New Deal, puts and calls are an expensive speculation. Puts and calls are sold in units of 100 shares and generally limited to the stocks traded on the New York or American Stock Exchange. But in Clara's day and in mine, an investor could buy stocks on the slimmest of margins. For $50, an investor could gamble whether 100 shares of General Motors would go up or down on any given day. Puts and calls attracted the professional speculators and the gamblers, for in the early twenties the market had not yet become the middle-class paradise it was to become five and six years later, when the waitresses, bootblacks, mechanics, and taxi drivers found that by taking advantage of the margin, they could all become Wall Street investors. Puts and calls were a minor operation compared to J. P. Morgan or Lehman Brothers. Still, puts and calls began to enjoy a growing popularity.

One of Clara's daily clients was named Bertha K., the wife of a successful surgeon. Puts and calls possessed Bertha. Compulsively, she played every day. Her gambling enraged her husband. He forbade her to leave the house with her purse. So Bertha would hide $30 under her hairpiece and pirouette before him, waving her empty arms, telling him she was going to Saks Fifth Avenue to charge a few frocks. Down she'd come to 50 Broad Street, extract the money from under her hat, and buy a spread. She told me confidentially one day, "I never go to bed without a spread."

C. Goldhurst Company sold puts and calls all over the nation, to investors in Iowa, in New Jersey, as well as in Canada, and in Mexico. The list of investors was essentially the business, and that was what Randolph Rose had entrusted to Clara, plus some office furniture. Clara listed the 200 most active stocks and circulated the price of puts and calls to these clients. Experience and intuition told her the price for every put and call, and her success was evidenced by her volume of business, in excess of $300,-000 a year.

Wall Street regulars called her the "voluptuous siren of puts and calls." She had to install a wooden rail in the office to keep back the men who came to buy options and flirt.

As the business grew, Clara had to add someone to help her. She hired me. I never suspected the disaster to which this step would lead. I couldn't wait to become a broker. If Clara hadn't sold puts and calls, I would never have had a chance on Wall Street. There were, no doubt, jobs for immigrant Jews down there, but none that would have interested me. With the entrée Clara gave me, now I, too, was a broker. I stood in line with Oliver Broom, an old-time speculator, who tapped me on the shoulder and said, "You look like Jacob Schiff. You act like Jacob Schiff. You will *be* Jacob Schiff." He pointed his finger to give this prophecy emphasis. I hope he did better with his stock speculations than he did with predictions.

I had a girlfriend named Rosie Bell who lived in Elizabeth, New Jersey. I always thought if she hadn't lived in Elizabeth, she would have been the mother of my children. Her father was a tailor. He was so impressed with my advance I didn't even need to bring the box of Loft's Candy when I called. He introduced me to all and sundry as a Wall Street broker, even though I tried to explain on occasion I wasn't quite yet a broker.

At C. Goldhurst Company I had to keep a wary eye on the

fluctuations of the day. If a stock started a quick rise, we often had to buy it to protect ourselves with those who had placed calls on it. I also researched all the stocks Clara listed. Research consisted of reading all the financial sheets, looking up records, and relying on hunches and impressions. My hunches and impressions were to our advantage most of the time but not always. I advised our clients that Lackawanna Steel was the buy of the year at $22 a share, "buy of the year," being an exaggeration I often permitted myself. But damned if Lackawanna Steel didn't become the buy of the year. It went from $22 to $40 in a day, and Clara's usual good humor deserted her.

"I keep a ticker in the office so you can read it," she screeched. "We have a big board so you can study it. You have wiped us out, Herschele, wiped us out." These sentiments continued as Lackawanna Steel resolutely climbed. At last it became unbearable. To the amusement of Clara's staff, I simply ran from the office.

Lackawanna Steel did almost wipe us out, but we survived, and a great many things did go our way. I sent out a newsletter which we called *From 10 to 3 in Wall Street,* every day, and while it wasn't living literature, it was more interesting than most of the market sheets. I used to write headlines that rivaled any I have ever seen: NOAH WAS PREPARED FOR A RAINY DAY—ARE YOU?

I am positive I was the first to use "wise" as a suffix. "Market-wise" was a favorite expression of mine, a dubious honor.

Our investors responded. One customer even sent in a poem paraphrasing Edgar Allan Poe's "The Raven" so impressed was he with my literary expertise:

> Once upon a midday dreary
> On Goldhurst's tip I bought some Erie.
> Suddenly there came a falling,
> Came a falling and a calling
> For more margin. Erie rose never more.

The C. Goldhurst Company newsletter brought me into contact with Big Bill Ebel, who wanted me to publish a newsletter for his firm as well. Gladly I set to do it, in the process becoming Big Bill's pal and later partner. Big Bill bet $1,000 every morning on whether the first quote of the day was up or down from yesterday's closing. If he was caught short thousands and thousands of shares, he yawned. "One thing I learned in this business," he would say, "and that is that tomorrow's another day."

What made Big Bill interesting was the way he could pinch pennies once the market closed. I waited with him one night in a pouring rain which melted his straw skimmer and made our summer suits soggy. The sewer gurgled like a maddened Mississippi. Yet Big Bill kept waving off empty cabs. New York City taxis used two different metering systems in the 1920's. A red meter cost more, but the cab could traverse the five boroughs; a white meter cost less but was restricted to Manhattan.

Bill and I wanted a cab to go to the Astor Hotel. As often as the expensive red meter pulled up, Big Bill waved him off, shouting, "Gyp taxi, gyp taxi." It took us more than a half hour to find a white meter. The trip cost him 80 cents and dry cleaning.

Often we would adjourn to the Golden Eagle Restaurant in Greenwich Village. With our meal we ordered a bottle of champagne for which the Golden Eagle charged us $20.

"Why should we pay that twenty dollars?" Big Bill asked me one night. "We can buy a case from the bootlegger and bring over our own bottles."

We bought a case of champagne, paying $8 a bottle, which we kept in Big Bill's office. The next time we adjourned to the Golden Eagle, Big Bill produced the bottle from his coat, gave it to the waiter, and said, "Put this on ice. We'll want it with our dinner."

The waiter bowed. Nor did he say anything when he filled our glasses. But when we paid the bill, we found a new entry: "Corkage—$20."

One of the workers populating Big Bill's office was a redheaded stenographer named Cassie R., whom everyone called Big Bill's downtown wife, though Big Bill was at pains to deny this was the nature of their relationship. He always said, "I'm taking care of her. I'm really like her guardian. Poor kid, she needs someone." One afternoon he gave his little ward a diamond bracelet. She wrapped it around her wrist.

"Aren't you going to say thank you?" Big Bill asked.

"It's nothing but another service stripe, Bill," she said, "and I've earned every one of them."

There was a greater familiarity among brokers on the Street

in the early 1920's than there is now. I never met J. P. Morgan or Thomas Fortune Ryan, but I did meet Bernard Baruch one afternoon who was cordial and polite to me as he consummated a million-dollar deal in Ben Bloch's office. I considered myself in the presence of a great Jew and an even greater Wall Street shark, and I was properly deferential.

Forty years later, when I interviewed Baruch in Charlotte, North Carolina, I recalled that meeting. His memory was crystal-clear. He even remembered what stock he was trying to corner. When we parted, he said casually, "Why don't you build yourself an estate? Buy Allied Chemical and Dye. It's a solid company."

I worried about the advice all afternoon. Should I tell my friends, or should I not? This was a tip from Bernard Baruch who, through with advising Presidents and content to sit on a Central Park bench in a big floppy hat, was still the same shark. What if it went down? What if it went up? I told no one. Allied Chemical and Dye did well enough.

I once watched Jesse Livermore selling United Drug Company short. United Drug I believe was then at $3 a share, and Jesse Livermore was selling thousands of shares at $2.50.

"Mr. Livermore," I asked, "you are selling so many shares short, where do you think United Drug will go?"

Livermore looked at me and said, almost snarling, "When they are sick, they die." A few weeks later United Drug went broke, was taken off the big board, and sold for pennies over the counter. Another killing for Jesse Livermore.

He was a spare man with rimless eyeglasses and a ready wit, sardonic perhaps, and cynical, but certainly expressive. He always sold short. His first killing came when he sold the Union Pacific Railroad short and the San Francisco earthquake made his hunch pay off.

He was the great Wall Street bear until the Securities and Exchange Commission ruled that Wall Street was not a public preserve.

One of Livermore's pet tricks was to operate a pool. Together with three or four other sharks, he would select a stock and run it up by wash buying. Wash buying is the process whereby the pool operators keep buying from one another. The ticker tape records heavy orders, and when the stock hits a certain high, the operators turn and sell it to the public. They came near selling the sky itself to the innocent and the wide-eyed.

I wasn't particularly close to Livermore, but I saw him frequently downtown. As often as I saw him, he was with a beautiful woman. He had three wives, and he once boasted the one hobby he indulged was hopping into bed with a handsome lady. That and making money were the only two things he never found boring.

The Crash changed his way of living: It wiped him out. He came back, was wiped out again. He even wrote a book, *How to Trade in Stocks,* but since he wrote it when he was broke, he couldn't offer himself as witness to its truth.

In 1940 he shot himself in the men's room of the Sherry-Netherland Hotel. He owed more than a half million dollars in lawsuits. He had written his own epitaph: "When they are sick, they die."

I used to play chess with Guy Loomis, who had made a career of selling blue-sky stocks. They called them blue sky because that's about all the customer bought for his money. Loomis had a genius for selling thousands and thousands of fake oil stocks at $1 a share. One of these stocks was called Group Number 1 Oil. The company made the biggest oil strike in the history of Oklahoma. The strike surprised no one more than Loomis. He spent a desperate two days trying to buy back this stock. Tears flowed from his chin when Group Number 1 announced its strike publicly and he hadn't succeeded in getting any of the stock back.

There was a clerk named Mahoney who worked out of a window taking orders for the Curb Market. Mahoney was stealing eighths and quarters from each sale—which is to say, if he got a report a stock was sold at fourteen and one-eighth, he would record the sale as fourteen and three-eighths. He would pocket the difference and split it with the broker.

The gambit proved so successful and simple that pretty soon Mahoney was coming to work in a big, shiny Pierce-Arrow limousine. In the morning, Mahoney had the chauffeur park the car in front of Fraunces Tavern. There he shed his beautiful camel's hair overcoat, hung up his cane, removed his spats. Then he hitched up his sleeves with rubber bands, put on a frayed jacket, tugged on his cap, and walked the rest of the way to his window.

One day his boss called him over and said, "I hear you're making a pretty penny for yourself. I hear you're making twenty thousand dollars a year."

"The rumor I am making twenty thousand dollars a year is all wrong," said Mahoney. "I am making seventy thousand a year." And he left his cap in his window and walked to Fraunces Tavern, got into his car, and retired permanently.

Jay Fogel was another broker I knew who came a cropper. Jay was a lawyer training with Laughlin and Company. He stole money from an estate he was managing and invested it in the market, buying thousands of stocks on the thinnest of margins. One afternoon the market declined, and old man Laughlin said to Fogel, "We need more margin. Otherwise we will have to sell you out."

If they sold him out, Jay knew he would never be able to repay the money he had "borrowed." Fogel turned to Laughlin and said, "I want to see the next sale on Baldwin Locomotive." He was gambling with his life on that stock. If it were up, maybe he would get the money back. If it were down, he had no chance. The next sale was down. Fogel walked over to the window, opened it, and plunged down seven stories to the street.

I remember an odd character named Tarshis who came from Johannesburg, South Africa. From the other end of a room, Tarshis could tell by the sound of the ticker tape what stock was reported. Tarshis was a margin clerk, and every once in a while he would bellow, "This is where you folks pay your money, at this window, and then you walk over to the big board and try to get it back." Tarshis told the whole story of Wall Street: Try to get even. Which is about what I learned from my experiences, that and never to buy stocks whose destiny you have to follow in the newspaper.

I thought Wall Street would be my life's work. The coincidence of Clara and Randolph Rose I was sure had determined my career. I suppose that coincidence did, unfortunately. That coincidence determined other events, too, one of them the happiest in my life.

Just before Randolph Rose set Clara up as his satellite corporation, he had hired a stenographer named Genevieve Gallagher. Genevieve was 99 pounds with a waist as thick as a thimble and big brown buttons for eyes. When Clara moved down the hall, Genevieve moved with her. I stood beside her the day we could see the members of the Curb Exchange dancing in exultation because, for the first time, 1,000,000 shares had been traded. I noticed Genevieve went downstairs every morning at ten o'clock to buy a Coca-Cola. As if by accident, I went down right after she did. Casually, I joined her. I remember the outrage which suffused my whole being one morning when the elevator operator turned to me and said, "She already went back up."

PART II

Chapter 8

GENEVIEVE Alice Marie Gallagher—everyone called her Tiny. They called her Tiny because she was small as a baby, little as a schoolgirl, diminutive and petite as a bride. I brook no doubts about it—she was and is an Irish beauty with black hair, brown eyes, and beautiful lines in her face.

Her diction is flavorful. Babies always "corked off" to sleep. When people bored her, they became "spiritual Saharas." When she wanted to finish something in a hurry, she gave it "a lick and a promise."

She is the wittiest woman I have ever met. Some years ago a cousin of hers died, a ne'er-do-well who had managed to accomplish in this life only his own and his wife's misery. Tiny's brother confessed he was unable to compose an appropriate eulogy for the funeral. Tiny thought it over. "Why don't you say if Cousin Austin had ever had any money, he would have been a real sport?" We had been amicably separated for several years when my first book, *Only in America*, was published. I asked her if she had read it. "Pretty good book," she said. "Are you going to read *my* book?"

"What book?" I asked.

"A sequel. It's called *Lonely in America*."

Genevieve is the daughter of Hugh and Emma Nolan Gallagher. Hugh Gallagher was born in Archbald, Pennsylvania, in 1865. His father, Henry, had emigrated from Ireland during the potato famine and got a job as a stoker in the Dickson City Stone Works in Dickson City, Pennsylvania, before moving to Archbald. Archbald is roughly nine miles north of Scranton in the anthracite coal region. Hugh Gallagher was a wholesale confectioner, a six-foot Irishman noted for his good looks and his kindness. He traveled throughout Pennsylvania selling candy, and as often as he returned on a Friday evening, he was met at the station by scores of children who followed him all the way home. He walked the entire distance with his hands plunged into his pockets. But when he reached his front gate, he would turn and distribute the candy and gum to the kids.

In 1909 a fire razed his warehouse. By the time Hugh Gallagher came back from a selling trip to Harrisburg, the fire engines had departed and only a few curious passersby watched the still glowing ashes. All that was left of Hugh Gallagher's business was four blackened walls. On the curb, his daughter Genevieve waited, tears coursing down her face. Everything was gone, the vats of chocolate, the mints, the huge cookie tins, everything. All that survived the fire were Luden's Cough Drops, which had charred but not melted. Scranton kids used to dig through the ashes to find them, scrape the black off, and spoil their dinner.

It wiped him out. Genevieve said he never really got back on his feet. He was a man who had always lived on the right side of the tracks. He didn't want to live on the wrong side so he moved his family to New York, where there were more opportunities. He got a job selling Lester Pianos. Later he sold the first gas ranges produced by Consolidated Edison.

He died of cancer of the throat in 1921. Tiny felt he spent the last decade of his life in melancholia. He was without question a good man, charitable and decent, yet when hard luck befell him, none of the people he had befriended over the years came to his help, save for Milton Hershey, who made the famous candy bar and never pressed Hugh Gallagher for the money he owed.

Genevieve's mother was Emma Nolan. She married Hugh Gallagher in 1892. She was born in 1868 in Oxford, New Jersey, the daughter of Joseph Nolan, who manufactured stove parts. Joseph Nolan was also an inventor and an engineer. He devised the floating grain elevator still in use on the Great Lakes, he invented the flange for the railroad wheel, and, during the Civil War, he helped engineer the turret of the ironclad *Monitor* which bested the Confederate *Merrimack* at Hampton Roads, Virginia, in 1862.

Emma Nolan, my mother-in-law, was the first woman to be

graduated from the Bloomsburg State Teachers College in Bloomsburg, Pennsylvania. She taught in the public schools of Scranton until she married. Then she went into business with her brother, operating the Crystal Star Laundry for the next twenty years. She was an indomitable woman. She ran a business in the 1900's and ran it successfully in a day and age when most women were never allowed to know their own minds.

Her efforts, coupled with those of her husband, produced a household which always employed two maids. The Gallaghers owned a summer home in Lake Ariel and some scattered realty in Scranton. Their quality of life, if not luxurious, was certainly comfortable. In New York Emma worked first for *Field and Stream* magazine and later took a civil service job with the Prohibition Enforcement Agency under Joseph Mildenberger, who was so incensed over the passage of the Volstead Act that he expected no one in his office to fulfill any assigned duties.

Emma Nolan Gallagher died in 1960, ninety-one and a half years old. To the end, she had all her faculties. Only her sight was failing. Up to the time of death she was still visiting the museums to look at the paintings and the sculptures.

Genevieve came from a family of six children, each born two years apart. The first was Eleanor Gallagher, who taught music in Scranton until she married John Burnett, her childhood sweetheart.

Jim Gallagher was next. He served in the Air Corps in World War I, was badly gassed, but recovered. He spent most of his life at sea, and during World War II he used to ship out on the New York to Murmansk run. He was torpedoed twice but survived both sinkings.

Then came Tiny, born in 1898, followed by Dorothy. Sooner or later every member of the Round Table Literary Club who wasn't married fell in love with Dorothy Gallagher, who was attending Hunter College when I first met her. She married John Deegan in the late 1920's. Sadly, she died of a brain tumor on New Year's Eve, 1944.

Hubert Donald Gallagher was born in 1902. He was graduated from New York University and went on at night to get his master's degree from the Columbia School of Business. He went to work for a Jersey City bank which folded during the Depression. Twenty years later Hubert Gallagher bought the assets of that bank, which I guess proves that the business world does have its romantic side. Hubert taught business courses at night in St. Peter's College in Jersey City until he enlisted in the Army in 1942. He was discharged as a bird colonel. He and his wife, Nina, live in Jersey City, where Hubert is president of the First New Jersey Corporation.

Nolan Gallagher was the last of the family. He was the captain of the George Washington High School football team, and I took Tiny one Thanksgiving Day to see him play. Nolan was a splendid halfback, and at the end of the second quarter George Washington was way ahead. But something happened in the Madison High School locker room at half time, and despite Nolan Gallagher's Herculean efforts, George Washington went down to defeat. He served in the Air Force. Now he is the production superintendent for American Cyanamid in Pensacola, Florida.

Genevieve Gallagher, my Tiny, was graduated from St. Cecilia's Academy in Scranton, where she studied violin. After St. Cecilia's she went on to Lock Haven Teachers College, where she majored in musical supervision. She finished her work there in 1918 and got a job supervising music in the State College, Pennsylvania, public schools. Because the family had moved to New York, Genevieve came on, too, and promptly got a job with Clara Goldhurst and Randolph Rose.

On our first date, I took Genevieve to the Golden Eagle. While the Golden Eagle wasn't the fanciest restaurant in New York, the food was excellent and the service prompt. I heard customers say to the waiter, "Could we have our dinner soon? We are on our way to the theater," and the waiter would reply, "If you are in a hurry, sir, may I recommend you come another evening when you have more time?" Many times I ordered a dinner there only to have the waiter shake his head and say, "I didn't think it looked that good when it came in." The cuisine was plain American, and the management accommodated those who wanted a cocktail with liquor served in coffee cups.

Genevieve and I liked each other. She said she'd like to go out again. We went to the Deauville Club, a speakeasy on Fifty-ninth Street, which had once been the home of Isadora Duncan. It was a famous speakeasy with beautiful decor, white tablecloths, and gold chandeliers. Charlie Hanson, who was married to the actress Lillian Walker, owned it. The Deauville was always filled with showfolk.

At the entrance I rapped on the door, and an eye behind a peephole scrutinized me. I passed. Tiny and I went in. Most of the big speakeasies went through this ritual more for the pleasure of their guests than for their own security. One of the reasons the Deauville never worried about a raid was that it was Mayor Jimmy Walker's favorite hangout.

We stayed there late that evening. When I took her home, the front door to the apartment house where her family lived was locked, and Tiny didn't have a key. Rather than wake everyone up, she took a room in a nearby hotel.

I said, "Don't you think you ought to call? You'll be out all night. Your mother will be cross. She doesn't even know me."

"My mother won't be cross," Tiny said. "She doesn't know you, but she knows *me*."

We went to the theater often. We saw Jeanne Eagels in *Rain* and Ethel Barrymore as Portia in *The Merchant of Venice*. We saw John Barrymore in *Hamlet* and *Richard III* and in *The Jest* with his brother, Lionel. We saw *Rio Rita* and the *Ziegfeld Follies* and Walter Hampden. Once a month we went to the opera, where Tiny was always taken with the divas like Rosa Ponselle and Florence Easton. She cried when Tosca sang "Vissi d'arte." Tickets were easy to buy. A man went right up to the box office for seats. One of the minor regrets in my life was that when I could afford the best seat at the Metropolitan Opera House, tickets were unavailable.

Tiny and I saw each other several times before I met her mother and family. The Gallaghers lived then at the Ivy Court Apartments on 107th Street between Amsterdam and Broadway, the first of the high-rise apartments which began to lend prestige and tone to New York's West Side. In my time, West End Avenue, Riverside Drive, and the side streets were the respectable upper-middle-class neighborhoods of New York City.

We all got along well enough; the Gallaghers were generous and polite people. I outraged Hubert once when I told him a man named Gallagher had shot Mayor William J. Gaynor, and he red-

101

dened and said, "That's a lie." But we settled the argument by calling the New York *Times*, and sure enough a man named Gallagher had taken a potshot at the mayor. All the Gallaghers save Tiny were Republicans. Emma teased us one night about a Tammany scandal, which led me to remark, "Tammany put more coal in the cellars of the poor than all of Scranton ever mined."

That eight-room apartment was always filled with brothers and sisters and laughter. There was an upright piano in the living room, and almost all the Gallaghers could play an instrument. Dinner there was often followed by a band concert. Like most of the Irish, the Gallaghers have a family that is legion. Emma could trace the history of cousins three and four times removed with the accuracy of a professional historian.

My father had friends and a few relatives, but no family network surrounded us. Not only did Emma Gallagher keep track of everyone, but she had read Dostoevski. My father had always exhibited a certain impatience with the affairs of the world: He undestood my brother Max, but he refused to understand basketball. He loved Clara, but when she tried to explain puts and calls, he shushed her.

I cannot re-create the moment in which I decided I wanted to marry Genevieve. Anyone who gets married feels he participates in an inevitable progression. I know I left the Ivy Court one night passing under the arch which let me onto the street. I waited for a taxi, decided to walk, realized I would have to find the subway, and ended by going back to the apartment house to stare at the lighted windows on the fourth floor, knowing she was there. I loved her until it hurt. I loved the home which sheltered her, I loved her brothers and sisters, I loved her widowed mother, I loved hearing Genevieve play the violin, I loved the delightful prospect of her, and I loved God for being a maker of marriages.

I had often thought of marrying an Irish girl. I traced this impulse to Oscar Geiger, who lived so happily with Nina Daly. I wanted to emulate Geiger. Tiny made it easy. Jewish boys on the Lower East Side loved the Irish. The Irish came here already speaking the language—to their advantage, for they quickly filled all the local offices. The Irish were the policemen, the customs inspectors, the firemen, the trolley car conductors, the ward heelers and the aldermen—the people who were authority to immigrants. The Irish were also fighters. They were strong. Nothing seemed more American to me than marrying an Irish Catholic.

And nothing seemed more American to me than making money, which I believe is *the* basic American impulse. I was in a business then where I could make money and make money fast. In a hotel room in Atlantic City on my honeymoon I counted up my assets—cash, stocks, and personal property. I was worth now more money than my father had ever seen. I was sure I would make more and more money as time went on—$20,000, maybe $30,000 a year! I forgot that my brother Jake was running a hotel, working eighteen hours a day trying to bring home $100 a week, worrying all the time about negligent bellboys and incompetent elevator operators.

It was indeed a happy time. America emerged from World War I as the greatest world power, and we all knew it. There wasn't a single national issue to bother Tiny and me. The cities had begun their growth toward megalopolis, but they were still new enough to hide the despair and misery they necessarily house. I should have remembered my mother's injunction: "It's bad when things are too good."

Genevieve and I had known each other for almost a year when she told me she would have to go back to Pennsylvania for the next two school semesters. To receive her teaching certificate, she had to complete two full years in the Pennsylvania school system, and the certificate was supremely important to her. In 1924 she taught music in a school in Cresson, Pennsylvania, the little town where so many had sought refuge from the Johnstown flood years before.

We corresponded, and she came to New York every other week. As soon as she had her certificate, she was hired by Henry J. Kugel, who ran a fashionable prep school in Harrison, New York. The Kohut School was for rich Jewish boys. Its faculty was predominantly Christian. "That's what the parents want," said Mr. Kugel. "The Jewish middle class wants a Christian faculty."

I asked Tiny once, "What do you teach those boys up there who pay a thousand dollars a semester?"

"If nothing else," she said, "I teach them to take their hats off in elevators, to open the door for a lady, and to stand behind the chair until their mother is seated." I thought those were pretty good things to teach.

On the way home from the Army-Navy game in 1925, I asked Genevieve to marry me. The proposal came as no surprise. She said yes.

But it wasn't as simple as it sounds, not by a long shot. Jews didn't marry Gentiles, nor Gentiles Jews, with any frequency.

Emma Gallagher said she didn't think Genevieve ought to marry a Jew. Genevieve said she had made up her own mind. Emma advised Tiny to think it over, not to hurry. Our marriage worried Emma Gallagher, and the first chance she got, she took a trip to Scranton, where she confided in one of her cousins, a judge named Edward Kelley.

Kelley considered the prospect and said, "I've practiced law all these years with Jews. They are good family men. I know a lot of Irishmen, Emma, who will make Tiny a bad husband. Maybe the Jew will make her a good one."

With the exception of my falling asleep and snoring loudly during a midnight mass, to the distress of Genevieve and the active indignation of Emma, the question of Jewishness was raised and settled with that trip to Scranton.

I had a harder time of it.

"I'm going to marry Genevieve Gallagher," I told my sister Matilda.

"Gallagher?" asked Matilda. "That's not a Jewish name."

"Genevieve is Irish."

"How can you be so selfish?" Matilda said.

My father looked coldly at me and said, "Oil and water do not mix." I told him I wasn't interested in Talmudic philosophy, and he asked, "How dare a son make a decision without asking the father?" I said I wasn't in the *shtetl,* and angrily he ended the discussion with, "Better you should have been a good Jew than a wise guy with a necktie on your throat every day in Wall Street."

My brother Jake's eyes swiveled around his lobby, lighting on the tattered davenports, the mismatched rugs, the garish chandeliers. "You're only doing this," he said, "because you don't understand the agony of a second mortgage." I told him I was determined, and he said, "A Jewish wife can make as much trouble for you as an Irish one. But you're not asking my advice, are you?"

While my father had little sympathy for the marriage, he did not actively oppose it. What distressed me was when his friends would ask me, "What are you doing to your father?" I wasn't in truth doing anything to my father. I was going about my own business, and I suggested they go about theirs. It distressed me when Jews called Tiny a *shicksa*, as it must have distressed her when Catholics called me a kike. Tiny always encouraged me as a Jew, once insisting I accept the appointment as secretary of a Red Bank, New Jersey, synagogue. I was outraged by the disapproval. I was right. A succeeding generation laughed at these inhibitions.

Still, intermarriage is not a normal process, not a process where boy meets girl and they get married. The Jew is compelled often to bring something to the union besides himself. The Jewish lawyer doesn't marry the Gentile partner's daughter, he marries the Gentile secretary from Tenth Avenue; the Jewish merchant doesn't marry the sister of his competitor, he marries one of his bookkeepers.

Nor was there any reason why we shouldn't make common cause. Our backgrounds and religion were dissimilar, but still, as an Irish Catholic girl in Scranton, she had felt that impenetrable condescension of the Protestant majority.

Yet my family's hostility was a tangible fact. Matilda spurred it on, which I could never understand because we had never been that close. Clara liked Tiny, and she couldn't understand Matilda's animosity either. In perspective I think the animosity wasn't as monumental as I thought. It was probably gossip. Lovers expect the world to attend them and only them.

Genevieve told me she would have to be married by a priest, for which I had to have a special dispensation since I was a non-Catholic. To get this dispensation, I signed an agreement promising to rear our children as Catholics. I felt then and feel now that this is blackmail perpetrated on two people by a third party. Any man will sign a piece of paper to get the woman he loves.

Who knew in 1926 there would be a Hitler six years later? Who knows in youth that this world doesn't take long to turn completely upside down, that the future we were all so sure of in 1926 on one afternoon in 1929 literally disappeared?

I signed the agreement. I reneged on it and succeeded not in revoking it but only in confusing my sons. Genevieve could not understand my breaking a promise, so she only succeeded in confusing them further. The boys, however, survived this confusion, just as they survived the confusion of the modern public school.

We were married on March 21, 1926 before Joe McCormack, the marriage clerk of New York. George Geiger and John Duff stood up for me, and Dorothy Gallagher was Tiny's maid of honor. On April 10, Father Prunty married us in the vestry of his church in Harrison, New York. We were married at noon, and at seven that night Emma Gallagher gave us a reception at the Vanderbilt Hotel in New York. Tiny wore a white marquisette dress, and a one-inch band of fine rhinestones in her hair matched the rhinestone belt.

All the members of the Round Table were there, as well as some of Tiny's colleagues from the Kohut School. Mr. Kugel, the headmaster, made a short speech in which he congratulated me and said how lucky I was. Mr. Geiger also rose and congratulated me, the groom. But the occasion was too much for him. Here before him was fertile ground. He spent thirty minutes explaining the single tax.

There were also a few friends of mine from the Lower East Side, and several of Tiny's relatives made the trip from Scranton. One of them, her cousin George O'Brien got drunk and was found two days later walking along Fordham Road in the Bronx wearing kilts. George always had a lot of trouble at parties. He was a lawyer, and some years before he had been accused of removing the pillars of coal from beneath Scranton's streets. The mine operators always left pillars at certain intervals in their tunnels so the streets wouldn't collapse. This coal was tempting to George, and he set up a dummy corporation and took it out. He was a good lawyer because the indictment was quashed. Thinking about that indictment at parties was too much for him.

None of my family attended. Clara insisted she would go and

defied Matilda and my father. As she was about to leave the apartment, Matilda tore the dress off her back. The single tax, the missing George O'Brien, and prejudice. Hardly an auspicious beginning.

Chapter 9

AFTER Genevieve finished the school year at Kohut, we rented a small furnished house in Larchmont, New York. The reason for Larchmont was a realtor named Addison Rogers. I told Rogers I wanted a place with open air, like the Grand Concourse in the Bronx. He put his hand on my shoulder and whispered, "You don't want to live on the Grand Concourse. Not an up-and-coming businessman like you. You want to live in Larchmont."

"Where is Larchmont?" I asked.

"There is no place else," he answered.

For $1,000 I rented a house with a porch, screens, two bedrooms, a kitchen, and a living room in Larchmont, the only place there was. Genevieve showed me how to run a lawn mower. There was even a garage, for which I thought I certainly must provide a car. I became a commuter long before anyone ever heard of a gray flannel suit. Every morning on the seven thirty-two I played bridge with three Irishmen, all brothers, named John, Jerome, and James Kennedy.

I brought Big Bill Ebel home with me one night, and Genevieve had her first fit of wifely pique: "Why can't you warn me?" She recovered her good temper when Big Bill spread $500 in $20 gold pieces on our living-room table as a wedding present.

We were no sooner settled than Genevieve told me we were expecting our first child, who would probably be born in January. Suddenly the rented house was too small. I looked up Addison Rogers again, and he said he had just what I needed. It was a brand-new house, the foundation just laid, out on Larchmont Avenue.

"You know, of course," Addison confided, "that Larchmont Avenue is *the* social center of Larchmont."

No, I didn't know that. What I also didn't know was that dear old Addison was the Cyclops in the Larchmont Ku Klux Klan. His name was always in the letters to the editor column protesting the inundation of un-American Poles and Italians into the sacred confines of the city limits. It was my cash which let me pass muster with him.

The house cost $17,500, and I paid $5,000 down, taking out a purchase-money mortgage for which I promised to pay the balance within three years.

Genevieve and I drove over every weekend to watch the carpenters and the plumbers and the electricians fit the house together. I knew little about houses or architecture. My sole contribution to these expeditions was the purchase of a sign which read MR. & MRS. HARRY GOLDHURST, which I stuck in the lawn. Genevieve knew everything. She dared haggle with carpenters and instruct flooring men. As we approached one Saturday, I heard one of the workers yell, "Watch it! Here she comes!" When she asked the foreman if the trim was as specified, nine workmen froze while the contractor explained the plans to her.

We moved that September. The living room had a cathedral ceiling. The house spawned three levels. Not only did it boast the first colored-tile bathroom I had ever seen, but the kitchen contained the first electric refrigerator in the neighborhood. Our friends used to come to admire these two innovations, as neighbors used to come to admire the first television set thirty years later.

Emma Nolan Gallagher used to come up as often as she had the chance and help my wife make curtains and bedspreads. I assisted in outfitting the nursery.

What we had was a certain vogue which is, in the end, what normality is. "Normalcy" was the catchword of the era, except President Harding didn't know he meant normality. The trouble with vogue is that it passes. In fact, the normality of the twenties passed a lot faster than the economic and social distress of the thirties. Vogue leaves a placid swell behind it, one you can hardly see. That house of which I was so proud is today a television repair shop. One of the walls has been pushed out to accommodate a large window, and the insides of sets, the wiring stiff and spatially uncoordinated, disfigure the grimy, dusty black-lettered window.

There were 6,000 people in Larchmont, two apartment buildings, and a railroad station. There was also, right at the end of our street, a famous speakeasy called The Monkey House. Abe Levine owned it. He called it The Monkey House to celebrate the spot where Enrico Caruso pinched Mrs. Vanderbilt—the Central Park Zoo. Caruso got himself arrested because Mrs. Vanderbilt didn't recognize him.

Abe's speakeasy was in the basement, about ten or twelve steps below the sidewalk, but no stranger to Larchmont environs could miss The Monkey House. It was always marked by the presence of motorcycle policemen out front, save when the cyclist was relieved by a uniformed pair of cops in a patrol car.

No women were allowed. When a suburbanite did make the mistake of bringing along his wife, Abe gave him alternatives: He could bring little wifey home and come back later himself, or he could have the motorcycle cop out front drive little wifey in the sidecar.

"Watch me undress that ten-dollar bill," Abe would say. It was the motto of the place: "Abe, undress this bill." Abe had an eminently respectable clientele. Bill Fallon, the "Great Mouthpiece," drank there, and it was in The Monkey House I met John McGraw, who always took the train up from Manhattan when the liquor ran low at the Lambs Club. McGraw was often joined by Charles A. Stoneham, who had just bought the New York Giants.

I remarked elsewhere that one by one all the big-timers who frequented The Monkey House fell by the wayside after 1929. Abe Levine survived. He wound up with all the money. The Monkey House now has a fancy casino name and covers acres and acres of the best land in Westchester. Armies of uniformed footmen, bellboys, and waiters attend the guests, but the policeman's motorcycle is still parked out front.

Abe was always nice to me. Before I got too drunk, he would telephone Tiny and say, "He's getting that way." Tiny always said, "I'll meet the sidecar out front."

On Columbus Day, my father, Matilda, and Clara came up to visit us. We all embraced and kissed and chatted, although only Clara and I had been on speaking terms four months ago. Things

110

proceeded smoothly until we were interrupted in the middle of the afternoon by the arrival of several friends, nameless now but drunk then. I don't think my father had ever entertained a drunk. He saw them on the Lower East Side, of course, the tramps and bums plunging into the gutter, feebly trying to support themselves on lampposts or car fenders, but I don't think he ever suspected a man who wore a suit and a hat and had his shoes shined would drink. His eyes kept widening. He looked at me in amazement.

"They can't be Jewish friends?" he whispered.

"They can be and are," I replied.

"Are there Jewish neighbors?"

"Yes," I answered.

"It's a *shanda* [shame] to them."

Tiny and I used to go into New York every weekend that fall. We always stayed at the Theresa Hotel in Harlem, which was run by Love B. Woods, who died in 1967. A four-course luncheon cost $1.25 in the Theresa dining room. (It was to the Theresa that Fidel Castro retired when the luxuries of the Waldorf-Astoria dismayed him during the United Nations plenary convention in 1960).

I was in Madison Square Garden that May night when Joe Humphreys, who announced the fights, came out and, lowering the microphone to his chest, said, "Ladies and gentlemen, let us stand up now for a moment of silence for that brave young man who is flying the Atlantic all alone tonight." Then Jack Sharkey beat Jim Maloney.

We hung a photo of Lindbergh and his *Spirit of St. Louis* in our boys' bedroom. It stayed upon the wall until 1940, when Lindbergh began making anti-Semitic speeches for the America First Committee. Without comment, Tiny took the picture down, and she never put it back up.

Both Genevieve and I were in deep sympathy with Sacco and Vanzetti and the injustice which claimed their lives. Tiny urged me to send a sizable contribution to Ruth Hale, Heywood Broun's wife, to aid in their defense. We went to hear Edna St. Vincent Millay's spirited polemics on Sacco and Vanzetti's behalf.

My son Richard was born on January 4, 1927. Tiny delivered him in New York City Hospital. The nurses told me it was a boy, and I danced a little bit. Then the nurses went and told Tiny she had married a silly man. It was the first boy on my side of the family. No wonder I danced.

My brother Jake would father three girls. In fact, when his third daughter was born, he refused to announce it. He went to the Hotel Union Square and sadly tore up the list of people he intended to invite for the *bris* (circumcision). I remember him telling my father, "Lily is all right. Lily is fine. She'll be home in a couple of days."

My father said, "It's not so bad, Jake. So it's another girl. Is that so bad?"

"Lily is fine," said Jake.

Harry junior was born on November 15, 1927. Genevieve was unaware that Jews do not name children after living antecedents or relatives. She was set on a junior, so I never mentioned the prohibition. Ever since, people have asked me why I, a spokesman for Jews, allowed a son to be named after me. I always reply, "You got a hell of a nerve asking me that when you're eating a shrimp cocktail."

On August 8, 1929, my third son, William, was born. I wanted to call him Thomas so the boys would be Tom, Dick, and Harry, but Tiny dissuaded me. We compromised on William Thomas Goldhurst. By this time Tiny and I had moved back to New York City, to an eight-room apartment at 260 Riverside Drive.

On Christmas Day, 1927, my oldest boy took his first step, and Harry junior, just an infant, attempted his first smile. Christmas Day and houses in Larchmont and children named junior are admittedly all middle-class values. Yet these values manifest themselves in generation after generation. Only the middle class has spread them around. Baby's first step will always be more important to Daddy than any number of riots junior might want to throw at Columbia.

Middle-class values have been mocked, jeered at, scorned, and dismissed. Yet they have persevered despite wars, police, and depressions. It must have been wearying to have been a serf in feudal times, and it must have been equally terrifying to have been a kulak when commissars ruled. It is never bad to be a member of the middle class.

The sad thing about the three Goldhurst boys was that they were the only boys on both sides of the family. My father would never celebrate a grandchild's bar mitzvah, and there were no

Gallaghers to carry on the name. Our boys created a certain contention and envy. The very thing Genevieve and I had going for us was to become a source of unpleasantness. Out of little boys grow men who maintain their own house. Everybody, it seems, wanted to instruct these boys what kind of house to maintain.

Chapter 10

W<small>HEN</small> Big Bill Ebel offered me a partnership in his brokerage, I left C. Goldhurst Company, and when I married, I left Big Bill. I walked in one morning and said, "Bill, I want to set up on my own."

Bill said, "Half the money in the bank is yours at the end of every business day. Good luck." By the middle of 1926 I was in business for myself. Since C. Goldhurst Company was already a well-established firm, I thought that calling my firm H. Goldhurst Company was an encroachment on Clara's reputation. So I used another name, Kable and Company.

I met Charles Kable through Hubert Gallagher. Charlie and Hubert were classmates at New York University, and the first time I saw Charlie Kable, he and Hubert were singing football songs in anticipation of NYU's beating Fordham the next day. Kable was twenty-seven years old, wearing a mustache to make him look older. He had lost his patrimony in the Florida land boom, and he was eager for the job when I offered it to him. I explained I wanted a nominal, not an actual, partner, that I wanted to use his name for the business, and that I would pay $100 a week.

Kable and Company opened for business in June, 1926, at 32 Broadway. It offered customers stocks and bonds on the partial payment plan. There were a certain selection of stocks I promised customers they could buy on a given day at the prevailing market price and that these stocks would be transferred to their name after they had paid the full purchase price in twelve equal pay-

114

ments over the year. I deducted my full brokerage commission from the first payment and stated that $100 was the minimum order I would execute.

On the first day I reached the office at eight thirty and waited for the telephone to bring me my opening order. There were eight desks in the suite, all with glass tops, a swivel chair at each. There were three new typewriters. There was a ticker tape in both rooms. Portraits of Ralph Waldo Emerson and Henry David Thoreau hung on the wall of the inner office, mine, and General "Black Jack" Pershing and Abraham Lincoln hung in the outer office, the staff's. Just before the market opened, I got my first order. The phones rang all morning. I do not think I ever had time for lunch during the next few years.

Between 1923 and 1929 anybody could open an office in Wall Street. Virtually everybody did. There wasn't a soul in America who didn't know that stocks kept up a steady advance. There were even those who believed if the advance lasted long enough, there would come a day when nobody ever needed to work again.

My commissions were such that in succeeding months I owned my office furniture free and clear. I even added two new employees, a secretary and another bookkeeper which made Kable and Company number ten in all.

Taxicab drivers bantered stock tips with traffic cops. A druggist filled prescriptions and dispensed market quotations. Farmers in Iowa and Kansas bought on margin. A cautious man thought of a long-term investment in terms of weeks, a month at the most.

Several of the customers whose portfolio I serviced at Big Bill's came over with me when I started Kable and Company. For $1,000 I bought names from the Hoffman List Brokers and circularized potential customers all over the country. I advertised. As soon as I made a profitable investment for one customer, dozens of his friends, relatives, and neighbors gave me money. The partial payment plan was a success, although it was only a sophisticated method of dealing in puts and calls.

One of my biggest customers was in Atlanta. Over a period of time he kept increasing his installments. His name was H. E. B. Smith, and he called the office often, wanting to know what the day would bring. He sounded like an easygoing man. When he told me he was coming to New York for a dental convention, I insisted he stop by. I remember my shock when I discovered that

115

H. E. B. Smith was a colored man, beautifully dressed and mannered.

I doubt that any sympathy for Negroes had ever invested my thoughts up to that time. Immigrant Jews might well understand more poignantly the cruelty of prejudice and bigotry, but they were in such haste to adapt themselves to the prevailing customs and traditions of their new milieu that they were more than capable of ignoring the sufferings of others. Of all my friends, only John Duff worried about the disabilities forced on Negroes. There was a philosophy I remember, attributed rightly or wrongly to Harold Ross, the editor and founder of the *New Yorker*, who, when asked why he didn't hire Negroes or publish their poems and stories, thought awhile before answering, "Because they're either funny or dangerous." Perhaps that was my attitude, too.

But H. E. B. Smith was neither funny nor dangerous. He was a member of the middle class. Over luncheon we discussed our homes. He had a corner lot of which he was very proud, and he had made substantial improvements on the house; I told him about my Larchmont realty, whose grass I had learned to mow the previous September.

Another of my customers was Father Aloysius Beck, a Roman Catholic priest in Cleveland, Ohio. When I asked him once if he used his profits to help the poor, he stared at me in wide-eyed astonishment. "My God, man," he said, "a priest still has a widowed mother and a brother at Western Reserve who wants to join a fraternity." I had two other priests, Reverends John Marsalick and Gregory Kulczycki of the Greek Orthodox Church. My most famous customer and good friend was James Cannon, Jr., the Bishop of the Methodist Episcopal Church, South. One of the few nice things we can say about the Wall Street of the 1920's was that in our frenzied quest for profits we traversed religious differences with a democratic impunity.

Bishop Cannon and I enjoyed a symbiotic relationship in the beginning. The more famous and powerful he became, the more I relished his patronage. The more I relished his patronage, the more profits he realized. But that symbiotic relationship was soon to undergo a terrible reversal. The more I got into trouble, the more he was implicated, and the more his implication, the deeper my trouble.

Trouble descended because Kable and Company was a bucket

shop. A bucket shop is a brokerage which accepts orders and payments from customers to buy or sell stocks but which does neither. The broker throws the order in the bucket and puts the money in his pocket. He waits until the stock rises or falls, depending on which way he thinks it will go, before purchasing or selling. Thus, if a customer, say, wants to buy Hudson Motors which is selling at $100 a share, the bucketeer gambles Hudson Motors will go down. He does not execute the buy order on the day the customer instructs him to. The stock falls to $97. The bucketeer buys. He has made his commission, delivered the stock as ordered, but he has lied, and for his lie he pockets an extra $3 a share. If a customer wants to sell Hudson Motors at $100 a share, the bucketeer, thinking the stock will rise, again waits. When the stock hits $103, he sells. The customer pays the commission, receives the money he anticipated, but again the bucketeer has pocketed an extra $3 a share at his customer's expense. In other words, I was betting against my customers, instead of actually buying or selling stock. *My* bet was always that the stock would go down.

I recall the day I realized that bucketing an order wasn't the risky proposition the other brokers said it was. Big Bill Ebel and I went to a funeral in Brooklyn, and while we were there, we thought we'd look at the Macklin Furniture plant. Macklin Furniture was coming on the exchange the next day. We had heard it might be a good thing. It had been a family-owned company, but now, for the first time, it was going public. After traipsing up and down a neighborhood filled with empty lots, we finally located the Macklin Furniture Company in a shanty beside a viaduct. Tin cans and garbage littered the area. Some of the broken windows in the shanty were covered with burlap. The Macklin Furniture Company made barstools for speakeasies. It couldn't have furnished the patio of an unemployed mechanic, let alone fill orders for a third-class hotel. No matter what it opened at the next day, it was bound to go down.

Bucketing every order to buy, I made a sweet profit a week later when Macklin Furniture not only went down but vanished. I thought: *Maybe they are all inflated—General Motors, United States Steel—all of them. We are reading figures out of a ticker tape instead of counting inventory and adding up sales.*

With Kable and Company I started bucketing orders for Hudson Motors as a matter of fact. Hudson Motors I knew was surely

117

as inflated as Macklin Furniture. The stock kept fluctuating—up a point, down a few more—down more than up, to my advantage. I did not bucket all the orders for stocks, but I began bucketing a great many. The market was going to go down, I knew it was going to go down, and I wanted to be on top when it did.

Charlie Kable kept questioning me about this practice, to which I facilely replied, "We do not have to purchase the stock until the customer makes the final payment." Charlie knew what I was doing. He was a nervous fellow, and as an officer of Kable and Company, his signature approved these practices. But he was not incorruptible. He did not want to leave his job, for I had increased his salary and rewarded him with bonuses from time to time when the books showed profit. Charlie solved his dilemma by falling sick with an inconvenient regularity. He would come down with pneumonia, develop nervous tics; his hands would shake when he signed checks, and he suffered migraine headaches.

What a sissy, I used to think, for that is precisely what a wise guy would think. While no Charles Ponzi, pyramiding one investor's money to pay another, still I was the wise guy and my customers were the suckers. Like most wise guys, however, I was the sucker after all. As I can attest, wise guys do not learn this lesson overnight. They learn they are the suckers much later, usually before grim-faced parole boards.

Did I rationalize? Of course. After all, I wasn't cheating widows or orphans. This money was the money of speculators, gamblers. Everybody bought on margin, paying only a fraction of the cost. They talked about their profits which were into the thousands when the original investment totaled at best $500. They talked about profits in the *hundreds* of thousands when the original investment totaled $3,000. In the 1920's the margin was 10 percent and sometimes not that. Today the margin is 70 percent, and no brokerage firm accepts an order on margin unless the buyer has an account of $2,000 or over.

Charlie Kable kept getting sicker and sicker. I used to tell him facetiously that he needed a stay in a sanitarium. "Everybody is selling short," I told him, "even my sister Clara, and she is as smart about the market as they come." Indeed, Clara was selling short, for I had persuaded her. But she wasn't bucketing orders; she was just going broke. Clara thought there was no one as smart as her little brother, so she took my advice; she who had advised

118

every customer never to sell short in a bull market—Clara sold everything short. Issues like Montgomery Ward, Chrysler, Bush Terminal, United States Steel surged ahead, indifferent to my prophecies. The surge ruined Clara's once-profitable business. She had to declare voluntary bankruptcy. She had assets of $100,000 and debts of $200,000. Judge Lewis Fawcett enjoined Clara to cease and desist selling stocks after Hamilton Ward, New York State's attorney general, brought charges of insolvency against her.

In the late spring of 1928 it was my turn. I guessed wrong on Wright Aeronautical. I had puts and calls on 6,500 shares. I had accepted these orders when the stock was fluctuating between $110 and $115 a share. The majority of stockholders began to exercise their options to sell when the stock hit $240 a share. I had bought none of it. These profits were enormous, and I knew I could not meet them. I tried to repay these customers the amount of their original investment, first by mortgaging my home for $10,000, then by borrowing from friends. That did not work. To protect stocks I had legitimately purchased, I decided I, too, had to declare myself a voluntary bankrupt.

Once I declared my insolvency, creditors and customers began to complain. They mailed their credit sheets to Hamilton Ward, and after studying them, Hamilton Ward gave these to the United States Attorney for the Southern District of New York, who at that time was Charles H. Tuttle, once called the "darling of the New York City Republicans." Mr. Tuttle was a native-born New Yorker who had the misfortune in 1930 to run for governor against the "darling" of the Hyde Park Democrats—Franklin D. Roosevelt.

Mr. Tuttle sent two deputies to Kable and Company. They were armed with a search warrant, and they confiscated my books and files, jockeying the steel cabinets over the threshold on a wooden dolly, moving them down the hall to the elevator.

"What an annoyance!" I complained. Charlie Kable was white and ashen. I had to make him sit down. He couldn't pull himself together when we, as officers of the company, had to pay off our employees and comfort the sobbing secretary.

I had to go home and tell my wife I was in trouble.

"What kind of trouble?" she asked me.

"Business trouble," I answered.

"Are you going to work it out?" she asked.

119

"Sure," I said, believing it. "It'll just take a little time."

A month later I was served with a subpoena which instructed me to appear before a United States commissioner to answer to an indictment a grand jury had returned. I retained a lawyer named Philip Samuels, a former judge, who said, "Don't worry about it, Harry. We'll work it out." Everyone kept thinking I was going to work it out. Alas! Americans always think work will solve anything.

I was indicted in New York on Section 215 of the Federal Code, charged with using the mails to defraud. I had written depositors that they had a credit balance with Kable and Company when neither the firm's nor my bank account could justify this statement. I wrote many of these letters to customers when stocks which I had not bought paid dividends. Often in these letters I suggested they increase their investments, and often they did. I touted them on other stocks, often worthless, which I had purchased long before at lower cost.

The indictment was a thunderbolt, not because it shouldn't have happened to me, but because so many other houses that had perpetrated the same fraud I had were going out of business. Grand juries were not returning indictments against them for their partial payment plans. Contractors were selling houses on the partial payment plan and never building the foundations. People made partial payments for their vacations to hotels which didn't exist. At 32 Broadway, four bucket shops went out of business on the same day. Whenever the market went up, it ruined dozens of bucket shops. When the operators went bankrupt, they moved across the hall and started another business with a different name.

To seek and get an indictment was an unusual move by a federal prosecutor. In the first place, the money in a bankrupt bucket shop was gone. In the second place, the federal prosecutor had no surety he would gain a conviction. There was a chance a jury would decide I was not compelled to buy those stocks until the final payment had been made. It was a fine point, a technicality, but it was there nevertheless. While the indictment surprised me, it didn't frighten me at all. I wasn't even concerned when I went to the Deauville Club that night and Charlie Hanson stopped by the table to say ominously, "Watch out for Charlie Tuttle. He is an ambitious man."

I couldn't imagine what spurred Tuttle on. Something was spurring him on, however, and I was not to find out what until a year later. Had I asked my partner, Charlie Kable, I could have learned. But then I never suspected Charlie had stolen valuable confidential files.

Nothing happened after the indictment. Philip Samuels said, "When it comes up—if it comes up—we will take care of it. Go about your business."

Since I had mortgaged the house, Genevieve and I rented it to cut our costs and took an apartment at 260 Riverside Drive. When I said meekly I was sorry she had to leave the house she loved, she said, "We'll be back here. I'm not worried. We'll save our money and pay off everybody and come back here and be somebody."

In the meantime I had to make a living. I started another company, which I called Cosmopolitan Fiscal Corporation, which proposed to sell the stock of Cosmopolitan Variety Stores of Canada, a department store chain owned by my father's cousin Noah Waterman, who had helped my father emigrate to Canada.

My next mistake was to hire Joe Radlow, who was to become the most notorious Wall Street stool pigeon of the 1930's. But I needed a partner who could serve as president of the corporation since I could not because I was under indictment. Joe had been involved in shady deals all his life, and when it came his turn to answer for them, he started to detail everybody else's, to save himself a jail term.

He was a short, ruddy-faced, tubby man with blond hair, and before he became a professional witness, he was a famous eater. Joe could knock off a nine-course dinner at noon and over coffee work up a tear in his eye over a steak he had had two months before in Asbury Park. No question about it, Joe Radlow was a trencherman. He was also a bucket shop expert, and we bucketed many orders for Cosmopolitan.

Then, one noon, Joe finished his meal and went down to the United States Attorney's office and told them I was again using the mails to defraud. Again I was indicted. Again my lawyer said, "Indictment is just another way of enjoining you from doing business."

I cannot explain my perversity. I did not feel guilty, only uncomfortable that a grand jury charged me again. I was not chastened, only irritated that the United States Attorney kept annoying me. I once said of Charles Tuttle to Big Bill Ebel, "What's the matter with the man? Doesn't he *know* the market's going down?"

I was arrogant, and I was arrogant in the way only the young can be arrogant. The arrogance of the young is a direct result of not having known enough consequences. I didn't realize there were consequences. There had never been consequences before; why should there be consequences now? I was like the turkey that every day greedily approaches the farmer who tosses him grain. On a November Wednesday the turkey runs to the farmer again—to lose his head for the effort. *But the turkey is not wrong.* It is just that no one ever told him about Thanksgiving.

A week before I was to go before a referee who would adjudge Kable and Company bankrupt, the New York *World*, on Thursday, June 20, 1929, carried the front-page right-column headline:

BISHOP CANNON REVEALED AS A BIG CLIENT OF STOCK
HOUSE ACCUSED OF FRAUD
Judson Campbell, Kable's Lawyer, Disclosed Stock Deals
After Charles Tuttle Refused Him Access to Books

The newspapers told me at last what it was that spurred Charles Tuttle on. He had the record of Bishop Cannon's stock deals. Bishop Cannon was big time. He was a big-time minister and a big-time politician. He had just helped defeat Al Smith, and he had helped prolong Prohibition. No matter what Bishop Cannon did in those days, it was news. That he was gambling in the stock market was big news. That he was gambling through an indicted broker was headline news.

Charles Tuttle had discovered that Kable had sold the record of Bishop Cannon's stock transactions to the New York *World*. The *World* through its editor, John Tennant, who had bought the file, probably told Tuttle the newspaper would sit on the story until it felt the absolutely devastating moment in which to release it had arrived.

The moment had arrived. What was at most a sordid little back street story about a bucket shop was now a major scandal. A Wall Street punk had to testify under oath within the week, and there was every chance his testimony would implicate a Methodist bishop now at the zenith of his political power.

On the day the bankruptcy hearing got under way, there were 100 reporters in the hall. They crowded the small hearing room, all of them bending forward to catch the name of Cannon.

Chapter 11

Bishop James Cannon, Jr., of the Methodist Episcopal Church, South, was the most successful prohibitionist who ever lived. Not only did he spend forty years drying up the United States, but by 1929 he was trying to dry up the whole world.

The Bishop, for so I always referred to him, was born in Salisbury, Maryland, in 1864, the son of a prosperous merchant. He attended Randolph-Macon College in Virginia; married Lura Bennett, the daughter of the college president; was graduated from the Princeton Theological Seminary; and, in 1888, heeded his call by becoming a Methodist circuit rider in Charlotte County, Virginia.

I never understood the genesis of his hatred of liquor. He was a humorless man; one of his friends once remarked that few had ever seen the Bishop laugh and none had ever seen him smile. I suspect that like most humorless men, he had to make life into a crusade to make sense of it. The Bishop crusaded against the demon rum and the Roman Catholic Church. And he crusaded against them because any true knight-crusader must possess an absolute ignorance of his enemy. Knights are not really expected to find the Grail; they are expected to find the dragon.

What made the Bishop more than an anachronistic crusader and crackpot was that he was canny and astute. He was an intuitive politician and a born businessman. He took over the *Virginian*, a moribund Methodist newspaper, and not only turned it into a profit maker but made it as well into the powerful political voice of the rural South. To meet his competition, Cannon had to publish a Sunday edition. When the strict Methodists worried about the Bishop's doing business on Sunday, the Bishop solved this moral dilemma by taking his name off the masthead.

The trustees of an impoverished girls' boarding school importuned Cannon to become principal. The Blackstone Institute in Blackstone, Virginia, was without a curriculum, without teachers, and virtually without students. The trustees apologized that they couldn't offer much of a salary. Cannon relieved their anxiety by declaring if they let him handle the school's business accounts, he would find a way to pay his own salary. Ten years later the Bishop had made the Blackstone Institute into a prestigious and reputable school. And he had also provoked several Methodist ministers into charging that he was lining his pockets with the school's profits. But then, the Bishop never said he wasn't after profits.

The Bishop could cut corners, financially as well as morally. I first met him when he stayed at my brother Jake's Hotel Union Square. I often wondered why he preferred the Union Square, whose clientele was drawn from the Yiddish theater, to all the other fancy uptown hotels. I came to the conclusion that he was a womanizer and wanted a hotel where he would least likely be recognized and embarrassed. But this discovery, as I say, came many years later. He started to make himself into a political force when he joined the Anti-Saloon League in 1901. In 1901 the Anti-Saloon League was a joke. But the Bishop soon enough, in his own humorless way, made sure the folks realized the Anti-Saloon League was no laughing matter.

Once Prohibition came to America, it seemed to many of us to come as the result of a moral fervor which had suddenly inspired the country. On January 16, 1920, when the Volstead Act became law, I remember the crowd scene in front of Gold's Liquor Store on Broadway at Forty-second Street, where the Rialto Theater now stands. Gold's stocked the finest liquor in the world, brandies bottled in the time of Napoleon, vintage wines from France, scotch which boasted service on the table of George V.

Gold moved every bottle out to the sidewalk in wicker baskets. "Going out of business," he advertised. "Every bottle $1." Six months later, of course, those bottles were worth $20, and a year later the going price for prewar whiskey was $50. Peter Salvin, who ran the famous Salvin Restaurant, told me on that January day he thought his wine cellar was well enough stocked to accommodate diners for the next year. But Salvin sold out that wine cellar on January 16.

Prohibition's crucial fault was that it was not a moral fervor; it was a political reform. That is why it failed so ignobly. The trouble with Prohibition as a political reform was not only that its adherents were losing power but that Prohibition ended where it began. The prohibitionists did not promise that we would all blossom into perfect health or that we would get more work done because our heads were clear or that we would improve the gross national product; they promised that the family was forever secured because we all would become supreme moral beings. Within weeks we realized we were anything but that. Within the year our divorce rate began to rise.

No law, not even Nero's proscription of the Christians, made as many honest citizens into lawbreakers as Prohibition. Dudja Silverberg, my father's pious friend, was noted throughout the synagogue as an honest man. Like an impatient evangelical angel, he sped to my father's house to instruct us how to make slivovitz, the prune brandy all the Mikulintsyers loved.

"You need only prune juice, a raisin, and sugar," said Dudja, measuring the components into a jar. He sealed it. "That's all there is to it, Herschele. Then you let it stand for three weeks."

"How can Herschele let it stand for three weeks?" asked my father dryly.

Every Monday and Friday a bootlegger came over to Big Bill Ebel's office looking like a Philadelphia lawyer, an expensive leather briefcase in hand. He would write out our orders, and the next day a florist's truck would draw up to the building, and in the bottom of the basket of a beautiful, if often wilted, floral arrangement was the scotch and champagne and gin.

The forces of reform fail to comprehend that law is not enough to make a man moral. One of our naïve ex-Presidents once remarked law is not enough to change the hearts of men; we might add, nor can it keep him sober. A law that cannot be enforced is no law at all. To start with, the Prohibition Bureau had to police a 3,000-mile border between the United States and Canada. It would have needed a standing army to police the Mexican border alone, not to mention the Atlantic and Pacific seaboards.

But the prohibitionists hated alcohol to such a degree they were sure all of us hated it, too. Bishop Cannon always called liquor "the scourge of mankind." He didn't think poverty was a scourge, or crime, or illiteracy, just liquor.

While the Bishop didn't bring about Prohibition single-handedly, single-handedly he mustered the energies of the Women's Christian Temperance Union, the Methodist Board of Temperance, Prohibition, and Public Morals, his own church, as well as the Baptist, and plotted the political course they all pursued. Like any reformer who wants to succeed, from Martin Luther to Mao Tse-tung, the Bishop adopted a strategy of one against a thousand and the tactics of a thousand against one. He committed his forces only in isolated areas and only when he outnumbered the enemy; he fought the main battle only when all those isolated areas formed a vast host behind him.

In 1901 the Anti-Saloon League was using its resources to bail out Carrie Nation as often as she was arrested for hatcheting saloons; its publications ridiculed known drunkards and recounted *ad nauseam* the evils of John Barleycorn. The Bishop changed that. He transformed the Anti-Saloon League into a lobby which populated the legislative hall of the Virginia Capitol urging legislators to pass an enabling act so that communities could vote whether or not to make themselves dry. Prohibition started with local option. League members would invade one county at a time, agitating for the referendum. They started with the backwoods, where they had little difficulty in persuading unsophisticated Methodists and Baptists that Prohibition was an earthly salvation. On election day voters went to the polling place accompanied by the ringing of every church bell and carillon in the county.

One by one the counties voted for local option. When enough of the counties had voted dry, the Bishop moved for statewide laws. Though these counties were populated by illiterate Fundamentalists, still they elected the majority of state representatives and senators. These backwoodsmen began to clamor for state prohibition, for the Bishop had convinced them that liquor was the sin of the cities, the peril of the rich. As a matter of fact, even when I knew him, he always referred to the urban population as

127

"the knights of the little brown jug." It is no distention of the truth to state that the one-mule farmer and the overworked yeoman have always been jealous of the city man. Poor people are jealous people, particularly when poor people realize they are marginal, as the countryfolk could not help realizing with the advent of the industrial twentieth century.

Prohibition hurt the cities. So did the Mann Act, which made it a crime for a businessman to transport his secretary across state lines for immoral purposes. But as H. L. Mencken once pointed out, Congress, in its wildest dreams, never considered making it a federal crime for a farm boy to drag a fifteen-year-old virgin into the barn. Rural virgins ran their own risks.

When Virginia voted itself dry, Cannon moved on to other Southern states. By no means do I insist this was an easy or facile process. It meant increasing propagandizing, campaigning, agitation. It meant compromise. There is the notorious legend of Bishop Cannon and his aide, needing one vote for the passage of an enabling act, seeking out a missing legislator, rescuing him from a bawdy house, giving him a belt of whiskey to pull himself together, and racing in a horse-drawn carriage to the State Capitol, where the legislator hiccuped yes. Nor did the Anti-Saloon League insist on total prohibition. Many counties and states opted for a limited prohibition, one quart a month per citizen or the simple prohibition of alcoholic spirits distilled out of state. As long as the Bishop could get any law on the books, he was satisfied.

Part of his success was due to his instinctive restraint. He never menaced a legislator or an elected official as long as he would vote his way. It was a cynical program, but he knew Southern legislators were smarter and more cynical than their constituency. Only when he had achieved immense power did he commit himself against a candidate who was an antiprohibitionist, and then the Bishop brought ruin upon himself.

For that is what the Bishop was accumulating as Prohibition gained momentum—power, raw, unvarnished political power. Virginia legislators were at first surprised and then dismayed to learn that after they had made the state dry, many committee appointments had first to be screened by Bishop Cannon. Party bosses had to consult the Bishop about the advisability of some nominees for high office. Nothing distresses a politician like the knowledge that his own vote has invited another hand to share the pie.

128

To call Prohibition a bandwagon is to dignify it with a certain joyous atmosphere which it did not emanate. Prohibition was a juggernaut. It didn't want supporters; it demanded disciples. William Jennings Bryan, when he was Woodrow Wilson's Secretary of State, in the years before the Volstead Act became law, still refused to serve wine at diplomatic receptions. That decision is all that distinguishes his secretaryship.

By 1915 national Prohibition had certain prospects. Accordingly, Prohibition became a headier brew than any liquor ever distilled. State legislators outdid themselves in legal sophistry and poetry. Indiana made it a crime for jewelers to display pocket flasks. Alabama proscribed the distillation of anything that "looks like, tastes like, smells like, or foams like beer." Mississippi declared it was against the law to distill alcohol "in the land, in the air, below ground, or under the sea."

The last push Prohibition needed came with World War I. The Anti-Saloon League argued the country needed wartime Prohibition to preserve vital food byproducts. The Anti-Saloon League meant malt and yeast. The brewers protested. Bishop Cannon, in the pages of the *Virginian*, noted how many of these brewers had German names. Wartime Prohibition became national Prohibition when Senator Warren G. Harding, convinced by the ever-persuasive Cannon, sponsored the move to have the Senate consider the Eighteenth Amendment. Twenty-seven states had already passed prohibition laws of their own. The drys needed only another nine. Within a year these states ratified the amendment. In all, forty-six states fell into line. Only Connecticut and Rhode Island refused ratification.

One day the country woke up, and no one was ever going to have a drink again, a resolve that lasted until noon.

But the Bishop's work was not done. While he told me he eventually expected the Nobel Prize for Peace, he was quite aware that where he had recently only *approved* the Democratic nominee for governor of Virginia, now he could *name* that nominee. The professional politicians had to accommodate him—which they did until 1928, when the Democratic Party nominated Alfred E. Smith for the Presidency.

Chapter 12

ADMITTEDLY, I am giving the Bishop the short end of the argument. He was an absolutely sincere and dedicated man. He firmly believed that when he finally enforced worldwide prohibition, the cupboard doors would open and nothing but good men would spill out. Which is to say he was a fanatic, but then, in this century, people have been fanatic about far more destructive reforms than prohibition. I found Bishop Cannon a gentleman and a brave gentleman. He was always loyal. Nothing ever flustered him. The Bishop never whined, and he was more than capable of fighting his own battles.

He was a spry man with a white mustache who always carried a burnished walnut cane; later he used a crutch, for he lived with a painful arthritis. He wore high shoes which had buckles, and he always wore long woolen underwear, winter and summer. He had immense presence—he was important and he knew it—but I never found him overbearing.

My brother Jake had promised to treat this Virginia minister to a luncheon at Luchow's, which was right around the corner from the Union Square. Jake invited me along. Luchow's was an exotic adventure to the Bishop. He spent an entire evening in my home in Larchmont exulting over the delights of some kosher dill pickles Tiny served him. Years and years later he still remembered those pickles. Until 1924, when I met him, I am quite sure the Bishop had never heard of puts and calls. I began to sell the partial payment plan with an instinctive vigor.

The Bishop said, "I've traded and sold all my life, but I've never put money into the partial payment plan. What do you think would be a good start for me?"

"It depends on what you like to invest," I answered.

"Say a couple of thousand."

I invested this money in Chicago and North Western Railway stock, and some months later, when I sold it, the Bishop realized a profit of $17,000. He became a steady investor. As often as he came to New York from Washington, D.C., he stopped at the offices of Kable and Company.

There were many reasons why this business relationship became a fast friendship. I liked the Bishop, humorless though he was. And he liked me. The Bishop did not like many people, but he did like Jews. He always introduced me as the son of a rabbi, as though my presence, as a direct descendant of the prophets, somehow cast a luminosity on him, a Methodist. The bigotry and prejudice that animated his soul about Catholics never clamored about Jews. Like any businessman, I catered to my good customers. Bishop Cannon was an excellent customer making substantial investments. Last, I was awed by the Bishop. He had made Prohibition happen. Because he made it happen, he was familiar with powerful men in America.

As well as the Bishop of the Methodist Episcopal Church, South, Cannon was the Methodist Bishop for South America and for the Congo. He made trips to his bishoprics, too, despite suffering malaria and tropical fever. When he told me his plans for bringing prohibition to the Congo, I was impressed. Any man is fascinated by another who wants to take over the world.

He came out to the Larchmont house several times. I used to call Genevieve and ask her to hide the cocktail shaker and secrete our liquor in the pantry behind the tins of flour and sugar and coffee. The Bishop admired Tiny. The first time he met her, he turned to me and said, "Harry, you have outdone yourself." When my first son was born, the Bishop said, "You should name your first son Richard. I named my first son Richard." And so I did.

The Bishop was always interested in meeting people. Several times he asked me to introduce him to Oscar Geiger. One Sunday we did go up to that Harlem apartment. Here were two men whose minds grappled all their lines with a single dedication. Unfortunately for the social event, they were dissimilar dedications. Oscar tried to instruct the Bishop on the justice of the single tax. The Bishop leaned forward in his chair, chin on his cane, ankles crossed, until Oscar took a breath. Then the Bishop proceeded to instruct Oscar on the heroic crusade of the temperance movement.

"It started at Oberlin College, in Ohio," the Bishop said. "Glorious Oberlin gave its name to the temperance movement, the Oberlin Movement . . ." I leave it to my reader to imagine what kind of afternoon it was.

On the way home, far from breathless or intellectually exhausted, the Bishop expounded on Oscar Geiger's virtues. "He could have been President of the United States had he devoted himself to practical politics," the Bishop said.

Of Bishop Cannon, Oscar Geiger said dogmatically, "He's a nut."

If Bishop Cannon thought John Barleycorn was the Devil, civilization's bête noire was the Pope. Demon rum and the Roman Catholic hierarchy were the Bishop's alpha and omega of all evil. Cannon was an anti-Catholic, not of the Ku Klux variety, ready to burn a cross on the lawn of a Catholic church, but he harbored a typical, if paranoid, suspicion of Rome, as he called Catholicism. The worse thing he could say about another Protestant minister was, "He has one foot in Rome." He told me in all seriousness that he had it on the highest authority that Joseph Tumulty, Woodrow Wilson's private secretary, had maintained an open line with the Vatican during World War I over which he leaked all our military secrets.

When I pointed out that the Pope was an Italian and that America and Italy were allies and that we had won the war, the Bishop brushed aside my logic. "Rome is after world dominance," he said with finality.

Anti-Catholicism has too often unfortunately proved to be a social grace, which is why the Bishop got away with it.

The Bishop was an anti-Catholic first because he was jealous. It is not true that a Roman Catholic priest exercises an iron control over the actions and attitudes of his parishioners, but the Bishop thought he did. It is not true that Catholics agree on every subject, but the Bishop was sure Catholicism was a monolithic discipline intent on denying freedom to all. Bishop Cannon was positive that the Roman Catholic Church would destroy the traditional separation of church and state. Conveniently, he chose not to remember that he exercised as prestigious an influence and as willful a power over his congregation as any medieval Pope, that the Bishop had no hesitation in invoking police power to see that a movie house in a Southern town stayed closed on Sunday, and that he had easily forced the inclusion of Protestant prayers in the public school curriculum.

The Bishop was also an anti-Catholic because he was a Southerner, a man born in the last homogeneous society in America. Catholicism in his mind was identified with the Irish, the Italians, and the Poles who were not Anglo-Saxons and who were therefore not proper people. Catholics wouldn't fit into the rhythm of rural America—the Irish who came to America during the potato famine, the Italians who succeeded them, and the Poles were poor, poverty-stricken. Nothing threatens middle-class values like the poor minority group demanding its fair share. The Bishop and other Southerners might not articulate this fear, but social displacement terrified them.

Bishop Cannon might have carried these prejudices with him as innocuously as he carried his watch in his vest pocket but for the fact that by 1926 it was obvious that Alfred E. Smith, four-time governor of New York, was certain to win the Democratic nomination for the Presidency. It was painfully obvious to the Democratic Bishop Cannon that Smith was going to be hard to stop. I say painful because Al Smith was not only an ardent Catholic, but also a Tammany man and a wet. Smith had succeeded in having the New York legislature memorialize Congress on the need for modifying the Volstead Act, and to Bishop Cannon, this was tinkering with the universe. In his editorials in the *Virginian,* Bishop Cannon served notice that he was not going to let the foreigners in the cities elect a Catholic who would open the floodgates of immigration and destroy Phohibition.

The key word here, of course, is "cities." The Bishop was astute enough to realize the country was in the process of transferring power from the rural to the urban areas. Since the Bishop had spent a lifetime reciting the litany that the city was the harbor of sin, the blight on the American body politic, that transfer would surely limit his power. As a matter of fact, though Al Smith did lose the election in 1928 by a substantial margin, still the

Democrats for the first time carried the ten largest cities by a plurality of 38,000.

What lent a shady, if nonetheless persuasive, substance to the Bishop's prejudice was Al Smith's naïveté. Until it was too late, Smith did not realize that anti-Catholicism wasn't restricted to the Ku Klux Klan. In 1926, when Giovanni Cardinal Bonzano, the papal legate to the Eucharistic Congress in Chicago arrived in New York, Al Smith and Mayor Jimmy Walker greeted him at City Hall and knelt to kiss his ring.

This public display of reverence enraged the Fundamentalists. Bishop Cannon called Al Smith "this wet Knight of Columbus and Chamberlain of the Pope." Cannon promised, "If they nominate Smith at the convention, I will beat him at the polls."

The Democrats who convened in Houston in 1928 did indeed nominate Al Smith. Immediately, the Bishop convened a meeting of the anti-Smith Democrats in Asheville, North Carolina. These Democrats decided against a third candidate and pledged their support to Herbert Hoover, the Republican.

The Bishop didn't raise the religious issue; he waved it like a flag. He insisted he did not oppose Smith because Smith was a Catholic; he opposed Smith because Smith was intolerant, that Al Smith and the Pope had declared good, loyal Protestant Americans were "strangers to the hope of life and salvation." There wasn't much in this vein the Bishop didn't say, and I feel it is tiresome to repeat it now.

Southerners listened. On election day, 1928, thousands of them "went fishing." Herbert Hoover carried Virginia, West Virginia, North Carolina, Florida, and Texas. Though the Democrats had carried the cities, for the first time the Republicans had breached the Solid South. The Bishop was flushed with his new and very real power. Where he was only naming governors, now he was ready to name Presidents. Though he contributed substantially to Al Smith's defeat, I do not believe the Bishop's role was a crucial role, although many at the time said it was. If the Democrats had nominated Dan'l Boone, they would have lost. Our prosperity was unprecedented, and the Republicans were responsible. When the smoke pours from the chimneys, the American people do not change national administrations.

With the election over, however, the Bishop, because of his organizational genius, still had control of a large political apparatus which he had no intention of dismantling. Professionals like Governor Harry Byrd and Senator Carter Glass of Virginia who had worked loyally for the Democratic nominee realized nothing for their energies. The Bishop controlled the patronage because he had an intimate relationship with the new Hoover administration.

Bishop Cannon was making enemies, but he was used to that. He had bested enemies before, triumphing even against other bishops, who once tried to prevent his elevation to the episcopacy. The ministers were convinced the Bishop was nothing but a horse trader. The ministers learned to live with him. But the politicians vowed they wouldn't, and the politicians were no amateurs.

William Randolph Hearst didn't like Bishop Cannon, or Joseph Pulitzer, or countless other editors, who were tired of defending their patriotism when Bishop Cannon attacked them for supporting Al Smith. Nor were the citizens of the city ready to admit that the Southern yeoman was the paradigm of democratic America. Yet all his enemies had against the Bishop was that he was an apostle of an asthmatic morality which would have bored the pants off Billy Sunday and Anthony Comstock. He was a sanctimonious psalm singer, superior and unctuous.

That was all they had to have against him.

Chapter 13

In the December, 1928, issue of *Current History*, Bishop
Cannon undertook to analyze why Alfred E. Smith was defeated:

> The deliberate denunciation by Smith and Raskob [John J.
> Raskob was Smith's Catholic campaign manager] and their fol-
> lowers of those opposing the Governor as intolerant bigots who
> were hypocritically using Prohibition and Tammany as a cloak
> for their bigotry undoubtedly fanned the flames of opposition to
> Governor Smith and aided in his overwhelming defeat. Smith and
> Raskob themselves issued orders to run the red herring of religious
> intolerance across the trail.

Having divested himself of these sentiments, the Bishop went
on to announce that the anti-Smith Democrats would nominate
Dr. William Moseley Brown as their candidate in Virginia's
gubernatorial election the next fall. Dr. Brown was also the Republican candidate. The Bishop did what Al Smith never intended: made religious tenets the basis of political control.

It was the last essay the Bishop was to write as King of the
Mountain. From June 20, 1929, on, in all his editorials the Bishop
was fighting for his religious and political life—and he was losing.

Once the New York *World* published the story of Bishop Cannon's speculations, every other paper picked it up. The headlines
on that Thursday in June varied, but the tenor was the same
in all of them: Bishop Cannon was gambling and was gambling
through an indicted broker.

The Bishop called me from Washington, D.C., that evening, by which time Philip Samuels, my lawyer, and I had ascertained how the *World,* an evening paper, had got hold of the story.

I told Cannon, "Charlie Kable, my partner, stole your confidential file listing all your transactions. He stole it over a year ago. He sold it to the *World* for four thousand dollars."

A brief pause. Bishop Cannon said, "Harry, they are trying to get me over your body."

"You think the papers will keep it up?"

The Bishop didn't sigh, nor did he equivocate. "They will keep it up," he said.

He was right. The New York *World* lost interest in the story after the bankruptcy hearing, but Hearst's New York *Journal* had a story from the first day right through my trial. Neither the Bishop nor I merited headlines every day, but we got them often enough. If we were not in the headlines, we were still in the news for a two-inch column in the back pages. The New York *Times* ran more than twenty-five stories ranging from the page one headline DEALINGS WITH KABLE AND COMPANY EXPLAINED BY BISHOP CANNON to a one-column "Legal Comment on Stock Deals" which was in the financial section one Sunday months later.

A newspaper story is a hammerblow to the heart. For the first time I realized I might have to go to jail because all the editors asked rhetorically, "If Goldhurst was indicted a year ago, why hasn't he been tried?" No judge was going to nol-pros the case or put it over for the next calendar or the next until the court finally forgot me. Jail frightened me, not for the time I would lose or even for the numbing routine of incarceration, but because I knew a jail sentence was irrevocable, as irrevocable and as menacing as the doctor's discovery of a malignant cancer.

These editorial questions are the precise prodding a United States Attorney General may not like but will certainly heed. And the newspaper stories made it impossible to gull Genevieve any longer. I tried to explain to her that if it weren't for Bishop Cannon's involvement, none of this would have happened. Each time I essayed this explanation I felt less and less like a political martyr. At last she cried. It wasn't just Harry Goldhurst: I had a wife and two children, a third on the way. Where would she go? How would they live?

I saw Charlie Kable the next Thursday, June 26, when we

appeared before a referee who would certify our bankruptcy. I was with Philip Samuels, and Charlie Kable was with his lawyer, Judson Campbell. When I saw him, quivering and nervous, I asked, "Kable, why couldn't you have given me a chance to buy that confidential file? I would have paid you more than the New York *World*."

Knuckles in his mouth, he turned away.

The bankruptcy hearings lasted almost three full days, an inordinate amount of time for so simple a legal process. The referee knew from both a state-appointed and a private auditor my liabilities and assets. My liabilities represented 90 percent paper profits because I couldn't pay off the tremendous rise. Most of the customers had long since received their out-of-pocket investment.

The reason the hearings lasted as long as they did was because Edward Benoit, the lawyer for the state-appointed receiver, was intent on eliciting from Kable's and my testimony that Bishop Cannon was a silent partner in our brokerage, that he received commissions for steering customers to us, that Kable and Company used the Bishop as a lure.

None of these innuendos was true. The Bishop was a customer; that's all that he was. But Benoit, following the lead of the newspapers, tried to implicate him in Kable and Company's corruption.

Kable testified that he had never handled the Bishop's account or any of the accounts. He said he was no more than an office boy. He said Goldhurst had introduced him to Cannon on several occasions, that Goldhurst bragged about knowing the Bishop, that the company extended an excessive credit to the Cannon account.

Over the next two days I testified that it was Kable and Company's practice to extend credit to good clients, as it was the practice of every brokerage. I stated that the United States Attorney General from the books he impounded could testify that Kable and Company never made a check out to Bishop Cannon except for profits legitimately realized from the sale of stock. Moreover, I said the United States Attorney General had a complete list of the customers of Kable and Company and could verify that not one enjoyed any special friendship with Bishop Cannon, which made it hard to believe he had steered them. Last, I pointed out that I had mailed hundreds of circulars to prospective clients in the last three years, had spent hundreds of dollars in advertising, yet neither these circulars, my ads, or letters addressed to specific customers ever mentioned the name of Bishop James Cannon, Jr.

Benoit admitted the defense and announced he would not subpoena the Bishop for testimony. But during his examination he discovered that I had executed orders for the Bishop which he had authorized on Sundays. It was obvious from the books and the correspondence the Bishop had ordered 330 shares of Lehigh Valley stock on Sunday, October 16, 1927. Going back and forth over the ledger, Benoit discovered the Bishop had issued several other orders on a Sunday. To the Methodists of the South, Sunday is a pure white color never to be soiled by affairs of the world.

Finally, when Benoit questioned me about bucketing orders, I demurred. I said I did not have to buy the stock until the final payment was made. The demurrers were those of a man uncomfortably pinned by knowledge of his own motives.

My testimony therefore did not completely exonerate the Bishop morally. The Bishop was the great foe of liquor. He was also the great foe of gambling in all forms, having urged the General Conference of the Methodist Episcopal Church, South, in 1922 to adopt unanimously a resolution condemning all forms of gambling. He who denounced daily the traffic in bootleg liquor had been detected in bootleg gambling.

Bishop Cannon's first response was to charge there was a Roman Catholic conspiracy to discredit him and Prohibition. Curiously, the two public figures who made no comment at all about my indictment or the Bishop's speculations were Alfred E. Smith and John J. Raskob. As a matter of fact, if there was a conspiracy to discredit the Bishop, it was a Methodist conspiracy, and it was headed by Senator Carter Glass of Virginia and Governor Harry Byrd, who wanted John Garland Pollack to succeed Byrd as governor.

But the case had exploded in the North, in New York, and the North was wet and Democratic. What the Bishop's ledger revealed was that during 1927 and 1928 Kable and Company bought stocks for him worth $447,000 and had sold them for $486,000, all on the partial payment plan, which cost Cannon an investment of $2,500.

"Instead of reading stock market reports," said an editorial in the New York *Times*, on June 22, 1929, "it would be better if

Bishop carried with him the injunction of the Apostle that a Bishop should be 'not greedy of filthy lucre . . . not covetous. . . .' "

The Bishop devoted himself to a more reasoned defense of his stock market transactions. Soon after the bankruptcy hearings closed, he published an 18,000-word polemic which he called *Unspotted from the World,* the title of the Methodist discipline. He distributed one copy of the pamphlet to every newspaper and distributed another 50,000 to his adherents. His arguments were trenchant, but he had as much trouble explaining why the partial payment plan wasn't marginal buying as I had trying to explain why I didn't have to purchase the stocks until receipt of the final installment.

Among other things, the Bishop argued:

> For forty years I have engaged in business transactions of various kinds. I have openly bought and sold houses and lots, timber and stumpage, coal, cotton, and bank stock and stocks and bonds listed on the New York Stock Exchange, first in Richmond from my personal acquaintances, Col. John P. Branch and Mr. Langbourne M. Williams, both Christian gentlemen, at the head of Richmond Stock Exchange houses.
>
> I learned of the monthly installment purchase plan of Kable and Company. I thought the firm to be a reputable firm, and bought and sold some stock through it. . . . I thought I was buying stocks for investment, buying on the partial payment plan, as any man may. I did not know there was any gambling by the company. . . . I do not feel that I did anything wrong in buying stocks on the partial payment plan, and I certainly did not intend to gamble.

To which the *Wall Street Journal* replied on June 25: "He must have known after a few transactions that he was not investing or even speculating; he was betting on the turn of the market . . . if this sort of thing can be described as buying stock . . . then drawing one card to an inside straight is a conservative investment."

There is no doubt the Bishop was gambling: I knew it and he knew it; Edward Benoit knew it; Carter Glass and the public knew it. A year later the Bishop admitted gambling at his church trial. The United States Senate Lobby Committee had got hold of the Bishop's file from Tuttle's office and under pressure from Carter Glass made that correspondence public.

On Friday, June 13, 1930, the New York *Times* published this correspondence in its entirety. I reproduce a few of these letters. They evoke a sad irony. In the beginning the Bishop *was* gambling; at the end he only *thought* he was gambling because I was bucketing some of the orders.

Cablegram, Oct. 4, 1927

From Cannon to Kable and Company, Jersey City—Richmond sending 600 whether sell Lehigh high, rebuying 300, reaction, advise.

Cablegram, Oct. 7, 1927

From Cannon to Kable and Company, Jersey City—Cable close market direct Western Union, São Paulo, till next Friday, adding Drug, Gleasonite, other quotations; option 2,000 motors expiring Thursday.

Cablegram dated Oct. 15, 1927

From Cannon, São Paulo, to Kable, 32 Broadway, New York City—Cable immediately opening, low, high, close quotations Motors Thursday and other quotations requested. Is Gleasonite collapse permanent? Quote Drug.

Letter dated Dec. 10, 1927

From James Cannon Jr. to Mr. Goldhurst, written on the stationery of the Board of Temperance and Social Service, Washington, D.C.: "My Dear Mr. Goldhurst: I came down to Richmond today and managed after a hard struggle to land $400 which I am enclosing by draft. I am being kept on edge and fearful of flop in the Paige, Butterick, Puerto Rico and Moon have conspired to induce pessimism. I started to wire "sell 17½" but thought surely would make 18. If it seems 17½ will be high on Monday sell at that and repurchase if wise. But do not get caught on a slump or I shall think all our ventures are hoodooed.

Sincerely yours,

Send all communications to Richmond promptly. Any reaction and it will be forwarded. But do not send any excitable gram.

Telegram, dated Dec. 12, 1927, from Cannon, Birmingham, Ala. to H. Goldhurst, Kable and Co.,

Your wire Washington forwarded. Never wire Washington unless I give definite instructions. Always causes unpleasant complications. Write Richmond, where secretary understands how forward. Cannot send anything more 'til return Richmond.

Letter, dated March 1, 1928

From James Cannon, Jr., on the stationery of the Anti-Saloon League of Virginia, to H. Goldhurst.

I find your telegram on my return to Richmond. I am sorry not only for my own sake, but for yours, that you are not a prophet of the first grade. I do not know from whom you get your information, but they are evidently not prophets of the first grade, and with the exception of the Paige and the Northern Ohio (which, by the way, was doing very well when I last noticed it) all of our stocks have gone back and wallowed in the trough of the sea. I wonder what is going to happen to Interborough Rapid Transit? I saw that it jumped up 2 or 3 points the other day, but no sales were quoted today. The issue in it seems to be very uncertain.

I am writing this, however, especially to emphasize the fact that I am not in a position to take such expensive stocks. If I had been free when Texas went down to 21 I would not have hesitated to have bought 1,000 and sold it at 23 or 23½ and bought it back again as conditions indicated. I was disgusted to see today that Continental Baking A had tumbled down one-third. Continental Baking B, of which I got 700 shares, has gone down nearly to 4. Do not try to reach me now until I wire you. I am leaving Richmond for the South tonight. Do not wire to Richmond or to Washington until you hear from me again, which will probably be next Wednesday.

Affectionately and sincerely. . . .

The General Conference of the Methodist Episcopal Church, South, held in Dallas, in May, 1930, tried the Bishop on the charges that his stock speculations brought his high ecclesiastical office into disrepute. The Bishop admitted to his jury he had speculated but now acknowledged his transgression and asked for and obtained the forgiveness of the conference. By that time, with the Depression full upon us, even Methodists must have realized any minister who had played the stock market in the 1920's certainly got more than was coming to him. They all knew too many devils to select one for stoning.

Cannon's stock speculations with Kable and Company were not all that crippled his political power. In July, 1929, while the Bishop was trying to allay suspicion that he gambled and gambled on Sunday, the New York *World*, this time joined by the Chicago *Tribune*, published the story that in 1918 the United States Food Administration held the Bishop guilty of hoarding flour during the war. This time the editors didn't have to buy the story: Senator Carter Glass, who had instituted the charges when he was a member of the House of Representatives, forwarded it free of charge.

The Bishop, as head of the Blackstone Institute, purchased 650 barrels of flour in the spring of 1917. He sold these barrels later in the year at a profit. In *Unspotted from the World* the Bishop said his only concern was that the girls in his charge had enough to eat. Carter Glass, who also owned a newspaper, The Lynchburg *News*, effectively demolished the excuse by citing the amount of flour purchases made by other women's colleges. The Bishop's idea of a proper diet for his charges, concluded the *News*, was 309 loaves of bread a year per girl.

The Bishop was immune from prosecution, if indeed he was a hoarder, because the Lever Food and Fuel Control Act did not become law until August, 1917, several months after he bought the flour. Ten years before, a technicality spared him prosecution; a decade later, there was no technicality to spare him the publicity.

Within the year the Bishop again outraged his constituency. On July 15, 1930, in England, the Bishop, now sixty-five, married Mrs. Helen Hawley McCallum. There was nothing in this action to provoke scandal; Lura Bennett Cannon had died several years before. But the Philadelphia *Record* published the news that on several occasions Mrs. McCallum had accompanied the Bishop abroad as his "secretary." The *Record* also published his correspondence with the forty-year-old widow. Not only had the Bishop settled an allowance of $200 a month on Mrs. McCallum, but he had settled it on her before Mrs. Cannon died.

The Bishop managed all at once to get himself in trouble with money, food, and women—which was more trouble than any that ever afflicted alcoholics I have known. There was more trouble yet to come, trouble that would keep me in jail longer than I expected.

Chapter 14

AFTER my son Billy was born in August, Genevieve and I moved to a small apartment in Jersey City. We went to see her mother, Emma Gallagher, and I had to tell her there was a good likelihood I would go to jail before Christmas. Emma heard me out and said, "We'll pray for you, Harry." My wife's mother owned a large three-story house on Jersey City's Woodlawn Avenue, and she said there was room enough there for Tiny and the three boys. At least that much was settled, that my wife and family had a place to stay.

Philip Samuels and I discussed my prospects. Samuels said, "All trials do not result in convictions. All convictions do not result in jail terms. Jail terms are occasionally overturned on appeal. Appeals can often consume two or three years." But he warned me it was an expensive proposition. I had some money saved, but I had no prospects if I was acquitted or if my sentence was suspended. I was heartsick at the thought I would have to borrow large sums again from Clara and Jack and Hubert Gallagher and others.

I worked at the Hotel Union Square. One morning a woman whom I shall have to call Vivien Black telephoned. I had taken Vivien to dinner and the theater some years before. She was a green-eyed, dark-haired girl, precociously smart and aggressive. She was a lawyer. She told me, "I've read about your case and I think I can help you with it."

"How?" I asked.

"I'm a dollar-a-year woman with the United States Attorney General's office. I work right down the hall from Charles Tuttle. Meet me at Klein's dress shop in half an hour. I'll tell you how."

After half a decade of bucketing orders, I wasn't about to turn moralistic, not when I was facing the penalty of imprisonment. I would have done anything to escape jail. No corruption would have scared me off.

Surreptitiously, I met Vivien among the dress racks where busy sales clerks and customers crowded. We stood by a cash register, and without ado, I asked, "What have you got?"

"I can give you the outline of the prosecutor's case. It will show you everything they've got against you. Give it to your lawyer, and he'll be prepared for any challenge."

"How much?" I asked, quite aware that Vivien wasn't doing this out of any misplaced longing for me.

"I want ten thousand dollars," she said.

"I haven't got ten thousand dollars."

Vivien walked over and inspected a dress. She took it off the rack and held it up and surveyed herself in the mirror. She walked back to me. "Can you get five thousand dollars? It's got to be at least five thousand dollars. It's too dangerous to do for less. Yes, it will have to be five thousand dollars and a nice bracelet."

"When?" I asked.

"Better do it as soon as possible. Say Friday. Do it while I have the chance."

I had $5,000. I borrowed some more money from Jack and bought a platinum bracelet. I met Vivien that Friday by the same cash register with the same salesgirls treading back and forth. She carried a black briefcase. I handed over the cash and the bracelet in a hatbox. She extracted a thick folder from the briefcase. She counted the money.

Philip Samuels started to look the outline over, raised his eyes quickly to me, then went back to his study. When he finished, he turned the papers over and, pointing his finger at me, said, "I'm not going to ask you where you got this. Don't tell me. There's some facts in here you never mentioned."

"I didn't think they were important." I shrugged.

"Unimportant facts always complicate matters. I tell that to all my clients. The ones who take it to heart are walking around. The ones who don't are in Dannemora."

145

The bribe had saved me. I was sure of it. But then I was running amok. Though apparently composed, I was running amok out of panic, out of hysteria, out of conceit, too. When I was young, I knew I wasn't smarter than the school principal who questioned me on why I missed my class. But now I was smarter and had made the arrogant assumption that this time the principal would not catch me in my lie.

Bishop Cannon helped slow down my frenzied career. We met a few weeks before my trial in the Herald Square Hotel. Up until that June day when the *World* put us both on the front page, the Bishop had been a friend of sorts but more of a celebrity to me. An important man to know, perhaps a man able to fix things from time to time when a friend needed something fixed. Therefore, a man to defer to, to cultivate. But since the story of our troubles broke, the Bishop had proved himself a real friend. He never said some of the things he could have said to mitigate his own involvement. He didn't say Goldhurst had cheated him, that he thought his conservative investments were in a portfolio. The Bishop said of me only that he had found Goldhurst an intelligent and capable young man, coming from a religious family, with a good wife, and that he was sorry for me. And he was sorry, sorrier for me than he was for himself.

"I think our trouble is beyond repair," said the Bishop in the hotel lobby.

"I think I'll do all right at the trial," I said.

The Bishop shook his head. "I doubt that, Harry. I just talked to Ellamarye Failor. Ellamarye was a student of mine at Blackstone Institute. Now she's an assistant to the Attorney General in Tuttle's office."

It was on the tip of my tongue to tell the Bishop about Vivien Black. I waited.

"Ellamarye," he went on, "said she hoped I wasn't trying to intercede on your behalf because if I were, she'd have to report it to the Attorney General. I said I wasn't. I simply wanted to know if Tuttle really was going to prosecute this case. Ellamarye said he certainly was, that he was going to call a hundred witnesses if necessary, that I would be the first witness and I would have to tell the truth about you. You know I do not want to do that."

146

The schoolboy finally turned his eyes to the principal. The game was up. I knew it was up. The whirling and dodging availed nothing.

"Bishop," I said, "perhaps I will plead guilty."

"I was going to ask you to do just that," Cannon said. "If you plead guilty, we will get this story out of the newspapers. You will spare me the rigors of being called as a witness. Lastly, you will probably receive a lesser sentence."

"Did Miss Failor say what she thought I would receive?"

"She said she never heard of a federal judge sentencing a first offender who pleads guilty to more than a year and a day for mail fraud, which deprives you of your voting rights but means you can reasonably expect parole in seven or eight months."

Separation from Tiny and the children, I thought. The ignominy. But I *could* end the publicity. And seven or eight months was not forever.

"I will plead guilty," I said to the Bishop.

"I'm always ready to help you, Harry. And one of the ways I can help you is to take a trip to one of my bishoprics. Brazil will do. It will be a nice, long 'trip by steamer with no reporters."

Philip Samuels said it would be a wiser move not to tell Mr. Tuttle I would change my plea, to answer guilty when the judge asked how I pleaded. This stratagem would put the prosecutor at a disadvantage.

My trial was set for the morning of Thursday, October 17, 1929. Genevieve wanted to come with me. I asked her please not. It wasn't bravery that made me go alone. I heard men over the next years insist to guards they would not see their visitors and turn to explain to fellow convicts, "I don't want her to see me this way."

The judge was the Roman Catholic Francis Coleman, who bore no love for Bishop Cannon. Coleman had been waiting in eager anticipation for the Bishop's turn on the witness chair. Forty years later it is hard to re-create the events of that morning. Samuels and I were surprised that Charles Kable pleaded guilty. Later Samuels whispered to me, "That's his reward for selling the Cannon file. Of course!" I prefer now not for me to recount the story of that morning but to substitute the account of the New York *Times,* which is objective and complete:

Kable and Co. Head Pleads Guilty
to Federal Indictment in
Stock Fraud Case

– – – – –

GOLDHURST MOVE SUDDEN

– – – – – – –

Kable, Held to Have Been Used Only
as "Front" for Concern, Gets
Suspended Sentence

– – – – – – –

Charles W. Kable and Harry L. Goldhurst, who operated the
investment concern of Kable and Co., pleaded guilty yesterday
before Federal Judge Coleman to an indictment charging them
with mail fraud and conspiracy. Kable received a suspended sentence without obligation to report at stated intervals, and Goldhurst, the actual head of the company and in full control of it,
was sentenced to the Atlanta Penitentiary for five years.

It was Kable and Co. which handled the stock dealings of
Bishop James Cannon, Jr., of the Methodist Episcopal Church
South. Several months after the indictment was filed in April,
1928, Bishop Cannon's name appeared as an active client of the
company through a complaint made by Judson Campbell, attorney for Kable, because United States Attorney Tuttle would
not give him access to the books of the company.

The fact that Kable and Goldhurst were to plead guilty was
kept secret until the plea actually was made. Robert E. Manley,
Mr. Tuttle's chief assistant, told Judge Coleman that Kable's part
in the operation of the company was negligible and that he had
only been used by Goldhurst as a "front." He said that data gathered by investigators showed that Kable and Co. had collected
$444,095.85 from investors. To show the activity of the company in
rounding up persons with money to invest, Mr. Manley said that
in a ten months' period the company spent $48,362.64 in tele-
phone and telegraph service, $27,579 for postage, $19,620.26 for
stationery and printing and $77,752.92 for salaries and commis-
sions.

Mr. Manley explained that the policy of the company was to
sell securities on margin and on installment payments, but that
no stock was ever bought. He asserted that where an investor asked
for his profits he was induced to switch his investment to some

worthless stock owned by the company that was described as sure of yielding quick and larger returns. Out of about $59,000 chargeable to stock purchases, Mr. Manley said, only $29,000 represented investments in listed stocks and bonds. The remainder represented only speculative issues. It was also charged that Goldhurst had private accounts with brokers which he carried with money taken from investors with Kable and Co.

Mr. Manley pointed out that at a time when the company listed on its books securities with a value of $2,328,000 sold under contract it was under obligation to customers for $408,000 and its bank balance was only $1,100. He told the court that the company bought shares worth only 10 cents and less and sold them to customers at 80 cents, and that another stock with a market value of about $3.50 was sold to customers for $5 a share.

The company filed a petition in bankruptcy in May, 1928. Schedules showed that the liabilities amounted to $226,000 and assets to $24,000. After the bankruptcy Goldhurst began business in the Transportation Building as the Cosmopolitan Fiscal Corporation. Orders came in, it was said, for the purchase of this stock but deliveries were never made. Then the Federal authorities had him and the Fiscal Corporation and others indicted.

When Judge Coleman read the sentence, the worst had come to the worst, and the worst is every bit as bad as a man imagines it will be.

In Jersey City, when the reporters congregated around the Gallagher home, Hubert came to the porch. "Will Mrs. Goldhurst make a statement?" they asked.

"She has no statement," said Hubert.

"Will you make a statement on the sentence?" they asked.

"I will not," said Hubert. "I will make a statement that it is time for all of you to go back to your city editors and write your stories."

Before the judge pronounced sentence, Philip Samuels made a speech for mitigation. He told Judge Coleman I was penitent and that I had a family whom I loved. As Samuels spoke, Robert Manley, the prosecutor, looked over to our desk casually. His eyes widened in wonder. There on top of Samuels' other papers was the outline of Manley's intended prosecution. Manley even rose to get a better view. Satisfied that those papers were his own handwriting, Manley turned and whispered passionately to his aides.

I moved from the courtroom through a long hall accompanied by two policemen, into an elevator, then to a police wagon, which carried me to the West Street House of Detention, where I surrendered my clothes, my hat, my cuff links and wallet. I received in return work pants and a blue denim shirt.

I didn't have long to wonder what Robert Manley had made of the outline he had seen on Philip Samuels' desk. Charles Tuttle was waiting for me at the West Street Jail. Before I was led to a cell, I was taken to an anteroom, and there was Mr. Tuttle, the outline before him. Manley had retrieved it from Samuels as soon as the trial was over.

"You had better tell me where your lawyer got these," he said.

I had absolved Bishop Cannon; now I had to absolve Philip Samuels. "I gave them to Samuels," I said.

"If you tell me who gave these to you and why, I promise to recommend you for parole. If you do not tell me, I will not. I will find out anyway, and I will put her in jail."

He thought it was Ellamarye Failor, Bishop Cannon's student. This was not succeeding in keeping things out of the newspapers at all.

I said, "Vivien Black sold me those papers. I gave her five thousand dollars and a platinum bracelet."

Tuttle jobbed the papers and put a rubber band around them.

"What are you going to do to her?" I asked.

"We'll ask for her resignation. And we will insist she resign from the bar as well. And if she doesn't comply, we'll put her in jail."

I never saw Vivien Black again. She did as she was told. So did I—for the next several years.

Chapter 15

Iɴ the West Street Jail, I shared a cell with George Graham Rice and Luigi Pachuko. Rice had been convicted of mail fraud, as I had, and Luigi was an unfortunate rum-runner whose ship sprung a disastrous leak which forced him to signal the Coast Guard for rescue. The three of us stayed in West Street for two weeks, and then with 112 other convicts we were taken to Pennsylvania Station, where we embarked on a prison train bound for Atlanta.

The train had one mess car, in which we ate standing up, and three cars which contained only three-decker canvas cots. There were no windows. Before the train began to grind from the platform, we could hear the guards lock the doors. The doors opened at the penitentiary. The guards manacled us together by twos, and we marched down a wooden ramp and across a bare field to the big steel gates, which opened to admit us. On the walls I could see the turrets which housed the machine guns, and I could see blue guards parading the ramparts, each cradling a shotgun. Along the walls were huge spotlights, which at night always played over the compound below.

Inside the prison we went through a large warehouse, where two busy convicts issued each prisoner two denim outfits and two sets of underwear. We waited in groups of six to take our turn to shower. We went through another room, filled with files, cameras, and fingerprinting apparatus. I faced the camera forward and turned my profile and learned my number in the federal penal system was 32510.

Warden Adderholt stepped forward. He said, "I did not send you here. The courts did. While you are here, I am your custodian. I did not make the rules. The federal government did. I expect you to obey them."

I was assigned to a cell on the third tier, where I met "Shorty" Shaw and Johnny Baldwin. Shaw told me he was serving a twenty-year sentence for kicking in post offices. He had kicked in post offices all his life. "It's my hobby," he said. He cased a post office, and if he could find entry, he would burglarize it at night, stealing money orders and postal notes. If he could not find easy entry, he pointed a gun at a postal clerk and ordered him to hand over the cash, the money orders, and the postal notes.

Johnny Baldwin was also serving a long sentence. He was convicted for bank robbery. In 1952, Johnny Baldwin showed up one afternoon at the *Carolina Israelite* in Charlotte. He needed money, and he threatened to reveal my past unless I gave it to him. I told Baldwin to come back the next day because I would have to borrow the cash, and after he left I went downtown to the offices of Charlotte's police chief, Frank Littlejohn, who had once captured the desperate Roger Touhy. When I told Littlejohn about my jail record, he said he already knew, that every police chief in the country kept a list of everyone in town ever convicted of a crime. Chief Littlejohn found out where Baldwin was staying and went over to the hotel. Littlejohn told Baldwin it would be a wise move to take the next bus out of town, which, as Littlejohn had ascertained, was leaving within the hour.

"The carrying of men from hope to hope is the greatest antidote to the seeds of discontent," wrote Sir Francis Bacon. Whether this quote is exact or not, I don't care. It is the way I remembered it. Surely Bacon was thinking of men in prison. Prisoners serve one day at a time. In jail, everyone is innocent or the accidental victim of the courts.

"My family is working on my case," they say.

"I won't be here long. My lawyer is sure the appeal court will reverse the sentence."

"I have connections," they boast, "important connections, who'll fix this for me."

One prisoner gives another a sympathetic ear and offers no advice. Henry Smith used to tell me over and over again the details of his case. He had shot and killed the man who seduced his wife. But the murdered man was a postman, and Henry Smith invaded the post office to kill him as he was sorting mail, which made Henry Smith's assault a federal crime. Henry was always sure a state court would have acquitted him, and I always agreed with him that indeed he would never have been convicted in a Louisiana courtroom.

The Atlanta Penitentiary was filled with Southern boys convicted of distilling or selling or possessing moonshine whiskey—white lightning, as they still call it. To this day, in my home state of North Carolina, illegal moonshining is still the third biggest industry despite the disclaimers of the State Chamber of Commerce. The Southern boys were terribly disadvantaged by the federal Prohibition law. Before the passage of the Volstead Act the state agencies used to destroy their stills, fine them a few hundred dollars, and lock them up for three months. Once moonshining became a federal crime, the federal judges of the South, who were almost to a man fanatical prohibitionists, imposed maximum sentences.

Judges A. M. J. Cochrane and John McClintock locked up half the population of Kentucky and West Virginia. Cochrane was infamous for having sentenced a man to three years in a federal penitentiary because the defendant had a mash stain on his vest.

A Jewish lawyer named Samuel Goldstein in Cincinnati heard of Cochrane's abuses and presented himself to the bench as an *amicus curiae*.

Cochrane asked Goldstein his purpose, and Goldstein explained he was present to protect the rights of the defendants. Cochrane asked him to come forward, and as soon as Goldstein did, Cochrane said, "I'm giving you three years in the federal penitentiary for contempt of court." It took Goldstein several years of appeals and arguments, and it cost him a small fortune before he had that contempt citation reversed.

McClintock was as mean as Cochrane. He, too, was a circuit judge, traveling the districts in West Virginia. Often his courtroom was a clearing in the backwoods areas. He would say to all the moonshiners, "Those pleading guilty, step over here. Those pleading not guilty, over there." When the defendants had divided themselves, McClintock would say, "I'm being lenient with you

153

who plead guilty. I'm giving each of you only three years." As soon as court reconvened, a great many defendants changed their pleas.

The Justice Department once assigned McClintock to one of the benches in Manhattan when the presiding judge died suddenly. The New York bootleggers, part of the organized crime syndicate, had as a matter of custom pleaded guilty and paid a fine of $100. That first morning McClintock presided he came near dealing a deathblow to the Mafia. He handed out ten-year sentences as easily as a pool shark sinking nine balls. At noon the Justice Department had to call on the New York City police to disperse the eight sedans which lined the street, each sedan with at least one man holding a machine gun, awaiting McClintock's exit from the court. In consideration of the judge's life, the Justice Department sent him back to West Virginia and made do with another jurist. The night McClintock died, there was sustained cheering from the cells in the Atlanta Penitentiary.

My job in Atlanta was to keep the books for Mr. Cook, the prison's chief engineer. It was one of the premium jobs—premium because it demanded no physical exertion—and I fell into it because I could read and write. The premier skill in prison is literacy. Because I could read and write, I also taught school, and in Atlanta I succeeded in having several men master the rudiments of writing, arithmetic, and reading.

On some Saturdays the Jewish prisoners were allowed to attend shul, which was held in the vast dining hall. Rabbi David Marx of Atlanta came out as often as he could. He was a large man, well spoken, sympathetic, and he always offered to communicate with any members of our families if we wished. Rabbi Marx fifteen years before had accompanied the coffin of Leo Frank to Brooklyn after a Southern mob of vigilantes had kidnapped Frank from prison and lynched him. Twenty-five years after my release I was to describe the role Rabbi Marx played in the Leo Frank case in my book *A Little Girl Is Dead*. The rabbi was then deceased, but Herbert Haas, one of Frank's lawyers, the only central figure in the case who still survives, let me read some of the rabbi's correspondence. I never told Mr. Haas I knew Rabbi Marx, but when I read over those old letters, the memory of that prison shul returned and made me shiver.

After a year in Atlanta, I was transferred to the prison barracks

154

at Fort Meade, Maryland. Meade was a Regular Army post populated by only a small complement of soldiers. The federal prisons were overcrowded, and the Justice Department decided to transfer honor prisoners to these almost deserted military installations. At Meade, I lived in a barracks with more comforts; I ate in an Army mess hall where the meals were varied; there were no bars on the windows. We mustered in the morning for roll call, and in the evening we mustered to hear the soldiers stand retreat at the flagpole.

The warden's name was Cornelius Fish. I worked in his office making the daily report and keeping the books. The atmosphere was less rigid. There were guards, but they were few. Fish used to talk to us about many casual subjects. In fact, on several occasions Fish asked me if I had any tips on the market.

"My Wall Street days are over," I told him.

"I'm not going to hold it against you if it goes down," Fish said.

"I'm here," I replied, "because I bet the market would go down. I was absolutely right. Any stock I quote is bound to go down. I quote Coty. That puts you ahead of the game, Warden. If there are three thousand stocks, you only have to bet on two thousand, nine hundred and ninety-nine going up."

After several months, Warden Fish detailed me to Colonel Fuchs, the camp commandant. Fuchs told me there were three barracks on the post filled to overflowing with books. These barracks had been laden with these books since the close of World War I. Thousands of people sent books to the American Expeditionary Force. Colonel Fuchs said he had no idea what to do with them. He lay awake nights hoping a fire would consume these barracks and relieve his worry. Perhaps I could catalogue them? He was willing to set these barracks aside as the beginning of a post library.

I wrote to the Library of Congress and asked for a cataloguing system. I studied it, and with two other prisoners I began to sort these books and shelve them. The colonel's description was accurate—the barracks were laden. The books filled the space from floor to ceiling, packed in. We had to struggle with several wheelbarrows of living literature to make space where we could stand in one of these barracks.

Cataloguing books took me several months. There were hundreds of novels by F. Marion Crawford and Marie Corelli, who must have been the Mickey Spillane and Grace Metalious of their day. How extensive a library Fort Meade has today, I do not know. But however extensive it is, I made the first material contribution.

In July, 1931, I came up for parole. The parole board that heard me out consisted of two men and a woman: the chairman, Arthur D. Wood; his assistant, Irvin B. Tucker; the third member, Amy N. Stannard, had a face so scarred by acne that it looked as though a grenade had exploded on the tip of her nose. They asked if I had a job: I said I was going to work for my brother Jake as a hotel manager. They asked about my home: I told them about my family. I answered all the questions they put to me about my crime. After considering my application, the parole board said they would parole me on April 15, 1932, which cut fifteen months from my sentence.

Unfortunately for me, the board's decision became a news item: CANNON'S BROKER WINS PAROLE. Senator Carter Glass saw it and rose to the floor of the Senate and denounced this remission of time. Senator Glass was still keeping the pressure on Bishop Cannon.

There were many important Democrats who gave Bishop Cannon money in 1928 to wage the campaign against Alfred E. Smith. Carter Glass wanted to know their names. Bishop Cannon had no intention of naming any of these men. Carter Glass charged that Cannon had diverted money from the Methodist Church to help defeat Alfred E. Smith. This Bishop Cannon had not done, but to have done so was a federal crime. The Bishop could be tried under the Corrupt Practices Act. Carter Glass called into being a Senate investigating committee.

The Lobby Committee of the United States Senate wanted to know two things from Bishop Cannon: the names of those who gave him the money to fight Al Smith and the names of those workers to whom Cannon paid the money. Defending himself, Cannon volunteered to testify. When the committee, chaired by Senator Thomas Walsh of Montana, put these two questions to the Bishop after a lengthy cross-examination, Cannon, supporting himself by his crutch, rose and read the following statement: "I respectfully state that having answered all the questions addressed to me by the committee on which I volunteered as a witness, I shall now withdraw. If the committee desires to subpoena me, that is all right."

With that he turned and started to hobble out.

The Senators protested he was not released.

"I'll be at my office if you want me," Cannon snapped.

With that he was gone, the first time a private citizen had defied a Senate investigating committee.

Senator Carter Glass didn't like it, but he thought long about subpoenaing the Bishop. In the end, Carter Glass never did cite Cannon for contempt, as he could have, nor did he ever subpoena him. But every time he could, Carter Glass tried to discredit Bishop Cannon. My parole was one of those chances.

My brother Jake went to Washington to see Senator Glass and plead my case before him. Glass met him in his Senatorial offices.

Jake asked, "Why are you doing this to Harry? He has served his sentence. He has a family to support. What good will keeping him in jail do?"

"If your brother wants a parole," said Carter Glass, "have him tell me about Bishop Cannon's women."

Jake came to Fort Meade to see me. He reported this interview.

"Now what in the world," I asked, "do I know about Bishop Cannon's women?"

On October 12, 1931, Carter Glass made public a letter he had addressed to William De Witt Mitchell, Herbert Hoover's Attorney General:

Frankly, I think the very integrity of the Department of Justice is involved in this matter and it was for this reason, and not from idle curiosity, that I sought access to the files of the Parole Board. A simple recital of the facts in the Goldhurst case will reveal my meaning.

The indictment of this bucket shop adventurer was made, as I recall, in May, 1928. For some reason, for which there has been no credible explanation, trial of the man was deferred from time to time over a period of fifteen months. Goldhurst is said to have repeatedly assured his partner in the bucket shop that the indictments would be dismissed through the intervention of certain powerful persons, one of them disclosed as a chief patron of this illict gambling concern.

It was also ascertained that Samuels, one of the attorneys for Goldhurst, had employed as attorney of record Bishop Cannon's Washington lawyer, a former professional associate and then office-mate of an influential Virginia politician. This Washington attorney, as soon as he learned the real nature of the case, promptly withdrew.

About this time it was disclosed that the United States District Attorney for the Southern District of New York had confided the conduct of this case to a former female student of Bishop James Cannon, Jr., the prelate who was alleged to be sufficiently influential to have the indictments against Goldhurst dismissed and who was afterward revealed as an extensive operator in Goldhurst's bucket shop.

Not until these astonishing facts were brought to the attention of District Attorney Tuttle in a savage protest by a citizen of New York was the case taken from the hands of this former student at Bishop Cannon's school in Virginia and a definite time fixed for the trial of Goldhurst.

The letter of this New York citizen bluntly charged that an Assistant District Attorney in Mr. Tuttle's office had been the recipient of enumerated costly gifts as an inducement to pigeonhole the indictments. Significantly enough, this shocking charge was not denied by the District Attorney in his letter of response.

Up to the moment this grave accusation was made Goldhurst had pleaded not guilty to the charges against him. At a public hearing before a referee in bankruptcy he vehemently declared his innocence.

Overnight his plea of not guilty was changed to a plea of guilty on various indictments, each carrying a prison penalty of five years, aggregating thirty years or more; made concurrent and Goldhurst was sent to the Atlanta Penitentiary for only five years.

At the time it was stated that the prelate and the politician above referred to had an interview with Goldhurst at a hotel in New York City, immediately after which Bishop Cannon, to the amazement of nearly everybody in Virginia, where a hot political campaign, largely precipitated by him, was in progress, sailed for Brazil.

It was stated at the time that Goldhurst, in order to avert the necessity of summoning Bishop Cannon as a witness in his case and thus revealing the prelate's gambling transactions, had consented to alter his plea and confess his crime upon the promise of a nominal sentence, to be afterward reduced to parole or outright release.

As a matter of fact, all the papers raided and seized in Goldhurst's illicit bucket shop had, after a visit by Bishop Cannon and one of his attorneys to New York, been tightly sealed and access to them denied by the United States District Attorney even to the referee in bankruptcy. They remained sealed until unearthed by an investigator for a Senate committee.

Whether there was a compact in New York, as alleged, which promised clemency to this swindler in compensation for averting the appearance in court of his ecclesiastical client, I am not in a position to declare; but, regardless of whether the alleged agreement was actually made, the undeniable fact is that the reported terms of alleged compact have been officially carried out.

In short, Goldhurst was among those favored convicts who were transferred from the Federal prison at Atlanta to open camps for accessibility to their friends and relatives. He is now at Fort Meade, near Washington, and has been, by the Parole Board, ordered released next April.

I find among the list of those asking and approving this action the name of former United States District Attorney Tuttle, who had distinctly declared in the face of Senator Norris's threatening resolution that he would oppose the release of Goldhurst.

I also find the name of former Assistant District Attorney Manley, who prosecuted the case after it was taken out of the hands of Bishop Cannon's protégé and who must have had full knowledge of the reasons actuating Goldhurst in changing his insistent plea of not guilty and, at the last moment, in order to avert an open trial, confessing guilt.

These facts are not confidential, and I cite them here because the New York papers recently published the fact, a fact now confirmed by your letter to me, that these officials recommended clemency for Goldhurst. You will thus observe, I trust, that my request to examine this file was not prompted by idle curiosity, but by a desire to ascertain whether the pursuit of justice had been arrested by sanction of public officials to save from serious embarrassment a certain ecclesiastical politician.

The fact that Goldhurst is to be released in the circumstances cited gives color to the persistent report of a sinister agreement to this end, and it would seem that the Parole Board should have more carefully inquired into the facts before acting.

You may be sure that I care nothing about clemency for this bucket shop swindler, notwithstanding he is alleged to have compounded the felonies of which he pleaded guilty with bribery of an official of the court. In these things Goldhurst simply engaged in pursuits which appealed to his depraved taste; but his release from prison, if it so occurred, as the result of a bargain to shield an offender more responsible to society should, I submit, receive unqualified condemnation from the Department of Justice.

The officials who recommended clemency were Charles Tuttle and Judge Coleman. They made their letters public on October 14, 1931:

TO THE EDITOR OF THE NEW YORK TIMES:

Ordinarily I would not feel it incumbent upon me to reply to statements made in the course of a political contest in Virginia, but your editorial in this morning's paper which refers to the correspondence between Senator Glass and the Attorney General, with reference to the prosecution of Mr. Harry L. Goldhurst while I was United States Attorney in this district, contains such unjust references to myself that I am, by this letter, laying the facts before you in the hope that you will give them equal publicity.

In the first place, it is news to me that the public was never "entirely satisfied" with the sentence of Mr. Goldhurst to five years in the Atlanta Penitentiary. On the contrary, that was spoken of at the time as, with but two exceptions, the severest sentence which was imposed in the Federal court in this district in a mail fraud case. There was no agreement with the District Attorney, and the District Attorney made no recommendation to the court.

The case was not under the charge of any "protégé" of Bishop Cannon, but on the contrary was under the charge of Robert E. Manley, the chief assistant in my office, who was under instructions from me to prepare the case with the utmost care. There was no "delay" in the bringing of the case to trial. As everyone knows, during that period there was a great shortage of Federal judges in this district; usually only one judge was available for the trial of cases; and our criminal calendar was more heavily congested than in any other Federal district in the country. Furthermore, the preparation of a bucket shop case for trial is a matter of great detail and requires extended study of voluminous books and records and much minute investigation.

Mr. Goldhurst did not, so far as I know, "suddenly" change his plea of guilty. He merely did what many other defendants do when convinced that the trial can have but one ending, and that he may somewhat shorten his sentence by a plea of guilty and thus save the time of the court.

Last May, after Mr. Goldhurst had been in the Atlanta penitentiary for a year and a half, I received a letter from the present United States Attorney asking for my opinion as to whether he should make any recommendation for or against a parole. Under the Federal statute a prisoner becomes eligible to parole after the service of one-third of his sentence, and such parole is usually granted where the prisoner has a record of good behavior and of no prior convictions. The circumstances under which I then recommended parole are set forth in a letter which I received this morning, without any solicitation from me, from Judge Francis J. Coleman, judge of the District Court, who sentenced Mr. Goldhurst. I enclose a copy of that letter herewith, and you will please particularly observe the following sentence:

"Accordingly, I sent for you and I can distinctly recall your appearing in my chambers and finally yielding to my persuasion and promising to recommend parole. . . . I can recall distinctly being nettled by what I thought was a too great severity on the part not only of yourself but of Mr. Manley, who presented the matter in court."

I make Judge Coleman's full letter part of my present letter to you.

I think on studying the foregoing presentation of facts you will agree with me that your editorial has, in its implications, done me gross injustice.

CHARLES H. TUTTLE

New York, Oct. 13, 1931

Judge Coleman's Letter to Tuttle

Mr. Charles H. Tuttle, 15 Broad Street, New York City

DEAR MR. TUTTLE:

My blood boiled this morning when I read the insinuations against you in the newspaper accounts and comments on the Goldhurst case. The conclusions intimated are so utterly unjust to you that I cannot restrain the impulse to express my sympathy and indignation.

You will recall that it was I who sentenced Goldhurst to a five-year term. In arriving at that determination I did not intend, nor did the law contemplate, that he serve five years, but merely that he be incarcerated for at least one year and eight months. After his sentence, his wife appeared before me and presented with her three little children so tragic a situation that I believed the public interests would best be served by releasing Goldhurst at the end of the minimum period of incarceration contemplated by law under my sentence—namely, a year and eight months. Accordingly, I sent for you and I can distinctly recall your appearing in my chambers and finally yielding to my persuasion and promising to recommend parole.

Unless you have lost some of the sense of humor you had when I saw more of you, you must be tickled by the irony of being accused of partiality toward Goldhurst. I can recall distinctly being nettled by what I thought was a too great severity on the part not

161

only of yourself but of Mr. Manley, who presented the matter in court.

The newspapers say that some young woman on your staff alleged to have been a parishioner of Bishop Cannon handled the case. Bob Manley must smile at that when he thinks of the days and nights of labor he put in on the case and the strenuous arguments he presented in court. However, situations like this, I suppose, are inherent risks of holding public office.

Faithfully yours,

FRANK J. COLEMAN

P.S.—You, of course, are at liberty to make any use you wish of this letter.

New York, Oct. 13, 1931

Bishop Cannon gave out a denial which ran to several newspaper columns. The Bishop was never pithy. He said in part of Senator Carter Glass' statements, "These accusations I brand as absolutely false and the statements of a cowardly politician . . . who hates me because I opposed his political ambitions in Virginia and led the movement which defeated his effort to give the electoral vote of Virginia to Alfred Emanuel Smith."

Bishop Cannon and Carter Glass had more than defined the contest; they had determined its crux—over my head. Carter Glass had his way. The parole board revoked my parole, citing in its reversal that it did not know I had been indicted for the same crime a second time or that I had attempted to bribe a member of the United States Attorney General's office. Attorney General William Mitchell absolved Ellamarye Fairlor of any complicity in my case.

Warden Fish came to my barracks on the evening of December 11, when the parole board had notified him of its revocation, and he said, "Goldhurst, the parole board is taking it back. It's no go."

There's not much a man in jail can say to his warden except, "Thank you for telling me." There are disappointments in this world so devastating we do not know how we can possibly survive them. Perhaps we survive them, as I survived this disappointment, because we have no choice. A man cannot go to pieces in jail, nor can his fellow convicts shoulder any of his troubles. I knew that night I would have to serve the whole of my sentence, one of the few federal offenders who had to do so. I knew I would have to serve three years and eight months and twenty-two days, which

162

is exactly what I served. The federal penal regulations provide that a prisoner receives so many days off each month for good behavior, and I knew exactly the time the law and the federal prison authorities would subtract from my sentence.

Three years, eight months, and twenty-two days after Judge Coleman sentenced me, Warden Fish gave me a new blue suit, a pair of used but shined black shoes, and $10. A guard took me to the train, and a few hours later I saw my wife and sons standing beside the gates of one of the train platforms at Pennsylvania Station.

By that time, of course, Carter Glass had lost interest in Bishop Cannon. The Senator would never have to worry about the Bishop or the anti-Smith Democrats again. Franklin D. Roosevelt had swept the country, making Carter Glass one of the most powerful Senators in the history of the Congress. He wasn't about to waste his time now with has-beens.

Chapter 16

W HILE I was in the Atlanta Federal Penitentiary, I heard from Bishop Cannon several times. He wrote me a note which I received during my first week. He wished me well and said he knew I would make it, that my life was not over; there were great prospects waiting.

In February, 1931, Bishop Cannon sent his representative, Sidney Peters, to see me. The Bishop was preparing his defense for the charges brought against him by his church. I signed a deposition in which I said that Bishop Cannon was entirely ignorant of Kable and Company's operations, that he was merely a customer and lost his money as did other customers.

Cannon let me know that after five days of hearings and two hours of deliberations by the twelve men who constituted his jury, Bishop William Newman Ainsworth, on the church steps, with the rain soaking his robes, read the conclusions submitted to the church elders: There was no need to try James Cannon, Jr.

After I was released, the Bishop faced trial under the Federal Corrupt Practices Act. A grand jury had returned an indictment against the Bishop and Ada Burroughs, his private secretary, charging they had conspired to misuse money entrusted to them during the election campaign of 1928. The Bishop had appealed the indictment through all the lower courts and to the Supreme Court itself, which ruled out eight of ten counts.

I spent almost two full days with him in Washington, D.C., where his trial was scheduled for April 9, 1934. The Bishop thought the federal prosecutor would accuse him of spending money contributed by the anti-Smith Democrats for stock market gambling. We went over his accounts with Kable and Company. We spent almost fourteen hours in a room in the Mayflower Hotel going back and forth, I explaining what happened to *this* money, he remembering where he had earned *that*. To fortify myself, I had secreted a bottle of bourbon in my briefcase. As often as I adjourned to the bathroom, where I carefully locked the door, I took a healthy swig. After nine hours of constant study, I couldn't find my briefcase for one of my retirements. I kept searching the room, muttering "I've got to have my briefcase because I've got to go to the bathroom."

Finally, the Bishop handed the satchel to me with a snort: "Here is your fumigated formaldehyde."

He and Miss Burroughs were acquitted. The trial attracted no headlines, and no one was surprised at the verdict. By this time the Bishop's attitudes toward Catholicism had mellowed. He told me he saw more ominous threats to the world than the Pope. The rise of Hitler was a worsening danger, he suspected, than ever alcoholism was. He worried about the spread of Japanese militarism. He wrote letters constantly to President Roosevelt and Secretary of State Cordell Hull urging that the United States make a commitment to England and offer aid to China. In these efforts, curiously, he was joined by Senator Carter Glass, who was, if anything, more alarmed than the Bishop.

When the General Conference of the Methodist Episcopal Church, South, convened in Memphis in 1935, Bishop Cannon was instrumental in pressing for the unanimous passage of the resolution condemning Hitler. The Methodists did pass this and became the first non-Jewish national organization to condemn the Nazis.

Bishop Cannon had met Hitler the year before, when he was returning from the Congo; he wanted to pay a visit to the Methodist bishop as he passed through Munich. Two storm troopers appeared at the hotel, the Bishop said, and informed him that the Führer, a teetotaler, would like to meet this famous American Methodist. Cannon drove with them to Munich Brown House, where the storm troopers parked in front of the house in which Hitler had his headquarters. Cannon told me there were at least fifty steps proceeding from the sidewalk to the front door. His

165

arthritis was so painful he told the storm troopers he couldn't climb to the door. Hitler came down to see him, and the two men talked in the limousine.

Cannon asked Hitler why this treatment of the Jews.

Hitler replied that Polish Jews came into Germany at the beginning of the Depression and exchanged money, exploited the unemployed, and starved the poor. Cannon asked, "Herr Hitler, did Einstein change money? Is Bruno Walter exploiting the unemployed?"

Hitler did not answer.

Before the start of the war the United States and Cuban governments refused to allow the steamship *St. Louis* to disembark 900 German Jews in either Havana or Baltimore. Cannon tried his best to have some responsible authority in Washington find a loophole. When the *St. Louis* finally steamed back to Germany with its human cargo, all of whose lives were obviously forfeit, Cannon wrote a letter to the Richmond *Times-Dispatch* which Arthur Morse quotes in his recent book *While Six Million Died:*

> . . . the press reported that the ship came close enough to Miami for the refugees to see the lights of the city. The press also reported that the U.S. Coast Guard, under instructions from Washington, followed the ship . . . to prevent any people landing on our shores. And during the days when this horrible tragedy was being enacted right at our doors, our government in Washington made no effort to relieve the desperate situation of these people, but on the contrary gave orders that they be kept out of the country. Why did not the President, Secretary of State, Secretary of the Treasury, Secretary of Labor and other officials confer together and arrange for the landing of these refugees who had been caught in this maelstrom of distress and agony through no fault of their own? . . . The failure to take any steps whatever to assist these distressed, persecuted Jews in their hour of extremity was one of the most disgraceful things which has happened in American history and leaves a stain and brand of shame upon the record of our nation.

An Emergency Conference to Save the Jews of Europe convened in New York City in July, 1943, Bishop Cannon one of the conference's sponsors. He chaired the panel on religion which called on the Christian Church of the United States and Europe to demand immediate action to rescue the Jews under Nazi domination.

One of the reasons the Bishop was able to lend his energies and what remained of his prestige to this charitable and Christian effort was that Herbert Hoover and Franklin D. Roosevelt broke his heart. Roosevelt's platform in 1932 demanded outright repeal; Hoover equivocated but obviously intended to ask the Congress for modification of the Volstead Act if elected. Roosevelt, of course, won. The Eighteenth Amendment barely outlasted Herbert Hoover's stay in the capital. By March, when Roosevelt was inaugurated, 3.2 beer was legal.

The Bishop tried to tell the lame duck Congress it was violating its oath to support the Constitution. No one heard him, nor were any of the incoming Congressmen and Senators disposed to listen. When Roosevelt, on March 13, 1932, asked the Congress to legalize the manufacture of beer and other alcoholic beverages, Bishop Cannon called him "the Apostle of selfish individualism as opposed to the general welfare."

The news that finally informed him his old sweetheart was dead was Congress' allowing the sale of beer on Army posts when the Selective Service Act became law in 1940. Still that sweetheart occupied his thoughts every day. To a prohibitionist meeting in Atlanta he said, "Carrie Nations by the thousands should rise up and smash the speakeasies of New York City." The last years of his life were spent in agitating for prohibition reenactment. He wrote letters to state senators and got up petitions demanding referenda on liquor sales.

Virginius Dabney, in his excellent biography of the Bishop, *Dry Messiah,* writes that one of Cannon's last public pronouncements was a letter to the Richmond *Times-Dispatch* complaining that the paper had no right to drop the comic strips "Prince Valiant" and "The Phantom."

I saw him in Richmond, Virginia, two weeks before he died. He had just sold the last of his property and he was living in a shabby hotel suite because his wife was convalescing in California. He had dissipated a fortune in legal suits against Hearst and Time-Life and assorted Congressmen. He was badly crippled. He could move only the first two fingers on his right hand. He told me he was sure prohibition would return immediately after the war. He remembered the dill pickles Tiny had served him eighteen years before.

Two weeks later, he got into his long johns, buckled up his high shoes, and made his way to Michigan to attend what must have been the last meeting of the Anti-Saloon League. He died there, in Chicago's Wesley Memorial Hospital, on September 6, 1944, a few weeks short of his eightieth birthday.

PART III

Chapter 17

WHEN I got out of prison, my brother Jake offered me $50 a week as the manager of the Hotel Markwell. I thanked him but said I was going to work for a newspaper.

"Well," said Jake tactfully, "I've just acquired the hotel, and it might do for you for over the summer, until you land what you want, of course."

I took the job on the condition that I was liable to leave at a moment's notice between now and Labor Day. But the Hotel Markwell at 220 West Forty-ninth Street between Broadway and Eighth Avenue is where I made my living for the next five years.

The Markwell was built in 1902 as a resident hotel for wealthy families. It was furnished originally with ornate beds and Louis XIV chairs and escritoires. Its suites consisted of two and three rooms, but as newer hotels went up around Manhattan, the rich Markwell clientele began to move away. In 1918, Mr. Walen Green of Virginia took it over and renovated it, dividing the suites into single rooms, catering to the transient trade. With the advent of the Depression, Mr. Green fell behind in his taxes and mortgage payments, and the New York Savings Bank took the Markwell over.

In the early years of the Depression, New York banks owned all the hotels. In that flush of gorgeous optimism the 1920's inspired, hotelmen built hotels as fast as they could. With the Wall Street Crash, these hotels emptied. The management of the newly finished Waldorf-Astoria used to go around at night, putting on lights in the empty rooms, so that potential guests, if there were potential guests, wouldn't think they were registering in a haunted house.

My brother Jake took over the Markwell in 1932 for a low-interest rate. The banks were tired of the hotel business and were anxious to turn these establishments over to professionals. Jake's hope, of course, was that with tight management the Hotel Markwell would pay the interest rates on the mortgage and he could hang on until times got better. Maybe. It was always "maybe" with the hotelmen in the 1930's. Conventioneering did not enjoy the vogue or the tax remission it does now. In fact, when the American Legion decided on New York for one of its conventions, Fiorello LaGuardia boasted of a political coup. The legionnaires were never worth the trouble, though. I remember lecturing five of them that dropping paper bags filled with water from the windows of the Markwell onto the heads of casual passersby hardly honored the heroic memory of the American Expeditionary Forces.

The Markwell did not present an imposing façade. It was a small hotel—120 rooms, ten stories high. Its marquee did not quite extend from the sidewalk to the curb. The guest who signaled a cab in rainy weather got wet. But the Markwell was respectable, and it was staid.

Eight stone steps mounted from the sidewalk to the front doors, which swung inward. On their glass panes in gilt was a heraldic crest with the scroll above reading in old English script MARKWELL and the scroll below *Bonus—Melior—Optimus.* In the middle of the shield, however, were the heads of two obviously hungry wolves.

To the right was a lobby with three leather couches and three matching morris chairs. There was a large round table, on which I deposited at 8 A.M. two copies of every morning paper and at 2 P.M. two copies of every evening paper. Against the wall was a fancy writing desk, the only furniture salvaged from the old, more opulent Markwell. It contained Hotel Markwell stationery and picture postcards which unfolded to show New York scenes.

The lobby floor was covered by an Axminster rug. The two windows which let on to the street boasted an expensive cornice and corduroy draperies. The windows would have been bare if Tiny had not insisted that cornice and draperies were precisely what the lobby needed to set off the exquisite leather of the couches and chairs.

The Markwell had no dining room, but below the street level was a bar which Jake leased to a concessionaire. Back of the oblong registry desk was an elevator, the door of which held a large pane of wired translucent glass. The barrier gate was a burnished yellow metal, which in the morning gleamed with the sunlight as often as the elevator opened. A green light signaled up and a red light down.

Behind the registry desk were the banks of pigeonholes for mail and messages and the switchboard. Next to these stood a safe, the combination of which I never remembered, so it was never really locked. Anything really valuable a guest deposited I locked in my desk drawer. In the rear was my office, where I kept the books. Around the corner from the elevator was a second, smaller lobby. It was in this lobby that Jake and I later installed a pinball machine which became the Markwell's biggest profit maker when the pinball rage swept the country.

I fell into the business naturally. Jake had been a hotelman for more than twenty years. An uncle, Koppel Berger, operated the Hotel Normandie at Broadway and Thirty-eighth Street. With no more than seventy English words in his vocabulary, Koppel Berger made a fortune letting rooms to actors. In the early years of this century fancy hotels did not accommodate actors any more than fancy churches accommodated them. Koppel had a sign in front of the Normandie, ACTORS WELCOME. Koppel was one of the few hotelmen who catered to the theater. Frank Chase at the Algonquin always did, and there were one or two others, but by and large, hotel clerks turned actors away. Actors broke down these barriers when movie stars began to make more money than the President of the United States. Koppel Berger was the first member of my family to make a good thing out of civil rights. Once, when a vaudeville troupe managed to beat their bill, I said to Koppel, "Those rotten acrobats took a lot of money away from you," to which he replied, "Yes, but I have taken a lot of money from other acrobats."

Koppel coined the legendary retort to the irate guest. A fellow came in for a room late one night, when the hotel was almost filled, and Koppel said the only room left cost $2.

"But you've got one dollar and fifty cents on the sign," said the guest.

"Go sleep on the sign," said Koppel, shrugging.

Koppel was one of the hotelkeepers who fell afoul of the Committee of 15. The Committee of 15 consisted of members of the New York Establishment who banded together to form an anti-vice crusade. One of the ways they fought vice was to cite hotelmen who let rooms to women without baggage and to couples who were not married.

When Koppel read his citation as one of these men who would encourage vice, he asked indignantly, "Why me? Macy's sells them lingerie. Gimbels sells them cosmetics. Bloomingdale's sells them black net stockings. I sell them a room, and I'm the one the committee wants to arrest."

At the Markwell we also accommodated actors and actresses, some of them well-known old-timers, others who were to become famous later, but all of whom had one thing in common—they were broke. Henry Chesterfield of the National Vaudeville Artists paid the room rent for a number of them out of a relief fund. He would come in once a week and settle up with me. Some of the actors and actresses were on Federal Theater projects collecting a check for $26.80 every week, which was just enough to keep them going.

There was a mystery about their tenancy, however. Why would these show people stay at the Markwell for $8 a week when the newly built, first-rate Manger Hotel (later the Taft) advertised rooms for $30 a month?

Ah, I saw the reason for this every day. In the Markwell the actor could cross the street and buy a container of coffee and a cinnamon bun and carry it through the lobby to his room. The actor could walk out of the Markwell with a bundle of laundry or a suit dangling over his shoulder. Despite the cheaper $30 at the much better hotel, an actor or actress could not cross the lobby on personal errands. He would have to call room service, and instead of 15 cents for a container of coffee and cinnamon bun, it would cost, even in those days, closer to $1, including the tip for the bellboy, and no actor could very well carry his bundle through the lobby of the Taft on his way to the Chinese laundry.

To the left of the Markwell was the Forrest Theater, where one of our guests, Maude Odell, played Sister Bessie in the original troupe of *Tobacco Road*. Miss Odell died in her dressing room not long after the play opened, and Vinnie Phillips took her place, continuing in the role for another two years. James Barton, who played Jeeter Lester in this company, also stayed at the Markwell for a while. I remember shaking hands with him when he checked out to move to more comfortable accommodations when the play caught on.

I gave away hundreds of free tickets to *Tobacco Road*. The usual practice among theatrical managers when a show was near folding was to hand out free passes to all the hotel managers, who would distribute them to the guests and out-of-towners. If enough people went to see the show, the producers hoped that word of mouth would keep the production running. This practice worked with *Tobacco Road*, whose future looked dim indeed until one of the national organizations dedicated to improving public morals condemned it, and then *Tobacco Road* went on to the longest run in theatrical history, making a millionaire out of the itinerant lawyer who put up a pittance to help get it started.

Across the street was the Ambassador Theater. Walter Pidgeon, who was playing in *The Night of January 16*, used one of the Markwell rooms to change his clothes. Dick Powell, who was the master of ceremonies at a Chinese restaurant, also stayed at the Markwell before he became a Hollywood success. In those days Mr. Powell was a cold, austere man, but a decent one, a straight-from-the-shoulder fellow. He used to send me a box of cigars at Christmas, and no matter how convoluted my travels in later years, those cigars always caught up with me. There were Christmases when I wished he had sent me the $20 those cigars cost.

I used to stake Frank Fay to long-distance telephone calls. Fay was a heavy drinker, and his wife, Barbara Stanwyck, had kicked him out. He would go on binges, work himself into a crying jag, and then beg to use the phone to see if she would take him back. After he scored a tremendous success in *Harvey*, I learned that Fay had made some anti-Semitic remarks at an Equity meeting. The news disappointed me. Jews, including me, had shown him some of the few kindnesses he had known when he was down-and-out. A lawyer named Harry Oshrien always lent him money and paid his room rent when no one else would.

Pauline Boyle, a theatrical agent, who had helped the careers of Spencer Tracy, Pat O'Brien, and Ralph Bellamy, lived in the Markwell, and whenever these actors came to New York, they always stopped off to see her. Another guest was Florence Walker. Miss Walker operated a sight-seeing bus, the only commercial vehicle permitted to pass through the gates of all the major racetracks in the world from Aqueduct to Havre de Grace. This exclusive privilege had been given to her for life many years before by one whom *Time* magazine would call her "great and good friend," the famous private detective Captain William Pinkerton. Miss Walker knew every owner, trainer, breeder, jockey, and bookmaker in the East. During the last three weeks of her life, however, her Italian bus driver and I were the only visitors she had at Bellevue Hospital. She wrote a note leaving me a set of ivory poker chips that had once belonged to America's greatest gambler, Henry Canfield. Since I never play for stakes, I passed them on to a friend.

One afternoon I got a telephone call from a good friend who asked, "Could you do me a favor? Could you give Lillian Lorraine a room for the night? Just till she sobers up?" Lillian Lorraine had been a famous *Follies* beauty, a rival for the affections of the great Ziegfeld himself. In fact, Lillian Lorraine is the only woman Billie Burke mentions in her autobiography.

But Lillian Lorraine had a drinking problem, one she brought with her onstage, and it proved to be her downfall. During one of the numbers in the *Follies,* Lillian tripped while she was drunk, fell down a long flight of stage stairs, and hurt herself badly. Now she was living with a kindly Negro woman in Harlem who had been her hairdresser a few years before.

The Markwell gave Lillian a room in which she slept off her drunk. She said good-bye the next morning. Lillian Lorraine, a little past her prime, with too many drinks in her, was still beautiful—an almost wispy blonde with a deep laugh. A few months later she went back to the liquor, and this time someone took her to the Actors Chapel of St. Malachy's Church on West Forty-ninth Street. Father Leonard, the pastor, tried to help this beautiful, though wretchedly sad, woman. He told her actors were usually generous people, and if she gave him a list of people who remembered and loved her, maybe they would help her pull herself together.

Miss Lorraine headed her list with William Randolph Hearst,

continued with Vincent Astor, went on to Eddie Cantor, added a few more of the great and near great, and finished with Harry Goldhurst, manager, Hotel Markwell. Father Leonard read it over and remarked of me, "He's the only live one on it."

Father Leonard came over to the Markwell and asked me if I could put Miss Lorraine up for a few weeks while he tried to interest some of her friends in rehabilitation. I did.

While she was there, I went to Lindy's Restaurant and met Fanny Brice. No one ever said Fanny Brice was anything but a dear, generous woman, and remembering this, I walked over to her table, introduced myself, and told her about Lillian Lorraine. Would she help?

Fanny Brice looked me over and said, "Now I'll tell you something, Mr. Goldhurst. A year ago I took Lillian down to Altman's and told them whatever she wants, give her two, send the bill to me. Then I got her a room at the Midtown Hotel and told them the same thing. A week went by, and I got a call from the Midtown's hotel manager, a man just as nice as you. He said, 'You're too decent a woman to let them do this to you, Fanny. Lillian Lorraine has sold all the clothes and all the jewelry to the bellhops for gin.' I was no better off than when I started. Neither was Lillian."

After a few weeks Lillian was strong enough to try it on her own. Sometime later she won a settlement from Metro-Goldwyn-Mayer. In the movie *The Great Ziegfeld* the producers included a scene in which a drunken chorine fell down onstage. The situation was unmistakably modeled after her, and the movie people settled. A lawyer got most of it.

The last time I saw Lillian Lorraine was after I had left the Markwell and was working at the *Daily Mirror*. The copyboy came over and said, "There's a lady outside says she has to see you." I went down and met this poor woman in the back of a taxi, the driver threatening to take her to the nearest police precinct because she could not pay her fare. She was drunk and disheveled. I gave the taxidriver $10 and told him to take her where she wanted to go, and she reached forward and gave me a faint wave. I did not hear of her again until I read her obituary in one of the Charlotte Sunday papers.

To the right of the Hotel Markwell was the Paradise nightclub, where Paul Whiteman, Johnnie Hauser, Goldie, Pingatore, Ramona, and Jack Teagarden entertained nightly. Some musicians lived in fancier hotels, but Whiteman's band always stored their instruments in the Markwell's basement and changed their clothes on the day rate in its rooms. Many a Whiteman musician gave me his money for safekeeping when he was going on a binge.

I was more than friendly with Jack Teagarden, who was a drunk. I helped him over one or two bad periods. We used to spend hours talking in the lobby, Jack trying to stay away from whiskey until the evening stand was over. I have been an opera man all my life and more or less looked down on jazz musicians and singers. Jack Teagarden changed my opinion. I listened to him talk and I heard him play—he was one of the great trombonists—and he converted me, not from opera but to jazz.

The last time I saw him was in New Orleans in 1960. I was there making a speech, and the newspaper told me he was performing in one of the city's nightclubs. I went backstage, and he threw his arms around me, musicians being generous in their emotions as in everything else. We spent most of the night together, and Jack told me every time alcohol got him down, Bing Crosby, who used to sing with the Whiteman band, would write a meaningful note to someone in the theatrical or broadcasting world, and Teagarden would get a job right away. Teagarden said Crosby had no special feeling for him; it was just Crosby's general practice. It saddened me to learn that Jack Teagarden died a few years later, aged fifty-eight. The paper said he died of pneumonia.

Not all the actors and actresses at the Markwell were on their uppers, and even when they were, they had amazing reservoirs of dignity. Bessie Dwyer was an actress in her early thirties with red hair and a voluptuous figure. She was unfailingly polite, industrious, and kind. It was a pleasure to see her come through the lobby.

The day clerk, Ross Peyton, was fascinated with her good looks and personality. One morning, when Bessie came downstairs to pay her bill, Peyton leaned over the counter, put his hand down her dress, and squeezed her breast. Bessie didn't start; she made no movement; she simply tolerated Peyton's affections. Two or three times his hand bounced her breast. Then he withdrew his hand with a smile that made his face look like a cracked plate. He presented the weekly accounting.

Bessie said, "Take five dollars off that bill."

"Whaddya mean, take five dollars off?"

"I won't pay the bill unless you take five dollars off."

"Why would I take five dollars off?" whined Peyton.

"For the free feel," said Bessie. "Why do you suppose you're going to take five dollars off?"

Peyton hurried through the subtraction, the smile long vanished. His amorous adventures with Miss Dwyer came to an abrupt end.

The Markwell always got guests when there was a fight at Madison Square Garden on Eighth Avenue and Fiftieth Street. The Markwell faced what sportswriters called Jacobs' Beach, the ticket agency from which Mike Jacobs ran the prize fighting business in New York. Mike Jacobs on more than one occasion rented a room in the Markwell for a secret conference. Not too long before, Jacobs had taken over the fight game from Tex Rickard, the first big boxing promoter. More important, in the 1930's, Mike owned Joe Louis, the heavyweight champion of the world.

I had known Mike Jacobs since I was a boy visiting the Hotel Normandie, where Mike operated a small counter with a big sign reading OPERA TICKETS. On occasions, Mike used to give me a spare ticket. From that inauspicious start Mike Jacobs became one of the most successful ticket brokers in New York. When Joe Louis had a fight at Madison Square Garden, Mike used to rent the front store in the Brill Building across from the Markwell. For one of these fights, the sale was slow, and I wondered aloud to a sportswriter in the lobby if Mike Jacobs would have any crowd in the Garden for the fight.

"Wait till Friday," said the sportswriter. "That's when all the Negroes get their WPA checks. Jacobs will have a crowd all right."

On Friday the line stretched around the block.

Mike Jacobs was of medium height. He was toothless, and he was a heavy drinker, as heavy a drinker as I ever met. His brother, Jake, never took a drink. Jake peddled chrysanthemums at the football games to the college boys and girls. He spent his life eking out a meager existence while his brother became a rich sporting promoter. Sometimes Jake would come up and hang around Jacobs' Beach, and it was often hours before Mike acknowledged his brother's presence and then only with a curt nod.

Mike Jacobs lived in Red Bank, New Jersey, when I, too, lived there. I called on him when the Jewish congregation elected me as the chairman of the United Palestine Appeal, which was what the UJA was called before Palestine's partition by the United Nations. The Jacobs home was on an impressive piece of land near the Shrewsbury River. No Englishman would have trouble playing cricket on the lawn. A servant admitted me and led me to the living room, which was three times the size of the Markwell lobby, as neat and well arranged as a picture in a home furnishing magazine. The only thing out of place was the bottle of bourbon on the table, out of which Mike and his wife, Essie, were drinking.

I explained my purpose.

Mike said, "I give everybody five bucks—the Red Cross, the Boy Scouts. I'll give you five bucks, too."

I once let a room to Jack Johnson, the first Negro to win the heavyweight championship. Johnson was working in a flea circus on West Forty-second Street, and he needed a night's lodging. I took him in, beret and all, and the next morning five or six non-paying guests raised hell with me about giving a Negro a room. This was my initiation into the civil rights movement. Jack Johnson, the man who beat Jim Jeffries, couldn't pay for a room in a second-rate hotel without irritating guests who hadn't half his courage.

I felt sorry for Johnson. It wasn't his own vices that did him in, not the drinking, the wenching, the gluttony. Jack triumphed over these as he triumphed over his opponents. It wasn't vice that brought Jack Johnson down, it was the antivice crusade. A Chicago judge gave Jack Johnson a year and a day. The judge sentenced Johnson on the charge of consorting over state lines with a white woman who, though she was most willing, said Jack seduced her. The defense lawyer forgot to emphasize that Johnson was also paying room rent for the woman's mother and sister.

Poor Jack Johnson. His own character lent credence to these charges. He was proud, arrogant, careless, often irresponsible, a man ill-prepared to carry the burden of self-esteem for his entire race as Joe Louis did and, a generation later, Jackie Robinson.

When I went to the fights at the Garden, I always ate at Jack Dempsey's Restaurant, not to be confused with the present Jack Dempsey's, a highly respected tourist attraction on Broadway. The old Jack Dempsey's Restaurant was financed by Jack Amron, a "Mr. Broadway" whose name rarely got into the papers. Amron also owned the Hollywood nightclub. He knew everything there was to know about the restaurant business, but he was going broke with Dempsey's.

"How come?" I asked him.

He was a small, dapper man with a pencil mustache and one prominent gold tooth. He pointed to Dempsey's, and he said, "There I give them a wonderful steak dinner for two dollars and fifty cents, and business is lousy." He turned and pointed to the Hollywood Nightclub, where later the Greyhound Bus Terminal would house thousands of sleepy soldiers and sailors. "At the Hollywood Nightclub I give them food for five dollars which is not fit to eat along with three naked dancing girls. Moral, Mr. Goldhurst: Bare teats beat good food."

While the people at the Markwell, in 1933, were mostly actors, we had an open-door policy. Groups involved in a particular line of work always live at a particular hotel. Burlesque girls always stayed at the Hotel Peerless, and if you were looking for a carny you'd find him at the Cadillac.

The cardsharks came to the Markwell, a fraternity all the Markwell's own. I knew them and listened to a thousand interesting stories. They plied their trade on the big steamships. Occasionally two of them would go off with their beautiful luggage only to return later with the explanation: "The purser tipped us off—no one with real dough on this trip." A few years ago I was coming out of Macy's, and I heard a fellow call me, and sure enough he was one of these old-timers. We talked for a bit, and when I told him I lived in Charlotte, he said that he had a profitable "connection" down there: "Stops at the Waldorf and he's a wonderful score." Hotel managers do not reveal names.

When the cardsharks returned from an ocean voyage, they went straight to the typewriter in the lobby, even before shedding their overcoats. They wrote a letter and took it over to the post office and sent it "Registered mail, return receipt requested." The letter was to the American Express Company: "Gentlemen: On an ocean voyage on the *Queen Mary* on such-and-such dates, the undersigned won the following money orders in a series of poker games from the following people."

They listed the serial numbers, amounts, and the names of the former owners of the money orders. This was for their protection. Usually the first thing the sucker did when he hit dry land was to send a telegram to the American Express Company that he had lost his money orders, and would they please stop payment on same and send him duplicates? American Express showed the sucker the registered letter and informed him there were possible criminal aspects to his recent behavior. Losing money orders in a poker game was not within the express company's jurisdiction; it was not in business to protect suckers. The sucker would have to seek relief elsewhere—which he never did.

I learned pinochle playing with one of these fellows, whose name was Andy Anderson. One night he was losing consistently, and I said to him, "Anderson, you're so far behind, I'm going to turn my back and let you pick yourself a hand. Maybe you'll get even."

"Hell, Goldhurst," Anderson said, "if you're going to let me pick a hand, you can look all you want."

No chambermaid ever had to dump the *Morning Telegraph* or any of the racing forms into the wastebasket of a room a cardshark let. Cardsharks avoided bets and odds and points as other people avoid measles. Once in a while they played cards in the Markwell lobby. Only whist.

"Is that game really exciting?" I asked, incredulous.

They turned and stared at me to a man. I suddenly realized they were looking at a mark. They could beat me at old maid; they could probably beat children at old maid without compunction.

There are only three types of people who give a hotel manager trouble—nonpaying guests, whores, and paying guests. Let me describe the paying guests.

Jack Fitzgerald was the advance man for the rodeo, and he stayed at the Markwell when he came to New York to get the promotion going. Fitzgerald handed me a thick envelope which contained $300, proceeded to busy himself in the newspaper offices and the ticket agencies, putting up the posters and collecting the celebrities who would attend opening night. Every evening after five he adjourned to the Markwell bar, where he gave the bartender instructions never leave the glass empty. Every other day the barboy would present himself at the desk with a penciled note from Fitzgerald: "Please give the bearer fifty dollars." By the time he was ready to leave for Springfield and points north, the $300 was depleted.

I added up his bill and presented it for his inspection. "Valet—$5; laundry—$3.50; room—8 nights at $2—$16."

"You're charging me two bucks a night?" he asked.

"That's the rate," I said.

"Why don't I get a rebate for staying here? What about one dollar and fifty cents a night? You get the rodeo folk because of me."

"You have spent three hundred dollars on whores, liquor, and dice and you are demanding a four-dollar rebate?" I asked.

Among the regulars at the Markwell was Mike-the-Horse, the model for Damon Runyon's Harry-the-Horse. Mike-the-Horse was a man who, at a moment's notice, could get you anything from a girl to 100 shares of New York Central preferred, no questions asked. On the police blotter where his name appeared from time to time, he called himself Alfred LeRoy. As he told me once, however, "My real, real name is Joey Abrams, from Coney Island originally."

Whenever the police pulled him in for questioning, he invariably asked the Markwell to go his bail. Since just as invariably he usually owed us a month's rent, I felt compelled to hunt up a bondsman. He was a witty man, and I suspect the precinct cops pulled him in for their amusement.

He and several friends sat in animated discussion one evening in the Markwell lobby. Something was up, and Mike-the-Horse was almost *hors de combat* because he was accompanied by a show girl. One of his friends came over to the desk and said, "Mike-the-Horse wants to shake the bimbo. Write out a fake telegram and bring it over. Say in it his uncle has died and the lawyer must see him to settle the estate."

Mike-the-Horse took the telegram from me and in mock surprise said, "Oh, my goodness. My uncle has died and I must go immediately to the coast to settle his estate. There's not a moment to spare."

The ruse was more than successful. The young lady sighed and asked, "What time does your train leave, Mike?"

It was the one response Mike-the-Horse hadn't anticipated. His eyes crossed, and his tongue stumbled all over his mouth. Finally he said, "My train? My train leaves at twelve sixty P.M."

"What the hell kind of a train is that that leaves at twelve sixty

P.M.?" she demanded. Pretense walked right out of the lobby and up toward Central Park.

The tourists could drive those of us at the desk to absolute despair. They never stopped stealing. They stole everything: towels, sheets, pillowcases, blankets, Gideon Bibles, and electric bulbs. The Markwell is probably the only hotel in the world where a guest once stole a medicine cabinet off the bathroom wall.

What made me nervous were the many things which go on in hotels every day. I was only too well aware of my personal vulnerability, and of course, I leaned backward in the conduct of the Markwell's operations. I established a direct line of communication with Lieutenant Coy of the Forty-seventh Street Police Station, the headquarters used to film the movie *Detective Story* with Kirk Douglas. I recalled that when Wilson Mizner managed a Broadway hotel, he notified his guests that there would be no smoking of opium in the elevator. I put this same order into effect from the first day.

I had trouble with only one guest, Frank Jones, who had been a vaudeville hoofer in his early days. Now he was forty years old, still slim and handsome. He earned $100 a week dancing with the mistress of a fat and rich subway-building tycoon. Jones played, in today's parlance, "the beard." Thus, if the tycoon's wife or his wife's lawyer spotted them, the tycoon pretended he had just happened by while two handsome young people were having a good time. Jones got the job because he owned a set of evening clothes. The tycoon paid him the $100 in the hallway of his girl's apartment.

Jones smoked opium and I was sure of it.

Opium smokers do not consider themselves addicts. They call it a pleasure smoke. What stopped me from throwing Jones out of the hotel was that I had no evidence, and more, he always paid his rent and never entertained female guests. One day, when Jones went to the racetrack, I had a friendly narcotics expert examine his room. There was no doubt he smoked opium. Everything smelled of it. But where was the evidence? Smoking opium involves elaborate preparation, evidence which is hard to hide. First of all the pipes—with their yard-long stems—and then the burner, resembling a Bunsen burner, which roasts the opium pellet, and the tongs to lift the roasting opium pellet from the

184

burner to the pipe. The opium smokers call this apparatus a lay-out, and it is bulky. But we never found a trace of it. Jones stayed.

Years later, in the 1940's, I learned where Jones had stashed his opium layout. He told me. The hotel had a horizontal sign running down the entire length of the ten-story building reading, with blinking lights, *H O T E L   M A R K W E L L*. The broad bottom of this heavy neon sign was directly outside Jones' room. Somehow he had had a tinsmith cut a panel in the side of the sign, and all he had to do was lean out of the window for the opium pipes, burner, and tongs. I looked at him as he told me this, and I saw his black teeth and yellow skin and lopsided walk, and I thought to myself, *You put one over on us, but, brother, you can have it.*

At least every other day I walked across the lobby and gave Broadway Rose a dollar bill, upon receipt of which she left the lobby. Broadway Rose was an ugly old woman with straggly hair who affected sleazy clothes smelling of camphor and sweat. She wore her stockings rolled around her ankles. A dollar was cheap price to pay to have her leave the hotel alone.

She didn't make all her income from desk clerks. She would wait outside a fashionable restaurant until a respectable couple exited, and then she would throw her arms around the man and screech, "My long-lost husband! Why don't you come home to your children?"

It was hard disengaging a set of shoulders from Rose's desperate grasp. Men protested, men became flustered, men were outraged, but still a crowd gathered to watch the drama. The victim paid more than $1. He paid $2, sometimes $3. Broadway Rose went her way, swishing her false teeth.

I had no sooner started my career as a hotel manager than an employee of another hotel offered me $300 if I put him on as a bellhop at the Markwell. Why would a man offer me a $300 bonus for a job which paid at best $12 a week? Obviously, to run whores in and out of the hotel. I took the necessary steps to eliminate this source of revenue by putting into effect three new rules: No room was rented to a "single" woman after 9 P.M.; no female could "visit" a male guest after 9 P.M.; and no "couple" could get a room unless they had baggage.

No hotel manager, especially a novice, is radically going to affect the Life, as whores like to call their profession. I am quite sure we rented many a room to couples whose luggage contained only a couple of bricks. Nor could I very well question the virtue of every woman who wanted to let a room at a reasonable hour of the day or evening. Many times we registered a woman at midnight who showed us her Equity or Vaudeville card. The only thing I did stop was the practice by which the bellboys made more than the management by pandering.

An interesting whore, in fact, lived in the Markwell for many years. Mary Waldenziak was a Hungarian with jet black hair and green eyes and a certain attractive and indefinable style. She was as exciting as a foreign spy met on an ocean liner. Mary paid her rent on time; she never flirted with a man; she never entertained one in her room. She did business only with clergymen and only with clergymen at religious conventions.

Miss Waldenziak subscribed to all the religious periodicals and bulletins, and whenever a conference was announced, she made a reservation at one of the hotels in that city. She traveled the entire Northeast from the White Mountains to Baltimore, from the Poconos to Asbury Park. She just waited in the lobby, and the incoming clergymen spotted her, and by the weekend she was back in the Markwell.

She told me she had eliminated all the risks of prostitution. No man got drunk in her room; no one beat her up; no one welshed on his fee. She said, "Clergymen come in the door with their cock in one hand and ten dollars in the other. Their whole ambition is to get in and out as fast as possible."

She had a son who was going to Bellemont, a fashionable private academy in Pennsylvania, and she had an enormous store of religious information. She knew who was ascending the hierarchical ladder, what the burning theological issues were, who was transferring to another parish. Later she joined the Tabernacle Church at Fifty-sixth Street and Broadway, and she was one of the prime movers in the Ladies Auxiliary because of her arcane knowledge about religious wheels within wheels.

The streetwalkers always tried to register. We knew most of them by sight. One of them came in one night, and I signaled the clerk no. He told her politely the hotel was filled, but she had caught my signal and turned from the desk and approached me, smiling. I thought she was going to plead for a room. She wasn't pleading for anything. Less than a foot away, she swung her pocketbook, which had a metal clasp, and caught me flush in the face. I went to the Polyclinic Hospital, where the doctors had to take a piece of my glasses from my left eye.

At 3 A.M. I took a telephone call, and the desk clerk said, "There's trouble in three o one, Harry." I dressed and hurried over, and together the clerk and I went up to 301, opened the room with a passkey, and saw a big man pounding and screaming on the locked bathroom door. He was yelling, "Come out of there. I'll kill you if you don't come out, you goddamn bitch."

He faced us, livid with rage, his fists bunched. Fortunately I recognized him. He was a horse cop, a mounted traffic policeman who guided the theater traffic at night.

I said, "If you leave quietly, I won't tell Mayor LaGuardia about this."

Within minutes he was gone.

From the locked bathroom, she asked us timidly, "Is it all right?"

She was stark naked when she came out, her nose was bleeding, and her eyes were black. She dressed tearfully, and we went downstairs, and I bought her a cup of coffee, and she composed herself. She was in town, she told me, to start a theatrical career, and she had a date with Major Bowes tomorrow. Would Major Bowes notice her black eyes?

Twenty-five years later, in Ivey's Department Store, I recognized her when she presented a book for my autograph. She was married and had a son in East Carolina State College. She said she'd had a few dates with the cop until that night, that he was all right except when he got drunk.

"What happened with Major Bowes?" I asked.

"He made me take the sunglasses off," she said.

I have reprinted too many times the story of how I was a $300 angel for the Midget Melodrama to repeat it in full here. Suffice to say, Lester Al Smith, a handsome young actor who was Ralph Bellamy's movie stand-in, stayed at the Markwell and persuaded me that we could make a fortune with a repertory theater in which the audience could drink beer and munch pretzels. To ensure our success, we would not use legitimate actors, but midgets.

The reasoning was that a midget repertory company had been one of the successful attractions along the midway of the Chicago World's Fair two years before.

My role in this scheme was to advance $300 in six weekly installments for the rehearsal halls and to house the midgets in the Markwell. Lester Al Smith was to stage, light, and design the scenery for our initial presentation, the melodrama, *No Mother to Guide Her.*

This venture allows me to boast that I helped produce the shortest run on Broadway. Many a show has closed after one performance: *No Mother to Guide Her* closed on opening night after only two of its three acts.

Seventy-four people, forty of them guests of the hotel, were in the audience. The midgets all talked at once. Our piano player, Ann Clark, kept her hand snaking to the top of the piano for another belt of whiskey to sustain her during the ordeal. As often as she had to swallow, the audience heard one-handed musical accompaniment.

By the time Ann passed out the midgets were quarreling about who was upstaging whom and never even noticed the audience walking out. Mercifully the curtain came down.

Only the New York *Post* reviewed *No Mother to Guide Her,* which Al read aloud to me before departing the next morning for a job in Syracuse. I was left with the midgets, who were left high and dry. Since I was one of the show's backers, they hounded me for the remainder of their rehearsal pay. They even deputized a committee of three to call on my wife. I could only say, "Genevieve, I am not even going to *try* to explain this."

Eventually, I had to make my peace with Mr. Williams, the theatrical agent who had recruited all our little people. I gave him a complete history of my relatively remote connection with the production, proved to him I was merely a glorified hotel clerk, that I couldn't possibly pay the cast, and he took it with surprisingly good grace. He only wanted to know Lester Al Smith's address.

I tell these stories because they were the good times. The good times were few and far between. The Depression ravaged us. It nearly devastated the rural population, and it stripped the urban population of hope. I remember trudging to my apartment house one night. A driving sleet chilled me the second I left the subway.

Trouble with the Markwell's boiler system had kept me late, and the boys would be in bed when I reached home. If I wanted anything that night, I wanted the cab fare for the six long blocks I had to walk.

One morning, while I was walking down the stairwells on a tour of inspection, I was at the landing on the eighth floor when I heard a famous old vaudeville actress named Mamie Russell talking. She was scraping loose plaster from the wall. She and her companion were waiting for the elevator, and the companion was saying, "What do you want to do that for, Mamie?" I could hear Mamie spreading the plaster with her cane, and I heard her reply, "Let those damn Jews fix the place up."

I got downstairs as quick as I could to tell Jake, whom I suspected was naïve about these things.

"For heaven's sake, Jake, this woman hasn't paid her rent in months—"

Jake smiled. "Aw, she's a nice old trouper. She doesn't mean any harm."

"She doesn't mean any harm." This was 1937, and this is where we came in.

Chapter 18

Sometime in 1930 the men began to build their shanties on Riverside Drive. They threw up little shacks made of discarded pilings, or tar paper, or the corrugated tin they had scrounged from the dumps. Riverside Drive in the early thirties from about Ninety-eighth Street to the George Washington Bridge was a gigantic ash heap, the one place in New York from which the cops had no interest in chasing the unemployed. The men were not hoboes, bums, or outlaws; they were men who streamed to the city from the rural areas seeking work of any kind.

In the cities the insurance companies kept going; the printing presses ran; the white-collar workers went to the office every morning. They worked for lower salaries, and they worked Saturdays, and overtime pay was as fantastic a notion as space travel. At least in the cities there was work. There was nothing in the country. The men who operated the reapers, who had pruned trees, milked dairy herds, flocked to the cities. The cities herded them along the garbage dumps and the ash heaps, hoping against hope no one would see them, and if no one saw them, the Depression would go away.

It was a futile hope. The Depression was here to stay. These men cooked their dinners in cans suspended over makeshift spits. They warmed themselves burning cardboard cartons and discarded wooden boxes. They milled around their ash heap, stamping it into a compound as hard and as slippery as glass. These men finally disappeared when Robert Moses began rebuilding Riverside Drive into the long green park it is today. I have no idea where they fled, but one spring they were gone, in their place the green benches, the new water fountains, the curving paths. These men were one of the sights and sounds of the Depression.

Another sight was the soup kitchen on Eighth Avenue set up by a private company, where good-looking men, some with brief-cases in their hands or under their arms, stood in line. They paid five cents for a bowl of soup. Stale bread, the slices stacked like books on library shelves, was free, as much as they could carry. Many a slice went into that briefcase.

Millions of people saved pennies for a cake of ice once a week in the summertime—not ghetto people, but people in the mines and in the hills and in the factories and the cotton mills, working people. I came across a 1934 catalogue for a North Carolina furni-ture manufacturer in which there was a photograph of a ladder, the caption beneath reading: "A ten-year-old can now fix looms." The platform ladder was designed to accommodate a child who was hidden in a closet when the labor inspector came. The pay in the cotton mills was 25 cents an hour for adult workers.

The movie houses on West Forty-second Street which charged 10 cents at 9 A.M. admitted thousands of men, hopelessly looking for jobs. They lined up in the morning and spent the whole day inside, warm, anonymous, lulled by the romantic images of a never-never land, seeing the show over and over again, for 10 cents.

My brother Max was working for the New York Stock Exchange in 1929. After the crash in October the exchange fired the un-married men first. Out went Max. He got a job right away with the Metropolitan Life Insurance Company as an agent with a debit, better, just better, than no job at all. For a lot of these men, how-ever, the job turned out to be much more than a refuge, Maxie included. After almost forty years, the income from his renewal premiums sold in those years is more than substantial.

The first thing Max did was run right down to sell Jake, who was operating three hotels in Manhattan, all of which dealt with many people who could be prospects for insurance. This is a natu-ral procedure with all insurance agents—see the rich uncle, the successful brother, the sympathetic friend, sell that first policy, and tell him to recommend you to his friend.

Jake held up his hand and said, "No, sirree. Go out and sell insurance to strangers. If you are still in business a year from now,

191

I'll really go to work for you." Max did just that, and Jake came through as he had promised. But it was hard. There were many mornings Max put one foot after another to the cold floor to start the day realizing he faced despair and futility.

During that first year Max sold a policy to a wealthy Negro who ran a betting parlor. Wally Bims was a Harlem fixture who made hundreds of thousands of dollars in the nickels and dimes of bettors; twenty or thirty of them would put together to bet a horse on the nose or across the board. Wally had a family, and he wanted to insure his life so that he would leave an estate. He was only forty-six, but no big company, not the Metropolitan, not Penn Mutual, not Aetna, insured Negroes. Insurance companies wouldn't sell Negroes policies, for that matter, until after World War II, then only because the companies and unions who subscribed to the salary allotment and pension trust programs insisted it was too much trouble to start dividing employees.

In 1930 Wally Bims listened to reputable companies refuse him. The more they refused, the more he wanted insurance. He approached Max. He wanted a $50,000 ordinary life policy. The premiums were astronomical, but Wally didn't care. Max scouted all New York for weeks and finally came upon a small company which three Jewish brokers had formed, the Fidelity Insurance of Queens. Their eyes lit up, too, when Max told them of Wally Bims' offer. The three partners held a serious conference with Max in a Chinese restaurant below their office, and after the *moo goo gai pan,* they said, "Go ahead, Max. Sell it."

Wally paid his first premium. Two weeks later, when a long shot Wally had neglected to lay off came home, Wally solved his problem by dropping dead of a heart attack. Max had to tell the three partners at Fidelity Insurance they, too, had made a wrong bet.

It was after five when he got there, the secretaries gone, the office deserted save for those in the conference room. The door was ajar. Inside, Max could see the three men in animated discussion. He waited for them to finish. One of the partners turned and saw Max. The three men stopped talking. The president of the Fidelity Insurance looked at his other two partners, then back at Max and nodded no. Max nodded yes. The three men nodded no. Max kept nodding yes. They spent five terrifying minutes nodding at each other, Max said, each nod spelling disaster for the Fidelity Insurance Company of Queens, New York.

My middle boy, Harry junior, got a summertime job delivering groceries for Mr. Cole. Mr. Cole paid him 50 cents a week, and Buddy made perhaps another 75 cents in tips. One week, when Mr. Cole paid Buddy, the cashier of another store looked at the coin and said, sorry, it was counterfeit. Buddy ran back to the grocery store and told Mr. Cole the 50-cent piece was false.

Mr. Cole said, "I paid you two quarters."

This is probably the saddest story I remember of the Depression, a grown man arguing with a boy to get out of redeeming a bad coin.

To Jewish communal affairs I'm a Johnny-come-lately. The people I associated with, who came to my house, were newspapermen, or nonnewspapermen, interesting people or bores. I never paid the slightest attention to who was a Jew or was not a Jew.

One evening in 1935, on behalf of the shul, I went to a meeting convened by Rabbi Stephen S. Wise who announced he was forming a committee to boycott the goods of Nazi Germany. Dr. Stephen Wise said, "Hitler means to kill all the Jews in Germany and in Europe."

I could understand removing Jewish officeholders; I could understand disenfranchising them; actually to kill them was incomprehensible. But Rabbi Stephen Wise said it, the leading rabbi in America. He said, "Hitler means to kill the Jews of Germany, every man, woman, and child in Germany."

Dr. Howard Tannenbaum followed Rabbi Wise and outlined a program for implementing this boycott of German goods. I went up to the platform and said, "I'd like to join."

From that moment on I was in Jewish communal life. I sat down and read the *Universal Jewish Encyclopedia* from *A* to *Z*, which took me three months. I also read Dr. Milton Steinberg's books, and Herr Heinrich Grätz's *History of the Jews,* and the works of Theodor Herzl.

As a member of the boycott committee I was to approach department stores and urge them to stop buying from Germany. I had a little success. In Gimbels, the managers told me that they sold Dresden china by the barrel loads. If a lady broke a dish or a cup, Gimbels had to help her replace it. Macy's told me the store sold many parrots from Germany. There was some success in the Boy-cott Nazi Germany Committee, but I did not achieve it.

Anti-Semitism is a constant of the Western culture, an incurable disease with two areas of infection. First is deicide, the killing of Jesus. No matter how far the Pope of Rome and the Protestant churches go in trying to correct this libel, it still is the supreme inspiration for anti-Semitism. Anti-Semites drink it in with their mother's milk.

Economic affairs is the secondary infection. If the crops fail, if a devastating war leaves the country helpless, if there is unemployment, poverty, hunger, the people will seek a scapegoat on whom to blame all their troubles.

Carl Sandburg told me, "I don't understand anti-Semitism. I found it among poets and among hoboes. I heard it among Socialists and radicals, and I heard it in the fancy homes of the rich."

Once, when Tiny sought a summer home and answered the advertisement of Dan Beard, the founder of the Boy Scouts of America, Beard, not sensing her Jewish connections, told her how exclusive the neighborhood was; there were no Jews. Tiny told him, "That's too bad; my husband needs a synagogue pretty close to where we live."

Anti-Semitism, both native and foreign, was changing Jewish attitudes, too. Nor were they subtle changes. On June 19, 1936, before 45,000 people, Joe Louis and Max Schmeling fought a heavyweight bout at Yankee Stadium. Max Schmeling was the ex-heavyweight champ who won his title lying down when Jack Sharkey fouled him and lost it standing up when Jack Sharkey won on points. Schmeling was an 8 to 1 underdog.

Schmeling was in minor disgrace with the German Propaganda Ministry for having signed a contract to fight a black man. Goebbels himself called for a boycott of the North German Lloyd Lines for scheduling an excursion from Bremerhaven to New York for the bout.

In the fourth round Schmeling knocked Louis down with a tremendous right to the jaw. As the fight continued, the roar of the crowd made it impossible for either fighters or the referee to hear the bell. Arthur Donovan had to take hand signals from the timekeeper to separate the fighters. Louis was heavy-footed, and Schmeling was hurting him. In the twelfth Schmeling hit him with another right, and Louis was out when he hit the canvas, not turning until Donovan, the referee, reached the count of eight.

Schmeling's victory was one of the greatest upsets in the history of boxing.

Joseph Goebbels sent a telegram which read: TO YOUR WONDERFUL VICTORY MY HEARTIEST CONGRATULATIONS. I KNOW YOU FOUGHT FOR GERMANY. IT IS A GERMAN VICTORY. HEIL HITLER. Goebbels also ordered the boycott against the North German Lloyd Line canceled.

When Schmeling returned home, Air Force planes saluted his ship. *Der Angriff,* the Nazi paper, printed an interview in which Max declared that the fight was the supreme test of white supremacy. If it weren't for Hitler and Germany, Max declared, he wouldn't have won. Hitler invited Schmeling and his actress wife, Anny Onder, to lunch.

Max was a Nazi, and at the moment the Nazis were unstoppable, in Spain, in the Rhineland, soon in Austria, and now in Yankee Stadium. Schmeling's victory brought other forces into play. The idea had always been that the championship should belong to a white man. Well, a white man was near winning it, except he had reservations not only about colored men, but a great many other white men. For the first time, I realized how important a colored man could be. He carried my hopes with him. He was an improbable ally.

But I had other improbable allies. I went into a cigar store in Red Bank, New Jersey, where I met the priest, Father Graven of St. Dominick's. After bantering with the storekeeper, we walked out, and I said to Father Graven, "That's a pretty good fellow, that storekeeper." The priest leaned to my ear, and he said, "Pretty good fellow, eh? I saw him lead a bunch of Ku Kluxers around my church two Saturdays ago. They went around and around and then burned a cross up on the hill."

In 1937 Joe Louis won the title from James J. Braddock, the Cinderella man of boxing, who refused to sit on his stool at the beginning of the eighth round, telling his seconds, "I won it in the middle of the ring; that's where I'll lose it."

On Wednesday night, June 22, 1938, Louis and Schmeling fought a return bout, again at Yankee Stadium, this time before 80,000. All the Jews at the Markwell went. This time, the North

German Lloyd Lines left Bremerhaven with bands playing Wagner arias.

As a hotelman in his last days—for I was soon to go to work for the New York *Daily Mirror*—it was one of the biggest weeks New York had during the Depression. People came from all over to see the fight. Over a three-day period New York took in $3,000,000, a fantastic amount for the Depression years.

With the bell, Louis shuffled from his corner and with left and rights started bouncing Max's head as though it were on hinges. With a right, he turned Max Schmeling around and knocked him into the ropes. As Max bounced back, Louis delivered another right mid-back, just below the ribs. Where no one could hear the bell in the first fight, this time everybody in the stadium heard Max Schmeling scream. The mouthguard shot from his mouth in a rising arch and landed rows and rows from ringside; I understand the ushers and the ballplayers still look for it in center field.

Schmeling got up, and Louis knocked him down again with another left and right. No one could see the punches, but we could hear them landing against Max's jaw. This time, when Schmeling went down, he started to crawl away. Arthur Donovan, without counting, stopped the fight as Schmeling's arms and knees gave out in center ring and he lay there, comatose. It took the Germans more than a half hour to revive Schmeling, and it took three days for him to convalesce in a New York City hospital. His jaw had been dislocated, and Louis' punch to the body had almost separated his vertebrae, all in two minutes and four seconds of the first round.

In the dressing room, the reporters asked Louis if he bore any personal animosity toward Schmeling. Louis thought over the word "animosity" for a few seconds and said, "Well, I just didn't like some of the things he was saying."

Joe Louis was our champion. Our other champion was Franklin D. Roosevelt. Joe Louis heartened us. Franklin D. Roosevelt saved us.

In 1936, Genevieve and I and the boys lived in River Plaza, New Jersey, right across the Shrewsbury River from Red Bank. I used to take the famous Blue Comet commuting train to the city and home. Every afternoon, from early spring until late fall, the boys would wait and watch for the Blue Comet to streak across the railroad viaduct extended over the Shrewsbury River.

River Plaza was originally a row of expensive homes on the south bank of the Shrewsbury River, all the homes mounting a bluff, all of them on extensive land with expensive gardening. Red Bank, New Jersey, was the home of Eisner's Uniform Company. In World War I, River Plaza was suddenly dotted with the bungalows of factory workers turning out uniforms for the American Expeditionary Force. Many of these people in River Plaza stayed on at Eisner's when the war ended. They were the Calts and the Hendricks, the Petits and the Gillises, men who were supervisors and foremen in the big brick factory just over the steel bridge, now manufacturing police and Red Cross uniforms, surgical gowns, and football jerseys.

Consequently, River Plaza was now a larger community with only two classes: the old families—the Forresters, the Sherwoods, the Blakes, the Russells—and the factory hands whom I have named, the two communities divided by Nut Swamp Road, which ran past Shadow Dam to the River Plaza schoolhouse, a mile away, across from which were the Russell orchards.

I rented a house for the summer on the Shrewsbury River on the right side of Nut Swamp Road, in line with the other grand homes lining the water. I rented it from a man named Edward Von Kattengale, who was the postmaster of Red Bank, the only Democrat I ever met in desperately Republican Monmouth County. The house had fourteen rooms and a porch around which literally my boys could roller-skate. In the the dining room there was a gilt-edged mirror 12 feet high by 6 feet wide. There was a giant staircase from the entry hall and a kitchen stairwell in the back. Von Kattengale charged me less rent than I paid for a New York apartment. But Von Kattengale wasn't all heart. He owned a Plymouth franchise and was forever selling me used cars which either lacked windshields or carburetors or spare tires. One of those cars the family called the *Holy Ghost,* Von Kattengale being *the Father,* and I, of course, *the Son.*

River Plaza was not a microcosm in which to describe the 1936 elections. River Plaza was, as I have described it, a little universe all its own, as staunchly Republican as though Herbert Hoover had been crowned king and the Depression had never happened.

One of our friends was Charlie Mott, a plumber, who lived three blocks away and with whose kids our boys played. In 1931, Charlie Mott sat on his front steps with a loaded shotgun in his

197

lap. A serviceman from the water company came. Charlie Mott pointed the shotgun at him and said, "I have a six-months-old baby in that house. You try to shut my water off and I will kill you." The serviceman walked away. Charlie Mott, who owed $4, kept his water on.

The Roosevelt administration succeeded in paying the World War I veterans a bonus, and with his money Charlie Mott bought a truck and became a plumbing contractor. The New Deal even provided work. Charlie was the plumbing contractor for several of the post offices beginning to dot the main streets of little towns in the area. In 1936, when we discussed the coming election, Charlie Mott, sporting a big Landon sunflower, insisted, "Taxes is too high under Roosevelt."

Our neighbors to the right were the Blakes. They were older people, childless, but kind and warm and generous. Mr. Blake was a bank president; Mrs. Blake a clubwoman. She was the president of the League of Women Voters, a secretary of the Fitkin Hospital Ladies Auxiliary, a past president of the Republican Women's Club. She was also a gardener with an unrivaled green thumb. Their house sat on two acres, all of which looked like Versailles. The gladioli always bloomed. The crocuses came up on time, and the daffodils were profuse. Over all this beauty, from time to time, one of our boys would tramp, playing cowboys and Indians, or going back for a fly ball, or trying to launch a homemade kayak. Mrs. Blake never voiced a complaint. When we apologized for the intrusion, she said she liked children and was especially partial to boys.

One year New Jersey enacted an antifireworks law, the passage of which reached the ears of Jim Gallagher, Tiny's brother, then a merchant seaman making port in Sydney, Australia. No firecrackers, Jim thought, would desolate his nephews, so he sent on the Australian variety of fireworks which resembled sticks of TNT. Tiny and I confiscated the goodies, but not before Bud and Dick got their hot little hands on a couple of sticks.

They inserted these firecrackers in the seams and knotholes of the Blake's garage. Buddy lit the firecrackers; Dickie ran away, arms over his ears, he who was later to become a paratrooper demolitionist. They did a beautiful job. The entire garage tilted with the explosion. Mrs. Blake tch-tched and said, "Boys will be boys."

It was hard to believe such a nice lady as Mrs. Blake with such a responsible husband would get into as much trouble as she did. But the trouble came with Roosevelt's election in 1936 when he carried the country by a plurality of 11,000,000 and forty-six of the forty-eight states, which led Jim Farley to remark, "As goes Maine, so goes Vermont."

Mrs. Blake, a public-spirited woman, was a poll watcher in the River Plaza firehouse. She knew the names and the faces of all the maids in all the big houses. As these girls approached the box with their folded ballots, Mrs. Blake would open them and say, "You voted for *him?*" The girls would take back their ballots and make an X for Landon, thereby effectively voiding their vote. Mrs. Blake also knew the faces and the names of those on whose houses her husband held a first or a second mortgage. She did the same thing with their folded ballots, nodding approval when the vote was right, staring incredulously when it was wrong. Mrs. Blake was not alone in this questionable, if effective, practice. Members of the Republican Women's Club were stationed at discreet precinct schools and firehouses.

Word of this behavior leaked to Mayor Frank Hague of Jersey City. Hudson County returned a thumping majority for Roosevelt, which made Hague the most powerful political figure in the state. Monmouth County had always been a thorn in his side since its Republican majority was helping keep J. Warren Barbour in the Senate. Hague wanted his man in the Senate, as is the wont of political bosses in every time and clime. In addition, Monmouth County Republicans were always threatening to sue Hague for corrupt election procedures.

Pretty soon Mrs. Blake and several of her dearest friends were looking into the steely eyes of state and federal voting referees trying lamely to explain. Ministers here and there leaped forward with petitions assuring all that Mrs. Blake and the others were a credit to their church and community. It looked black for a while.

Since I had been touring the community in the *Holy Ghost* with a Roosevelt sticker, Mrs. Blake asked me what I could do. No one had less influence with the federal authorities than I, but I promised to take the matter up with Von Kattengale. I suppose Von Kattengale asked Frank Hague, "You're not really going to put these silly little old ladies in jail, are you? Especially when they promise they'll never do it again?"

Another Red Bank friend was Gerard Alfred. Gerard Alfred was

Eisner's sales manager, selling carload lots to J. C. Penney's and Sears, Roebuck, making $25,000 a year when $75 a week was a living wage. Gerry and his wife, Grace, who were childless, had a dog named Trixie. When Trixie was sick, Gerry and Grace used to run around the roof of the apartment house comforting the poor animal.

Gerry came often to the Markwell with another woman named Peggy. Peggy went to Reno in October, 1936, to get a divorce. She was away for six weeks. While she was gone, Gerry got involved with another woman, Manila. Manila was a Hawaiian and had a daughter she was sure could get into the movies. Gerry thought so, too, apparently, because he bought Manila's daughter a vibra-harp which cost $600.

Peggy, the divorcée, returned, and Gerard was suddenly torn between a great many women; there was the comfortable mistress, Peggy, and the volatile, maternal Manila. And there was the wife, Grace, whom he really, really loved. Gerard didn't know what to do; his emotions, he told me, were completely shredded.

"Why not declare yourself bankrupt in women, Gerry? Tell Grace everything. Hold her hand and tell her you love her and that you're sorry."

"I couldn't do that," said Gerard. "It would kill her."

"You'd be surprised what doesn't kill women," I said. "When little Trixie passed on, it didn't kill her, did it?"

"Almost," said Gerard Alfred, wiping a tear in memory of the dog.

Gerard told Manila it was all over. Manila told him no soap. She was going to leave town for Hollywood as soon as Gerard paid the first-class fare for her and her daughter and the vibraharp. Gerard didn't have the money. He had Grace, he had his country club dues, and he had Peggy.

I promised to get him out of it and called up a friend of mine, Hymie Levine, top detective of the strong-arm squad. Hymie said he and his partner would go up and talk to Manila.

Election night, 1936, and Gerard and I waited in the Markwell lobby for Hymie. All the while we waited, Gerard kept telling me he hoped to hell Roosevelt wouldn't win because it was criminal spending all that money just to get votes. "Spending, spending, spending," he said with a sigh, "all to get votes."

Roosevelt's landslide caused Gerard dismay. Hymie caused him even more.

"We went up there," Hymie said, "and threatened to run her in for prostitution if she didn't leave town."

"And?"

"She said if we didn't get out of the place that minute she was going to call LaGuardia and we'd be back pounding beats in Queens. So," said Hymie, "we got out."

Gerard Alfred paid off.

In the middle of 1938 I finally got a job on the New York *Daily Mirror* through the efforts of Jack Lait, the columnist, with an assist from Walter Winchell. I did promotional writing and some reporting. I wasn't there a week when Jack Lait received an anonymous letter revealing I had been in jail. He called me into his office, showed me the letter, and said, "To hell with them."

One of my beats was Fritz Kuhn, the *Bundesführer* of the American Nazis, who was the director of Camp Siegfried and Camp Nordland for boys and girls in Sussex and Bergen counties, New Jersey, respectively.

Fritz Julius Kuhn, whose name was actually Friedrich Kuhn, boasted that he had accompanied Hitler and Ludendorff in the Munich Putsch of 1923. He had emigrated to America in the late twenties, become naturalized in 1934, and in 1935 set up the German-American Bund, whose members, he warned, were "useless to America if we deny our racial characteristics."

If poverty and unemployment and displacement were the chief terrors of the 1930's, the next menace was the growing ferment engendered by American Fascists and anti-Semites. I think we newspapermen made Fritz Kuhn into a larger menace than he was in fact, but that is not to insist he was harmless or that his Bundists were no more than grown-up Boy Scouts.

The Bundists outfitted themselves in blue and gray uniforms. They wore the gauleiter's chest belt and black boots with white piping on their overseas caps. Fritz Kuhn recruited them by speaking first to small groups of German-Americans at meetings held in private homes. One of these meetings, I remember, took place in the home of Carolina Meade, a teacher and a Shakespearian actress in New Milford, New Jersey. Miss Meade was no German, but she liked Hitler and disliked Jews. It was either Fritz Kuhn or Father Coughlin, and Fritz, after all, was in New Jersey.

Fritz Kuhn got the front page for the first time on the night of Hitler's forty-ninth birthday, April 20, 1938, when the Bund held a celebration in the Yorkville Casino on East Eighty-sixth Street. Yorkville, a Manhattan neighborhood extending from Eightieth to Ninety-eighth streets, from the East River to Third Avenue, has always been called Germantown.

Yorkville was the extent of Kuhn's influence in New York. The American Legion used to assign squads to follow Fritz around and report on his unpatriotic behavior. On the night in question, while Fritz was ranting against Roosevelt and America, a legionnaire stood up and shouted, "Is this America, or is this Germany?" Fritz's guard moved in on the man, and one blackjacked him. Several other American Legionnaires rose, put on their blue overseas caps, and the meeting disintegrated into a melee which necessitated calling the police.

One of the legionnaires I interviewed told me, "As far as the fight goes, it was a draw."

Fritz reached the zenith of his power in 1939, when the German-American Bund rented Madison Square Garden for a rally which they called the George Washington Birthday Exercises. Returning from Germany in January, Fritz prophesied that the rally expected to attract between 30,000 and 40,000 adherents.

The rally was a bold, outrageous idea. New York was then, and is now, a Jewish city, and countless numbers of organizations and individuals agitated for cancellation of the permit. A good half of the protests came from Gentiles, organizations like the German-American League for Freedom, from Protestant ministers and Catholic priests, and from the women's groups. The Jews sent an avalanche of nays into City Hall.

I was one of the reporters attending LaGuardia's press conference who heard him say, "As long as this meeting is conducted in an orderly and lawful manner with no violence and no preaching overthrow, it will be permitted. It would be a strange kind of free speech which permits only free speech for only those with whom we agree. That's the kind of free speech they have in Fascist countries."

On the night of February 20, 1939, LaGuardia dispatched 1,700 policemen to the Garden, but only 22,000 Bundists showed up, although the admission was free. While Kuhn was condemning the Jews, a young man named Irwin Greenbaum charged the platform. When Kuhn's bodyguard moved to intercept him with their blackjacks, the police stopped them and carried Greenbaum from the rally. The incident led LaGuardia to issue an order that no military regalia could be worn at rallies, so for Hitler's fiftieth birthday, Kuhn's elite guard had to forgo their black belts and their spears with fluttering pennants.

By the end of the year Fritz Kuhn was in jail, convicted by a New York jury of having misappropriated $1,217 of the Bund's money, which he used to pay the costs of moving his girl friend's furniture around the country. Her name, as I recall, was Mrs. Capen, and she was not instrumental in Fritz's trouble, except for letting his love letters fall into the hands of the New York district attorney. When read aloud in court, the letters revealed a fatuous fifty-year-old whose idea of passion was marching around a hotel room in his black boots, describing the wonders of the Thousand-Year Reich. As the judge admitted these embarrassing documents as evidence, I remembered the famous correspondent and political leader Boies Penrose's sage advice: "Never write a letter to a woman you can't cool a beer on."

The Bund, of course, insisted that its membership gave the money to Fritz to do with as he chose, that he could throw it down the sewer for all it cared, but the judge gave him five years, declaring that misappropriation was misappropriation whether the membership was crazy or not.

The man who frightened me most was Colonel Charles A. Lindbergh. I never covered a story about the colonel, I never met him, but I listened to those radio broadcasts, each one of which became more ominous for Americans and for Jews. Lindbergh frightened me because he was a legitimate American hero, he was respectable in a way Fritz Kuhn was not, and he was rich. He was also reasonable in a way Father Coughlin was not. A great many Catholics opposed Coughlin because he proposed in time of war to confiscate profits, as well as manpower. You can imagine what some of the rich Protestant munition makers thought of the proposal.

Lindbergh didn't make my hands shake with palsy, but he made my brow crease with worry. What he did was to disguise the moral issue of barbarism versus civilization in a realistic appraisal—that somebody was going to win the war, and we had to get along with that somebody, who was probably going to be Hitler. That this happens not to have been a particularly astute appraisal is beside the point. Who knew in 1940 that the English simply couldn't have been beaten in their home isle or that the Russians were going to chew up generations of Germans, sometimes chew them up in a matter of hours?

Lindbergh began his political career against American involvement in the European war with a radio speech in June, 1940, on the day the Nazis announced they had broken the Maginot Line, a day after Italy entered the war on the German side. Apropos of Roosevelt's remark that the hand that held the dagger had stabbed it in the back, Lindbergh said, "We are making gestures with an empty gun after we have lost the draw."

On August 4, the day General John J. Pershing, in a national radio broadcast, urged that the United States lend Britain fifty old destroyers, Lindbergh, before 40,000 people collected at Soldier Field in Chicago by the Citizens Committee to Keep America Out of the War, said, "We must cooperate with Germany if the Reich wins the war." He went on with his backstairs history to urge that we had lived with a Europe dominated by England and now we were going to live with a Europe dominated by Germany.

These speeches led Robert Sherwood, an intimate of Roosevelt's, to comment that Lindbergh was supported by "groups made up of people personally and completely American whose sympathies are with totalitarian nations and who wish to make us the Nazis of the western world."

Lindbergh's sympathies, however, were gathering momentum. The America First Committee had come into existence with the financing which permitted full-page ads in the New York *Times,* ads signed by such representative and respectable Americans as General Robert E. Wood, R. Douglas Stewart, General Hugh Johnson, Alice Roosevelt Longworth, John T. Flynn, Edward Rickenbacker, Henry Ford, and Chester Bowles.

Buttressing Lindbergh's speeches was the book *The Wave of the Future,* written by his wife, Anne Morrow Lindbergh, in which she suggested that reform at home was better than a crusade abroad. She opined, also, that "somehow the leaders in Germany, Italy, and Russia have discovered how to use new social and economic forces while we have not."

Every time Lindbergh spoke, more and more people listened.

They were indeed a small minority, but it was hard to discount the statement Lindbergh made in his radio speech of April 17, 1941: "If we can be forced into a war against our will, then the idea of representative democracy is dead and there will be little use of fighting for it abroad."

While the Greeks and English resisted the Nazis north of Athens, Lindbergh announced he was newly enlisted in the America First Committee. He let us in on this news in a speech delivered at Manhattan Center on Thirty-fourth Street between Eighth and Ninth avenues. Whereas the police had cleared Fiftieth Street of Bundists, 20,000 people stood on the curbs and listened to the public-address system as Lindbergh complained that London had misinformed its allies of England's strength. He concluded that American ideals could not survive an unsuccessful war.

It was obvious Lindbergh was readying a candidacy, whether for the Senate seat in Minnesota or the Congressional seat in New York no one knew, but this is what he was about. For all I know, Lindbergh may have thought he had a chance at the Republican nomination in 1944. He was on the move.

The day after Lindbergh's Manhattan Center speech, a reporter asked Roosevelt why Lindbergh wasn't called to the service. After all, Lindbergh was a colonel in the Reserve, and the Draft Act was summoning thousands of young men as inductees; National Guard units were already shipping overseas.

Roosevelt replied that during the Civil War, Lincoln did not call Vallandigham to colors. Vallandigham led the Northern Copperheads. A military tribunal, said Roosevelt, tried Vallandigham and, convicting the Representative from Ohio, banished him to the Confederate States.

Lindbergh resigned his commission immediately, which led Stephen T. Early, Roosevelt's press secretary, to ask: "He is sending his commission to the Secretary of War. That leads me to wonder is he sending his decorations back to Hitler?"

On September 12, 1941, the day Roosevelt ordered the Navy to shoot first if Axis raiders entered our defending zones, Lindbergh made a speech in Des Moines, Iowa, charging: "The three most important groups pressing this country toward war are the British, the Jews, and the Roosevelt Administration." Generously, he invited Jews to oppose the war because they would be the first to face its consequences, which sounded more like a threat than a welcome. "[The Jewish] danger," he said, "lies in their large ownership and influence in our motion pictures, our press, our radio and our government."

A month later he was in Madison Square Garden at an America First rally. The people in the galleries sang "Columbia, the Gem of the Ocean" over and over again. I stood in a hotel across the way watching 30,000 people who could not get seats in the Garden raise their voices in chorus.

The Depression started with men on bread lines and ended with the same men stamping around Madison Square Garden, cheering a sane, rational, courageous figure who thought if America could control the Jews, it would live happily ever after, as though there were no airplanes which could fly the Atlantic.

The anti-Semitism that menaced Jews in the 1930's diminished in World War II. The war unified the country. Thousands of young men who had served all over the world went from Army barracks into colleges. More, the war put money into people's pockets for the first time in their lives.

The economic revolution engineered by Roosevelt became the income revolution, and for the first time policemen and teachers, garmentworkers and mechanics, factory hands and poets, made enough to save money, acquire property, educate children, pay orthodonty bills.

Last, anti-Semitism abated because Americans are not *natural* Jew haters. One hears anti-Semitic remarks more than one would like, one is often distressed by patent anti-Semitism, but anti-Semitism has never been as respectable in America as it has been in Europe. There is no native anti-Semitism; all of it is of European variety, descended to us through the countless immigrants who bring it with them as my mother brought "Oh, what memories!" with her.

Since the beginning of this century, it has not been necessary to hate the Jew for what he allegedly did 2,000 years ago but for what he might do in the future, which is to take over the world by one or another political or financial stratagems.

As a matter of fact, anti-Semitism has little religious life anymore, thanks to the publication of the *Schema on the Jews,* in which the Vatican's Ecumenical Council decided to absolve the Jews from the guilt of having crucified Jesus.

There is no minimizing the goodwill and nobility of purpose

that inspired both Pope John XXIII and Pope Paul VI. For that reason, I published in my *Carolina Israelite* an open letter to the Jewish leaders of the world calling for a *Jewish* ecumenical council in Jerusalem. At that time the Jews could issue a *Schema on the Christians.*

It is our turn, I said, to forgive the Christians for the Inquisition, the Crusades, the ghettos, and the expulsions. I think we can also include forgiveness for the usurpation of property that continued for 1,600 years, the worldwide discrimination; we should also waive our annoyances at the barriers that guard country and city, fraternal and luncheon clubs, resort hotels, and college fraternities.

There is no reason for us to hold bitterness in our hearts because Crusader Godfrey of Bouillon drove the Jews of Jerusalem into the synagogue and set it on fire. There is no reason our Christian neighbors should be held responsible for the wholesale slaughter of the Jews in the cities on the Rhine by the Christians of the Second Crusade. Nor should they be held responsible for the murders perpetrated by Peter the Hermit and Peter of Cluny.

And why should we let the memory of the Inquisition haunt us?

This was one of the most widely quoted of my editorials which I believe buttresses my point that anti-Semitism is abating in America.

In Berlin during the 1960's one of the remarks Germans who had been to America always made to me was that they had heard the families with whom they visited remark that the one thing Hitler was right about was the Jews. The motive behind the statement was that they, the Germans, were wiser than the Americans because they knew that Hitler was wrong. We know, however, the Germans are liars, liars because they are guilty. No doubt some Americans said as much—but they are a small minority. One has only to study American foreign policy to realize Americans are not isolationist: It just happened that in two wars the enemy was Germany.

Americans do not think Hitler was right about the Jews, any more than they think some Arabs are right in punishing thieves by chopping off their right hand.

The victory Hitler wanted I believe he won. The next pogrom will start with the gas chambers. I doubt seriously that Americans are at all concerned with Jews as I write. We are all concerned with Negroes. The Jew does not need the Gentile's willingness of heart today; the Negro does. I believe the Negro will find it. I would like him to find it sooner rather than later, but I am convinced the black man will find it.

Chapter 19

I was in prison for nearly four years. Whether a man is gone because of a war, or because he must travel for his livelihood, or because he is in prison, four years eventually become crucial to a marriage. An absence that long can rend a marriage. A woman who has to run a home and family without her husband, will find when he returns that no matter how well she managed, there are things he would have done that she didn't do.

Tiny did not have much choice; she had to live with those who would take her in—her family. They sheltered her. They were kind and generous and warm, yet they held certain values to which I could not subscribe, just as I held values which to them were alien. While I was in jail, however, it was their values to which Tiny and my boys were constantly exposed. It is no one's fault but mine, yet none of us, I submit, applaud our faults.

When I left to serve my sentence, Tiny got a job right away with the Bankers National Life Insurance Company, which was located first in Jersey City and then in Montclair, New Jersey. She was a department supervisor. She confided in no one about me. Toward the end, when my time was almost up, she told her boss, who said that he was sure he could make arrangements to put me on as a salesman.

For as long as I was in prison, I begged her not to visit me, as indeed many other men beg wives, sweethearts and mothers, not wanting their loved ones to see them behind bars. Thus, when I did come home, and she told me excitedly I had a job with

Bankers National, she was naturally astonished when I replied I had no intention of selling insurance. That wasn't at all what I wanted. I was just past thirty, and I had decided in prison that life was not just something I was going to make the best of. I was sorry for what I had done but could not bring myself to put away ambition. I wanted to become a journalist and no more could have brought myself to sell insurance than I could have brought myself to go back into a brokerage.

Separations do that to people: They forget what each other is like. Three years, eight months, and twenty-two days is a long time. People change.

Let no one doubt Tiny's loyalty; she was a dutiful wife, a good mother, and a forgiving woman. To this day, she believes Charles Tuttle railroaded me.

What now intruded on our marriage was our religious differences. Tiny knew what Jews were, as I knew what Irishmen were. It didn't make much difference in 1926.

But now there was a difference, and the difference was Adolf Hitler. Hitler made people conscious of Jews twenty-four hours a day. We Jews realized that there were people who had never met a Jew but who hated and feared us. Where a hotel with a policy of a restricted clientele once made guests simply snobs, now it made them proud and secure. Hitler gave anti-Semitism a political career all its own. No longer was anti-Semitism a religious issue, and religious issues are often boring issues; now anti-Semitism was a day-by-day political tactic for many. Because anti-Semitism had become this, it made Jew after Jew more and more conscious of his Jewishness.

I was no different from other Jews; involuntarily I had learned I was different from other men, and voluntarily I tried to find out why. But it was hard for me to be a Jew with my children raised as Roman Catholics. Nor were they nominally Roman Catholics—since they had a Jewish father, it was determined by others they were to become more Catholic than the Pope.

Like most continuing arguments between husband and wife, this one started in bitterness. Tiny said, "You signed an agreement when you married me that I could rear the children as Catholics."

I admitted signing the agreement, but I also said, "We are not two partners arguing over profits. We are parents, husband and

210

wife. A lot of agreements go by the board with husband and wife. We do not hold each other to every promise."

"It's not fair for you to argue you did not know what you were signing," she said. "I explained it to you. The priest explained it to you. You said you understood."

"I didn't sign an agreement that I would hang a crucifix in the hall or hang a picture of Jesus in the bedroom, did I?"

With that, I threw them out.

Not the actions of a rational man, I admit. Men who sign contracts which are disadvantageous are rarely rational in trying to escape contractual clauses. Religion is, moreover, supremely dear to men. Jews have died over and over again for the faith, and Christians have willingly gone to the stake for their beliefs. So I was not always fair. I remember writing the boys a long letter belittling and condemning the Catholic Church, saying things about Catholics which are no more true than some of the things Catholics say about Jews.

Religion became more than a touchy subject; it became a divisive force moving us apart. Tiny may not have been particularly devout—I tend to believe Catholics who marry Jews are not, just as Jews who marry Catholics are not—but her family was. Their thinking had as profound an influence on Tiny as my family's thinking had on me. To add fuel to the fire, we had the only boys on both sides (in the 1940's, Max had a son named Larry). That my father would never sit on the dais in a shul and hear a grandson read the Talmud was a disappointment. While he was not fervently religious, he loved his family, and a bar mitzvah celebrates not only the admission of another man to the congregation but the whole idea and comfort of a family.

One Saturday night my son Buddy—Harry junior—told me tomorrow he and Richard were making their first communion. They had been studying the catechism for two months. As much as I recall of the matter, they had studied their catechism with a lady who taught retarded Catholic children. I suppose as Jews this qualified my boys for her classes.

Tiny had a sister who never stopped worrying about my sons' immortal souls. All of Tiny's immediate relatives worried about their faith. They worried: Would the boys make their first communion on time? Their confirmation? To what parochial schools would they go? I argued with Genevieve that her brothers, Hubert, Jim, and Nolan, all had attended public high schools; they had gone to nonsectarian colleges; why did it have to be my sons who went to Catholic schools?

"Can you imagine these boys going to St. Peter's Prep?" I asked. "Isn't it an absurdity to send little boys named Goldhurst into a Catholic environment?"

Their playmates told them they were Jewish; the nuns told them they were Jewish; certainly their uncles and their aunts admitted as much. The boys were already different in their way; why compound the differences?

To which Tiny would reply, "You married a convent school girl."

It was incomprehensible to me that the Gallaghers would insist these boys be arch-Catholics. It was, I suppose, incomprehensible to them that they not be. Still, it seems to me had I been a drunken Irishman who beat her, had lost my faith, no Gallagher would have dared interfere with the way I reared my family. They interfered because I was Jewish. The boys were uncomfortable in church, and the Gallaghers kept assuring them this would pass. It doesn't pass necessarily, and it had less chance of passing in the 1930's than ever.

Billy came home from St. Aloysius with a copy of Father Coughlin's *Social Justice*. Coughlinites hawked this magazine in front of churches and parochial schools. The anti-Semitism outraged me. Tiny cried and said, "I'm going to write to the bishop and ask him why he's letting this go on." I felt sorry for her then, very sorry.

At St. Peter's Prep School an Army major addressed the assembly, explaining the different components of the military services. When he mentioned the Quartermaster Corps, all the boys hooted, "That's where the Jews are." Buddy had to listen to this.

The Coughlinites were everywhere in those years. One of their favorite tricks was to station a small boy on the corner crying his heart out. When people gathered to question him, the boy would bawl, "A big fat Jew hit me and took all my copies of *Social Justice*." It was effective.

I do not mean to insist that all Catholics subscribed to the sentiments of Father Coughlin. I know they did not. But one Coughlinite was too much, and I thought it was trying enough to tolerate the presence of Coughlinites on the street without having to sit with them in class. I had no redress. I could have told a public school principal this was wrong and won the point. I couldn't tell a Jesuit dean.

Father Coughlin was a Canadian-Irish priest, a not unusual American phenomenon: He had a large following but no constituency. He made his broadcasts on Sunday afternoons at 2 P.M., and if professional football and television had come to us a generation earlier, we would never have heard of him. He was a "funny-money" man with quack prescriptions for our economic ills.

In 1936 he started a third party, the Union Party, which proposed the election of William Lemke, a Congressman from North Dakota, for the Presidency. Mr. Lemke didn't receive a tenth of the votes expected. Fewer than 1,000,000 people wanted him in preference to either Landon or Roosevelt. After this defeat Coughlin turned to the International Jewish conspiracy. He reprinted the *Protocols of the Learned Elders of Zion* in his *Social Justice*. He organized platoons of Christian Fronts, each platoon consisting of 25 dedicated men, all shabby, ill-educated, ill-informed, marginal people victimized by their own and by society's weakness.

While I am no authority on another man's motives, I do believe that one of the reasons Buddy, an experienced newspaperman, refused a transfer to the Army daily during the Korean War, insisting instead on staying with the artillery, is that as a Jew he had to offer proof of his patriotism. I believe one of the reasons Richard became a paratrooper in World War II was a similar desire to prove he was as patriotic and as brave as the next man.

Tiny had her side, too. I refused any accommodation. I used to tell the boys there was no God. I was an agnostic who never tired of preaching. Trying to decide which of contending parents has the truth is no way to guarantee emotional stability in children. In the end, I had my way, for the boys run secular households. I don't know that any of them go to church at all. Perhaps then my worry about what Catholicism would do to them was premature.

Still these issues die hard. In 1953, Richard succeeded in publishing his first piece, an essay describing the attitudes engendered in growing up between two worlds—Catholic and Jewish. *Commentary* magazine, which is subsidized by the American Jewish

Committee and is strictly for the intellectuals, published the article.

Because Richard was dealing with his father and his mother, he asked *Commentary* to publish the essay anonymously. One way or another, the editors knew he was my son, and they inferred that Richard Goldhurst was his pseudonym, to everyone's distress. I was annoyed and angry because in describing some unflattering attitudes about my family, he used Clara as an example, changing her name to Clair, which I did not think a particularly daring exercise of imagination. Tiny was angry because she thought he was not exact, that he was unfair, in describing some of her family's attitudes. She was angry enough, in fact, to write all her relatives *and mine* that she was not responsible for what Richard said.

Max called me to ask, "Harry, where in hell do I buy this magazine *Commentary*? I've been to four newspaper stands already, and they never heard of it."

Eventually, Tiny and I agreed that the abuse was more imagined than real. After all, the boy hadn't turned over the car; he wasn't in trouble with the police; he didn't have a girl in trouble. How irate can two people be over a son's contributing essays to an intellectual and arcane monthly? One of his Irish uncles, however, never talked to him again.

Richard was in the 11th Airborne Division during the war, one of the paratroopers who occupied Japan after the atom bombs were dropped on Hiroshima and Nagasaki. He was graduated in 1950 from Kenyon College in Gambier, Ohio, where he had majored in Greek and Latin and went to the Princeton University Graduate College. He took another degree, this time in philosophy at New York University, where he was a teacher. But he left the academic world and became an Off-Broadway stage manager and a television extra.

Later he moved to Hartford, where he arranged poetry series and movie series and helped stage such touring companies as the Inbal Dancers and John Gielgud's evening of Shakespeare, *The Ages of Man*. One of the first large fees I ever received for a lecture came through Richard's offices. I asked him once how he liked the job, and he replied he liked it fine, except sometimes he had trouble with his committee. When I asked him what was wrong with the committee, he replied they were all wealthy middle-aged Jewish ladies: "When one of them has a hot flash, *everybody* has a hot flash."

I hired Richard as my associate editor in 1958. He has collaborated with me ever since on the *Israelite* and on my books *Carl Sandburg, Forgotten Pioneer, Mr. Kennedy and the Negroes,* and *A Little Girl Is Dead.* He published his own novel in the 1960's, *The Deceivers,* and last fall, Dial Press brought out his second book, *The Dark Side of the House.*

Harry junior, went to Belmont Abbey College in Belmont, North Carolina, just outside Charlotte. He took a job one summer as a copyboy on the Charlotte *Observer* and step by step worked himself up until he was the city hall reporter. He was drafted in June, 1950, and assigned to the 29th Division. He spent two years overseas and was a master sergeant in a field artillery battalion.

From Charlotte the Knight newspaper chain sent him to Detroit, and after several years on the *Free Press* he moved to the Chicago *Sun-Times,* where he is the city hall editor.

His headlines are poetry. Billy Graham, the evangelist, came to Charlotte in 1949, at the end of the tobacco season, when all the farmers are in town, having sold their crops. That night at the revival meeting a pickpocket lifted the considerable "bakky" money from a grower. Buddy's headline was A ROLE IS CALLED UP YONDER. On another occasion a Charlotte minister ran off with two underaged girls. I have never understood the equation, but over the years I have noticed that ministers run away with one choirmistress or two underaged girls. The clergyman was apprehended in Nashville. Buddy described his return with the headline MINISTER TO FACE RAPE RAP.

I have relied on Buddy to edit and arrange my books of essays— *Only in America, For 2¢ Plain, Enjoy, Enjoy!, So What Else Is New?, Ess, Ess, Mein Kindt,* and *The Best of Harry Golden.*

William, the youngest, is an associate professor of the humanities at the University of Florida. He, like his brother Richard, was graduated from Kenyon College, in 1953, and took his MA in English at Columbia University. He taught at Ohio State, moved then to Newcomb College at Tulane, where he got his PhD. For several years he was a professor of English at the University of Puerto Rico before coming to Gainesville.

Billy is our F. Scott Fitzgeraldnik. He wrote *F. Scott Fitzgerald and His Contemporaries* in 1963, which World published, and he has been a steadfast subscriber and contributor to the *F. Scott Fitzgerald Newsletter*, founded by his friend and colleague Broccoli, whose name I can not resist including in this autobiography.

Billy had also published the textbook *Contours of Experience*, now in use in several colleges.

Billy is a *tummeler*. A *tummeler* is a personable fellow employed by the hotelkeeper in the Catskills to see that bored guests are constantly amused and distracted. The *tummeler* is a combination of court jester and acrobat, waxing enthusiastic about shuffleboard and horseback riding early in the day, playing the guitar and the piano when the guests, exhausted by their pleasure, lounge by the pool in the evening. The Catskills' loss is the academy's gain. Billy is captivating when he explains the verbal mechanics of a twelfth-century madrigal, the only man I know who, if he doesn't make twelfth-century madrigals as zesty as *My Fair Lady*, still keeps your attention.

When the boys were young, they helped fill the house with their friends. I realized nothing distresses a child like shame he feels for his parents. That compulsion to explain a mother or a father to a playmate may not be traumatic, but it is still painful. Tiny and I had an arrangement between ourselves that while the boys and the playmates were in the house, we would discuss only school and books, music and baseball. We would never disagree in front of the boys and their friends. I pass this advice along to those who want it: There are no secrets in a marriage, but you don't have to tell the children everything.

If my sons are men of substance who have saved their money and own their own homes because, as Tiny puts it, "They want to *be* somebody," then they have her to thank for it. Religious differences were not the only despair to invade our home.

In November, 1938, Tiny and I had another son, named Peter. Within a week of his birth Peter suffered a convulsion, the first of many he was to suffer during his life. He was badly retarded and spent almost all his life institutionalized. Despite brain and spinal operations, we were never able to determine the precise nature of his disability. Peter had a lack of brain cells, but why he lacked them we never knew.

He was nineteen when he died at the Wassaic Home in New York. When he was eight or nine, the presence of his mother so distressed him that she ceased visiting. Because Peter was never sentient, Catholic theology presumed he never knew sin, and the priest at Wassaic read the mass of angels at his funeral. If it comforts anyone, the mass of angels is all right with me. Tiny and Dick and Hubert Gallagher went to the funeral. Certainly this trip proved a sympathy and great kindness on Hubert's part since his only child, a son, had been stillborn a few months before.

It seems unnecessary here to try to detail the sadness and pity we felt for Peter. Parents who have undergone the same accident know the sadness and pity too well, and parents who have not cannot imagine them. It's one kind of grief to lose a son; another to have realized he never really lived.

Complicating all this was the fact that during the 1930's I was always broke. Money is often the ultimate factor in any marriage, and the lack of it is devastating. We did not know poverty—Tiny worked until we moved to River Plaza—but we knew that middle-class hopelessness of going nowhere, that hypocrisy of pretending we had enough when we knew we didn't.

Many times I came home on Friday night to say, "Tiny, the Markwell couldn't pay me this week." There would be no money in the house, and we would have to borrow from friends and neighbors, getting the money sometimes with a postdated check. With some of that money, I'd buy a bottle of liquor, which led Tiny to complain, "There might be no milk in the refrigerator, but there's a bottle of whiskey in the house." I did not bother to argue that liquor is one of the cheapest and most available of all anodynes, nor did I say that cold sobriety isn't much of a help.

There were mornings at the Red Bank Railroad Station when I did not have the $14.70 to buy the monthly commutation ticket. When the conductor stopped by my seat, I told him nonchalantly I had left my ticket at home. I paid him the single dollar for the ride. He always gave me a receipt, which the ticket agent would discount against the price of the commuter's ticket. I am sure the conductors were aware of the situation. I was not the only man in those days without $14.70 who needed the good graces of a train conductor to preserve his dignity. The conductors pocketed the $1, and the trip back and forth for the next twenty-five days cost $50, instead of $14.70. The most embarrassing aspect of the Depression was handing over that $1 with the aplomb of a man who has a million in the bank.

217

I used to cadge money from Tiny's relatives, from Hubert Gallagher and from Dorothy Gallagher Deegan. Sometimes I didn't have the courage to say I needed it. I had to have it to pay the fuel bill, so I'd kite a check, knowing it wasn't going to be good. It would take me months to pay it off, time extended me because these people were relatives and understanding. Many years later Tiny asked Hubert if he would like an autographed copy of *Only in America,* and he said, "I certainly would, though I have enough of Harry's signature on paper to last anyone a lifetime."

We had to demean ourselves often. We had to buy food on credit, and when our bill ran too high, we had to go to another store. When I had some cash, I couldn't frequent our usual butcher because he would expect some of the money to reduce our bill. I would go to a stranger instead.

Poor people do not stay together because they are in love. They stay together often because they cannot possibly afford to live apart; without money, life is dangerous and threatening. Living under a single roof may not banish these threats and dangers, it may not guarantee survival, but the single roof offers at least the next morning, though the night is spent in despair.

One of the reasons I went South in 1941 was that I got a job there which would enable me to send money home every week. By that time, anyway, I realized Tiny and I were estranged. When I went South, times had improved. Tiny went back to work, first as a bookkeeper in Ford's Edgewater plant in New Jersey, where she stayed until the war ended, and then as an office manager for a successful printer named Martin Linzer, for whom she worked for almost two decades. Martin Linzer could leave his office every day, sell his accounts, recruit new business, sure that Tiny could handle all the troubles that beset any printer: union difficulties, lost shipments, rush orders, and broken machinery. Within a week of Mr. Linzer's retirement in 1963 another printer named Fred Dubin implored Tiny to come work for him in the same capacity, and there she still works.

In 1961, Tiny and I signed a separation agreement. The separation, however, has always been amicable. I see her as often as I come to New York, and she never forgets my birthday.

When it came time for me to leave for the South, I went with the dreaded knowledge that I had failed as a man, a father, and a husband. All my hopes should have worked out, and not one of them had. I was smart enough; I'd gotten a good start, married a fine woman and had healthy sons. Now—nothing. I can blame circumstances only to a certain degree for these failures; the rest of the fault was mine. Perhaps I should have headed South promptly upon my release from prison. I would have done no worse there than I did in the big city.

I had learned some things, however. I learned that there is no center of gravity in American middle-class life. The carpenter will want to become the builder, and the builder the contractor, and the contractor will eventually want whole cities named after him. We are unable to find nirvana, the extinction of desire, its cessation, I suspect, because our glandular system works only as long as the prospect of more is there to stimulate us.

I also learned the things told me as a child were really true, the first of which is that there is only one woman in the world who will do. By no means do I insist that this woman will make you happy, but it is a corollary that subsequent women will make you no more comfortable. If you can't get along with the first one, you won't be much more successful with those who follow.

If we all lived in Plato's republic, and the state collected all the newborn and shuffled them off to a work farm, and we accepted this as part of the natural order of things, then I think we all should marry one woman when we're twenty, another when we're thirty, another at forty, and another at the turn of each decade. Fathers and mothers so far have insisted that they, and not the state, will rear their offspring. Which means the family is better off together than apart.

It is true that many men and women feel divorce is not so much a selfish as a sanitary matter, that without divorce they will lose their equilibrium. I worry about them. My heart always welled with pity for Tommy Manville who never understood the furniture of life. I remember an easy chair I hated. It was new and had usurped an older and more comfortable chair. I learned to live around that chair. I never sat in it. I never commented on how ugly I thought it. It partially blocked passage from the living room to the hall. I never said, "The damn thing is in my way." That chair was *there*. I imagine personal unhappiness much in the shape and substance of that chair—you must learn to live around it, trying not to notice it. If you insist on noticing it, you will have to sit in it.

God, insists the Talmud, is a maker of marriages. I thought I would let Him figure it out, and He has. Had I not let Him, I would have wound up just as unhappy as poor Thorstein Veblen, the eminent economist who outlined the drive toward conspicuous consumption in his classic *The Theory of the Leisure Class.* Veblen wound up teaching at a California university with a wife at one end of the campus and a girlfriend at the other.

"I'm not happy with your marital situation," the president of the university told him.

"Neither am I," sighed Veblen.

Chapter 20

Just why we thought the World's Fair of 1939 was going to bring a freshening wind into our financial doldrums no one to this day knows. The World of Tomorrow came and went and left us still shoaling. But the prospects of the fair excited everyone in New York, particularly the men with whom I was in close contact—hotelmen, newspaper reporters, restaurateurs, merchants—all thought New York would be inundated by hundreds of thousands of tourists, all the tourists recklessly spending money, all of us getting rich. Hundreds of thousands of tourists did not come, and of the thousands who did, few seemed disposed toward reckless spending. People came to the fair from Scranton, Pennsylvania, and went home the same day. Excursion trains brought in groups from Pittsburgh, who, as soon as they had seen the General Motors Exhibit, went back home on the same day, too. There were tourists who never touched the sidewalks of the city.

At the Markwell my brother Jake raised the rent of all his permanent tenants in the hope they would move. They obliged him. They left, bag and baggage. Most of the show girls and actors on Broadway fled to the upper Manhattan rooming houses, vacating their $8-, $10-, and $12-a-week rooms. Jake thought hotel-owners would get this rate once a night instead of once a week. After the World's Fair opened, Jake was promising to pay the cab fare back downtown if these actresses and actors would only come home again to the Markwell.

There was a lady tenant in the hotel named Hazel who lived in

221

a large, outside room which cost $9 a week. Frank Costello paid her room rent. In all the years I gave him receipts, he never went upstairs. He came in every Monday, paid the rent, and talked to Hazel over the house telephone. When Hazel came down to the lobby, he handed her an envelope. I suspected Hazel was the widow of one of Frank Costello's henchmen, but this was only a guess. Nobody asked Costello questions.

A few months before the fair opened, Jake told Hazel her room rent would be raised to $20. The following Monday Costello came into the hotel. After a few polite inquiries, Jake agreed to transfer Hazel to a smaller room which had ordinarily let at $7 but was now $12.

Some time elapsed. Costello said one morning, "Hazel, she tellsa me her old room it'sa still empty." Costello was right. The room from which the desk had chased Hazel was unfortunately unoccupied. Each Monday Costello reported this fact. About the fifth time, Jake said, "All right, Mr. Costello, tell Hazel to move back into the big room." Mr. Costello smiled as he phoned Hazel. "Hazel, go back to the big room and at the old rate, too."

The trouble with staging a World's Fair in New York City is that it is both presumptuous and absurd to invite people to come to the eighth wonder of the world, expose them to the Empire State Building, the Rockettes at Radio City Music Hall, the museums, the Metropolitan Opera House, and Carnegie Hall, and tell them they will have more fun out in a swamp called Flushing Meadows looking at the reproduction of a baby in embryo. It will not work. It did not work for the World of Tomorrow with its symbols of the trylon and the perisphere, and it did not work in 1964 for Peace Through Understanding with its symbol of the stainless-steel globe.

I myself had visions of becoming a successful public relations man through the World's Fair. While at the *Daily Mirror,* I conceived the idea of publishing a New York City directory to be distributed free to all the out-of-towners staying at the hotels. I could finance the directory by selling advertisements. There was no reason why I couldn't make a huge success out of this venture. I knew all the hotelmen, and my job at the *Mirror* gave me easy access to all the advertisers.

Damn it, it was a good idea—if only world's fairs were successful. When I broached the idea to the executives of Childs Res-

222

taurants, they hired me on the spot for a week's work. I was to escort one of their executives to all the hotels and introduce him to the managers. The executive would try to persuade the manager to tack up a plaque in the elevator reading THE NEAREST CHILDS RESTAURANT IS . . . and then proceed to give explicit directions for reaching it. Childs would be happy to pay a nominal fee for this privilege.

It seemed that every executive at Childs Restaurants was an Irishman, and the executive whom I escorted was named Mr. O'Hara. We went to the Chesterfield Hotel, and I said, "Phil Goldstein is the manager." We went to the Lincoln, and I said, "Abe Garfunkel is the manager." Then we went to the Midtown Hotel, and I said, "William Mahoney is the manager." O'Hara's eyes looked like two mazda bulbs. As often as we met an Irishman, O'Hara and he would spend two hours gossiping about whose sister was a nun and in what order cousins had taken priestly vows.

Between us, O'Hara and I sold a large number of hotels on the plan, and Childs invested a substantial sum in the manufacture of tasteful plaques which decorated many a midtown hotel elevator while a hunter could shoot deer in the empty restaurants.

For my directory I charged $50 a full page. I sold all the sightseeing tours, many of the restaurants, the movie houses, and many others. Optimistically I had 100,000 directories printed and distributed. I even paid for the signs which said TAKE ONE FREE.

The World's Fair peaked on opening day, with Franklin D. Roosevelt's address. From then on, it was downhill all the way. The patriots among the opening-day crowd discovered that the worker brandishing a sickle atop the Russian Exhibit was two inches higher than the pole from which flew the American flag. The Russians did not appear eager to chisel the worker down, so the fair authorities had to install a new flagpole two feet higher to preserve diplomatic protocol.

The only New Yorker who made money on the World's Fair was Billy Rose, who operated the Aquacade, where pretty girls in bathing suits swam ballet patterns in a big pool from which raked bleachers ascended. I met Billy Rose a few times before his death and told him once I was thrilled to meet a man who made money on the 1939 World's Fair.

"I thought of a cool place where people could sit down with their kids on a hot day," is how Billy Rose explained it. The

223

Aquacade neted him thousands of dollars every week. But he went on to tell me it wasn't all peaches and cream.

"I had to sue a man who was trying to horn in on me by calling his place Billy Rose's Concession."

"Did you win the suit?" I asked.

"No," said Billy Rose. "The guy defended himself in court by insisting his name really was Billy Rose and my name really was Billy Rosenberg. He told the judge I had a hell of a nerve suing him, and the judge agreed."

Dick, Bill, Bud, and I had come into the city one Saturday night, when we stayed at the Markwell so we could get an early start for a tour of the fair in the morning. As we crossed almost-deserted Forty-second Street at 7 A.M., the New York *Times* news billboard flicked on, and we read that England had declared war, and the French declaration was expected shortly. The World's Fair was throwing a party at the worst possible time for a celebration.

I did not become a successful public relations man. Throughout 1939, 1940, and up to 1941 I wrote and sold promotional advertising, first for the *Mirror,* then for the New York *Post.* At the *Post* I answered an ad for a promotional salesman to work in Norfolk, Virginia. The ad had been placed by the *Times-Advocate,* which wanted a space salesman able to write the copy, do the layout, and generally expedite the puffs the paper would publish during the year. A puff is a special section published, say, to celebrate the town's centennial birthday or the erection of a new civic center for which special ads are sold and special copy written.

The *Times-Advocate* offered appreciably more money than I was making, $60 a week. Hughie McKay, the publisher, hired me. I told Tiny this was a real chance. If I could succeed in Norfolk, perhaps we could move the family down there soon. With one suitcase, I took the Greyhound bus to Norfolk.

Before I reported to work at the *Times-Advocate,* I had resolved to change my name from Goldhurst to Golden. Virginia was Bishop Cannon's home state. He was still in the news. Changing my name, I guessed correctly, would save both the Bishop and me occasional embarrassments. I did not want to have to explain over and over again the extent of my relationship to the Bishop, nor did I want potential advertisers to know that the space salesman to whom they were giving orders had served a federal prison sentence. In New York City a man who wants anonymity can have it; this is not always true in the South, rarely true about anyone who has achieved notoriety. So I hid my prison record by adopting another name, the hiding of which caused me pain many years later, but for almost twenty years the hiding made many things easier.

I was at the *Times-Advocate* for about eight months, during which time I did a job for John L. Lewis, the head of the United Mine Workers. The UMW published an annual report of its activities for which I sold the advertising and oversaw its publication. As a consequence, I met Lewis several times, and we enjoyed each other's company. Coal was King then, and John L. Lewis was one of the three most powerful labor leaders in the country.

What surprised me about his accomplishments was his vast knowledge of Shakespeare. He was a supreme Shakespearian scholar and had probably committed to memory as much of the Shakespeare corpus as the great Kittredge of Harvard. He told me once with a wink that he had finally found the authority who explains the reasons for Hamlet's delay and for his melancholia. "A lady teacher out in Indiana," Lewis told me, "has it all down. Everything is due to the fact Hamlet doesn't want to get married. This lady proves it by correcting the punctuation. She says the line doesn't read, 'O all you host of heaven! O earth! What else? And shall I couple hell?' She says it goes, 'O all you host of heaven! O earth! What else? And shall I couple? Hell!' "

John L. Lewis had even mastered the Shakespearian phrase. The United Mine Workers were threatening a strike which President Franklin D. Roosevelt was trying to avert. Failing an easy solution, Roosevelt remarked, "A plague on both your houses."

Said Lewis, "It ill behooves a man who has supped at labor's table to condemn with equal venom the hostile neighbor and the genial host."

Of the union, he said, "The life of a miner used to be ten years in the pits. Now it's twenty-seven years. That is what I gave my men—seventeen years of life." As often as we discussed these matters, he worried about strip mining, which was just coming in then. Strip mining is coal mining without the pits; it is the process whereby machines scrape coal from the earth starting on the surface and plowing down.

"If no one stops it," he said, "the government will someday

225

have to spend millions of dollars to fill up the pockmarks all over the coal country."

Many years later, when my book *Only in America* was published, I visited Lewis in his home in Pittsburgh. He had retired, now an old man. I inscribed the book: "To John L. Lewis in memory of a pleasant association." When I asked if he missed the UMW, he reminded me of his prophecy. "I see where the government is spending even more than I supposed to fill up the holes the strip operators gouged. Yes, I miss it. If I were back, the public would know to the penny how much it costs them to let operators strip coal."

Toward the end of 1941 I received an offer from William Witter, the publisher of the Charlotte *Labor Journal*. He offered me a job selling space *and* writing editorials. Thus I came to Charlotte, North Carolina.

William Witter, whom everybody called Old Man Witter, was not quite five feet six inches tall. He was wiry and tough, without question the best journalist I ever met and without question the best drinker. Old Man Witter taught me how to drink white lightning, the famous bootleg whiskey of North Carolina—180 proof. There was a family in the western part of the state famous for distilling this corn liquor. The name of the family was Mull, and they delivered a gallon of white lightning to our offices every week. Witter put a teaspoon of granulated sugar into a glass, added ice, then filled half the glass with Mull's and half with water, sprinkling several lemon drops into the mixture. Behold! The finest drink in the world.

The gallon came in a porcelain cask which had a faucet. One summer day a girl came over from the Charlotte *Observer* with a mat we had been awaiting. She saw the cask, thought it was water, and filled up a Dixie cup before Witter and I noticed her mistake. Too late! She gulped it, coughed like a garroted Spaniard, and passed out soon afterward, dead drunk.

The Charlotte *Labor Journal* was on College Street, housed in the Chatham Building, owned by the man who manufactures Chatham Blankets. It was the official newspaper of the American Federation of Labor in North Carolina, and we published weekly. It was eight pages, half of which were editorials and reports on the labor movement in the Carolinas and half of which was advertising.

My father, Reb Lebche himself.

My mother.

The house I was born in, in Mikulintsy in the Galician province of the Austro-Hungarian Empire. The photograph was taken by my father on a trip there in 1928.

Me with Sister Clara. 1922.

Sister Matilda.

Brother Max, the insurance m and his wife, Ann.

Graduation Day at P.S. 20. I am the fifth one from the right, bottom row.

This is me as a student at CCNY and a member of the Round Table Literary Club. September, 1921.

On the roof of a Lower East Side tenement. Our orchestra: Harry Cantor, violin; Harry Golden, mandolin; Joe Cantor, clarinet; and Maurice Maisel, flute.

Me as an "athlete." 1923.

Genevieve Alice Marie Gallagher **Goldhurst.**

The Gallaghers, from left to right: Dorothy Gallagher Deegan, Jack Deegan, Evelyn Reilly Gallagher, Billy Goldhurst, Dick Goldhurst, Emma Nolan Gallagher, Hubert Gallagher, Buddy Goldhurst, Harry Golden, Mary Deegan, Tiny Gallagher Goldhurst. 1937.

The Larchmont house.

Richard, Harry, and Genevieve. 1928.

Sons Harry junior and Dick when they were young.

The three boys, Billy, Harry junior, and Dick.

The three boys: Dick, Bill the professor, and Harry junior.

Me with Harry junior and Dick. 19[

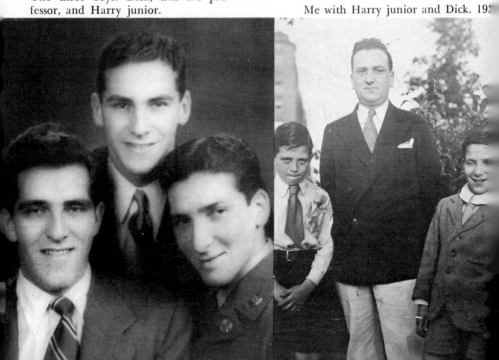

With the Mother Superior of Sacred Heart College at Belmont Abbey.

Premier David Ben-Gurion at a press conference on the eve of the Eichmann trial.

Autographing *For 2¢ Plain*, B. Altman's New York store, with my brother Jacob. Seated is May Hartman, the widow of Judge Gustave Hartman.

The party celebrating the sale of the 250,000th copy of *Only in America*. From left to right: Eleanor Rask, public relations director of the World Publishing Company; me; Genevieve; Ben Zevin, president of World; Mrs. Zevin. On the far right is Bill Targ, my editor; the rest are people from the staff of World. 1959.

Carl Sandburg and me in my office in Charlotte, North Carolina. *Photo/Declan Haun*

Carl Sandburg and me. Carl wrote about this picture: "We have just finished our matinee at the vaudeville house, had a good dinner and on the way to the Chinese laundry to get our laundry."

Photo/Don Hunter

Hubert Humphrey, David Dubinsky, and myself.

Addressing a joint labor council in Charlotte, North Carolina.

At a North Carolina Writers' Conference. From left to right: me, Clara Bell, Mack Bell, Burgwyn Mebane, Inglis Fletcher, and Bernice Kelly Harris.

Reception in the White House in honor of the hundredth anniversary of the Emancipation Proclamation.

Given to me by Ethel Kennedy, Christmas, 1968.

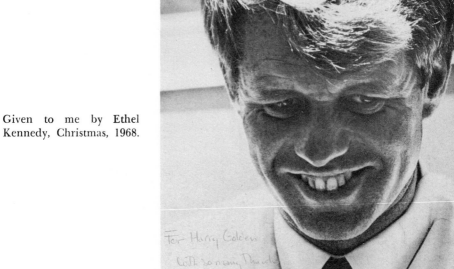

For Harry Golden
with so many thanks
from
B

Greeting President Johnson at a reception of editors. When I passed Mrs. Johnson, she said, "I've been a fan of yours for years."

Senator Jacob Javits and me.

Photo/Associated Photographers, Miami, Florida

Genevieve and me.

In Charlotte, North Carolina.

Photo/Tom Walters

The *Carolina Israelite* building.

The *Carolina Israelite* building after the fire.

With my secretary,
Maureen Titlow.

Photo/Tom Walters

Reading the last issue of the
Carolina Israelite.

Photo/Tom Walters

William Witter had been a newspaperman for forty years. Had he ever been able to overcome alcohol, he would have become governor. He was politically brilliant. Without the aid of polls, without recourse to the apparatus of the public media, he could predict within 1,000 votes why any election will go a certain way and the reasons why. I never knew him to be wrong.

Old Man Witter was married to Lula, a big, buxom woman who hated liquor with a passion Bishop Cannon might envy. Sunday was deprivation for William Witter because little labor news transpires and there was no need to open the office. He was constrained to stay at home. He always warned me on Saturday of my Sabbath duties: "Golden, on your way into town tomorrow morning, leave a bottle of Virginia Dare in my mailbox. Hear?"

Lula made William Witter account for every dollar. She doled out to him in exact amounts the change he needed for cigarettes, for lunch, for the newspaper, and she reviewed the checks he wrote for the expenses of the *Labor Journal*.

A local candidate named Strickland stopped at the office one afternoon during the campaign and paid Witter $150 in cash for a full-page advertisement. Strickland's appearance was propitious because Lula was out on a shopping tour. With the money in his pocket, Witter started to usher Strickland out of the office.

But Strickland was a garrulous fellow, who wanted to reminisce about the old days and how he had first run for public office in 1901. Witter kept laughing at the old clichés, always maneuvering Strickland closer and closer to the hall door. Before Witter could accomplish this purpose, Lula came steaming up the stairs, entered, and said casually, "How *you*, Mr. Strickland?"

"I just gave your husband one hundred and fifty dollars for a full-page ad, Miz Witter," Strickland said.

Resignedly, Witter took the crumpled bills from his pocket, laid them on the rolltop desk, and gave me the look Napoleon must have given his generals after Waterloo.

One night walking home, Witter stopped under the railroad viaduct which bridges College Street for one last snort before he came under the ever-watchful eyes of Lula. As he savored the white lightning, rolling it around his mouth, one of the water pipes overhead sprang a leak, and drops cascaded on Witter's suit. He looked into the road and said to himself, "Raining. Can't go home in this." He finished his bottle and fell asleep under the viaduct.

William Witter's daughter, Betty Phillips, called me one afternoon and said, "Mr. Golden, Father died today. Can you come out here right away?"

"When is the funeral?" I asked.

"Thursday."

"Why do you need me tonight?"

"We really do, Mr. Golden," she said.

Out I went, though it was far from a convenient trip for me. Betty and Lula served me coffee, and I talked to Frank Phillips, a Charlotte banker, Witter's son-in-law. Before he died, Witter had whispered to Mr. Phillips, "Have Golden write my obituary."

In the obit, I noted how William Witter, former linotype operator, the editor and publisher of the Charlotte *Labor Journal,* scrupulously obeyed an injunction served on him many years before. When he was a labor organizer, the Charlotte *Observer* had won an injunction enjoining Witter to walk on the other side of the street from where the newspaper's offices were located. Witter was proud of that injunction. He always crossed the street when he came to the *Observer.*

At labor conventions I attended, he was always introduced as "Old Man Witter who brought bread to the strikers at Shelby twenty-eight years ago!" Invariably the convention chairman approached and lifted up Witter's pants leg to expose an ugly scar. "That's the bullet wound Bill Witter took helping the strikers in High Point."

On one of these occasions, Mrs. Witter snorted to me, "Bullet wound, my foot! He got that when he broke his leg running out of an old-timey whorehouse."

Let no one doubt that William Witter played his part. Charlotte was better for his presence. So was the South. So was I.

I learned the Japanese had bombed Pearl Harbor in the boardinghouse room on Emerson Street in Charlotte. When I heard the radio broadcast, I remembered a letter I had written to my old boss Hughie McKay a few weeks before. I had said, "Japan will take the Philippines at the same time that Hitler bombs Hampton Roads, our naval base."

Hughie always took my predictions seriously, and he wrote that week, "Well, Golden, so far you are half way right. What do you suppose happened to Hitler?"

A young schoolteacher named Elizabeth Farrar lived down the hall from me. She was engaged to marry a fellow who had been drafted the year before. He expected to be discharged in February. That night at our boardinghouse supper table Elizabeth began to cry. She wondered when he would ever get out of the Army, when they would ever be married. There wasn't much the rest of us could say to comfort her. All of us knew it would be a long war. Yet Elizabeth's distress brought home the urgency of war to all of us: It was depriving two young people of what was a reasonable expectation in life.

A year later, however, Elizabeth married another fellow. I still meet her from time to time in downtown Charlotte, and she is inordinately proud of her grandchildren. I'll bet she never thinks of that young man who was stationed at Fort Bragg in 1941, only 50 miles from Charlotte. If he survived the war, I wonder how much he ever thinks about Elizabeth.

PART IV

Chapter 21

I WAS thirty-nine years old when I arrived in Charlotte, North Carolina; it was late at night at the Greyhound Terminal opposite the Charlotte post office. The WPA built the post office in the 1930's. It has an acre of lawn fronting it, shaded by tall trees. It is three stories high, federal courts occupying the upper floors. There are three entrances. The floor is marble. Standing desks opposite the postal windows line the center of the floor.

In a Southern town, in those years, a post office was more than a federal building. I myself have been in and out of the post office twice a day for twenty-eight years. I used to meet many of the businessmen in Charlotte there, for they came in to pick up their mail twice a day, too.

On hot Sunday afternoons, when I went to pick up the New York newspapers, I would see perhaps 100 men lounging on the lawn benches or along the low granite wall which surrounds the building. In talking to these men, I learned everything that had happened in Charlotte. In fact, many exciting events took place in front of the post office. Tom Jimison, an old newspaperman in Charlotte, stopped at the post office on his way home from covering a story in Asheville. He had a satchelful of bootleg whiskey, one of which was intended for me and Old Man Witter. As he swung the satchel, it hit the wall and the whiskey bottles broke. The police immediately arrested him. He was bailed out by Governor Cam Morrison. Cameron Morrison, one of the most successful Tarheel politicians, had been a Congressman, a member of the

Senate, and governor. He had also married a former nurse and widow of Mr. Watts, the tobacco tycoon, who had inherited millions of dollars, putting Cameron Morrison on easy street.

Before marrying Mrs. Watts, Governor Morrison had courted the widow of George Vanderbilt at Asheville, North Carolina. Cam was a tobacco-chewing man, and one day, while he was traveling with Mrs. Vanderbilt in her limousine, the window was so clean that he thought it was open and he let go with a splash of tobacco juice, and that ended the romance with Mrs. Vanderbilt.

All the whores frequented the post office. On a weekday evening, dozens of salesmen repaired to the post office to send in their reports to home offices in Cincinnati or New York or Chicago. The minute a whore saw a man drop that brown envelope in the brass out-of-town slot, she knew that he wasn't a cop and that he was probably lonely. The cheap night rates for long distance did more to subdue prostitution than all the vice crusades ever mounted.

As long as I have lived in Charlotte, I have never been able to determine its complex geography. No matter where I go, I always start out from the post office. If I am coming from my friends the Wallases on my way to visit the Wheelers, I always go back to the post office and start all over.

If you want to feel the milieu William Faulkner tried to create in his novels about Yoknapatawpha County, study a Southern post office on a hot afternoon when the heat bounces from the earth like a miasma and dogs dare not cross the street for fear of getting stuck in the melting tar. Idle men talk about the "niggers," Wall Street, and the best place to buy or steal a hound dog.

In 1941, Charlotte was 85,000 people in a city which encompasses a vast amount of land. In 1969 there were still huge vegetable farms and dairies within the city limits. During the 1930's, spurred on by their booster morality, the city administration kept absorbing more and more of the Charlotte perimeter, even though it was often to their disadvantage to do so, for it meant the installation of pipelines and telephone wires; it meant new schools and more policemen, more roads and parks. Charlotteans always nursed dreams of making their town the biggest city in the state, and the strategy of the 1930's proved more than successful. Charlotte now has more than 250,000 people, making it one of the largest cities in the whole South. It houses the branch offices of

234

virtually every major national concern from Avis to Xerox. It is also one of the major textile centers.

What has always fascinated me about Charlotte was that I was able to turn the stereotype inside out. I have been enthralled as I watched the Presbyterians, Methodists, and Baptists chase the buck. The Protestants *do* have all the money, and they go at it with an intensity unknown anywhere else in the civilized world.

Charlotte has four colleges: the University of North Carolina at Charlotte; Central Piedmont Community College; Queens College for women; and Johnson C. Smith University, a Negro university. Davidson College, where Woodrow Wilson went to school for a year and from which Dean Rusk was graduated, is 12 miles away.

Charlotte was the Confederate navy yard. One section of the city is still called the wharf. Confederates seized the Union ammunition and stores at Newport News and transported these overland to Charlotte. Since the South never managed to set in operation a shipbuilding yard, the stores were still intact when the Civil War ended with General Joseph Johnston's surrender to General William Tecumseh Sherman in North Carolina. The Confederate States of America maintained their mint in Charlotte, and the building is still preserved, known now as the Mint Museum, which has become the city's cultural center for theater and art.

There are more churches per capita in Charlotte than any other city in the Western world save Glasgow, Scotland. The worst traffic jams afflict the city on Sundays, when the pious venture to church. More policemen are on duty on Sunday than on any other day. Providence Road, where the churches line up one after another for a half mile, looks like a gigantic parking lot. The churches make the city physically attractive, even if our venereal and crime rates are out of proportion to our population. The land the churches occupy is usually extensive, and so the city seems filled with small parks.

On the night I arrived, I checked into the Willard Hotel. The next morning, when I went to work, all of Charlotte that I needed was contained in a few blocks. Looking over a Southern town is a strange sensation for any New Yorker. The tallest building in Charlotte was, I believe, the Barringer Hotel. Every other building was short and squat, although the spires of the churches towered. It was hard to realize I was in the center of the city and not on the outskirts. Life in a Southern city is never congested, the pace is more leisurely, which I think makes the girls prettier if not as stylish as the girls in the big cities, but the excitement of the city itself is never intense. I saw the Little Pep Delmonico and the Oriental restaurants, the New York Café and the S & W Cafeteria. Around the corner was the drugstore and the two movie houses and the public library. The only thing lit at night was the poolroom. The one oasis was the Dixie Newsstand, which sold the New York City newspapers and books. There are a dozen bookstores in Charlotte which sell only Bibles, prayer books, and commentaries on Jesus, just as there are dozens of publishers who issue only religious materials.

Belk's, Ivey's and Efird's were the three big department stores in Charlotte. Belk's was Presbyterian, Ivey's was Methodist, and Efird's was Baptist. George Ivey ordered the shades pulled down on his first-floor windows so that the Lord's Day would not be desecrated by any hint of commerce. His store sold neither playing cards nor cocktail glasses, which led me to ask editorially, "George, why are you selling beds?" Mr. Belk built fences around every Presbyterian church in North Carolina. Mrs. Belk once donated a chapel to Queens College and she asked David McConnell, legal counsel for Belk's, to help prepare some appropriate remarks for the occasion. David, my good friend, asked me what I thought; I wrote a short speech on the spot. Thus it was that an unwitting Mrs. Belk used my words in addressing herself to 1,000 virgins who listened to her dedicate a chapel to Jesus Christ.

On my first parabola around Charlotte I noticed an empty store between Efird's Department Store and Belk's. Efird's owned the empty store, and Mr. Efird let the store deteriorate, painting its windows black, never making repairs, letting refuse pile up just so people would know there was a difference between his store and Belk's. Belk's eventually won. When Mr. Efird died, Belk's absorbed both the empty store and the department store in its chain.

Since I was working for the Charlotte *Labor Journal,* this qualified me as the only Jewish newspaperman in town. Often church groups asked me to participate in panel discussions. One of these panels tried to define the importance or unimportance of cul-

236

tural differences among Jews, Protestants, and Catholics. I did the best I could to hold my end up. When our panel discussion was over, the audience asked questions. The first question was: "Why do the Jews have all the money?"

"Yeah, why?" chorused the audience.

I said, "You people down here have the Wachovia Bank, the American Commercial Bank, and the Union Trust Company. There is Ivey's, Efird's, and Belk's. In none of these companies are there Jewish stockholders, or even Jewish employees. Where is all the money?"

Southerners don't worry about Jews because Jews do not threaten them socially. When I first arrived down South, the Jews were a single proprietary class. They peddled clothes or they ran jewelry stores or they shipped peaches, but they were never employees angling for the vice-presidency of a corporation. There are few Jews in the South, and their contact with the Gentiles is through the power structure, with the banker who lends the money for capital investment, with the lawyer who draws up the contract, with the realtor who rents property, and with the income-tax expert. No hotel boasts of a restricted clientele because there are simply not enough Jews to go around.

Occasionally the country clubs worry about Jews. For years the Jews in Charlotte tried to join the Charlotte Country Club, the most luxurious and exclusive of the more than one dozen clubs in the area. For years the Charlotte Country Club said no. Finally, the Jews gave up and decided to build their own which they called the Amity Country Club. Simultaneously, Police Chief Frank Littlejohn ordered the Charlotte Country Club to remove its slot machines, which drastically cut revenues. The Charlotte Country Club's board of directors met in grave conference and decided to replace the slot machines with Jews—but it was too late.

What the South did worry about—and worried about constantly —was the Negroes. As I, a stranger to Charlotte, an immigrant in America, walked down the street, Negroes, whose parents had been in this country for two and sometimes three hundred years, stepped off the sidewalk and tipped their hat. When I went into the drugstore to buy razor blades, I never saw a Negro. And I am not talking about a Negro at the soda fountain, I am talking about a Negro who might also need razor blades. Almost half the Charlotte population, the colored half, was invisible.

There were not even balconies in the movie houses for the Negroes. When Laurence Olivier's *Henry V* opened in Charlotte, Mrs. Henry McKeithan, a Shakespearian scholar, whose husband taught English at Johnson C. Smith University, could not see the movie. She badly wanted to see *Henry V*, and it was I who suggested we borrow a white child whose nursemaid she could pretend to be. When the cashier saw Mrs. McKeithan holding the hand of a blue-eyed, blond-haired white child, she had no hesitation in clicking out two tickets. Not too long afterward, I used the incident in proposing the Golden Rent-a-Baby Plan, one of the many I proposed to resolve the impasse of integration.

Negroes could attend the two colored movie houses in what Charlotte calls the Second Ward, houses which played only Western and Jungle Jim serials with an occasional Tarzan picture thrown in.

No place could a man witness the senselessness of segregation as he could on the buses. Film distributors can make a living out of two sets of movie houses—one for white, one for colored—but no transportation expert can figure how to turn a profit out of two fleets of buses. One fleet has to do. The long seat over the rear wheels was always reserved for Negroes. Depending on how many whites were riding, sometimes Negroes could move forward two rows. I remember when a Cuban basketball team came to play in Charlotte, they were allowed to sit in the front of the bus. Paradoxically, all of them were darker than the Negroes consigned to the back. Many times I saw Negroes standing in the rear while the front was devoid of any passengers. There were other times when whites stood with the rear vacant. Gasoline was rationed during the war, so almost all of us relied on the buses for all transportation. On one occasion, a man and his wife, who were obviously visiting Charlotte from another area in the country, moved to the back. White passengers immediately told them, "That's the nigger section. You can't sit there." Dumbfounded, the man and woman stood until the bus reached their destination.

A white man could not rise to give his seat to a pregnant colored woman without the bus driver ordering both of them off. One night I resolved to sit in the colored section. The bus driver saw me in his mirror and yelled, "Hey, mister, there's a seat up here."

I said, "I'm sitting here."

He said, "There's a seat up front."

238

When I didn't move, he started to revile me and kept up a blue stream until I got off at the Willard. I doubt now that I proved anything except my ability to desecrate a hallowed custom.

When Martin Luther King, Jr., organized the bus boycott in Montgomery, he tore at a sensitive nerve. Whites did not realize they were going to have to share schoolrooms with Negroes; they always knew they had to share buses. That they had to share the space equitably for the same fare outraged the whites. The whites in Montgomery imagined they were superior people. Not to get more for the same money is no badge of superiority. As often as Martin Luther King, a truly humble man, argued that history was not an inevitable force, but a process which must be changed often, they heard him out incomprehensibly.

No, Southerners didn't worry about Jews; they put all their efforts into denying humanity to Negroes, depriving and dehumanizing other men because of their color. Justice for Negroes was a huge joke. I sat in a courtroom and saw two colored men, both bandaged as a result of a knife fight, come before the judge for trial. They pleaded guilty.

"Where are you from, boy?" the judge asked the first Negro.

"I'm from Charlotte, your Honor. I live in the Brooklyn area."

"And you," asked the judge of the second man, "where are you from?"

"From Rock Hill, your Honor."

The judge turned to the first defendant and said, "I'm giving you thirty days on the chain gang." To the second, he said, "I'm giving you six months. That's going to teach you Rock Hill niggers not to come around here cutting up our Charlotte niggers." The courtroom broke into wild laughter. But here was a criminal court judge, perhaps a stern and decent man, losing all perspective, all sense of fairness, because the defendants before him were Negroes.

Two Negroes who sued each other were also a source of merriment to juries, spectators, and lawyers. A Negro who sued a white man risked his life. When William Witter passed out under the railroad viaduct from too much drink, the police drove him home and helped Mrs. Witter get him to bed. When a colored man staggered, the police put him in jail.

What made me despair about the segregation I saw was not only the cruelty it inflicted on Negroes but the total self-corruption it inflicted on white men. William Witter had given his life to the labor movement. He championed workingmen when bricks and bats broke up picket lines. Yet when I told him how unjust and inequitous segregation was, he looked up at me and said coldly, "Don't pull that stuff around here, son."

I have known great liberals in the South, men who went down the line with Roosevelt, the NRA, the TVA, the war, Medicare, Social Security, who still, on the subject of race, say "nigger." Herschel Johnson, ambassador to Brazil, the envoy to whom the Doenitz government of Germany made the first overtures for surrendering the German Army, Herschel, a sincerely religious man and an avid reader of philosophy, said to me when the Supreme Court ruled against school segregation that he was afraid of the "mongrelization" of the races.

Once I traveled around North Carolina with a colored welfare worker named Frank Larkin. I was doing a piece for my paper on illegitimate births, and Mr. Larkin agreed to help me get some statistics and interviews with Negroes. We left Raleigh on a blistering hot day in August. Halfway toward our destination in Greensboro, he said, "Let's stop off at my uncle's farm, which is right around the bend."

We stopped. Mr. Larkin introduced me to an old, white-haired man who came down to the gate. The heat was blinding. The sun was equatorial. One thing I wanted was a cold glass of well water. I could see the shaded well from where I stood, but the old man kept us at the gate and never invited us in.

We said good-bye and continued on our way. Mr. Larkin asked, "I suppose you're wondering why he didn't invite us over the threshold."

"Yes," I replied, "I am wondering."

"Well," said Mr. Larkin, "the old man has been saving up most of his life to buy his daughters a baby grand piano. He'll be damned if he'll let any white man see that a nigger owns a baby grand piano."

I was forced to remember that those Negroes in Charlotte who went downtown had no place to get a cool drink of water either, that if a little colored girl had to go to the bathroom, her mother simply had to take her home, for there were no rest room accommodations for Negroes.

A Negro could get a glass of water in New York City. Negroes rode the subways. Long before I left New York, Adam Clayton

Powell had organized the first boycott of the chain stores on 125th Street and had won concessions from the bus lines. I registered Negroes at the Markwell, and a decade before that John Duff and I had a drink one night with a colored judge at a political club. Chicago had sent De Priest to Congress in 1928, the first Negro elected to the House since the end of the Reconstruction. The North was no paradise; living in the South taught me that. But Northerners weren't proud of their ability to oppress Negroes. The oppression was there, but it was an oppression not institutionalized.

Admittedly, I was naïve. One of the words always in Tiny's vocabulary was "fair." Living with her made "fair" part of my vocabulary, too, and part of my sons'. The South was not fair. Now I must admit I have been unfair in my life, always, however, for my own advantage. Other men I have known have been unfair for the same reason. We knew we were unfair. We were sorry we were unfair, but we knew we gained by it. The South did not gain. The South suffered. Southerners were never cynical about the bromides they uttered on behalf of their way of life. They were never skeptical about the phrase in the Pledge of Allegiance "with liberty and justice for all," although the evidence that there was no liberty and justice for half the population was before their eyes every minute of the day.

That they could not see this has made them victims of countless other difficulties, not related to the colored question. The fiercest fighters for the separation of church and state in the South are the Baptists. The Baptists want secular schools because mistakenly they believe all efforts at religious instruction come from Rome and the Catholics. These Baptists have never listened to a Board of Education meeting long enough to realize it is the Presbyterians and Methodists who believe prayers should be recited by schoolchildren every morning and an hour of the school day set apart for religious instruction. The Baptists have inured themselves against seeing this through long and steady practice. If a man believes that "liberty and justice for all" describes America, even though his presence on the sidewalk makes a dozen Negroes evacuate it, he is never going to see much of anything.

Time, of course, has made my conscience more articulate, my objections more precise. As much as I remember of my impressions when I first came South is that the segregation I witnessed which made me an involuntary accomplice nagged me. It was not as nagging a concern, say, as an impending jail sentence, but it was there. It was nagging to ask a colored man directions unselfconsciously and have him reply, "Boss, I just don't know." It was nagging to realize he was afraid of me. It was a nagging experience to ask the janitor to sweep our office and have him reply, "Yessah, yessah." It was nagging to realize that in asking a man to sweep the office, I had become Simon Legree. It was nagging to realize the first public high school for Negroes in Charlotte was opened in 1928, and it was not a new school but a dilapidated structure abandoned by whites. I submit it is nagging for anyone who has ever raised a child to realize that as late as the 1960's a little colored girl who had been hit by a car lay bleeding for more than an hour on a Charlotte sidewalk because a good Samaritan mistakenly summoned a white ambulance.

In short, I was vexed, morally vexed and perhaps morally vexed for the first time in my life. I used to address Negro groups in churches and clubs. I gave the commencement address in a colored high school, the first white man to do so; I was not a mayor, or an elected official, or a man with a vested interest in the community—just a newspaperman trying to eke out a living. I had been asked to deliver the address because I had made it my business to find Negro friends. I went out of my way to meet Negroes, not an easy task, for the Negroes regarded me with suspicion and the whites thought I was insane. I persevered. I made friends with professors at Johnson C. Smith University and with colored ward heelers. Perhaps I made friends with no more than twenty, but it was twenty colored men more than others knew.

There was no ferment then; Negroes had always lived this way. Many thought they would always live this way, but not all.

Two of my friends for as long as I have been in Charlotte are Fred and Kelly Alexander. Both were born in Charlotte, Fred in 1910, Kelly in 1915. Their father was Zechariah Alexander, who worked for the North Carolina Mutual Life Insurance Company.

Zechariah told his sons never to leave Charlotte, to stay, to try to do something for the community and their people. Zechariah abandoned the insurance business and opened the Alexander Funeral Home so that his boys would have an inheritance and remain. Education, said Zechariah, was the key. "You can't beat the whites with money. They have all the money. You can't beat

242

them physically; they have the police and the Army. The one thing the white man fears is the Negro mind. Education is life."

Fred Alexander was graduated from Lincoln University in Pennsylvania, and Kelly was graduated from Tuskegee.

Zechariah Alexander always fought for Negro rights. Fred tells me his father always took him to meetings. The program usually listed "Master Fred Alexander in a Recitation."

James Steere, a white banker, and Zechariah Alexander, in a protest for civil rights, succeeded in having the Myers Street School padlocked in the 1920's, a ramshackle, wooden firetrap, the elementary school to which Negro children were consigned. Charlotte had to build a new school. Fred Alexander planted the elm tree on the walkway standing at its full growth today.

Zechariah organized a Better Boys Movement, agitating to get the Negroes into the Boy Scouts. Until the Better Boys Movement, a Negro could not join the Boy Scouts. The merchants would not sell a colored kid a Boy Scout uniform. The Alexanders won the fight. In the 1928 annual parade honoring the Mecklenburg Declaration, Negroes marched. First came the white Boy Scout leaders, then the white Boy Scouts, followed by the Negro leaders and then the colored Boy Scouts.

On May 20, 1929, Zechariah Alexander suggested to George Houston, a white Boy Scout leader, that kids with the flags could possibly parade together. Charlotte had its first taste of integration. Negro and white Scouts paraded together, each boy carrying an American flag, which provoked little protest.

The only equipment the Negro schools received was what the white schools discarded. When the white school got a new stove, the old potbellied one was installed in the Negro school. Negroes got nothing without court action or the threat of court action. Negroes won recognition by the Associated Charities, a citywide Community Chest for the first time in 1930, and for the first time poor Negroes got relief.

The Alexanders admit that their father had an advantage. He didn't work for whites. He and his two sons could agitate and speak out for Negro rights. It was hard for whites to discipline them.

In 1940 Fred Alexander went before the school board to ask that business courses be given in the Negro high schools. Dr. Harry Harding, superintendent of schools, wondered, "Why?

They can't get a job." Fred Alexander said, "Did you ever stop to think, Dr. Harding, that if boys and girls were trained in business courses, there may come a time when jobs will open up to them?"

It was in 1940 that Kelly Alexander received a charter for an NAACP chapter. He became the president. Now he is the president of the state organization and was elected to the national board in 1950.

The first test of constitutional law was started in Charlotte by its NAACP: *Leeper v. Charlotte Park and Recreation Commission.* The NAACP won in the North Carolina Superior Court. Spottswood Robinson argued for the local. Mr. Robinson is now a judge of the Federal Circuit Court in Washington, D.C. The victory opened up Revolution Park, golf course, swimming pool, and all facilities to Negroes.

The Alexanders then agitated against police brutality. Whites threatened to blow up their funeral home. The Alexanders recruited thirty Negroes armed with shotguns to guard their place.

It was nothing in those days for a cop to storm the shanty home of a Negro and break everything inside. One Charlotte cop used to frighten a Negro woman into having sexual relations with him. The Alexanders used their thirty deputies to surround her house. The cop had to use his gun to get through the hooting Negroes; as he ran away, the cop dropped his hat, in which his initials were stenciled. The Alexanders sent the hat to the Baltimore *Afro-American* weekly, which printed the story with a photograph of the revealing initials.

The NAACP had stiff opposition in the 1940's. It was looked on with contempt, charged with being Communist-inspired. Membership cost $1, but most of the Negroes working for white people wouldn't reveal their names and requested that no mail be sent to their homes. Negro teachers who joined the NAACP were always frightened. Fred Alexander says many gave him money but refused to accept a receipt for fear of exposure.

In 1942 Fred Alexander was the head of the Negro Division of the Associated Charities. He insisted Negroes get credit for their contributions. He insisted on the same system for the Negro YMCA supported mainly by Negro funds.

When the Negroes began to register in large numbers, the power structure quaked. Since large Negro registration would result in the election of three or four Negro councilmen, the North Carolina legislature abolished the ward system and made election subject to a citywide vote.

Kelly Alexander ran for the City Council, but he was "the NAACP candidate." The second time he ran, he would have won election, but the Democrats put up a "bandana head" to split the Negro vote.

The NAACP brought Dr. Martin D. Jenkins of Howard University to do a school survey of Charlotte. The survey showed marked inequities in the separate but equal concept. After a bond election, all the funds were used to build four super high schools for white students. The Negro schools got nothing. The NAACP protested. It was difficult to get the cooperation of Negro school principals. One principal visited Kelly, insisting first that they go inside by the back door so he wouldn't be recognized.

The Alexanders agitated for Negro police, and Charlotte appointed two as *special officers,* neither allowed to take merit examinations. The NAACP argued for full police status and won.

Many Negroes and most whites looked on Kelly as an agitator. Mecklenburg County was and is a seat of Ku Klux Klan terrorism and harassment. Threatening phone calls are a daily occurrence. Negro maids and chauffeurs working for white people were told not to associate with Kelly Alexander.

Along came Victor Shaw, in the late 1940's, who was the first mayor to show concern for Negroes. They registered in huge numbers and voted for him. The NAACP agitated for housing, and Victor Shaw prevailed on a builder to build Double Oaks, a large Negro housing complex. Fred Alexander was hired to manage the project, which he still does today. Negroes were welcomed to the City Council meetings during Shaw's administration.

Next, the Alexanders took up the matter of the county home. Whites had the front brick facilities, and the Negroes had the wooden homes in the back which looked like old plantation shacks. The NAACP argued. A new building was finally erected. Then the Alexanders threatened Memorial Hospital with a lawsuit unless Negro doctors, Negro patients, and Negro employees were integrated.

With the Supreme Court decision in 1954, the NAACP began educating Negroes. There was a built-in attitude among many colored people against Negro children going to white schools. The

NAACP went door to door explaining to parents the meaning of the decision, working night and day to get the promise Negroes would send their children to white schools.

Those were difficult days before the 1954 Supreme Court decision. Negroes were completely out of any decision making. They were cut off from community life. The majority of the Negro homes were on streets which were not paved. Recreation facilities were bad, and Negroes were always short-changed on public improvements. The elite among the Negroes were not the educated men but the Negro waiters in the clubs, and the Negro bootleggers were the only affluent. A few teachers and a few doctors lived nicely. City, county, and state governments did not employ Negroes except as janitors. Negroes did not work in the huge textile industry of the area. David Clark, editor of *Textile Bulletin,* wrote editorials in those days insisting it would be a tragedy for Negroes to go into the textile mills. Their entry would result in Negroes marrying the sisters of white mill hands.

The great affliction of the American Negro comes through the failure of the American society to educate him for participation in everyday life. Land-grant colleges educated Negro preachers but never provided education for other professions. This system deprived the Negro of financial resources, the leverage for political action. Registration of Negro voters was financed by foundations, and many Negroes didn't register because the candidates were always racists.

These are a cavalcade of small triumphs which do not quite add up to a victory. The Alexander brothers have given their lives to achieving these accomplishments, and new prohibitions flourish as soon as the old prohibitions are exorcised.

Fred Alexander is light-colored, a handsome man with a mustache who stops into the office at least once a month, more usually two or three times, to tell me of our progress. In 1964 he won election to the Charlotte City Council, which outraged the North Carolina legislature. Fred had won by bullet voting, by which Negroes with a choice of seven candidates, voted only for Fred. The legislature proposed to make bullet voting against the law. The attorney general of the state dampened this enthusiasm with the reminder that no sensible candidate who ever ran for a multipost office ever requests anything of wife, mistress, employees, and constituents but that they vote only for him. The idea of bullet voting is not as old as the idea of elections, but it is perhaps only a few minutes younger.

In his post as a city councilman, Fred's strategy was to represent Charlotte as a whole, to devote himself to the problems of downtown parking, municipal reservoirs, bond issues for schools, the reorganization of the police and fire departments, and only secondly to be a Negro council member.

He won reelection in 1966, and the first request he made on behalf of his Negro constituents was that the fence which divides the municipally owned cemetery into white and colored sections be removed. The proposal lost. One of the councilmen argued that the Civil Rights Act did not include cemeteries.

In 1942 the election of a Negro to the City Council was undreamed of. I knew it would happen, though I never expected it would take twenty-four years. Over and over again I told Negroes about the Irish and Jews in New York who were hostile to each other but who were united by Tammany for mutual political gain. Until World War II, however, the situation in the South was separate but equal. Everything was separate, and few, very few things were equal. But the most important thing *was* equal— poverty. There was separate but equal poverty. The Negro had nothing, but neither did the majority of whites. The Negro consequently stayed quiet. Once the white man could join the Lions Club, buy a washing machine, own a car, then the Negro asked, "How about me?" He is still asking.

I had faced discouragement myself, but this racial situation was far more discouraging than anything I had weathered. When I joined the National Association for the Advancement of Colored People, there were three whites who went to the chapter meetings: Hermann Cohen, a textile broker; my good friend, Marion Cannon, who was related to the family who owns Cannon Mills; and me. The strategy we discussed then with Kelly Alexander was always toward education. Kelly bent might and main to interest the Charlotte hierarchy in education: The churches were always silent; the charities never had enough money for the Negro education; the businessmen were preoccupied.

I had no money and thought I was powerless. Had I had $1,000,-000, I would have been equally powerless. Marion Cannon had extreme wealth, and the best she accomplished in those years was the writing of letters to the editor, which most of the time were never published.

But coming from the railroad station one night, I shared a taxi with a colored man. There were never any black cab companies in Charlotte within my memory. The white man who shares a cab with a Negro sits in the front seat. Customarily the first man in the cab gets out first, and on this night the colored man got off at Johnson C. Smith University. He paid his fare, and the cabdriver gave him change. As we drove off, the cab driver kept muttering, "Goddamn Roosevelt. That goddamned Roosevelt."

"What have you got against Roosevelt?" I asked.

"Did you see where that nigger wanted change for a five-dollar bill? Where did a nigger ever have five dollars before Roosevelt?"

When the Charlotte newspaper carried the news in April, 1945, that the Roosevelt funeral train would pass through town a little after midnight on its way to Washington, D.C., I went down to the Southern Railroad Station about eleven o'clock. I found it impossible to get within a block of the terminal. I have never seen so many mothers with infants in their arms. They, too, had come to wait for the passage of the train through Charlotte. It was a long wait. As the train which carried Roosevelt passed through, I could hear whispered prayers. I edged through the crowd and saw dozens of Negroes on their knees, hands clasped.

It was a slow exodus afterward. I waited. What fascinated me were the lights on both sides of the track stretching northward as far as I could see. These were the flashlights and lanterns of the rural folk who had walked down to the tracks to see the passing train.

I shall always remember those Negroes praying at the Charlotte Railroad Station and the rural folk coming out to wait for the funeral train. They came and prayed because the President who died had attempted for the first time in the history of man to abolish hunger. This is the important and central fact of the Roosevelt career. People still starve in America, but there is no need for starvation. Natural forces do not emaciate children but man's clumsiness and obstinacy. The significance of Roosevelt's relief programs was not that he salvaged the Negroes but that these programs included the Negroes. Roosevelt was the President who made the Negro part of the whole.

Two hundred thousand Negroes went into the Civilian Conservation Corps; the Public Works Administration built schools, hospitals, and homes specifically for Negroes; Negro colleges collected federal education grants; and the National Labor Relations Board let Negroes vote in labor disputes. The WPA for the unemployed white was a stopgap; for the Negro the WPA was a momentous development in his struggle for equality. It was the first time in his history that the Negro received the same wages for the same amount of work as the white man.

Roosevelt was the man who lifted the cloak. It was because of Franklin Roosevelt that the people, white and black, who united in the civil rights protest no longer had to plead for equity but demanded it.

Chapter 22

AFTER William Witter died, I got a job selling advertising for the Charlotte *Observer*. I am not immodest when I say I was one of the best telephone salesmen in the business. I have sold thousands of dollars' worth of space. I sat at a desk with a telephone eight hours a day, receiving a 15 percent commission for an advertising contract. There are no tricks to selling space by the phone, just hard work. I could make at least forty phone calls every business day, and I could sell gas stations and grocery and appliance stores on weekends.

Certainly I was proficient enough to have returned to New York did I choose. But there was a compelling idea which kept me in Charlotte. That idea was to start my own newspaper. It wasn't that it was easier to start a newspaper in Charlotte than it was in New York—it is hard to start a newspaper anywhere—it was that the big story was in the South. The South was on the verge of a revolution—an industrial revolution which would change the entire social order. The war was hastening this revolution. The last homogeneous area of the country was about to transform itself and not transform itself gradually but suddenly and painfully, as the North transformed itself in the Civil War. As a newspaperman I sensed the story was all mine. I guessed and guessed correctly that the daily papers would miss the event completely, leave it alone, because to report this story meant describing the lot of the Negro. The black man invaded every area of Southern life; he intruded on every event and every situation.

When the Southerner realized at last he was in the middle of a revolution, he blamed Supreme Court Justice Earl Warren. The real reason I could report the story was I knew the man who started the revolution; it was James Buchanan Duke, the tobacco tycoon, who built the first power station on the Catawba River in 1906. Segregation can be maintained in a rural and agricultural society. It cannot possibly survive in an industrial and urban society. To deprive a city of colored buying power alone is devastating. In 1941 I knew that the Negro constituted one-third of all credit purchases. Today the Negro accounts for one-half. Sooner or later, as we all have learned, a ghetto or a slum explodes in violence. Colonial America produced intellectuals whose only education was in reading the Bible. A modern nation, let alone a city, cannot function without a universal program of public education. In a representative democracy, the voting blocs of a city exert pressures which must force accommodation. I could sense the shape of these impending changes.

I was prescient. The South industrialized faster than other regions in America for several reasons: ample land, equable climate, available labor, and the breakup of the family farm, which sent young people into the city and freed land for development.

Besides reporting this story, I wanted to make people aware of the way segregation had degraded Southerners and enslaved whites. Whites in Charlotte could see nothing except the back of the bus, nor could the Negroes see anything else. I have admitted my naïveté. I thought if I could start telling a small public about this outrage, their reaction would abolish segregation. A moral clamor would admit Negroes to the schools, the hospitals, and employment offices. I did not for a minute think I would be the first man to instruct Americans that a caste system was intolerable; I knew there were others, but I thought my voice would lend those other men support and help win assent from the public sooner.

I have two and a half decades of hindsight. The public responded eventually but slowly. The Negroes won their advances through the courts and not through public outrage, through politicians and not through moral fervor, through secular law and not through Christianity. Such advances as have been made did not come through basic decency but through federal law.

I started the *Carolina Israelite* with the intention of recruiting

Jews and Gentiles into the movement for civil rights for colored citizens. My influence has always been among white liberals. White liberals have indeed won significant advances for Negroes, but the true advances, the real progress, came, of course, when the Negroes mobilized themselves. We liberals in Charlotte, always the same people belonging to a variety of organizations, spent twenty years agitating for public accommodations for Negroes. When the colored students at Johnson C. Smith staged the first sit-in in 1960, they won their point within the month. The *Carolina Israelite* never aimed for a Negro audience, nor did it ever find one. Yet I believe my editorials were perceptive and sensitive, that they adequately expressed not only the sentiments and attitudes of Negro leaders but their strategy and tactics, too. I have been able to advise and counsel many Negroes, advice and counsel sometimes accepted, sometimes discarded. Such success as the paper enjoyed came in large part because I had the lines of communication open to the Negro community, and Negroes always found welcome at the offices of the *Carolina Israelite*.

I had two basic talents to invest in the *Carolina Israelite*. The first was memory. I remember everything I've ever read and everyone I've ever met and everything anyone has ever said. The second talent was what my mother called *zitsfleish*—the ability to sit working for hours at an end. I could sit at a typewriter for an entire weekend, get up once in a while for a drink, and go right back to work. I could sit still and think and write. My uninterrupted reading for a half century was an asset. When schoolboys write me about becoming a writer, I answer them, "To be a writer, you must be a reader."

"What kind of paper?" I asked myself. One like the *American Freeman,* published by my friend Emanuel Haldeman-Julius in Girard, Kansas. The *American Freeman,* the prototype of the *Israelite,* was a personal journal in which E. Haldeman-Julius discoursed on Socialism, atheism, literature, and a Philadelphia boyhood.

Haldeman-Julius was also the publisher of the *Little Blue Books* selling more than 300,000,000 for 5 and 10 cents each. Millions of these books were classics, and E. Haldeman-Julius created thousands of new bookreaders all over America.

Despite the fact that Haldeman-Julius thought of himself as an iconoclast, the vast majority of his books were reprints of the classics—the Bible, Shakespeare, Goethe, all the important authors from Aesop to Zola. The *New Yorker* magazine once called him "the cultural tycoon of the American midwest." *The Rubáiyát of Omar Khayyám* and Oscar Wilde's *The Ballad of Reading Gaol* were *Little Blue Books,* Numbers 1 and 2, and were published in 1919.

Haldeman-Julius was willing to print the works of skeptics and dissenters who often could find no publisher elsewhere. He put his imprimatur on the works of Margaret Sanger, Clarence Darrow, Will Durant, H. G. Wells, Upton Sinclair, Havelock Ellis, Morris Hillquit, and Bertrand Russell. No other publisher ever created so wide a reading audience; no other publisher ever carried so diversified a line of books, 1,700 titles in all; no other publisher ever sold so cheaply.

For several years I maintained a correspondence with Haldeman-Julius, all of which was unfortunately destroyed in a fire in 1958. Learning I was in Norfolk, then in Charlotte, Haldeman-Julius asked me to write him a *Little Blue Book* on the race issue, which I did. *Race* was a 4,000-word essay in which I explained my impressions of the changing order in the South. I said that the coming revolution would probably happen first in North Carolina because North Carolina had never had a slave and plantation culture. The slavers could not come to the North Carolina seacoast, known as the graveyard of the Atlantic. The only plantation culture in North Carolina was from Norfolk, Virginia, down and from Charleston, South Carolina, up. North Carolina, in fact, almost declared for the Union when Lincoln asked for volunteers.

Another *Little Blue Book* I wrote for Haldeman-Julius was entitled *Who Has the Foreskin of Jesus?* inspired during the Marian Year by the Pope's encyclical that Mary ascended into heaven with "bodily integrity." Since Mary ascended corporally, so must have Jesus, and I wondered what happened to his "integrity" after His circumcision.

With one of Haldeman-Julius' letters came an invitation to visit him at his farm in Girard. I went out there and met a little, short Jewish man who looked amazingly like Edward G. Robinson. He was an opinionated man, and the first thing he said when he met me was, "The bastards are after me."

"What bastards?" I asked.

"The clergymen, that's who," he said. "The rabbis, the priests, the ministers," he said, waving his hand out toward the Kansas wheatfields as though these enemies skulked there. Haldeman-Julius brooked no compromise. He was not an agnostic; he was an atheist, the number one atheist in America, the mantle having descended on him, he assured me, from Clarence Darrow. The two portraits in his living room were of Clarence Darrow and Robert Ingersoll.

His wife, Marcet Haldeman, was a Methodist, a niece of Jane Addams. When Emanuel Julius married her, he incorporated her name into his with the hyphen. She was a more than pretty woman, exceptionally intelligent, and she had written several *Little Blue Books* herself. It was obvious she adored her husband.

On that weekend, Charlie Chaplin was a house guest. Charlie often hid out at Girard when women troubles overtook him. Chaplin had become Haldeman-Julius' friend as I had through the *American Freeman*. The three of us were left-wingers, so over the weekend we repeated one another's dialogue, rising, each of us, to pound the table as we cried out for a second front.

The only disagreeable moment came when Emanuel brought up the subject of Konrad Bercovici, the fine short-story writer who had written the beautiful book *The Story of the Gypsies* which had earned him his reputation. Bercovici had given Charlie Chaplin the idea for the movie *The Great Dictator*. The movie had earned Chaplin money, and ten years later, Konrad, dead broke, wanted to be paid for his idea.

Charlie Chaplin writhed in his chair as Haldeman-Julius argued that this was no way to treat a friend, that all Konrad wanted was $5,000, which was cheap enough.

Chaplin told him to mind his own business. He never did pay until Konrad Bercovici won a court judgment, and then the $5,000 became $100,000. When I left on Sunday night, Haldeman-Julius whispered to me, "That Chaplin, what a fellow! He just doesn't like to pay, and there's no amount of trouble he cannot compound."

Until he committed suicide in 1951, Haldeman-Julius and I maintained a lively exchange of ideas. The only complaint he offered about the *Carolina Israelite* was that it wasn't atheistic enough. What overtook Haldeman-Julius toward the end was the realization the barricades had moved. He thought the Socialists had all the truth. Jack London was a particular hero, but Jack

London was also an anti-Semite. The ministers and priests Halde-man-Julius so roundly condemned were the very people who wanted to save Jews from Hitler.

When I reminded him once by mail that William Jennings Bryan, his particular bête noire, campaigned for an eight-hour day in 1908, Haldeman-Julius sent me a long list of Socialists and atheists who also wanted an eight-hour day. I returned the list with the notation, "William Jennings Bryan wanted an eight-hour day in forty-six states."

I digress to salute a man whose newspaper and writing greatly influenced my own. Haldeman-Julius was what Aristotle would have called the material cause of the *Carolina Israelite*. I took his newspaper format and style for my own, talking about food, liter-ature, and my own boyhood experiences, even including, as he did, fan letters from subscribers. Without Haldeman-Julius, I still think there would have been a *Carolina Israelite,* but it would have been a different paper, and I wonder if it would have been as successful.

Early in 1942 I took a short-term lease on an office in the Build-ers' Building on Charlotte's Trade Street, opposite my favorite landmark, the post office. I wrote the editorials at nights and over the weekends. By the time I was ready to go to press for the first run, I knew I would always need ninety typewritten pages.

My job on the *Observer* was a great advantage. I knew all the advertisers. Selling ads for the *Israelite* was easy because it was a monthly. I hoped for 40 percent advertising and 60 percent edi-torial copy. I bought lists from the Jewish organizations in New York, Chicago, and Los Angeles, and I bought lists from local brokers for North Carolina and Charlotte.

The Charlotte *News* printed 1,000 copies of the first *Israelite* and carried me on credit. I mailed out 800 free copies with the note that the subscription rates were $2 a year. Out of the 800, I received 200 subscribers. With the advertising revenue I could pay the *News* and the rent. The *Israelite* couldn't support me on its first venture, but I thought there was a good chance one day it would. It took me three years to make it a paying proposition.

I chose the name *Carolina Israelite*. Though the *Israelite* wasn't a Jewish paper as such, in the beginning I did include stories I got from the Jewish wire service. But calling my paper the *North Carolina Journal of Opinion* or *Golden's Report* was presumptuous. I had not been down South long enough to represent myself as an authority. More, people could voice the legitimate complaint "What is that fat little Jew doing coming down here to tell us about the Negroes?" I was in a Fundamentalist society, where all religion is considered sacrosanct. When Tarheels complained, they would still say, "That's just a Jew paper talking."

In that first issue, October, 1942, I led off with a Booker T. Washington epiphany on behalf of his fellow Negroes: "If you want to keep a man in the gutter then you have to get down in the gutter with him."

The recipe I included was Cato's cure for a hangover: six raw cabbage leaves.

On the *Observer* I had been traveling all over the state writing copy and selling advertising. I knew a lot of manufacturers and businessmen. On more than one occasion when I came into the office, one of them would say, "Golden, you're just the man I want to see. We had an argument about the Old Testament in our Sunday school class. I'd like your opinion."

I was, in effect, often the horse's mouth. This gave me the idea that the best job in the world was being the lone Jew in a Southern town.

When that Jew opens the store in the morning, he may not know it, but the folks automatically identify him with Jeremiah, Isaiah, Amos, and the Second Coming.

I went into a small town to address a Lions Club, and as usual my gracious hosts remembered not to serve me the ham which was on the menu for the day. Instead they brought me a chicken platter, which in their extreme generosity, they had prepared in pure country butter.

During the dinner, my host, the leading citizen of the town, told me that he had been anxiously awaiting my coming: "I asked Mr. Goldstein, a f-i-n-e Jewish citizen in our town, what happened to the Ark of the Covenant, and he told me to ask you when you came here to speak."

As I discussed the Ark with my host, I thought of poor Goldstein; with the bottom falling out of the textile machinery market, this fellow keeps worrying him about the Ark of the Covenant. But such matters are part of the daily life of the lone Jew in a small Southern town.

After the first edition was published, Burke Davis, an editorial writer for the Charlotte *News,* came around to the office one night and said, "That *Israelite's* pretty good." Burke Davis is six feet four inches tall with blond hair and looks the soul of the South, which indeed he is, having come out of Greensboro, North Carolina.

Burke and I became good friends. He was a newspaperman with deep liberal convictions, and he was the first Southerner I met who had liberal convictions on the race issue. Burke had been graduated from the University of North Carolina at Chapel Hill, and he told me his mother, a member of the United Daughters of the Confederacy, once pointed her finger at Frank P. Graham, the great liberal president of the university, and exclaimed, "You ruined mah boy!"

Burke got started in the newspaper business as a sportswriter. When he wrote a famous story about a dog who disrupted a football game, the editors put him on the desk right away. Burke met his wife, Evangeline, when he covered a tennis tournament in which she was one of the contestants.

Burke was the first Gentile who became my friend in the South. He was, in fact, the first Gentile to invite me into his home. At this time, Burke was writing his novel *Whisper My Name.* In it, he recounted the story of David Ovens, a Jew, who was an early partner of J. B. Ivey. When he first came South, Ovens became a Presbyterian. The Jew of *Whisper My Name* gets off the train in Charlotte, looks in the faces of passing Christians, and says to himself, "That's what I want to be, that's how I want to look."

As he worked away, Burke showed me the book, and I could sometimes advise him about the things a Jew would be doing when he was new to a Southern town. Burke Davis also corrected the impression that Charlotte was named after a Queen of England. Not so, Burke said. Charlotte took its name from a famous Colonial whorehouse. The city grew because of the traffic the whorehouse attracted. The name of the whorehouse madam was Charlotte, and the old expression was, "Let's go to Charlotte's." This information, though new, did not earn Burke any invitations to speak before the city's women's clubs.

Burke has realized his great talent and energy. He has written many excellent books, the most successful of which was *Gray Fox,* a biography of General Robert E. Lee. His book *The Billy Mitchell Affair* is the most objective account of the Air Corps general who was cashiered for proving airplanes could sink battle-ships. His inscription on my copy of *Whisper My Name* reads: "To Harry Golden, who started me in this business." Burke is now at Williamsburg, Virginia, historian in residence.

Burke and I played poker once a week with, among others, Harry Ashmore, then the editor of the Charlotte *News;* C. A. "Pete" McKnight, a young writer for the *News,* now the editor of the Charlotte *Observer;* and Legette Blythe, the novelist, who was then the city hall reporter, the job to which my son Buddy later succeeded. I can't remember the poker habits of any of these men, but I do remember ours was no different from any other game when it broke up at midnight: Everybody had lost $5. Important to me was the fact that these professional newsmen all liked my paper. They agreed they liked best what Burke called my "sudden death" dispatches, like "The safest way to register with a strange woman in a hotel, tavern, or inn is to use a Jewish name" and "They Never Met a Payroll: Copernicus, Galileo, Newton, Einstein."

I benefited greatly from this friendship with Burke Davis since he provided me with another window which let upon the articulate, educated Southern society. It was in the home of one of these men that I saw the first automatic record changer. One night we all attended a performance of *Don Giovanni,* not one of us having to rise once to change the records.

Through the offices of these men, too, the Charlotte *Observer* asked me to write a full page on Bernard Baruch and sell the advertising for it, which made me enough money to finance several editions of the *Israelite.* The reason for this assignment was that Camden, South Carolina, had planned a celebration in honor of Baruch's impending birthday. I went down to see Baruch at his estate, Hobcaw Barony, outside Georgetown, South Carolina.

Baruch wasn't home. I returned to my hotel, one of those old-fashioned two-deck affairs which could have served as a set for *Gone with the Wind.* At the mansion, the next day, I learned Baruch still hadn't returned, and I resolved to go back to Charlotte and write the page from references.

A chauffeur came into the lobby paging me as I was about to check out of the hotel. Mr. Baruch was home and would see me in the morning. I was invited to the Barony to spend the night. The menu was printed with a selection of three full-course meals.

A wine steward attended me, suggesting vintages. After my dinner, the majordomo, Mr. Leonard, asked if I would like to see a movie. In Baruch's study I saw *Destry Rides Again*. "Baruch loves that picture," said Mr. Leonard when it was over. "We show it over and over."

Breakfast was suggested again by a printed menu, and then I went to Baruch's study, where I explained the purpose of my visit. He complied graciously.

A few years later I wrote Baruch, reminding him of this event and asked for another interview, this time not as a reporter for a Charlotte paper but as a Jewish reporter for a Jewish magazine, *Midstream*.

"Come along," wrote Baruch. "I don't know how I can help you but I'll try."

He told me he was "bone-of-the-bone and blood-of-the-blood" of old South Carolina. I asked Mr. Baruch about Israel bonds, and he replied, "I buy American bonds." I asked him about Father Coughlin calling him the head of the Sanhedrin, and Baruch replied, "My wife tells me, 'Bernie, don't get into politics.'" Finally, I asked since he had advised so many Presidents, how about advising Jews? and he replied, "I do best in the high grass."

One day an officer of Davidson College, the Presbyterian school outside Charlotte, came to see me. He had a large, leather-bound volume under his arm, and he put it on my desk. It had inscribed in gold letters "Bernard M. Baruch." Davidson College was building a new dormitory dedicated to Woodrow Wilson, and since Mr. Baruch had been such a close friend of Woodrow Wilson, the college thought of asking Mr. Baruch for a donation. The president had selected me as the college's emissary.

I said, "You Gentiles all believe that all the Jews meet in some cellar once a week, Baruch, Felix Frankfurter, Danny Kaye, Einstein."

I said, "Wouldn't it be better if the president of your college went to see Baruch? Baruch would love that." The official said he thought I'd get a more sympathetic hearing.

"My friend," I said, "suppose you and I and Baruch were in a canoe and it capsized. I'm the only one who can swim, and I can save only one. Whom do you think I'd save? I'd save you, of course. You are younger than Baruch, and I know you. We are friends. You're a neighbor. Now if Baruch were the only one who

259

could swim and he could save only one, he'd save you, too. We'd each save you for a different reason. So go back to Davidson and thank God you're a Presbyterian."

Getting ready to put out the October, 1942, issue, I didn't begin to comprehend the many diverse people, all so different, I would meet and talk to through the *Israelite*. The paper did more than make me sophisticated, however. It immediately lifted me from that despondency in which I had lived since 1928. I forgot about the mark prison left on me, and I never thought of the weariness of failure which always plagued me. In later years when I told Jewish organizations, "You are never safer than when you are fighting for somebody else—when you fight for others, you build a wall of security around yourself." I knew it was true. It is still true.

When a heckler in Atlanta shouted, "What's a Jew doing down here trying to change the Southern way of life?" I replied, "I am trying to organize a Jewish society for the preservation of Christian ethics," and the audience rose and cheered me.

Chapter 23

B ECAUSE of the war there was almost no union activity in the South. There was never much union activity to speak of, but with unlimited war work in factories, in Army construction, on the farms, there was less than ever. I doubt that 10 percent of the working force in the South is unionized today. It was not 5 percent in 1943. The Southern worker made 60 cents an hour less than his Northern counterpart, and now he makes 72 cents an hour less.

In the pages of the *Carolina Israelite* I used to campaign for the unions. With the demise of the Charlotte *Labor Journal*, I was probably the only editor in North Carolina pointing out the necessity and advantages of workingmen organizing for their own interests. Anyone who lives in an emerging industrial society must realize unions will become as much a part of the landscape as skyscrapers.

The dominant attitude of the South toward unions was that they were Communist, not Communist-dominated, but Communist, atheistic, against God.

There were two reasons for this attitude. The Communists, first of all, were the most convenient scapegoats. Second, such Communists as there were were in the unions. Other than union organizing there was no place else for a Communist to go.

There have been strikes against the railroads, against the mining operators, against the auto manufacturers. The one great strike against the Southern millowners, the only strike in the

South with a national impact, took place in Gastonia, North Carolina, 20 miles from Charlotte—the Loray strike of 1929.

The Loray Mill was the largest single mill below the Mason Dixon Line, and the strikers were led by Communists, the chief of whom was Fred Beal. The factory was surrounded by a large picket fence, which was locked every morning after all the employees reported for work. Workers called the mill the jail. These mill hands put in twelve hours a day working the stretch-out system, whereby the worker kept himself ever on the run caring for more and more looms. In the Loray Mill, before the strike, the men watched twelve looms. Most manufacturers thought six looms were all a man could handle. Children were impressed into the mill at age six or seven because, as the mill management insisted, they liked work better than school. When the gate was unlocked at 6 P.M., the worker went home to a mill village, owned by the mill management, to a four-room shack he rented from the mill-owner; he bought his food at a company store and attended a company church.

Fred Beal talked these workers into a strike, and as soon as they walked out, the company foreclosed on their shacks and cut off their credit. National Guardsmen patrolled the streets. The strikers set up a tent city.

One night in May, 1929, the Gastonia police force raided this colony. The strike guards asked for search warrants. The police had none. In the scuffle, firing broke out, and Police Chief O. F. Aderholt was fatally wounded, dying the next morning. The incident broke the back of the strike. It released a wave of vigilantes. The strike leaders were arrested and all charged with second-degree murder.

In one sense, the strike failed because the strike leaders had an invincible ignorance about the mill hands. These mill hands were not educated in the ways of dialectical materialism. When the management accused Fred Beal of atheism, he proudly admitted it, a sudden-death admission in the Bible Belt.

Fred Beal and his codefendants skipped bail and fled to Russia. They were welcomed there as American labor martyrs. But what he saw there disillusioned Fred Beal. He returned to America, pleaded guilty to a lesser charge, and served ten years in the North Carolina Penitentiary.

When he was released, he applied for a job selling space for the

Carolina Israelite. I can only say of Fred Beal he was a hard nose, one of those men whom neither circumstances nor history will break. He was tough, his morale inviolate. He was an anathema to the Communist Party in America. He was truthful about what the Communist aims in Gastonia had been and equally truthful about what the Communist aims in Russia were.

He might have become one of the new American celebrities, recanting his Communist profession to chambers of commerce and women's clubs, but instead of going from the far left to the far right, he went to the center. He used to preface his remarks to audiences with the statement "I am a trade unionist." Needless to say, the chambers of commerce let go of him. Saying "I am a trade unionist" to the women's clubs was as shocking a disclosure as a discussion of the sex act. He was a failure as a lecturer.

As a space salesman, Fred Beal was adequate. I don't think he really made a living at it. I know he didn't make a living at *Israelite*. We talked often. He was one of the few men in whom I confided my own prison record. He told me once about the paradoxes he had found. He said, "To think, I was ready to give my life for men who eat flapjacks and bacon for breakfast. In Russia, every meal is black bread."

Fred Beal is one of the forgotten men of the labor wars. He had one brief flurry of publicity when he sued in federal courts for the reversion of his franchise, which he won. He died of tuberculosis in Lawrence, Massachusetts.

I have talked to Southern mill hands who told me, "Charlie Cannon who owns the whole mill is the same as me. He comes into the mill in his suspenders, and he always asks about my Aunt Jane."

In my editorials I used to try to point out that Charlie Cannon was not at all like the ordinary millworker. In the first place, Charlie Cannon owns the only unincorporated city in the Western Hemisphere—Kannapolis, North Carolina, the home of the Cannon towels. If Charlie Cannon doesn't own the street, it is not paved, nor are there fire hydrants on the curb.

Kannapolis is a feudal barony. No dentist, no doctor, or no accountant ever has more than a thirty-day lease on his office. Charlie owns the buildings. Charlie Cannon pays the firemen and the police. For all his democratic byplay in the mills, Charlie once told me, "I keep five cents an hour ahead of the bastards," meaning the minimum wage asked by the union leaders in the South.

Bedford Black, who once challenged Charlie Cannon's nominee for the legislature, to this day cannot buy a cup of coffee in Kannapolis. No restaurant will serve him. He has to drive out of Kannapolis to a diner on the highway.

Talking about Charles Cannon never annoyed Charlie. It certainly, however, annoyed the Jews. Not all the Jews, but some of them. It did not annoy I. D. Blumenthal, a wealthy manufacturer, nor did it annoy Moses Richter, a wealthy millowner. It annoyed the Jews who owned the stores, the middle-class Jews. These Jews used to tell me the Gentiles would punish them because of the *Carolina Israelite*.

I pointed out that I was barely selling 100 copies of the paper in Charlotte. The argument availed nothing. These Jews insisted I should give up the paper. That was the long and the short of it, and I should give it up without recompense, they said, because I was hurting all the Jews.

"How am I hurting all the Jews?" I asked.

"Because the Gentiles think you speak for all of us."

I told them that one day Bertha Helms, a mill lady who was the shop steward at the Cone plant, came to the *Carolina Israelite*, carrying a big box under her arm, which she deposited on my desk without invitation. "Here, Mr. Golden," said Mrs. Helms, "you get me my money back from Seymour's," a small dress shop in Charlotte.

"What do I have to do with Seymour's?" I asked. "I don't even know him."

"He's a Jew, isn't he?" Bertha replied.

I called Seymour, who said to me that Bertha was out of luck.

"She's going to put her complaint on the mill bulletin board if you don't make a refund," I said.

Bertha got her money back.

I thought it was obvious that Seymour spoke for all the Jews when he sold an ill-fitting dress, just as the jeweler who sold a wedding ring at usurious interest spoke for all the Jews. Since every Jew was speaking for all the Jews, why select me as the one to keep quiet?

The deputation from the middle class still thought I should fold up the paper, which I simply wouldn't do. "If the Ku Klux

Klan burned crosses outside, I wouldn't close down. Four shop-keepers aren't going to have much more luck."

When I wrote a letter to the editor, the telephone at the *Israel-ite* would start ringing at sundown and continue until midnight. It was always Jews on the other end. These letters were always subtly encouraged by the editors who were my friends, and they suggested such improbable programs as killing all the dogs or rec-ommending that the First Presbyterian Church on Trade Street be moved to the outskirts of the city to make room for veterans' housing.

The Jews told me I was *"dain-gerous."* It was bad enough to enflame the Southerners over the Negro; to enrage them by urg-ing a massive union movement was worse. "But now," said the Jews, "you're fooling with their churches." I had every intention, I said, of recommending as well that the Jews move the temple to accommodate the veterans.

They said, "Golden, you are insane."

What outraged these Jews really was that they had no moral argument against the editorials which appeared in the *Israelite*. Their outrage was compounded by the fact that while I was alone in Charlotte, I was not alone elsewhere. Jewish fraternal and so-cial action agencies were beginning their admirable agitation for Negro civil rights.

The Jews in Charlotte were angry enough about the matter to send a delegation to the American Jewish Congress. The delegates warned Dr. Israel Goldstein that if the AJC did not withdraw its lawyers, who served as *amicus curiae* in several civil rights cases, Charlotte Jews would cut off their annual allocations to the com-mittee.

Before he showed them the door, Dr. Goldstein said no one was asking the Jews of Charlotte to become crusaders, least of all the Negro. But the least they could do was not annoy or threaten the B'nai B'rith, the American Jewish Congress, or the American Jewish Committee, which felt compelled to take a stand on the race issue.

For a long time, and perhaps still, many Jews in the South have been frightened at the prospect that abolishing segregation means bad news for them. The Union of American Hebrew Con-gregations once went so far as to refuse to support the Supreme Court decision which ruled against segregated schools.

The Jews could not dissuade the national organizations, nor could they dissuade me. They did not subscribe to my paper. I did not care what any nonsubscriber said. They did not compose a significant advertising bloc. I would often argue with some of them, "Look who we have on our side. Harry Truman. The Supreme Court. The Constitution. Every decent man in the country."

They sighed, "Golden, you just don't understand the South."

I told the American Jewish Committee in a convention in New Orleans, "The time has come for the Jew to fight for democracy when it is not he who is the primary target. I think every Jew in America should contribute his money, expertise, and energies to help the Negroes."

They laughed.

I do not mean to suggest the Southern Protestants were much better. My advertisers were Protestants, but they didn't care what I said because they didn't read the paper. The Jews who wouldn't subscribe did read it.

Nor do I mean that all the Jews in Charlotte ostracized me. Indeed not. Bea and David Wallas were always loyal friends, and Sanford and Elizabeth Rosenthal, and Hermann E. Cohen. And others, many others. One Jew complained then that I came to too many of the temple affairs. It was embarrassing. I was controversial. After the publication of *Only in America*, he complained I didn't lend my presence to the temple affairs often enough. *Gurnisht helfin*, a favorite phrase of my father, which means "Nothing helps."

The man who saved me from the rancor of my fellow Jews was Frank Porter Graham, then the president of the University of North Carolina at Chapel Hill. Graham wrote me a letter saying he liked my paper, he liked what I was doing, and he asked if I were free on a certain Saturday, would I care to visit him?

I met several professors that afternoon, and we discussed the need for doing something to alleviate the crime of segregation. We talked Shakespeare, too, and the Roosevelt election. A photographer, as was customary, took a picture of all of Dr. Graham's guests. When that picture appeared in the Charlotte *News* on Monday, the Jews ceased and desisted. They figured if I had tea with Dr. Graham, I was kosher.

Dr. Frank Graham, teacher, U.S. Marine, university president,

War Labor Board member, Truman appointee to the United Nations Secretariat, was one of the men who helped draft the Social Security Act in 1935. He is a peppery man, not tall, but strong, with a square face and strong, work-worn hands. He looks like a perfect coxswain for a rowing team. Tarheels called him a "nigger lover" and a "union man." To this charge, Frank Graham, despite the tumult of Southern politics, used to answer yes.

Governor O. Max Gardner asked this history professor to take the post of university president in 1930. In his inaugural address, Graham promised, "I dedicate myself to making the university a stronghold of learning and an outpost along the frontier of mankind." Which is precisely what he did.

It was Dr. Graham who invited Dorothy Maynor, the colored singer, to give a concert at Chapel Hill. He ruled the audience be desegregated. Miss Maynor gave her recital on what was an exceptionally hot evening. Before she began, Graham helped some students open the auditorium windows. David Clark, the segregationist publisher of the *Textile Bulletin,* wrote, "Even Frank Graham couldn't stand the smell of the niggers. He had to open the windows."

Whenever my critics complain, all Harry Golden ever did was jump on the bandwagon, I think about this editorial and Dr. Frank Graham. It steadies me. "What bandwagon?" Dr. Graham would want to ask. In those years he was always in debate with his trustees. He survived them and built the university as it should be built, because after Walter Hines Page, Woodrow Wilson's ambassador to England, Frank Graham was the most illustrious and prestigious North Carolinian of his age.

To say we became the best of friends is not accurate. Dr. Graham numbered Presidents of the United States among his best friends. But I saw him often, and he always made me welcome. It was at his home that I met Jimmy Street and Noel Houston, who became my close friends. James Street lived in Chapel Hill and was a successful novelist. The most popular of his books was *The Velvet Doublet,* which re-created the life and times of Christopher Columbus. Among his other books were *The Biscuit Eater* and *Tap Roots.* Toward the end of his life he turned to history, writing innovative books on the Revolutionary and Civil wars.

Jimmy Street was born in Laurel, Mississippi, and started out in life as a Baptist minister. Liquor put an end to his calling, and he worked for several years as a newspaper reporter. Liquor was rapidly putting an end to this calling, too. In eighteen years Jimmy had worked for eighteen newspapers. He lost a job on a big-city daily and realized he had just about run out his string. So he went to the newsstand, he told me, and bought the *Saturday Evening Post* and counted every word in each of the short stories. They all were 3,000 words long. Jimmy wrote a short story which contained exactly 3,000 words, and the *Post* bought it immediately. Jimmy called it "Nothing Sacred." It has served in its time as two successful motion pictures and one more than successful musical. He liked telling this story of his first start, and he always finished it with the ringing declamation, "David O. Selznick is the greatest Jew in the world."

"Why is David O. Selznick the greatest Jew in the world, Jimmy?" I asked.

"David O. Selznick paid me twenty-five hundred dollars for the rights to 'Nothing Sacred.' When I signed the contract, he saw I was drunk. I grabbed that twenty-five hundred, but Selznick was such a gentleman he did not ask me to sign the contract which would have awarded all the rights to his studio. So now I have a gilt-edged annuity. I get seven hundred dollars a week from the musical *Hazel Flagg*. Harry, I am wrong. David O. Selznick is the greatest Jew in *history*."

I never saw Jimmy Street take a drink. He was as long as I knew him a member of Alcoholics Anonymous. When a man in trouble called, Jimmy jumped to help, sometimes grabbing his suitcase and running to the bus terminal. At a writers' conference in Asheville once, the Baptist ministers, who were also holding a conference at Ridgecrest, asked Jimmy to address a seminar on alcoholism.

Jimmy hesitated.

I said, "It doesn't seem much to ask."

Standing in front of the lectern, Jimmy swept his gaze over the collection of ministers. "You have asked me to come here to instruct you what to do about drunks. These are my instructions. Leave them the hell alone."

Jimmy Street had strong convictions about integration. One afternoon, he insisted I accompany him to the ice-cream parlor in downtown Chapel Hill. "It's very important," he kept telling me, "very important."

When we reached there, he said, "Look. Two Negroes sipping sodas. I knew it would integrate, and I wanted you to see." I heard him address a writing class at the university. He said, "You Southern boys have to forget Sambo. You cannot write about Sambo with Dr. Ralph Bunche in the United Nations."

When Jimmy died, he was buried in an Episcopalian service. I wondered why a onetime Baptist turned atheist would choose an Episcopalian ceremony. The reason why was simple. Jimmy came home one Sunday and told his wife, Lucy, "I just learned that the Brother Yates, the Episcopal chaplain of the university, has made a wonderful sermon on integration. If I die, Lucy, make sure the good brother buries me."

Noel was a writer and a professor of English at the university. He was a native-born Oklahoman, tall and handsome and an excellent teacher. His students used to shake with his contagious enthusiasm. Noel was the first man who suggested I write a book made up of editorials from the *Carolina Israelite*. In fact, he had saved all the copies of the paper, and one Sunday he gave them to me with the essays he thought the best circled with a red pencil. I always took Noel's suggestions seriously but still managed to spend years not writing a book.

Noel and Jimmy died within a few months of each other in the late 1950's. I felt lonely, deprived of that wonderful triumvirate at Chapel Hill. For by this time Dr. Graham had moved on to the national and international scene.

In 1948, J. Melville Broughton, the senior Senator, died in office. W. Kerr Scott, the governor, in one of his most inspired moves, appointed Frank Graham to the seat. Kerr Scott was an eastern North Carolina farm boy who became one of the truly fine liberal politicians in Tarheel history. I say the appointment was inspired because Graham was not a force in North Carolina politics.

But Kerr Scott had supported the Truman candidacy in North Carolina, which was not a popular candidacy because of the civil rights plank, and now Scott wanted to be sure Truman had the support of a courageous and intelligent liberal in bringing the Fair Deal to fruition.

I passed through Washington several times during Frank Graham's tenure—I was lecturing occasionally—and when we both had the time, I would go over to the Senate Building and say hello. Waiting in the reception room, I saw Frank Graham saying good-bye to another Senator.

"That Senator's name is Joe McCarthy," Graham said to me inside his office. "That is the boy," said Dr. Graham, in mock amazement. "You are going to hear from him. He is the boy."

In 1950, Graham would have to face election for the rest of Broughton's unexpired term. He entered the spring primary expecting sure nomination. Because North Carolina is a one-party state, the Democratic primary is crucial for candidates. To win nomination, a candidate must win a *majority* of the votes in the primary. Should he win only a plurality, a runoff primary is scheduled between the two top contenders.

In the 1950 primary Frank Graham faced two opponents. The first was Willis Smith, a fifty-five-year-old lawyer who represented the utilities and the mills in North Carolina. He had never held public office, but he commanded more than sufficient backing for his primary campaign. Graham's other opponent was Bob Reynolds, the old isolationist Senator who had lost the seat in 1944. Reynolds had always been a red-neck Senator, and this time again, his constituents were the red-necks.

Dr. Graham asked me to help him in the primary. I attended the strategy sessions where the liberals Graham had recruited agreed the accomplishments of the New and Fair Deals were Graham's best platforms. I also published the newspaper which described Dr. Graham's background and qualifications. By this time Joe McCarthy had introduced politicians to the joy of anti-Communism, and the Smith forces were intimating that Dr. Graham was a Red. The headline I wrote read: FRANK GRAHAM IS AS DANGEROUS AS THE DECLARATION OF INDEPENDENCE . . . HE IS AS RADICAL AS THE BEATITUDES . . . HE IS AS REVOLUTIONARY AS THE BILL OF RIGHTS.

Dr. Graham won the primary by 50,000 votes, just 5,000 short of a majority. Willis Smith was undecided about filing for a runoff. But just before the time for filing expired, the Supreme Court read its decision on the *Sweatt v. Painter* case, ruling that a separate makeshift law school would not do and ordering the University of Texas to admit a Negro.

This decision provoked outrage in North Carolina. Learning that, Willis Smith had filed his petition for a runoff. Dr. Graham said ruefully to me, "While I am in absolute sympathy with the

270

decision, I do wish the Supreme Court could have waited one more day."

That decision provided Willis Smith with the one issue he needed—race. Willis Smith stumped for white solidarity, saying the only way to maintain it was to defeat liberals.

From Washington, D.C., Smith supporters set up a switchboard manned by twenty or thirty people who telephoned every doctor in North Carolina. "Frank Graham is for Socialized medicine," these operators said. "Make sure you vote for Willis Smith. Make sure your family votes for Willis Smith. Make sure your patients vote for Willis Smith."

David McConnell, my good friend, tried to distribute Graham circulars in Kannapolis, Charlie Cannon's own little backyard. Charlie Cannon had our messenger arrested at the mill gate on the charge of loitering. He had the second distributor arrested for vagrancy and the third for littering the streets. Finally, McConnell hired a little monoplane and showered the circulars on the exiting millworkers. Dave McConnell said, "Charlie Cannon missed the boat. He forgot to install antiaircraft devices."

Graham would have survived these techniques and the charge that he was soft on Reds and labor. He could not survive the charge he was for mixing the races.

A week before the runoff primary Willis Smith filled the state with flyers, on every one of which was a picture of LeRoy Jones, a nineteen-year-old Negro student whom Senator Graham selected as an alternate for possible appointment to the West Point Military Academy. Like all Senators, Graham sponsored a written examination, those taking it providing no background information about themselves, using numbers instead of names, all anonymous. Graham, on the basis of the test, appointed the top two men and named two alternates. One of the alternates was LeRoy Jones.

"This is what Senator Graham appointed to West Point," read Willis Smith's flyer. LeRoy's picture had been retouched to make the hair more kinky. This effective, if vicious, propaganda resulted in Frank Graham's defeat, a disastrous defeat, not only for Graham and liberal Tarheels but for many thousands of people around the world. The November election filled an unexpired Senate term, and Willis Smith took the seat immediately, according to law.

Pat McCarran, who helped author the McCarran-Walter Immigration Act, waited for Smith's swearing in before he asked the Senate to pass the act over Truman's veto. Originally, the one Southerner to vote against restrictive immigration was Frank Graham. Willis Smith's vote was the one vote by which the Senate overrode the Presidential veto. Willis Smith had the help of a Negro boy, the most innocent bystander of modern times.

LeRoy Jones made a valiant try but did not qualify for formal appointment to West Point. Willis Smith served eight months in the Senate, and then he, too, died in office. Senator Wayne Morse of Oregon told me he refused ever to speak to Willis Smith except when necessary on the floor of the Senate. He said he thought Willis Smith was a contemptible racist.

There was a schoolteacher who worked in Frank Graham's headquarters. She was a devoted worker who rang doorbells and talked into the telephone until late at night. She voted for Willis Smith in the runoff primary, and her explanation describes the reasons why Willis Smith swept the state. She said, "I voted for Smith because my father said you are going to fill the schools with niggers."

Before he left Washington, Dr. Graham went to see President Harry Truman at the White House. Truman stood up when Graham entered, spread his hands, and with a shrug said, "Frank, you told the folks too many things. You answered too many charges."

Not long afterward, President Truman appointed Frank Graham to the United Nations Secretariat as the mediator for India-Pakistan, a post in which the good doctor still serves his country.

Governor Kerr Scott told the press, "This campaign has set our state back twenty-five years." In a Labor Day speech before the North Carolina Federation of Labor (AF of L), Scott chided the delegates. "You were taken in by the racial bigots. You turned down the man who stood to do more for us, the common people, than any man in our generation." When the Negro delegates rose to applaud, Scott shook his finger at them and asked, "What are the Negro brethren clapping so hard about? There was no black or white in this campaign; it was mostly 'yellow.' You have four hundred thousand votes, but less than one hundred and fifty thousand of you came out."

When Kerr Scott some years later readied his Senatorial campaign, a reporter asked him if he was preparing himself for the "hot stuff" that decided the election in 1950. The rough-hewn Kerr Scott, the farmer from Haw River, smiled and said, "I'll take care of it, son. Remember I'm not as good a Christian as Frank Graham."

Chapter 24

Eᴀʀʟʏ in the evening of August 14, 1945, I heard Harry Truman tell the country by radio that the war with Japan was over. I ran down to the lobby of the Willard to wait for that first extra: ᴊᴀᴘᴀɴ sᴜʀʀᴇɴᴅᴇʀs. I shared the exultation of all Americans and the relief of all parents. My oldest son, Richard, was already in the paratroops, and my middle boy, Buddy, had just been accepted for the Navy Air Force. Buddy did not become a Navy pilot because with the end of the war, the Navy asked for a six-year enlistment. Tiny told me that Bud bundled together all the airplane magazines he had saved for years and put them on the dumbwaiter with the sigh *"Sic transit gloria mundi."*

What was the greatest of all adventures for the generations which succeeded my own ended for me in a Charlotte hotel room excitedly talking about the victory with other friends also in their forties. Though we were stirred and committed to the war, it touched us less than the Depression, touched us less because we were older and because despite the ravages of the Depression, the country was strong, powerful, and, in this instance, magnificently responsible.

With the war's end I was sure of two things: I was positive the nation would enter into a phase of unparalleled prosperity. All the consumer goods had been off the market, and all needed to be remade. The making would provide unlimited jobs and the jobs provide unlimited money. I was also sure that civil rights for the Negro would be implemented immediately. The returning Negro veteran would be treated differently from the way the Negro veteran had been treated after World War I. In 1920 America recorded its greatest number of lynchings. Many of these lynchings were inspired by the sight of a discharged colored veteran wearing his old Army uniform in the bitter winter. The sight of a Negro in uniform infuriated Southerners. An Army uniform is a symbol of equality.

I was aware, too, that on the highest political and military levels there was already talk of integrating the Army. Had the war lasted longer, say, another year, without doubt the Army would have begun integrating white and colored units. The military had already found it was expensive and wasteful maintaining two different armies, one colored and one white, that it was inefficient scheduling white and colored battalions for the same duty at different times. And indeed, the military was integrated in 1948 by President Harry Truman.

In many respects my predictions were right. The populace did not get behind the move of the Negro for equality; the populace is not behind that movement now. Most people are not convinced that equality is a birthright. But the cases which came before the Supreme Court in the 1950's were, many of them, initiated in the 1940's. The courts *are* convinced every man is born equal.

My personal fortunes had undergone a distinct turn for the better. I was still selling space to support the *Israelite*, but in addition, I was writing speeches for politicians. Through the *Israelite* I had earned a reputation. Politicians are always in need of speech writers. Some of the work came my way.

I wrote speeches for Hamilton C. Jones, the Democratic candidate who won election to the House representing Charlotte in the 1940's. I wrote a brochure for Jones which so pleased him he said, "Golden, get me twenty thousand of this here paper. Get me ten thousand with the union label and ten thousand without."

Hamilton C. Jones would have won his seat with a larger popular vote, but at one point he spent several valuable days campaigning in his own behalf outside his Congressional district. In a nearby district there was another Jones, this one named Woodrow. When Hamilton C. Jones stumped there, telling the folks his name, they automatically thought he was Woodrow Jones' father.

Ham Jones was nothing if not ubiquitous. I passed through the checkout counter of the Colonial Stores one afternoon, and when I put my hand out for my change, I suddenly found another hand in it. By golly, it was Hamilton C. Jones soliciting a vote from his very own speech writer.

Once I was caught in the unenviable position of writing speeches for two candidates who were opposing each other. I was not, in this instance anyway, a charlatan. Charles Raper Jonas was the Republican candidate for Congress in Charlotte, and he asked me for a speech he could use to introduce Dwight D. Eisenhower when the general came to town. I was writing speeches for lawyer J. Chesley Sedberry, Jonas' Democratic opponent, on the issues of the campaign. I was at pains to make sure Jonas and Sedberry did not appear at the office at the same time.

Sedberry came as often as I prepared a new speech. Nothing would do but that he recite it to me for my appraisal. Sedberry's oratory bored me. To amuse myself, I thought I would include some ringing phrases just to pep up the recitation. Sedberry was going to make a speech at Steele Creek, a Fundamentalist Baptist farm community. For his peroration, I wrote: "It is no coincidence that the symbol of the Republican Party is the elephant, which clumps all the little animals underfoot, while the symbol of the Democratic Party is the donkey, the same blessed animal Our Lord and Saviour rode into Jerusalem two thousand years ago!"

Sedberry said, "That's the best thing you've ever written." I understand his speech met with violent and sustained enthusiasm. Sedberry lost, however, and that seat is still filled by Republican Charlie Jonas.

The late Governor Gregg Cherry stopped by my office one noon. He had been offered time to make a radio speech that night, and he asked if I could write it for him.

"Will six o'clock be too early for me to come back?" he asked nervously.

"Governor," I said, "sit right down there. When you leave here in a half hour, you're leaving with your speech."

I gave the carbon of the speech to Cherry's manager, Ben Douglas, the undertaker.

"How much?" he asked.

"Aw, nothing," I said. "I'm a Democrat."

"Listen," said Douglas, "I bury them and get paid. You write speeches; you get paid."

The speeches I most enjoyed writing were those for W. Kerr

Scott when he ran for governor and later when he ran a primary for the Senate nomination against Alton Lennon.

Olin Johnston of South Carolina asked me to write speeches for him, too, which I did. I asked him once, "Governor, how do you stand with the Jews in South Carolina?"

Johnston said, "Why, Harry, me and the Jews are just like that," and he crossed his middle finger over his forefinger to show this deep affection. "Do you know Tony Castellano in Charleston? Well, we're best friends. Course, he's an Eyetalian."

Olin was running for the Senate against Strom Thurmond. One of his devices was to hire a bus filled with Negroes which toured the countryside. Two gaily painted banners decorated each side which read WE WANT STROM.

On the occasion of Israel's independence in 1948, Olin was the Southern governor who stood before a Jewish audience and quoted from Ezekiel how God gave the Holy Land to the Jews. Lowering his voice, Olin said, "Of course, now that Israel has become a state, I shall be sorry to see so many of my Hebrew friends leaving South Carolina."

The Jewish businessmen down there are still shaking.

To digress momentarily, Israel's statehood was a mixed blessing to Southern Jews. I remember a headline in the Charlotte *News*: EGYPT CLAIMS TWO JEW PLANES. Brodie Griffith, the editor, called me and said, "Harry, what did we do wrong? Every Jew in the Carolinas is calling us with a complaint."

I said, "Change your headline to 'Israeli' planes, Brodie. It's a long, long story why the Jews are phoning you."

A good offer came my way from I. D. Blumenthal, a wealthy Charlotte manufacturer, who offered me a job as the advertising manager for several of his enterprises. I. D. made chemicals for autos and rubber goods, and he was about to start selling bottled mineral water to restaurants and factories.

Just outside Charlotte is the famous Midas Mineral Spring, which flows constantly and had been commercially bottled sometime in the past. I. D. acquired the property, which consisted of a small bottling plant and a small house, which he let to me. We worked hard at selling Midas Mineral Water, but even with the combination of I. D.'s expertise and my imagination it was no go. What market there was the established companies had already pre-empted. Again, the regular water in Charlotte is excellent. Last,

277

in the factories we discovered the workers do not drink water; they drink Coca-Cola.

One of the reasons I. D. hired me was that he was intensely interested in and concerned about the interfaith movement. He was an officer of the National Conference of Christians and Jews, and sometime previously he had bought Wildacres, a beautiful estate in the North Carolina mountains which had once belonged to the famous Ku Kluxer Thomas Dixon, who wrote *The Leopard's Spots* and *The Clansman*.

The Clansman was made into a famous movie, *The Birth of a Nation*. During the Willis Smith-Frank P. Graham campaign for Senate, the forces of Smith, to emphasize Graham's liberalism on the race issue, played this twenty-one-year-old movie every day in a theater opposite the Frank P. Graham headquarters. The great irony is that I. D. Blumenthal turned this establishment into a B'nai B'rith retreat for the interfaith movement, a meeting place for ministers, rabbis, and priests.

The first time I went up to Wildacres I was in a car filled with Baptist and Methodist ministers. Arriving, I. D. told all of us we would have to share rooms because it was late winter and one wing of the house had not yet been opened. My roommate was an Episcopalian who later became a bishop, the Reverend Matthew George Henry. One of the architectural oddities of Wildacres was that all the doors had half windows. From one bedroom an occupant could look through all the others. This startling feature made it hard on a man sequestered with Baptists who wanted a quick nip from his flask. I waited until dusk when all the Baptists gathered to look at the sun setting behind Grandfather Mountain. Bending low, I tipped the flask to my lips. At this moment, Bishop Henry walked into the room, which led me to exclaim, "Thank God! You're an Episcopalian!"

I. D. Blumenthal was devoted to the idea of brotherhood and lavished vast sums to encourage it. He worked hard for tolerance. His patience was saintlike. One Baptist minister, leaving Wildacres after a weekend of prayer, good food, and horseback riding, said, when I. D. presented him with a basket of apples, "Mr. Blumenthal, you would make a wonderful Christian."

I. D. Blumenthal tried hard to get on the board of directors of the Charlotte Associated Charities, and he made it. The first Jew so honored. At the first meeting of the board when they were to hand out the cards of the big givers, I. D. came out looking terribly defeated. I asked him why he was so sad, and he replied resignedly, "The *momzer* gave me all the Jewish cards."

Nevertheless, I. D. Blumenthal and his wife, Madelyn, inaugurated the first ecumenical project in the South.

At I. D.'s instigation, I once chaired the annual fund-raising dinner in Charlotte for the National Conference of Christians and Jews. I had two lovely assistants, Mrs. Goldstein, the wife of a Jewish merchant, and Mrs. Gurney, the wife of a Presbyterian banker. In the first week Mrs. Goldstein sold four tickets and Mrs. Gurney forty-six. In the second week Mrs. Goldstein, devoting all her time to the effort, sold ten tickets, and Mrs. Gurney in one day sold another forty.

The three of us met for lunch, and I asked, "Mrs. Gurney, you are so successful, perhaps you would tell Mrs. Goldstein just how you approach these donors."

"I tell all the businessmen in town I am selling tickets for the National Conference of Christians," Mrs. Gurney said.

"But it's the National Conference of Christians *and* Jews," I reminded her.

"But I can sell many more tickets if I say it's the National Conference of Christians."

After a year as I. D.'s advertising manager, I found the *Carolina Israelite* was self-supporting. I thanked I. D. for the work and said I was going to devote all my time to the paper.

The year was 1947. I was comfortable living in Charlotte. I felt it was my home. I was a fixture more or less. I was asked to review one of Harry Overstreet's books before the congregation of Christ Episcopal Church, the fanciest church in Charlotte.

I told my audience, "Before I review this book, I have a secret to tell you folks. If Jesus put Charlotte on His intinerary for the Second Coming, I would be His contact man. This is not blasphemy. In the first place, I am a cousin. In the second place, He would need an interpreter, for He probably doesn't speak this 'you-all' business. In the third place, He would want a trained reporter. He would want to know what in hell are Episcopalians."

I will always believe that if Galileo had used humor, the Inquisition and the Popes would have let him alone. One of the reasons the United States government never tried Carl Sandburg during World War I, when the government jailed all the other

Socialists, was that Sandburg was a poet and a humorist. I still meet Episcopalians who remember my preface to the book review. They say, "Hello there, Harry," with a gleam in their eye that signals, "Don't forget me, son."

"To create goodwill among the races," I wrote in my paper, "we Jews should provide all the Christians with blintzes, especially cheese blintzes."

The Smithfield, North Carolina, paper ran an editorial congratulating me on the recommendation and asked me: Would I eat ham? When I said I would, the editors sent me a big ham, with which I posed for photographs, and they accepted my blintzes, including the recipe the next day for their readers.

One of my subscribers was the then governor of Illinois, Adlai Stevenson. When he won the Democratic nomination for the Presidency in 1952, I wrote him a letter of congratulations and promised he could count on me for any support. Bill Reddig, the editor of the new *Democratic Digest,* asked me to come to East Libertyville, Illinois, Adlai Stevenson's home.

I was there a few days writing speeches with Harry Ashmore, Clayton Fritchey, Ralph McGill, and Mrs. Marshall Field, as well as Adlai Stevenson's son. One did not actually write speeches for Adlai Stevenson. I wrote what I thought on a variety of subjects, all of which concerned the South. Stevenson read each of these and extracted thoughts and ideas he thought would prove effective in his campaign. He would then write his own speech incorporating these suggestions.

I include an extract of one of these essays:

Memo to Governor Stevenson:
You asked: "If you had a fund with which to help better race relations in the South, what would you do?"

To start with, I would stick to one Idea—that I would not "intrude" upon any function of government: city, county, state, and/or federal. The Negroes are highly sensitive about this. About as sensitive as the immigrant Jews were fifty and sixty years ago.

If for example, the Strauses, Lehmans, Schiffs, and Warburgs had built us a school or a public library, we would have been terribly chagrined (here we go again, second-class citizens), because the Government was supporting the schools and libraries for the Gentiles "uptown," and why should a philanthropist have to build us a library?

But these noble men knew better. They did not "intrude" on the functions of Government. If they did build a school or a library, it was a religious school or religious library, and above all they created and supported the Settlement House, which I still believe to be the most valuable "invention" in all the history of social relations. Everything these men did for us was based on COMMUNICATION with Gentile America to help ease us into this civilization. There were classes in English, citizenship, and how to vote. The elderly immigrants took the bag of coal and the turkey for Thanksgiving Day from the Tammany district leader, but the immigrant's son eventually put the same district leader in jail for fraud.

And this is what I consider a great sadness—and I refer to the late Julius Rosenwald, one of our most distinguished citizens and a man of great spirit and nobility. I feel that if some experts from the University of Chicago came South and spent a year evaluating Mr. Rosenwald's great philanthropy, the results would probably be disappointing, and this is a pity because it involved many, many millions of dollars.

When I say the results would probably be disappointing I do not mean that in the sense of ingratitude. Far from it. The Negro leaders revere the name of Rosenwald, and they understand the kindness that prompted his service, but privately they will tell you that the building of rural school houses did little to establish the idea of first-class citizenship; and this is ALL the Negro wants. The State builds schools for the white people and so why should a rich man have to build our schools? This is an important factor.

Thus the Negroes in the rural sections of the South do not have a photograph of Julius Rosenwald in their homes. The first photograph they put on the wall was that of Franklin D. Roosevelt.

In the evening all we journalists enjoyed dinner with Governor Stevenson and then went up to bed. Stevenson's home was huge, filled with servants, and it included everything which would make a man comfortable. In each room was an intercom. I was already undressed and under the covers one night when Stevenson buzzed me.

I told him I was in bed, and he said, "Put on your robe and come over to my room. We'll have some champagne and talk."

I leaped from the bed and dressed, even tying my necktie. Stevenson was in an easy chair, papers piled on a table in front of him. He was wearing a smoking jacket with a cravat, and A.E.S. was embroidered on the lip of his slippers.

281

"I thought you said you were in bed?" he asked me when I appeared.

"Give me a drink, Governor," I said, "and I'll tell you the whole story. What ghetto boy ever had a bathrobe?"

During the campaign Stevenson spent two days in North Carolina. He traversed the state by a train which I boarded in Charlotte. The governor made stump speeches at every little station, and in the larger cities he went to the downtown auditorium or the merchandise mart for a longer discussion of the issues. We writers typed out speeches for each of these stops, emphasizing local issues, adding local color. One of the statements Adlai Stevenson made in all these speeches was that he could not say one thing about race relations in the North and another in the South. He always used the phrase "The Negro has to enter the open society of America."

On this trip, which lasted two days, I realized Stevenson was going to lose the South and, if he lost the South, lose the election. The crowds were sparse and disappointing. The Republicans in the South had the issue of the Negro, and they were beating us over the head with it. They distributed flyers by the thousands which effectively frightened the whites.

Southern Republicans also had the issue of the Korean War, which they exploited.

The prospect of defeat did not dismay Adlai Stevenson, nor did it force from him compromise. He remained unfailingly polite, clear, and witty. He was the one politician whose private life was as near his public image as is possible. He never had to search out appropriate quotes; they came to him spontaneously.

It was after his defeat by Eisenhower in 1952 that Adlai Stevenson and I became quite close friends. We were both inveterate correspondents, and we exchanged letters frequently.

January 10, 1955

DEAR MR. GOLDEN:

Every now and then I look through the Carolina Israelite and invariably end up in a gale of mirth or with a knitted brow—or both! I am your debtor, either laughing or anxious. Thank you most recently for "Bigger and Better Invocations"—because you really haven't heard anything yet until you have run for public office in a great state and a great country.

Now don't print this or I will have to believe all I have heard—
that it isn't safe for a politician to set pen to paper any longer. The
results, of course, are obvious. We politicians can no longer write!

Cordially,

/s/ ADLAI E. STEVENSON

January 21, 1955

Governor Adlai E. Stevenson
11 South LaSalle Street
Chicago, Illinois

DEAR GOVERNOR STEVENSON:

Thank you for your high-hearted comment on my writings.
Your letter was worth a thousand subscriptions. Your suggestion
that I do not reprint it is superfluous. I need your letter as "col-
lateral" behind all those other encomiums I print from time to
time.

Your observation that "politicians can no longer write" was successfully resolved by Sheik Nefzaoui in the sixteenth century. According to legend he wrote the great work "The Perfumed Garden" only because he wanted to stay out of politics. The reigning
Bey wished to appoint him to the exalted office of Cadi, the judge
of the high court. The Bey's will was the law of the land, and
Nefzaoui did not dare risk the royal displeasure by a refusal of the
honor and responsibility, and so he told the Bey he wanted to
write a book. The delay was granted, and the fellow stalled all
through the Bey's life, reporting progress from time to time. In the
end, however, he left us this exquisite piece of Arabian eroticism.
As Cadi of Tunis we would never have heard of him.

It would be wise however for politicians, before they start writing, to reassure themselves with Bill Nye that: "No living man has
heretofore dared to perform all he advertised."

I am enclosing a page from a recent issue of THE GREENS-
BORO DAILY NEWS—a feature story on the development of Tar
Heel journalism. I never cease staring wide-eyed at the wonders of
America. Less than forty years ago I was playing around the pushcarts of the lower East Side of New York, and now these Angles
and Saxons put me on their journalistic roster between a Confederate veteran and an editor who never wrote anything "that would
bring blush to a maiden's cheek." And an Adlai Stevenson reaches
down to an obscure little journal, with a letter of kindness and
—heart.

The next time you visit Mrs. Ives, set aside a half-hour. I'll drive over and we can chat about the Cadi of Tunis, Bill Nye and —America.

Cordially,
HARRY GOLDEN

In these letters we touched on a wide range of topics.

DEAR HARRY:

I know you prefer Sandburg—and so do I, bless his heart. But I am demonstrating my versatility by enclosing a piece I did at Robert Frost's 88th birthday. And they don't make poets like that any more either!

Yours,
ADLAI E. STEVENSON

DEAR ADLAI:

I had already read your beautiful tribute to Robert Frost and it warmed me all over. I love Carl Sandburg and I love Robert Frost for the many good hours he has given me.

But, unfortunately, I am a politician animal . . . I was cradled in Tammany Hall, and the first fifty-cent piece I ever saw came from Big Tim Sullivan, the Tammany sachem. (Big Tim's report to Boss Richard Croker: "Boss, Cleveland 1,948; Harrision, 3. I know the one Republican in my district, but I'll find the other two bastards if it takes me all year.")

And so I cannot help myself. Frost is a great poet and a good country philosopher, even though he has no distinguished prose style and no PRAIRIE YEARS will follow him into Valhalla. Neither do I believe that Frost's Coolidge is the equal of Sandburg's LINCOLN. Men must not only match their mountains, they must challenge and stretch their biographers—and Abraham is a much sounder and more heroic name than Calvin—or even Dwight.

I think I forgot to mention that Mrs. Ives was very gracious when I visited Springfield. The whole family came out to hear me speak in the high school.

Sometime this summer—June, July, August; perhaps I can come on up at your convenience.

Devotedly,
HARRY GOLDEN

In 1956 I worked for Stevenson again, this time with less hope than I had in 1952. In 1952 we had a chance. In 1956 we had none. In 1952 the chambermaid thought Dwight D. Eisenhower might take away her Social Security. By 1956 Dwight D. Eisenhower had expanded Social Security so the chambermaid could have her Social Security and Ike, too. It was impossible to beat Eisenhower in a three-month campaign. I knew it, and most of the professional politicians knew it. Everyone knew it but Adlai Stevenson. There is something about the pressures and excitement of running for President which lifts a man out of ordinary reality, lifts him up, makes him at moments a giant.

Coming into New York by train in late October, 1956, I said to Adlai as I prepared to disembark, "I hope I have the chance to visit you in the White House."

Stevenson said, "You will be my midnight snack companion at the White House."

I said, "I am the son of a mother who could not speak English. Only in America."

A few days after Dwight D. Eisenhower had defeated Adlai E. Stevenson again, I was in the office of Jonathan Daniels, a former press secretary for Harry Truman, editor of the Raleigh *News and Observer*. Said Jonathan: "My father, Josephus Daniels, went down the line for twenty-five frustrating years with William Jennings Bryan. I think, Harry, you and I are destined to spend our generation with Adlai E. Stevenson."

On that day I had received the following request from Adlai:

DEAR MR. GOLDEN:
Thank you, my dear friend, for your wire. If it pleased you to participate in my campaign think how pleased I was to have you.

And knowing your wit, humor and also, I think, your resilience, if your reflections on the campaign are not indecent, why not send them along to me and perhaps you'll not mind if I utter them before those smug, complacent, rich publishers who have just had their way with me, at the Gridiron Club post-election banquet in early December. Now let it never be said that you can help Stevenson with impunity.

Cordially,
ADLAI E. STEVENSON
P. S.   I would not ask for this if my own resources were not so depleted.

I complied and sent Governor Stevenson a speech which opened with the phrase "A funny thing happened to me on my way to the White House."

Passing through Chicago and New York, I saw Adlai as often as his schedule allowed. One time in Chicago, staying at the Sheraton, I got a call from Adlai inviting me over to his home. At dinner that night, I said, "Governor, after you called, I had an invitation from lawyer Kahn to come to his house to celebrate the First Seder. Tonight is Passover. I turned down lawyer Kahn because I'd rather be here."

Stevenson said, "Let's have a Passover right here."

I told the story of Exodus and asked him, "Why is tonight different from all others?" We even drank the ritualistic toast "Next year in Jerusalem."

On the night in 1960 that the Republicans nominated Richard Nixon, I met Stevenson at his aunt's home in Chicago. She had invited all the newspapermen friends of Adlai covering the convention to a late-evening party. That morning I had talked with John S. Knight, the publisher of the Knight chain—the Charlotte *Observer*, Detroit *Free Press*, Miami *Herald*, and the Akron *Beacon Journal*. Knight had said to me, "Your friend Adlai will get nothing from the Kennedys."

I confided this information to Ralph McGill, who said, "I'll call Arthur Krock, who's close to the Kennedys." When Ralph returned, he said, "Krock confirms this. Perhaps the best Adlai can expect is the ambassadorship to Guatemala."

Ralph kept insisting we tell Adlai.

"Leave the man alone," I said. "Why should we annoy him with this kind of news?"

At the end of the evening I saw Ralph waddling toward the front door with Adlai waddling behind him. Ralph beckoned me to follow, and the three of us adjourned to a huge utility closet where Stevenson sat on a trunk.

Ralph said, "Harry, tell him what John Knight said."

At this point I had no choice but to repeat that Knight knew the Kennedys at best were going to offer Adlai the ambassadorship to Guatemala. McGill said, "I have the same information from Arthur Krock."

Adlai sat there, mulling over the information, then said, "I always knew that Joe Kennedy hated me because of his Catholicism."

Consequently, Stevenson knew he was not to be Secretary of State after Kennedy's victory. He was reluctant to accept the post of Ambassador to the United Nations. It was better than the ambassadorship to Guatemala, Stevenson thought, but just better. It was a job that went no place and conferred no decision-making powers on its incumbent.

Frank Graham, however, wrote several of Stevenson's friends, saying, "You ought to persuade Adlai to accept. He can make it a jewel of a job." Among those Graham asked to write were Ralph McGill, Bill Baggs of the Miami *News,* and Mrs. Katharine Graham of the Washington *Post.*

I sent Adlai a telegram through his law partner Newton Minow:

DEAR NEWT: WILL YOU PLEASE SEE THAT THE GOVERNOR GETS THIS EXPRESSION FROM ONE WHO LOVES HIM DEARLY. THE UNITED NATIONS POST IS A TREMENDOUS OPPORTUNITY FOR WORLD PEACE, FOR AMER-ICA, AND FOR THE GOVERNOR. I KNOW HIM AND KNOW SOMETHING OF THE THINKING OF PEOPLE AROUND THE WORLD. IN MY TRAVELS I FOUND THAT PEOPLES EVERYWHERE ARE HUNGRY FOR A WORD ABOVE THE BATTLE, A WORD ABOUT EMERSON AND JEFFERSON AND THOREAU, AND WITHIN A YEAR THE COLORED PEOPLES OF AFRICA AND ASIA WILL LOOK TO ADLAI STEVENSON AS THE INTELLECTUAL SPOKESMAN OF THE ENTIRE FREE WORLD. HARRY GOLDEN

Two weeks later, I followed the telegram with this letter:

December 27, 1960

DEAR GOVERNOR:

When I sent the telegram urging you to accept the position of Ambassador to the United Nations, I had in mind something more than serving the new administration. Ambassador Lodge is a man of fine character but he followed through with the entire philosophy of the Eisenhower era, winning a debate a week and sweeping the loose ends under the carpet.

You should not be disillusioned. You are on the threshold of making a greater personal sacrifice than even the tasks of 1952 and 1956 in maintaining the prestige of the Democratic Party in two campaigns against a war hero whose name had become magic. Against anyone else the devastation would have been so great that the Democratic Party would never have returned in 1960, certainly not before 1968. The personal sacrifice you now are called upon to make is to lift up the thinking of the entire free world.

For this task ahead I feel that you need the wishes of so many of us for a New Year of Good Health and Good Fortune.

Devotedly,

HARRY GOLDEN

Two days later, Adlai replied:

DEAR HARRY:

I agree with you on the "sacrifice" but I hope I can do more than
that. "To lift up the thinking of the entire free world" is, however,
a considerable order. I'll need your help!

Thanks for the dope about that wonderful Mrs. Tillet.* I wish
I could see just where she fits; but be sure I will work on it, because I admire her deeply.

Yours,
ADLAI

Some of the last correspondence we exchanged was over the
Johnson-Goldwater election in 1964:

July 20, 1964

DEAR ADLAI:

The Goldwater movement should not have come as a great surprise. The time comes when the "newly arrived" take over from
the "aristocracy."

We Jews are a human seismograph, we feel the tremors first,
and everyone I have spoken to says the word without the slightest
hesitation: "Finally it's come—an American fascist movement."

The "newly arrived" live in constant fear of being displaced. I
see them all around me by the thousands—the contractors who, as
boys, stood in the manure pile to keep their feet warm, the fuel-oil
distributor, the developer, the tax lawyer, etc., whose mothers operated the rooming houses and the teacherages, and who now live
in constant fear, and what can I join today that will save me from
the devil—and the devil changes from year to year—Roosevelt, New
Deal, Pinks, Reds, Negroes, Jews, Aliens, Foreign Aid, Fluorida-
tion, UN, Unions, Truman, Walter Reuther, and sometimes all
the devils at once. They are all after him. Comes along a fellow
and says to the fear-ridden and the bored: "Let not your heart be
troubled," and whirls them away from themselves in hysteria—
and into his lap.

On the Lower East Side of New York we had a song about the
"newly arrived," to the tune of *Maryland, My Maryland:*

> The working-class can kiss my ass
> I've got the foreman's job at last.

* Gladys Tillett of North Carolina, who was soon appointed to Stevenson's staff.

288

It's been too long since we were together. (And that goes for Steinbeck and Walter Lippmann to whom I am sending copies.) God willing, I'll come up early in September. The President [Lyndon B. Johnson] wants a bit of work done so I'll be up North a good deal of the time. Of course I'll give you notice.

Devotedly,
HARRY GOLDEN

July 28, 1964

DEAR HARRY:

I don't know whether it's a fascist movement or not, but certainly the newly arrived took over, as you say. I pray they will let go in November.

I think you have hit it about right. Somehow, this curious character has raised the standard to which all of the fearful, frustrated, suspicious and hateful can repair for mutual support. That there are so many of them depresses me deeply. And ditto that they should come from the most recent beneficiaries of liberal democracy.

But I don't despair. "Prosperity" may not be enough, but peace lies close to the heart of every man—and especially every woman. Goldwater's path is straight to war.

Moreover, if we can stir around in the ashes of our old affirmations of national purpose, I think we will find some fire to warm the torpid spirits.

I have had enough experience to know better about the "people" by this time, but I am still convinced that there is more sense in the goodness than in the fear and ignorance around us.

Come soon; I will get John Steinbeck out of his mole-hole, and we'll attack the wagon ring—shooting from both hips!

Bury Goldwater!

Yours,
ADLAI

Adlai Stevenson died in London in 1965. I was in London not long afterward, and I went to the spot where his heart stopped beating—a few doors from the American Embassy.

Adlai Stevenson's influence will be a far greater influence than any other defeated Presidential candidate has ever exercised. Not Henry Clay, not William Jennings Bryan, not Wendell Willkie, not Thomas E. Dewey, ever exercised such lasting influence. It is true that Bryan succeeded to Woodrow Wilson's Cabinet as Secretary of State only to resign when Wilson drafted a strong protest to the German Kaiser. It is true that Wendell Willkie worked for Franklin D. Roosevelt and wrote a significant book, but his untimely death cut short his influence.

Stevenson succeeded to John F. Kennedy's Cabinet as Ambassador to the United Nations. Just how powerful and all-pervading an influence Stevenson has wielded was demonstrated after the Cuban missile crisis, when reporters Charles Bartlett and Stewart Alsop published an article in the *Saturday Evening Post* which purported to be the inside story of administration planning and strategy sessions. These journalists were critical of Adlai, charging that he had advised President Kennedy to go soft and negotiate with the Russians for the removal of the missiles.

But the story exploded in their faces. No one has to overhear administration councils under such conditions to realize men change their thinking from day to day and minute to minute. No doubt some of the men sitting in on these conferences called for war. But what was interesting is that these two journalists were charging that the man who counseled peace was suspect.

Even so perceptive a man as the late John F. Kennedy was amazed by the mail which inundated the White House following the story's publication. It ran 10 to 1 for Stevenson, and it was evident that the scare word "appeasement" apparently, did not terrify Americans. God help the world on the day when a Presidential council does not have a man willing to face up to the risks of peace.

There was a sadness about Stevenson in his later years. It was not that power eluded him—Stevenson knew why it had—it was rather that with the Kennedy administration of young men and new words America did not give Stevenson the sense of personal security he so richly deserved. Ed Murrow summed it up best for me in a letter dated August 3, 1960: "In England Stevenson would be in Parliament, lighting the hearts of the people of the free world, but here he sits around waiting for a few tired old friends to come in and have a drink with him."

Chapter 25

I stayed in a succession of rooming houses and cheap hotels that often made me feel I was living in Dickens' *Oliver Twist*. Sometimes I lived in the office, the kitchen a desk drawer, the bed a battered couch under whose cushions I buried the sheets and blankets. But one way or another the *Israelite* returned me a living. In early 1950 I saw a two-story house that would suit my purpose, but it was not for lease—only for purchase. So I asked my friend Sanford Rosenthal to buy the house, which he did. Sanford then told me to fix the rental at my own discretion. The postbellum frame dwelling at 1229 Elizabeth Avenue had an attic, a wide porch, and steep stone steps down a severely sloped lawn to the street. Upstairs became the living area, downstairs the office.

I perambulated around the porch in the spring keeping track of the dogwood blossoms. This perambulation earned me my one great insight into nature. Dogwood in the Carolinas always blooms on Passover. God is supposed to have pitied the dogwood, on whose wood Christ was crucified, by turning its blossoms into the most delicate and beautiful of spring—a Southern school myth. The Southern dogwood doesn't always respond to its symbolic role. If Easter precedes Passover, the blossom is still tight in its bud; if Easter comes after Passover, the blossom is about to become leaf. I intend to write an article on this someday if I ever start another newspaper. Above and beyond this sole insight, my perambulation around the porch earned me the honor of knowing John J. Parker, chief judge of the Fourth Circuit Court.

As the citizens of Königsberg could set their watches by the passage of Immanuel Kant to and from his study, so I could set my watch by the passage of a distinguished gentleman who passed by 1229 every evening promptly at six. He wore a Homburg, carried a cane, stepped briskly, the cane beating a steady rhythm. I nodded at him one evening, and he nodded back. The next evening he stopped and asked, "Do you want to take a walk?"

I fell in step. We exchanged names. He said, "I used to walk with lawyer Garrison. He's dead now. Then I used to walk with lawyer Plummer. He's dead, too."

"It's not much of a recommendation for my company, is it?" I asked.

"I like your paper," Parker said. He was every inch and fiber a judge. His sentences, always pithy, cut through side issues to the core of a discussion. They were always succinct. He could not waste time in small talk. Nor was he humorous. When, in fact, we did talk about Immanuel Kant, he prefaced our discussion with "Categorical Imperative—Nineteen fifty-three." When we talked about the Eisenhower administration, the judge said, "He's a Democratic President. Just as Truman was a prisoner of the opposition, Eisenhower is an unknowing hostage of the Democrats who elected him. He will continue the programs initiated by other Democratic Presidents. He will talk about balancing the budget. He will extend Social Security."

"Yes, sir," I replied.

Living in Charlotte, I could not help being aware of both Judge Parker's reputation for probity and his fate in our history. In 1930 he became the eighth man whose appointment to the United States Supreme Court the Senate refused to confirm. The first seven men were John Rutledge, 1795; Alexander Wolcott, 1811; John Spencer, 1844; George Washington Woodward, 1846; Jeremiah Black, 1861; Ebenezer Hoar, 1870; and Wheeler Peckham, 1894. The rejection of John Johnston Parker reveals in small part the agony of good men in the emerging South.

Herbert Hoover named Parker, the man he had considered for the Cabinet post of Attorney General to replace the late Associate Justice Edward Sanford, in March, 1930. Parker's nomination was the first from the Fourth Circuit in seventy years.

Forty-four years old in 1930, Parker had been a lifelong Republican, which made a Southerner virtually *sui generis*. He had campaigned twice for governor of North Carolina before his appointment to the federal bench.

Of the nomination, Lee Slater Overman, the senior Senator from North Carolina and chairman of the Senate Judiciary Commitee, said he naturally preferred a Democrat; if the seat were not to be filled by a Democrat, he could think of no finer Republican than John Parker.

William Green, president of the American Federation of Labor; Max Dyer, the secretary of the Central Labor Union of Kansas; and Walter White of the NAACP, among others, challenged Hoover's choice. Senator William E. Borah of Idaho, who served on the Judiciary Committee, said he, too, opposed Parker's appointment. The gravamen of the charge against Parker was that in upholding an injunction in the Red Jacket case he ignored the illegality of yellow-dog contracts and ignored as well that they were contrary to public policy.

A yellow-dog contract is one which a worker signs with his employer agreeing not to remain in, or join, a union as a condition of his employment. In April, 1927, Parker and two other circuit judges upheld the Red Jacket Coal and Coke Company of West Virginia in its suit for an injunction restraining the United Mine Workers from interfering with its operation by sending organizers among its employees.

Parker read the decision:

> There can be no doubt of the right of the defendants to use all lawful purposes to increase their membership. On the other hand, that right must be exercised with due regard of the right of the complainants. To make speeches or circulate arguments is one thing. To approach a company's employees working under a contract not to join a union while remaining in the company's service, and induce them in violation of their contracts to join a union and go on strike for the purpose of forcing the company to recognize the union or of impairing its power of production is another and very different thing.

Vainly Parker argued that he had followed the decisions of the federal courts which had adopted the rule that it is unlawful for one person to induce another to violate a contract into which he has entered with a third. President Hoover and Attorney General Mitchell agreed that Parker had no alternative but to rule as he had. Nevertheless, the opposition led by Senator Borah gained strength. There were impending Senate elections, and the politicians in Washington were coming to the realization that labor was a significant voting bloc.

Walter White of the NAACP charged Parker with having declared in his gubernatorial race in 1920 that the Negroes were not prepared to exercise their franchise and only a Republican governor could defend the segregation laws. This is not what Parker said at all. The Democrats in North Carolina in 1920 warned the constituency that if the Republican Parker won, he would organize the Negroes as a class. To which Parker replied he had no such intentions at all.

Despite the efforts of Senator Overman, Senator Borah, a powerful political figure, mustered enough opposition within the Judiciary Committee to report unfavorably on the nomination. The vote was 10 to 6. The Judiciary Committee, moreover, would not interview Parker. His only defense, therefore, was a letter he addressed to Senator Overman in which he said his decision in the Red Jacket case was in accord with the Supreme Court, that his decision did not prevent a man from joining a union or quitting a job.

On May 7, 1930, the Senate rejected Parker by a vote of 41 to 39. One can not help calling attention to the irony that in 1930 the Senate rejected John J. Parker as a Supreme Court Justice because he did *not* make law while in the 1960's the Senate complains of Supreme Court Justices that they *do* make law.

Had it not been for Borah's stubborn opposition, probably Parker would have won the Senate's consent. He was in court on the morning the vote went against him, and he interrupted the hearing to comment that while he was disappointed, he was also pleased that so many important and distinguished Americans had supported him.

The judge was never bitter about his rejection. He told me about it several times. The only time I heard harshness edge into his voice was one night when we were discussing Senator Borah, who had recently died, leaving an estate of $325,000. I asked, "How can a Senator whose yearly stipend is twenty thousand dollars leave so much money?"

"You have to understand something about some Senators," Parker answered. "Because they're Senators, they get a lot of tips along the way."

Parker was one of the associate justices at the Nuremberg trials of Nazi criminals. He was the judge second to Attorney General Francis Biddle. He told me the Nazi Hans Frank stood before the judges with tears in his eyes, crying, "If we had won, one thousand years would not wipe out our evil." One of the reasons for his appointment to the Nuremberg Trial Commission was that he was the chairman of the Philosophy Club of Charlotte, a unique organization. Dr. Will Durant, who has led our discussion on three separate occasions, once asked me, "Where did Charlotte ever assemble such a group as this? It is unbelievable that men so different, so smart, could meet in such stimulating discussion so often."

The Philosophy Club initially convened at the suggestion of Professor Horace Williams of the University of North Carolina, who thought it would be a fruitful experience for faculty members to study Hegel's *Philosophy of History*. The first meeting took place in the summer of 1912. The original members included Professor Williams; Frank P. Graham; Dr. Otho B. Ross, who has served as the Philosophy Club's secretary for the fifty-four years of its existence; and Fred Leinborth and Charles Tillett, both politically prominent in North Carolina.

Today the club numbers forty-two members, twenty-five usually in attendance at every monthly meeting. For as long as I have been a member, the club convenes in one of the small dining rooms of the Barringer Hotel on Tryon Street. Each member, in turn, is expected to deliver a paper on his particular expertise which occupies the whole of the evening. Thus, it was Judge Parker's paper on international law, later delivered at Harvard University, which brought him to President Truman's attention and led to his appointment to the Nuremberg bench. Dr. Claude Broach, of Charlotte's St. John's Baptist Church, who was a Protestant observer at the Vatican Council, says his interest in that congress was originally kindled by club member Father Cuthbert Allen, the abbot of the Benedictine monastery in nearby Belmont, North Carolina.

I was invited to the club membership in 1952. I have it on

reliable information that Judge Parker told the club, "We need another member. We need a Jew. I propose Harry Golden."

Until his death in the late 1950's, Judge Parker continued as chairman. He was succeeded by Herschel Johnson, onetime minister to Sweden, ambassador to Brazil, and deputy ambassador to the United Nations. Herschel was a kind, delightful man. The word which best described him was "cultured." He stopped often at my office and left a copy of Marcus Aurelius or Spinoza, and it was he who introduced me to *The Martyrdom of Man* by Winwood Reade. Judge Fred Helms succeeded to the chairmanship after Herschel's death.

The membership of the club invariably includes the presidents of the universities, the leading clergymen of the city, and those of us who do not wince when we are called intellectuals. They are Judge Francis Clarkson; Judge James McMillan; Father Cuthbert Allen; John C. Bailey, Jr., of Davidson College; Dr. William Beidler of Queens College; Dr. D. W. Colvard, president of the University of North Carolina at Charlotte; Dr. M. P. Jacobson, president of Winthrop College; Dr. E. H. Garinger, Charlotte educator; Kays Gary, Charlotte *Observer* columnist; Legette Blythe; C. A. McKnight and Brodie Griffith, newspaper editors and writers; Dr. Warner Hall of the Covenant Presbyterian Church; Dr. Claude Broach, St. John's Baptist Church; Dr. George Heaton; Reverend Charles Milford; Dr. H. Lee Lodge of the Presbyterian Hospital; Dr. W. S. Rankin of the Methodist Home; Dr. Don Rhodes of Davidson College; Dr. George Abernathy, dean of the Philosophy Department of Davidson College; Dr. E. L. Stoeffel, First Presbyterian Church; Bishop Herbert Spaugh of the Moravian Church; Dr. W. H. Williams, Sr., of the Baptist Church; Dr. Thom Blair of Christ Episcopal Church; Fred Helms; David M. McConnell; John Shaw; Francis Parker, Judge Parker's son; John S. Cansler, attorney; Judge William Bobbitt; Dr. J. R. Cunningham; John Paul Lucas, of the Duke Power Company; Dr. Carlyle Marney; and the late Judge Spencer Bell.

We tolerate no intellectual inhibitions. No member may interrupt another member's presentation, but—once delivered—criticism must be answered. After the Supreme Court decision of May, 1954, which declared school segregation unconstitutional, I spoke on why the decision would eventually benefit the South. Some of the members pressed me, then turned to John Parker and asked why America would tolerate the Court's changing its mind, particularly when it was a sociological, not a legal, changing of the mind.

Parker replied: "The Supreme Court made sociological decision in the *Plessy v. Ferguson* case in eighteen ninety-six when it ruled for separate but equal facilities. It has changed its mind. The Court has changed its mind about many things many times. It changed its mind about legal tender. It changed its mind about what constitutes a fair trial. It changed its mind about the Dred Scott decision. It has even changed its mind about yellow-dog contracts."

One of the members in exasperation sighed and asked, "What *do* you believe in, Judge Parker?"

"I believe in Jesus Christ and the Constitution of the United States," he replied, meaning every word of it.

These men are some of the most delightful I have ever encountered, and many of them I count as good friends. Father Cuthbert Allen once gave me an honorary LlD at the Belmont Abbey graduating ceremonies. George Abernathy slipped into a seat beside me one night and whispered, "August Claessens died." It surprised me that a Southern philosophy professor would know about a Lower East Side Socialist.

I have known Dave McConnell since we both worked in Frank P. Graham's Senatorial campaign of 1948. David was the youngest colonel in World War II. After serving in the Near East for three years, he was attached to General George Marshall's staff, and he can recall the day an aide told the commanding general that President Roosevelt had died. Marshall walked to the window, looked out, said, "Truly a great man." And with that, the general bent again to his work. David was secretary to James Byrnes when Byrnes was Truman's Secretary of State.

McConnell was the North Carolina manager for the Kennedy campaign in 1960 and for the Johnson campaign in 1964. As general counsel for Belk's Stores, he was instrumental in devising and implementing the program by which the chain quietly integrated its personnel. Now McConnell is the United States Ambassador to the United Nations Economic and Social Conference in Geneva, Switzerland.

Spencer Bell, who died suddenly in 1967, also sat on the Fourth Circuit Court. Generously he read the law portions of my book

Mr. Kennedy and the Negroes and advised me of errors. If that book enjoys any excellence, it is due to Spencer.

After a Philosophy Club meeting, I went up to Judge Francis Clarkson, who that day had sentenced a young newspaperman to five years when a jury returned a guilty verdict on a homosexual charge.

"Francis," I asked, "how could you send that boy away? Sending a homosexual to prison is like sending an alcoholic to a brewery."

"I didn't do it," Clarkson said sternly. "You did it. You Jews did it. You Jews prescribed stoning. All I did was cut down the severity. I gave him a break. I gave him five years."

These were some of the rewards of knowing John Parker. After a while he would tap his cane twice on the sidewalk. If I was not on a lecture tour, I always joined him. On one of our strolls, Judge Parker said to me, "I must have Simon on my court."

He was talking of Simon Soboloff, the Solicitor General whom Eisenhower had just nominated as a judge for the Fourth Circuit. Senator James Eastland of Mississippi, chairman of the Senate Judiciary Committee, threatened to hold up the confirmation because Soboloff, as Solicitor General, had argued integration cases before the Supreme Court and won.

We walked on. Parker said, "Harry, get hold of Senator Kerr Scott. See what he can do. As a judge I cannot possibly interfere."

Kerr Scott, on whose behalf I had often campaigned, was a die-hard liberal. Only the day before, I had come from the office of Irving Engel, president of the American Jewish Commitee, who was also distressed at the delay in Soboloff's confirmation. Engel, too, had asked me to see Kerr Scott.

With these urgings, I went to Washington and saw Kerr. I said, "Senator, the president of the American Jewish Committee, who has certainly helped us in our efforts in the South, is anxious about the appointment of Simon Soboloff. The Southerners are dead-locked about confirmation. Another dear friend from the court itself wants Soboloff. We think a favorable statement from you might help break this deadlock. And we suggest that some Jewish constituent write you how pious and just a man Simon Soboloff is. You can answer this letter publicly. You can say that if you were a member of the Judiciary Committee, you would be inclined to vote for Soboloff."

Kerr Scott said, "Let me think it over. See me in the morning."

We had breakfast. Kerr Scott said, "Harry, I talked to the leader. He told me, 'Us Southern boys are going to stick together against the nomination.' But tell your friends Soboloff will be confirmed!"

When I reported the conversation to Parker, he banged his cane on the sidewalk and shouted, "God bless Lyndon B. Johnson!"

Chapter 26

I knew in May, 1954, that the case of *Brown v. Board of Education of Topeka* would result in a milestone decision. I knew for a variety of reasons. I had close contact with the Charlotte NAACP which had expert legal advice. There was no doubt that this was *the* case. The tenor of the country indicated the way the court would rule. Had the Supreme Court upheld segregation, there would have been supreme disappointment at such a decision. It is true the country did not realize what great changes this ruling portended not only for the South but for the North, Midwest, and Far West. Even at this late date the country still feels Court decisions are remote, at a remove, from actual practice.

I knew *Brown v. Board of Education* would be a milestone decision because the handwriting was on the wall. Chief Justice Vinson had put the handwriting there while Earl Warren was still governor of California. One of the ironies of integration is that the South has been roiling to lynch Earl Warren when the real villain was Truman's appointee, Fred Vinson.

The legal assault on segregation which reached its massive proportions in the late 1950's began in the 1930's not with the charge that "separate" was unconstitutional but rather with the charge that "equal was not a fact."

In 1934 the NAACP (which has always centered its energies on winning the precedent-making decision) determined to begin suits against graduate and professional schools since it was patently easy to prove inequality in graduate education.

One of the first of these precedent-making decisions was the Gaines case of 1938, known technically as *Missouri ex. rel. Gaines v. Canada.*

Gaines was a colored law-school student whose education Missouri financed out of state. He argued that this practice denied him equal protection. The Supreme Court agreed, requiring Missouri thereafter ". . . to furnish him within its borders facilities for legal education substantially equal to those which the State there afforded for persons of the white race." Chief Justice Charles Evans Hughes wrote:

> Petitioner insists that for one intending to practice in Missouri there are special advantages in attending a law school there, both in relation to the opportunities for the particular study of Missouri law and for the observation of the local courts, and also in view of the prestige of the Missouri law school among the citizens of the State, his prospective clients.

However, Missouri did not admit Gaines to its law school. It interpreted the ruling to allow it to build a separate law school for Negroes. But the Gaines case was the beginning of the end of the separate but equal doctrine. "Separate" remained, but "equal" was examined ever more closely.

More cases followed. In 1950, in *Sweatt v. Painter,* the Supreme Court ruled that a separate, makeshift law school would not do and ordered the University of Texas to admit a Negro student. In the same year, in *McLaurin v. Oklahoma State Regents,* the Court held that a specially devised system of segregation interfered with the education of a colored graduate student at the all-white University of Oklahoma.

Mr. Sweatt had refused to attend a separate law school in Houston. The Supreme Court upheld his refusal, ruling he had to be admitted to the school at Austin. Chief Justice Fred M. Vinson read the majority opinion, noting the factors that make for the greatness of a law school: "Reputation of the faculty, experience in the administration, position and influence of the alumni, standing in the community, tradition and prestige." The Chief Justice went to the heart of the entire matter when he said that the Negro law school "excludes" 85 percent of the population of Texas, "and most of the lawyers, witnesses, jurors, judges, and others, with whom Mr. Sweatt would deal when he became a member of the Texas bar."

Chief Justice Vinson had more to say in the case *McLaurin v. Oklahoma State Regents*. Mr. McLaurin fought segregation rules forcing him and twenty-three Negroes to sit in different rows while attending classes with whites at the University of Oklahoma Graduate School. Holding a master's degree, he sought one as a Doctor of Education. Originally, he had been denied admission on racial grounds, but the Oklahoma legislature amended the state laws to allow admission on a segregated basis. Mr. McLaurin was required, the Chief Justice said, first to sit in an adjoining room away from the class, at a special desk on the mezzanine floor of the library, and eat at a different time from that of other students in the cafeteria. Later the situation was changed, and the graduate student was seated in a place railed off, a sign above reading RESERVED FOR COLORED.

Such restrictions, Justice Vinson, "set McLaurin apart" from other students and handicapped his graduate instruction, "impairing and inhibiting his ability to study, to engage in discussions and exchange views with other students, and in general, to learn his profession."

The Chief Justice observed that removing these restrictions would not "necessarily abate individual and group predilections, prejudices and choices." But, he added, the state would not be depriving Mr. McLaurin of the chance to "secure acceptance by his fellow students on his own merits."

Though my résumé is brief, it is still easy to see the tack the Supreme Court was taking. While the ruling the Supreme Court handed down in 1954 outlawing public school segregation was momentous, it was not surprising. The argument had found its secondary proposition: "Equal" was incompatible with "separate."

The Court that heard the argument of *Brown v. Board of Education* was made up of Chief Justice Earl Warren, Felix Frankfurter, Hugo L. Black, Stanley F. Reed, William O. Douglas, Tom C. Clark, Robert H. Jackson, Harold H. Burton, and Sherman Minton.

The principal spokesman for the South was John W. Davis, Democratic nominee for President in 1924 and veteran of more Supreme Court battles than any other lawyer in American history. Thurgood Marshall, chief counsel of the NAACP, key figure in a quarter century of legal combat on behalf of the Negro, pleaded the cause of desegregation. Another able lawyer, Assistant Attorney General J. Lee Rankin, spoke for the United States. Associate Justice Robert H. Jackson, convalescing from a heart attack, had left his hospital bed only that morning, so that all nine Justices could be together when the decision was read. His being there was the clue to the great event, but no one could be sure because the Court had not even given newsmen their usual advance printed copies of the opinion. So at 12:52 P.M., May 17, 1954, some 335 years after the first Negro slaves arrived in America and 91 years after the Emancipation Proclamation, Earl Warren, Chief Justice of the United States, began reading the Supreme Court opinion in *Brown v. Board of Education:*

"Segregation of white and colored children in public schools has a detrimental effect upon the colored children. The impact is greater when it has the sanction of the law; for the policy of separating the races is usually interpreted as denoting the inferiority of the Negro group. A sense of inferiority affects the motivation of a child to learn. Segregation with the sanction of law, therefore, has a tendency to [retard] the educational and mental development of Negro children and to deprive them of some of the benefits they would receive in a racial[ly] integrated school system."

Whatever may have been the extent of psychological knowledge at the time of *Plessy v. Ferguson,* this finding is amply supported by modern authority. Any language in *Plessy v. Ferguson* contrary to this finding is rejected.

We conclude that in the field of public education the doctrine of "separate but equal" has no place. Separate educational facilities are inherently unequal. . . .

The vote was unanimous. All the Justices said the same thing— Republican or Democrat, Jew or Gentile, Catholic or Protestant, Northerner or Southerner, liberal or conservative. There was no minority opinion. Only two of the Justices were Republican, Warren and Burton, while three of the seven Democrats were from the South; Black of Alabama, Clark of Texas, and Reed of Kentucky.

The South, however, did not realize what was going to happen. No matter what the Supreme Court said, Southerners were sure nothing would come of it. They paid little attention to Supreme Court decisions. Newspapers did not editorialize about this im-

303

pending decision; bar associations did not explain the consequences; educators were unprepared.

Discussing the *Brown v. Board of Education* case with my friends on the newspaper, I heard the invariable prediction, "Oh, Harry, the governor would convene the legislature immediately if the decision went against us. They cannot change the Southern way of life in Washington, D.C." When I argued that the Supreme Court indeed was going to change the Southern way of life, they became Biblical and sighed, "Wise men fill up their bellies with the west wind."

One of my friends was Kenneth Whitsett of Mecklenburg County. I met Ken while I was working for I. D. Blumenthal. Ken is an excellent artist, and he did the drawings and layouts for the Blumenthal advertising account. Ken is a charming companion, well informed and articulate about a variety of subjects.

The one subject we never discussed was race. The mention of the word "Negroes" drove Ken haywire. Ken Whitsett had no animosity toward Jews, toward Seventh-day Adventists, or toward subversives, for that matter. But the image of the Negro transformed him. Because I enjoyed his company, because I relied on him for advertising art for the *Israelite,* prudently I left the subject of race alone in his company.

We saw a lot of each other because Ken had an office a few doors away from the *Carolina Israelite.* On May 17, 1954, I walked over to Ken's office to commission him to do some artwork for the forthcoming issue. It was a little after one o'clock. I was unaware that the Supreme Court had ruled against school segregation. I walked into Ken's office with the copy and the rough sketches.

Ken rose from his chair, advanced toward me, and shouted, "You did it! You did it! You came down from the North and put the niggers up to it." He slapped me. Only then did I realize what had happened.

Ken Whitsett blames the Supreme Court for changing his way of life. But the Supreme Court did not make him abrogate a friendship. Nor is that all that changed for Ken.

Whitsett is a staunch Presbyterian. The Presbyterian Synod, in convention a year later, voted to obey and uphold the Supreme Court decision. Ken Whitsett called the pastor of his Presbyterian church, the church in which he had been baptized and instructed, the church in which his mother and father and grandfather and grandmother had worshiped, in whose graveyard many of Ken's antecedents were buried.

"How did you vote on the resolution?" Whitsett asked.

"I voted with the majority," said the minister.

"You are no longer my minister," said Whitsett.

He called the Presbyterian pastors in an ever-widening radius around Charlotte, asking each of them, "How did you vote?" At last he found a minister who said, "I voted no." This church is 60 miles from his home, but it is to that church Whitsett repairs for his devotions.

Unwittingly, perhaps, all these Southerners were changing their lives. Virginius Dabney, from whose excellent book I have already quoted, was widely regarded as a famous Southern liberal until the Northern newspapers asked him for an opinion on the Southern reaction. When he complied, the editors realized they couldn't use the editorial since it was nothing more than a rehash of the Southern backstairs biology which insists God made the races different colors to keep them apart.

On that May afternoon, I left Ken Whitsett's office exhilarated. I hurried over to Kelly Alexander in his funeral home. Kelly said, "This is the beginning of a new life for us." Together we went to see John Perry, the president of Johnson C. Smith University. He was also transported. The colored students had run from their classes when the news came, and they were clustered all over the campus, cheering and clapping and singing.

But the rest of Charlotte was quiet. There was a news story that night, but that was the end of it. The ministers did not discuss the ruling from their pulpits, nor did the school superintendents convene the Board of Education, nor did the local representatives offer political comments. In the South there was . . . utter silence.

I thought this silence was because the South was stunned. But I was wrong. The South was mustering its forces. It was going to preserve segregation. It was planning the strategy of noncompliance. Had the Southern governors and the responsible legislators set the pattern for direction of obedience, integration might not be a *fait accomplis* throughout the South, but in many areas it would now be institutionalized. The leaders did not do it. The leaders of the South created a vacuum, and into the vacuum came the white supremacists, the racists, the White Citizens Councils,

305

the Ku Kluxers, a sad price to pay for maintaining the Southern way of life. Many a Southern governor would pay anything today to rid his state of night riders, Ku Kluxers, and dynamiters.

In North Carolina, Governor Luther Hodges had just succeeded William Umsted, who died in office. I was on speaking terms with the new governor, for I had helped in his campaign for lieutenant governor. I asked him about the silence. He said it was deceptive. Underneath, he said, the people were seething.

"That is only your opinion," I ventured. "Maybe the people aren't seething; maybe they are waiting for direction."

In the fall of 1959, Governor Hodges told me he was going to a convention of Southern governors in Washington, D.C. LeRoy Collins of Florida, the chairman of this committee, had appointed Hodges to sum up the sense of the meeting on a network television program.

"I have heard from all the segregationists. I do not think I should go to the meeting without hearing the views of one integrationist," Hodges said.

I wrote this letter:

> These views I offer are not mine; they are those of Judge John J. Parker, a Southerner, whose credentials cannot be challenged. Judge Parker says the South is law abiding. He also says the Supreme Court is not going to reverse itself on this issue. Therefore, he says the Southern governors should accept these hard realities. Once accepted, it is reasonable for the Governors to ask the rest of the country to accept other hard realities. The South can integrate some schools tomorrow, some schools within the next decade, and some schools never. Working realistically, the Southern Governors can get someplace.

None of these ideas invaded Governor Hodges' television summation. Instead, the Southern governors promised intransigence. They proved as good as their word.

Southern states adopted a variety of legislative ruses to circumvent the decision. One abolished public education, a move which its State Supreme Court ruled unconstitutional. James Jackson Kilpatrick of the Richmond *News Leader* in Virginia suggested the relic of "interposition" forgetting interposition is only the prerogative of a sovereign state, of which there hasn't been one since 1789. Governor Orval Faubus of Arkansas called out the

State Guard to bar colored students from Central High School, citing civil strife as his motive. President Eisenhower sent in the 101st Airborne.

The most successful of all these attempts was the Pearsall Plan, initiated by North Carolina, named for the lawyer who proposed it in the state Senate. The Pearsall Plan provided:

The elimination of the compulsory attendance law to prevent any child from being forced to attend school with a child of another race;

The establishment of "Education Expense Grants" for education in private schools in the case of a child assigned to a public school attended by a child of another race;

A "uniform system of local option" whereby a majority within the school district may suspend or close a school if the situation becomes "intolerable."

Several of these provisions were patently unconstitutional, but one barricaded white schools against Negro attendance. It was the local option clause which put it up to the local school board to decide who would be integrated and when. The Pearsall Plan soon became known as freedom of choice, which gave the right to a colored schoolboy to declare he didn't want to go to a white school. Each colored applicant who wanted to attend a white school had to make a personal petition to the school board while his parents waited outside a closed door, sometimes for days, while the school board, all white adults, among them always a minister or two, questioned him.

"Aren't you happy with your own people?" is a question sophisticated philosophers can, on occasion, answer. A frightened ten-year-old colored boy often has a hard time of it. Preparatory to bringing the plan before the state legislature, the governor's Advisory Education Committee held open hearings in Raleigh in the summer of 1956. I was one of many witnesses invited to express my views. Another was Ken Whitsett, by then president of North Carolina's Patriots of America, Incorporated, Charlotte's White Citizens Council.

On the day I testified, the committee heard thirteen witnesses, eleven for segregation, two against, I and Dr. C. Maggs, dean of the Duke University Law School. The committee convened in one of the large chambers of the statehouse. The benches were

307

filled with reporters, and one of the TV stations had a camera and cameraman. The room had red rugs, burnished tables for the committeemen, and rows and rows of black benches for the witnesses. Ken Whitsett sat beside me.

One of the first witnesses to testify was the Reverend James Dees, an Episcopalian minister from Statesville. Reverend Dees said if God had wanted us to mix, he would have made us all one color. The exercised Reverend Dees kept on with this nonsense while the legislators solemnly attended him. I turned to Ken Whitsett and said, "That's the first clergyman I've heard speak so positively for segregation."

"Of course," said Ken Whitsett, "he's a real Christian. All those other fellows are for brotherhood." (Author Burke Davis heard the remark and reported it in the Greensboro *News*. The Reverend Dees was eventually forced to resign the pulpit of the Statesville Episcopal Church. Now the church has invited the Negro Episcopal Church to join it in a merger.)

In his turn, Dr. Maggs said, "The Pearsall Plan is unconstitutional." He argued strictly the legal implications of the plan. The committee heard him in cold silence.

My turn. I suggested the Golden Vertical Negro Plan:

One of the factors involved in our tremendous industrial growth and economic prosperity is the fact that the South, voluntarily, has all but eliminated Vertical Segregation. The tremendous buying power of the twelve million Negroes in the South has been based wholly on the absence of racial segregation. The white and Negro stand at the same grocery and supermarket counters; deposit money at the same bank teller's window; pay phone and light bills to the same clerk; walk through the same dime and department stores; and stand at the same drugstore counters.

It is only when the Negro "sets" that the fur begins to fly.

Now, since we are not even thinking about restoring Vertical Segregation, I think my plan would not only comply with the Supreme Court decisions, but would maintain "sitting-down" segregation. Now here is the Golden Vertical Negro Plan. Instead of all those complicated proposals, all the next session needs to do is pass one small amendment which would provide only desks in all the public schools of our state—no seats.

The desks should be those standing-up jobs, like the old-fashioned bookkeeping desk. Since no one in the South pays the slightest attention to a Vertical Negro, this will completely solve our problem. And it is not such a terrible inconvenience for young people to stand up during their classroom studies. In fact, this may be a blessing in disguise. They are not learning to read sitting down, anyway; maybe standing up will help. This will save more millions of dollars in the cost of our remedial English course when the kids enter college. In whatever direction you look with the Golden Vertical Negro Plan, you save millions of dollars, to say nothing of eliminating forever any danger to our public education system upon which rests the destiny, hopes, and happiness of this society."

Governor Hodges invited all the witnesses to meet with him when the meeting adjourned. On the statehouse steps, a reporter asked Ken Whitsett why he, the president of the Patriots of America, Incorporated, was walking along with Harry Golden, the publisher of the *Carolina Israelite*. Ken said, "Harry Golden and I have nothing in common but our friendship."

There were ten of us, I believe, who presented ourselves to the governor. Luther Hodges walked up to me and said, "That Vertical Plan is a great idea," and he threw his head back and laughed. He was, however, less complimentary about the absent Professor Maggs. He used such words as "Communist" and "subversive" and said the good professor was a disgrace to his profession.

When our meeting was over, I asked my good friend Jonathan Daniels, the editor of the Raleigh *News and Observer*, "Why the anger against Professor Maggs? He presented a reasonable and learned brief, whereas my Vertical Plan was much more provocative and emotional."

Jonathan said, "Golden, you're not a renegade, that's the reason. You are not a Southerner, one of us. Maggs is."

If the governor was laughing and jovial at my remarks, however, there were many of my advertisers and readers who were not. I had no sooner made the *Israelite* self-supporting than it began to go under when advertisers and readers canceled because of my defense of integration. An example from my paper in 1956:

THE RACE QUESTION IS A BASILISK
Definition—Basilisk: A legendary monster whose mere look was enough to cause complete paralysis.
Here is the South, with its strong heritage of freedom, which gave to America its concept of free government, the ballot and the

separation of church and state; where its ratio between the production of raw material and manufacture, is slowly but surely approaching the best balance anywhere in the world; where it possesses the best climate on the continent; the "most" American section of the nation; where its people "pioneered" the idea of America's responsibility in world affairs; where its legislators saved the Draft Act two weeks before Pearl Harbor; where its Congressmen saved the Lend Lease Act which helped rescue Western civilization; and where we may find some of the kindest people in this world. And now this great civilization stands paralyzed; and what is it all about? Here is what it is all about. It involves the possibility that NO MORE than eight per cent of the Negro school children of the South would be legally eligible to go to predominantly "white" schools. That is All this paralysis involves. Nothing, ABSOLUTELY NOTHING, more.

South Carolina cut out all my advertising after a speech at the University of South Carolina. I had been invited by the Unitarians, and I told them that segregation is evil, unconstitutional, and represents unequal education.

On the floor of the South Carolina state legislature, a member rose to ask why I was invited to speak at the university.

The president of the Unitarians explained that I had not been invited by the university to make an integration speech; I had been invited by the Unitarian group on the campus. Actually they weren't as worried about my speech as much as they were worried about the standing ovation the audience gave me.

Roughly, I had 16,000 circulation, half of it in the major cities —New York, Chicago, Los Angeles, Philadelphia. I carried two pages of national advertisers: Katz's Delicatessen had an ad in every issue of the *Israelite* ("Buy a salami for your boy in the Army"), and the New York publishers from time to time took out full-page ads. For thirteen pages of the *Israelite* I was dependent on local advertising. These clients ranged from the Duke Light & Power through WSOC-TV to gas stations in Florence, South Carolina, and mortuaries in Rock Hill.

The white supremacists began writing these fellows, and these clients began canceling their advertisements. The fellows who didn't get the hate letters still got the paper with their ad outlined, and often, after reading the editorials, they would refuse to pay the reminder of their billing.

310

In 1955–56, I had to borrow $4,000 to keep the paper going. I borrowed from friends, from Dr. Paul Sanger, from Sanford Rosenthal, and from George M. Ivey. After a year, the $4,000 was dissipated, and vigorous though I was, advertising revenue simply was not forthcoming. Not every Southern businessman and entrepreneur was against me. Many had limited advertising budgets. They advertised once a year in the Brotherhood or Israeli Independence Day or the New Year's issues. Some advertisers did stick with me and not out of sympathy or charity either, but because the *Israelite* brought them the return they paid for. The *Israelite* was a profit maker, strictly a business venture, but as circulation dropped, so did the rates for advertising linage.

When further publication looked fruitless, Irving Engel of the American Jewish Committee came to my aid. He sent me money to continue publishing. Joining with him was Senator Herbert H. Lehman, Edward Warburg, Kivie Kaplan of Boston, and others. In all, I borrowed $20,000 over a period of three years, all of which I was later able to pay back with interest when *Only in America* was published.

The time I gained with this money let me and my advertising manager, Ken Robertson, shore up our paper. On Saturdays and Sundays I stayed on the phone soliciting ads from any businessman who answered. Without *Only in America* I would still have paid off my debtors. It would have taken longer, but I still would have managed. I was contributing articles to the *Nation, Commentary,* the *Democratic Digest,* and many other magazines; from time to time, I was quoted by reputable journalists; all of this brought me lecturing dates. I put this income back into the paper, so I could continue to report the ever-fascinating study of the middle class coping with the twentieth century.

The first attempt at token integration in Charlotte came on September 4, 1957, when attractive fifteen-year-old Dorothy Counts entered Harding High School. A crowd of jeering teen-agers spat and hissed at her. During her second week of school these teen-agers reviled her in the halls and hit her with an eraser and a piece of tin. Inflamed bands of high school children followed her home every day. When her brother, Herman Counts, a twenty-year-old college student, drove to the school to pick her up, he was greeted with catcalls, and a rock cracked the rear window of his car.

Dorothy finally withdrew from the school. In the Charlotte *Observer* of September 11, 1957, her father, the Reverend Herman L. Counts, professor of Christian theology at the School of Religion, Johnson C. Smith University, made the statement: "It was with compassion for our native land and love for our daughter, Dorothy, that we withdrew her as a student from Harding High School."

With several members of the local Human Relations Council, I called on the Counts family. Our purpose was to urge the Reverend Mr. Counts to permit Dorothy to stay in the previously all-white school.

At one point Reverend Counts showed us a diary in which he had listed the names of the people who had called to express sympathy and compassion for Dorothy's ordeal. We looked over this list in wonder and chagrin. The list was a fair representation of Charlotte society, the white leaders of the religious, political, and philanthropic structure of our city. Why hadn't any of these people called the school board or the mayor or written a letter to the editor expressing their views? The embattled editors of the Charlotte *News* and the Charlotte *Observer* were hungry for such an expression. But none came—publicly. Such action would have meant a betrayal.

Chapter 27

WHEN I went to the University Settlement House on Eldridge and Rivington streets, I used to see a tall lady in the old-fashioned blue bloomers teaching the immigrant girls American dances. I knew she was a Protestant lady, one of the many volunteers from the New York aristocracy who lent their time and energy to the betterment of the downtown minorities.

When Franklin D. Roosevelt became President, I recognized this tall lady as his wife, Eleanor. I had occasion to tell her of this memory almost fifty years later. I met Mrs. Roosevelt at a civil rights meeting in New York. She said, "If you had watched more carefully, Mr. Golden, you would have seen my young husband call for me."

Not long after this meeting, I went with Mrs. Roosevelt to conduct a seminar at the Highlander Folk School in Monteagle, Tennessee.

In July, 1957, Myles Horton, the founder and director of this integrated school, invited me to lecture on political action at a symposium. At the time the Highlander Folk School was the only integrated school in the South. It was integrated only because it was a private school supported solely by private donations. Myles Horton, a longtime liberal, was a subscriber to the *Carolina Israelite* and had founded the school in 1954. He was motivated by a desire to see if an integrated school could function in a Southern state. To get the school going, he asked liberals and educators for contributions, and I was one of the many who responded with some money.

The Highlander School was similar to the Henry George School of Social Science, though on a far smaller scale. Its students were not pursuing a degree; many of them already held degrees. The students at the Highlander Folk School studied political action, race relations, trade unionism, and social work. There was perhaps a student body of 150, half of them white, half of them black.

The Highlander Folk School was a modest effort. Located in the highlands, it was remote from the large communities. The students conducted themselves courteously and made demands only of their own resources. But Tennessee was still outraged by the Highlander School's existence. Myles Horton had already been subpoenaed to testify before James O. Eastland's Senate Committee on Subversive Activities. Eastland kept asking over and over was Myles Horton a Communist, and Myles Horton kept replying, no, he was not. At no time during his testimony did Horton seek refuge in the Fifth Amendment. Yet his neighbors in Tennessee had no compunctions about accusing him of treason. Myles was fighting a long succession of suits, timely and costly suits. He was persevering, but he needed help. The authorities accused him and his students of everything from drug addiction to illicit sex. Neither Myles nor his students wanted to provoke anyone. The politics of confrontation was a decade away. Tennessee was making sure the Highlander Folk School was getting all the trouble it could handle.

The seminars Myles planned were well publicized, and certain liberal groups had responded with generous sympathy. Once invited, I felt I had no choice but to go. Myles said it was important.

The first person I met in the Chattanooga airport terminal was Eleanor Roosevelt. Lo and behold, this woman, who had just returned from Holland where she had dined with the queen, was also bound for this mountain school, which had at best primitive facilities: The classrooms and dormitories were uninsulated barracks built by the students themselves; the china was paper plates and the stemware Dixie cups. We ate from tables which were planks nailed over sawhorses.

Myles appeared and introduced himself. He drove us the 40

314

miles to Monteagle. It was a hot day. Blisters rose from the tar on the road, and the trees were as still as spears.

On the way, I told Mrs. Roosevelt that many of my friends and colleagues had advised me not to come to Monteagle. Mrs. Roosevelt said she, too, had received the same warnings. Myles interrupted to tell us that the Roman Catholic Bishop of Buffalo, New York, was a member of the school's board of directors. He repeated this information several times.

I said to Mrs. Roosevelt, "Every liberal should have at least one Catholic priest behind him. Behind me is the Bishop of North Carolina, Vincent S. Waters. Do you have a Catholic bishop behind you?"

She laughed and said, "No, Mr. Golden. I do not have a bishop. All I have to recommend me is that my husband was four times elected the President of the United States."

Race had by now become the tumultuous concern of the South. The North was being drawn toward this vortex. Mrs. Roosevelt and I both felt that going to the Highlander Folk School on Myles Horton's behalf was not a symbolic or rhetorical gesture but a practical one. We had a lot to tell these students and a lot to tell each other. And most important, we were at this moment traversing a state whose racial attitudes were rigid and uncompromising. We were on our way to an integrated school, which five years before was not only unthinkable but impossible. While the Highlander Folk School was not flourishing, it was surviving. That alone made it a magnet.

The school was pitched on the side of a small mountain. Trees surrounded the enclave, which numbered eight or ten barracks and three or four houses. Students ran all the facilities and performed all the services the little community needed. They had a mess detail, a garbage detail, a cleanup detail. Attached to the school was a corps of social workers, as embattled as the students.

Over these two days at Monteagle I first met Dr. Martin Luther King. Dr. King had just won the Montgomery bus strike, but he had not yet achieved the international reputation he later enjoyed. One of the photographs his enemies always circulated to prove Dr. King was a Communist was taken at Monteagle by a spying photographer hired by Governor Marvin Griffin of Georgia. As often as Dr. King was questioned about this photograph, which showed him lecturing before an integrated class, he would defend

315

himself with, "Harry Golden and Eleanor Roosevelt were at Monteagle, too."

This photographer took dozens of pictures over the course of the symposium. He concentrated on snapping pictures of white girls talking to colored men or a colored woman talking to a white student. Out of these pictures, Governor Griffin constructed a photographic montage which he distributed to every elected legislator in the South. The picture of me, however, shows me talking to a black nun.

Myles Horton was our host for the two days and two nights Mrs. Roosevelt and I were at the Highlander Folk School. The thrust of my argument to these students was that they must work toward a coalition. The American political system is based on coalitions. The farmers and the workingman still constitute a powerful bloc, and I told the students that the Irish, the Jews, and the Italians on the Lower East Side kept Tammany in power for many years. Effective coalitions do not need absolute sympathies, just a general recognition of similar interests. I urged these integrationists to work for a coalition with the union man. If the union man and the Negro ever joined forces, they would control the election machinery.

Going back to the airport, Myles described the relentless pressures Tennessee had brought to bear against him and the school. The state tried many devices to close up the school and failed in all but one: Tennessee is a local option dry state, and one police officer later claimed to have found a pint of bottled whiskey on the campus. The state was able to bring a criminal action, and consequently it padlocked the Highlander Folk School. Myles moved on to establish another integrated school in Tennessee, this time with better luck, for by the 1960's the laws were working for him.

During John Kennedy's administration, Mrs. Roosevelt invited me to dinner at her home in New York City. I was there with John Hersey, Art Buchwald, John Mason Brown, Laura Hobson, and Clark Eichelberger, the then president of the American Association for the United Nations. Mrs. Roosevelt was a delegate to the United Nations Commission on Human Rights. She asked us to lend enthusiasm to the cause of the United Nations, to pub-

316

licize its good works, and to encourage our readers to support the UN.

When we had finished eating, we moved back to the living room. Mrs. Roosevelt unclenched her hand and showed me a pill in her palm. She sighed, "Now what good is this little thing going to do for a big woman like me?" In her bedroom, on her night table were two pictures: one of FDR and the other of Adlai Stevenson.

I heard from her again right after John F. Kennedy had invited me to attend the civil rights seminar in New York City which was convened to help implement the civil rights proposals of the Democratic platform. When it was announced I was one of the delegates from North Carolina, John Warren, Democratic chairman of Mecklenburg County, asked, "Why did they ask an ex-convict to attend?" I recited this charge to Mrs. Roosevelt and said my appointment might be a disservice to the delegation.

She said, "Forget John Warren. You come." The North Carolina press, notably the Charlotte *Obesrver* and the Charlotte *News,* confirmed Mrs. Roosevelt's judgment.

At the meeting, which was chaired by John Kennedy, Mrs. Roosevelt said to me, "It's conventions like these which will break the cycle of white racism in America."

There is no need for me to detail how she championed the cause of the American Negro. These actions have already passed into American legend. As early as 1942, when she visited the Cannon Mills in Kannapolis, North Carolina, she remarked how shocking it was to see separate drinking fountains for whites and colored. These sentiments put North Carolina up in arms. It was this remark which gave rise to the rumor that the Negroes had organized thousands of Eleanor Clubs in the South. Never let it be said the South can't create its own ogres.

Talking to Eleanor Roosevelt made a man conscious he was in the presence of a great and noble woman. She was exceptionally smart, always tough with her opponents, but she laughed a lot. Her first cause in these last years was the United Nations, and race was her second. She gave them both all she had, bestowing on them her influence and her good sense.

The last time I heard from her was when she placed an emergency call to me in Charlotte. She said, "My doctor wants me to

317

go to the hospital. I believe it is a lot of nonsense, but I'm going. I have had to cancel a lecture at Alfred College. Would you go in my place? I have asked the president of the college, and he is pleased to accept you as a substitute." I went.

Two weeks later Mrs. Roosevelt was dead.

Chapter 28

MY friendship with Carl Sandburg was the most rewarding of my life. Carl was all-out for friendship. If Carl was your friend and your son was sick, Carl worried as much as you. If you were depressed, Carl wanted to share your depression as he wanted to share your exhilaration when you were happy. Carl, as a friend, accepted your entire universe, every star, jungle, and person in it.

Carl was also a rewarding friend because I deemed him a great American writer. I had read his pamphlets as a young Socialist in the twenties, read his biography of Lincoln, *The Prairie Years,* in prison, and his poem *The People, Yes* in the Depression. His response to me was that of one writer to another; he took me seriously as a writer long before I had ever published a book.

Carl Sandburg and family consisted of his wife, Lillian (the sister of the famous photographer Edward Steichen), called Paula, daughters Margaret, Janet, and Helga. The Sandburgs moved to North Carolina in 1945, after having spent several decades on the dunes of Harbert, Michigan, across the lake from Chicago. They came South because Carl needed a warmer climate and chose North Carolina because Paula, an animal husbandryman with a PhD and a Phi Beta Kappa key from the University of Chicago, wanted to see if she could raise thoroughbred goats on Southern soil, a farming venture never before attempted. At this she succeeded. One of the rooms in Sandburg's home is filled with the blue ribbons Paula won.

In the company of several other newspapermen I met Sandburg in 1948. We were interviewing him before a guitar concert at Davidson College just outside Charlotte. When I introduced myself, he said, "You're the fellow with the paper." This flattery encouraged me to write a letter saying I'd like to talk to him again. Sandburg replied:

DEAR BRUDDER GOLDEN:
We won't settle the problems of the world but you come on. I'll be glad to see you.

CARL SANDBURG

My motive was to talk to a man who had helped change and add to American literature and history. So I drove across the mountains to Carl's home, Connemara Farm in Flat Rock. This home, a Southern mansion which Carl purchased from the proceeds of the movie sale of his novel *Remembrance Rock*, was built by the secretary of the treasury of the Confederate States of America, Christopher G. Memminger. Memminger called the estate Rock Hill, and it was to Rock Hill that Memminger fled for refuge in the last tumultuous days of the Confederacy. Captain Ellington Adger Smythe changed the name from Rock Hill to Connemara. It was from Smythe's estate that the Sandburgs purchased the 240-acre farm.

From the porch of the house Carl could see the Appalachian range of the Great Smokies. Connemara crested a smooth upward slope that rose perpendicular for 500 feet. Bordering the base of the property was Big Glassy, the circular flat rock from which the town takes its name. The house itself is representative of plantation architecture: a huge cellar, two stories girdled by an enormous veranda, and an attic. The ground floor is divided into two sizable living rooms, in one of which Carl stored all his research materials and in the other of which he did his writing and reading. Books overflowed everywhere. They waited atop the piano and were stacked on the furniture. There were piles of them underneath the windows, and they were banked against the sides of the desk. Every inch of wall space was lined by filled bookshelves.

When I stood alone with Carl on his porch at Connemara and looked over this wonderful site and the beautiful old building, I said to him, "The old Socialist Victor Berger would turn over in his grave if he saw this."

Carl threw his head back and roared in laughter and yelled through the screen door to his wife, "Paula, Paula, he says Victor Berger would turn over in his grave if he saw this place."

We became close friends that afternoon.

It must be remembered that though there was a twenty-year difference between us, though Carl had grown to manhood in rural, small-town America and I in a tenement ghetto, still we had a lot in common. Both of us were children of mothers who could not speak English and Carl had written the first pamphlet analyzing the race question in modern urban America, *The Chicago Race Riots, July, 1919.*

Sandburg was still trying in the years of our companionship to understand how America could come to the solution of this ever-desperate issue. When Thurgood Marshall and I were in Carl's company at Connemara one evening, Sandburg asked the then Solicitor General, who had argued the integration cases before the Supreme Court, "Why did the Negro make his move for integration in the schools? Why not in health facilities, hospitals, and convalescent homes, for instance? Negro infant mortality is five times that of whites. People would have been less aroused."

Marshall replied, "We are a school-oriented society. If we desegregate the public schools of America, the whole pattern of racial segregation will inevitably collapse."

Part of Carl's fondness for me then grew out of his concern for the racial issue. He told me, "Harry, you're the most important man in America today. You are the only white man with popular influence devoting full time to race." Another time he said, "When I left Chicago, I left behind Mr. Robert Hutchins and Clarence Darrow. I thought I'd be lonely. But in North Carolina I got Harry Golden to the east and Ralph McGill to the south."

I had no sooner met him than he ordered thirty subscriptions of the *Israelite* to be sent to his friends. Faithfully he renewed these subscriptions year after year.

This was a significant gesture because all his life Carl lived with a poverty syndrome. Connemara was cluttered with everything Carl ever put his hands on. There were boxes of assorted string in the stairwells, and Carl still owned the first hat he ever bought. Paula Sandburg told me Carl's father saved bent nails, and Carl himself never threw out a pair of shoes. He was a great saver. He still had newspapers from 1912.

When he first began getting dates for his guitar and poetry recitals, Paula told me, Carl always instructed the chairman of the event to send him the railroad fare, not the ticket. Carl rode the rods or hopped the freights to many a lecture. When you offered him a cigar, he automatically broke it in half, put one end in his breast pocket, and smoked the other.

No matter where I traveled with him, Carl always knew someone who would put him up for the night and save hotel expenses.

Yet when he died, Carl left more than $1,000,000, not counting Connemara, which the United States government will purchase to transform into a museum. There were abiding and profound reasons why Carl was penurious. His boyhood was passed in rural poverty, and he never forgot it. Two of his three daughters have sad afflictions. Margaret, the eldest, suffers nocturnal seizures and has suffered them all her life. Margaret is a brilliant bibliophile, but year after year these seizures, for which there is no therapy, have drained her strength. Janet, the second daughter, stepped into the path of a car as a schoolgirl. Her skull was fractured. She could never overcome this disability, and Carl worried all his life that when he died, these two girls would not be able to support themselves. All his money went into a fund to provide for Margaret and Janet. Helga, Carl's youngest daughter, is, of course, a prominent writer and is married to the brilliant surgeon Dr. George "Barney" Crile, Jr., of the famous Cleveland Clinic.

Dinner at the Sandburgs' home was a Spartan repast. Carl never had an appetite. An ordinary omelet had all the splendor of French cuisine for him, and Campbell's Baked Beans and boiled hot dogs were a Sunday treat.

In Charlotte's Hearth and Embers Restaurant I watched this poet, who had won two Pulitzer Prizes and had addressed the joint Houses of Congress, enthuse over a baked potato into which the waitress had poured a dollop of sour cream with chives. He thought it such a culinary milestone he ordered a second potato. The Hearth and Embers Restaurant, incidentally, serves the guests of the Manger Motel. I always reserved the first-floor suite for Carl, and as a consequence, that suite is called today The Sandburg Suite and always reserved for visiting dignitaries.

I became a constant visitor to Connemara, after a while not

even awaiting an invitation but simply announcing my arrival. I was always at Connemara on Thanksgiving Day, Christmas, and the Fourth of July when we raised the flag and Paula, Margaret, Janet, and I would sing "Amerikay" while Carl accompanied us on his guitar.

> Torn from a world of tyrants
> Beneath this Western sky
> We formed this new dominion
> A land of liberty.
> The world shall know we're freemen here
> And such shall ever be
> Huzzah, huzzah, huzzah
> For free, free Amerikay
>
> Lift up your hands ye heroes
> And swear with proud disdain
> The wretch that would ensnare you
> Shall lay his snares in vain.
> Should Europe send invading force
> We'll meet her in array
> And fight and shout and fight
> For brave, brave Amerikay

What we did at Connemara was talk, Carl in his rocker, wearing his old newspaperman's eyeshade, I in the straight-backed chair opposite. We even prepared an agenda so that our discussions wouldn't ramble. A typical agenda included: (1) Richard Nixon; (2) Dwight D. Eisenhower; (3) Adlai Stevenson; (4) Socialism, Its Death and Future?; (5) Dorothy Day of the *Catholic Worker*. Dorothy Day was on our agenda on this particular occasion because she had been arrested in New York City for refusing to participate in an air-raid alert. Carl said, "She'll be needing some bail," and he forthwith interrupted the discussion to write her a check.

Carl had been a morning newspaperman. Consequently he had spent years working nights. Once his books began to support him, he found the old habits too hard to break. He never came downstairs before noon, and he went to bed in the early hours of the morning. On the other hand, I am an early riser, and often our agenda had to conclude when my eyes were red from lack of sleep.

I was on the second floor one predawn, on my way to the crow's nest bedroom, when I heard Carl below, crying agitatedly, "Harry, Harry!"

"What's the matter, Carl?"

"We didn't finish our agenda."

"What didn't we discuss?" I asked.

"We didn't discuss the death of Mike Todd," he said.

"We'll have to complete it in the morning, Carl."

"All right," he said resignedly. "But I want you to take one thought to bed with you. I wish it had been Cecil B. De Mille."

When I signed a contract with World Publishing in 1957 for a book of essays, the first person I told was Carl. I went up to Connemara and said, "I'm going to have a book out next spring."

Carl said, "I always figured there oughta be a book out of the *Carolina Israelite*."

One of our rituals at Connemara was the brisk walk from the house to Big Glassy and back. Much of the way was wooded, and on this fall day the wind was thrashing the leaves from the trees. On our way, I told Carl what I thought the book should contain. Back at the house, Carl said, "You know, Harry, you will need a picture for the jacket of the book. Since I have agreed to write the introduction, let us take the picture for the publisher."

He had carried a camera with him for reasons I couldn't determine until this moment. He handed the camera to Margaret and said, "Take a picture of me and Harry," which later, of course, became the jacket picture for *Only in America*.

"A book is the most satisfying experience in life," he said. Then he added, "Naturally your book will be a great success."

Paula Sandburg was as happy for me. Paula was always sympathetic to my aspirations. Carl had been a Socialist and a Socialist organizer until World War I, when he began to compromise his position. Paula never compromised. She was a Socialist then and is a Socialist now. She used to tease Carl that she had more politics in common with me than she did with him. When I bought a second house adjoining my first one in Charlotte, she said, "You are just a couple of old Socialists who are now North Carolina landowners."

This particular weekend ended for me with the arrival of Ed Murrow's advance men from CBS who were preparing Connemara for Carl's appearance on *Person to Person*. The Sandburgs were naturally thrilled by the prospect, and to show their appreciation and hospitality, they offered each of these men a pitcher of goat's milk. Carl and Paula loved their goats to a degree they couldn't see the CBS advance men choking on the milk. I had to tell him before I left, "Just because I drink the goat's milk doesn't mean everybody loves you as much."

Until *Only in America,* Carl was always worried about the *Carolina Israelite.* He used to urge me to keep it going, that I could not let it die. If Carl were still alive, I would not have closed the paper in 1968 because he believed in it so fervently. *Only in America* gave me a solid decade of solvency for the first time in my life.

"What are you going to do next?" he asked when the book was published.

Spontaneously I answered, "Carl, I'd like to do a book about you."

He took one rock on his rocker and said, "Go ahead."

"It's not that simple," I went on. "I need your help."

He took another rock. "You'll have it," he said.

With this guarantee I went to World Publishing and explained I'd like to write a book about Carl Sandburg. The editors were enthusiastic. They said there was no definitive biography of Sandburg.

"I don't want to write a definitive biography," I said. "I am not a definitive biographer. I want a *Carolina Israelite* type book, the subject of every essay—Carl Sandburg. I have no intentions of writing an objective book."

I reasoned that Sandburg's definitive biographer will have to spend two years at the University of Illinois, where his papers are collected, and another year at Knox College in Galesburg, which owns still more of his papers. That biographer will need another year traveling around the country talking to people who knew Carl at different times in his life.

I wrote *Carl Sandburg* through Carl and through Paula. One of the chapters I wanted to write was about their courtship and their love affair through the long years of their marriage.

"How does it feel to be the wife of a man like Carl Sandburg and the sister of a man like Edward Steichen?" I asked.

Paula just smiled.

Carl took off his eyeshade and said, "Well, why don't you answer the guy?"

He always kissed her hand when she brought food to the table, and she always kissed him back.

One of the privileges Carl gave me for the book were the unpublished chapters of his second volume of his autobiography, *Ever the Winds of Chance.* Some years before, he had published *Always the Young Strangers,* and I think when he let me use this subsequent material, he knew he would never finish it. I did incorporate all of it in the early chapters of *Carl Sandburg.* It is still amazing to realize that when Carl died, he left behind almost 3,000 pages of unpublished poetry and prose.

Writing this biography let me know more and more not only about Carl but about America, too. Carl was one of the first boys to enlist in the Army when the Spanish-American War broke out, and he went back to writing a newspaper column in World War II. In many ways, tracing Carl Sandburg's life was tracing part of the career of America during the first fifty years of the twentieth century.

December 22, 1959

DEAR CARL:

Don't forget your "date" with Olin Johnston's daughter. She's coming next Friday, an interview for her high school paper. Governor Johnston is quite a fellow. Did a bit of work for him—professionally—wrote speeches during his last campaign.

I've done a bit of detective work for you. Amazing that you had so many of the details correct about that Eugene V. Debs Memorial Meeting.

You were on the committee and James Oneal put you up at the University Settlement on the Lower East Side of New York. It seems to me that you might have written "Home Fires" after that visit unless you had been there before. The Settlement house is on Rivington Street. Your poem starts off:

"In a Yiddish place on Rivington Street . . ."

According to the record, you, James Oneal, and Jacob Panken, Socialist candidate for Governor, went to the *Jewish Daily Forward* to get the money for the use of Madison Square Garden. This was on October 16, 1926. Madison Square Garden had o.k.'d the Debs meeting for the Socialist Party. But the Communists got wind of it, hurriedly arranged a meeting of their own, and secured the Garden for the same night—October 26—for themselves. They did this by putting up cash, $1500, and the Garden management grabbed it. The Communists used a subterfuge name—The Workers Party. You, Oneal and Panken went to the Garden, and you convinced the management that the Workers Party was the Communist Party. The Garden management said that if you Socialists could bring $2500 cash the Garden would then be able to cancel the Communists "date" on a technicality and give the Socialists back their meeting.

The *Forward* gave you and your committee the money. The meeting was a big success, packed. The principal speaker was Morris Hillquit, of course. Norman Thomas opened the meeting.

When the Communists lost the Garden they organized a meeting of their own for October 23; the main idea was to have their meeting before the Socialists. They met in an auditorium called Webster Hall and the meeting was a terrible flop, a flop precisely because they had only one thing in mind, to be ahead of the Socialists and the speakers blasted the Socialists all evening. Debs was hardly mentioned.

At the Garden meeting, Hillquit referred to all of this Communist maneuvering and he quoted two or three public statements in which Debs said what he thought of Communists. Hillquit closed that portion of his speech saying, "Eugene V. Debs was no closer to the Communist movement than the North Pole is to the South Pole and the Communists know it. They would not dare to claim him for their own if he could speak for himself. The honest nature of Debs revolted against everything the Communists stand for."

The *Forward* says you and August Claessens took the money back to the *Forward*. You brought it in heavy bags of nickels, dimes, quarters, lots of pennies too. The hat had been passed in the Garden and more than enough was collected. The *Forward* contributed the money to the Socialist Party campaign fund in New York and Wisconsin.

By the way, have you read in recent years the speech you delivered from the rear platform of the Red Special during the presidential campaign for Debs? "We Socialists demand free text books for the children, wash-rooms for the miners, the 8-hour-day, and workman's compensation." Nixon could run on that platform today. Sic transit . . . See you New Years as usual.

Love,
HARRY GOLDEN

The hard work on the book, its actual composition, started sometime in 1959. Carl was soon in Hollywood, working for George Stevens at Twentieth Century-Fox on the film *The Great-*

est Story Ever Told. In Hollywood, they gave Carl Marilyn Monroe's dressing room—her "undressing room" he called it. He was full of admiration for George Stevens because of the producer's previous productions of *Shane, Giant, A Place in the Sun,* and *The Diary of Anne Frank,* but he wasn't at all impressed with Miss Monroe's "undressing room," which he found too fancy for his taste. The studio personnel transferred him immediately to a less pretentious room. Carl also insisted on being transferred from a $45-a-day hotel suite to a $25 one—even though he wasn't paying the rent.

During much of the composition of *Carl Sandburg,* Carl and I were at a remove. It was fortunate for me—I didn't have to show Carl rough drafts, only the finished chapters. We kept in touch by mail, telephone, and sporadic visits.

October 4, 1960

20th Century Fox

DEAR HARRY:

Good and sweet to have your letter. When in L.A. if you can't get to my odd lair in Bel Air, I will go to whatever hotel you are at very cheerfully and report to you the doings and didoes. You will be saying, I believe, that I am on a nice constructive piece of work. Paula says it is a new field that is challenging and good for me. I think you might enjoy an afternoon of four hours at a session of five rare fellows, headed by Stevens. And Jesus wept! yesterday comes the news—Harcourt Brace and the World and Ben Zevin all in a merger—and that we can talk over.

I send you deep and abiding affection.

CARL

October 11, 1960

20th Century Fox

DEAR HARRY:

Your letter comes along and is good to have. A suite at the Beverly Hilton sounds good. What Bill Targ says of the book is more than interesting. I am marking October 29 as our day and night. You may be sure if the manuscript comes along in early December I will give it a good reading and send you any comment I might have.

I have telegrams about a radio series for Kennedy to be taped by you and me here in L.A. I have no anxiety about it and it may work out. Anyhow I'm looking for your coming. You'll enjoy a look at the first office I have ever had, a large affair that was once the dressing room of Marilyn Monroe, and the door having my name in brass letters, this for the first time in my life. You will have campaign news that will interest me.

Ever yours,
CARL

19 January 1961

20th Century Fox
DEAR HARRY:

I should not forget to tell you I have a letter from Curtiss Anderson, Associate Editor of the "Ladies Home Journal." He was on "Better Homes and Gardens" when I did the article on the jet planes. He says, "Please do have Harry Golden send the carbon of your biography. As I told you I have already discussed this by letter with Mr. Golden suggesting there may be a chapter or two or more for us."

. . . and Harry, it sure would be right good to see you at Connemara.

CARL

May 29, 1961

20th Century Fox
DEAR HARRY:

A letter comes from our friend Joe Wershba with a paragraph we can share as follows:

"Harry Golden just came through for a luncheon speech to the Public Relations Society of America. He held them enthralled— and told them to their faces we're losing the fight for ideas because we're prisoners of racism. Best speech I've heard him give. He is without doubt one of the most effective public speakers today."

You don't need compliments. What's yours by right is not compliments. He has deep faith in you. He sees you as sometimes bringing faith or again as deepening an already deep faith. I will allow you desperate moments but never in your present form desperate moments about yourself.

Ever yours,
CARL

June 9, 1961

20th Century Fox
DEAR HARRY:

Enclosed are photographs of George Stevens and me at Connemara. I will try for some photos of the conference room and enclosed is the Fog holograph. Also I enclose a copy of a letter that came to me after the Associated Press story quoting me as favoring the shooting to death of anyone caught painting a swastika. I am also sending you four photographs made by John Bryson whom Stevens and others, myself included, rate as one of the few great photographers. He was an editor of Life at one time and has quit to free-lance. I want all possible care taken of these prints and there should be instructions to return them to me because they are so scarce. Incidentally, Bryson has a gifted young Jewish woman so skilled as a developer that she saves him much time and he praises her skill. I told him that I would like to meet her sometime. "She'll be glad to meet you. She thinks you hung the moon." I said, "That's the first time I ever heard that expression." He said, "It's an old saying in Texas." And, Harry, I keep meeting people who think that you hung the moon. That is a nice kind of "guilt by association." You gently but convincingly handled the matter of Bruce Catton going off-key in his history. The first three photographers you list I don't know where they are. Paula will give you over the phone the address of Fred Knoop. John Vachon took photographs of me and they are masterpieces of photography and are the only ones I have, I find. There are some remarkable photographs, an extraordinary series, along with cartoons in The Sandburg Range. You might ask Herb Mitgang of the New York Times for photographs out of the Gettysburg TV which was shown on April 13 and is to have a rerun on July 4. The Gettysburg TV is one of the best things that I have ever done in my life and the general saying is that it will be around a long time and will be seen by millions of school children. I'm sure Fred Friendly would run it for you at CBS in New York along with the early one that Murrow did at Connemara.

Ever yours,
CARL

June 14, 1961

20th Century Fox
DEAR HARRY:

The photograph of Bette [Davis] and me was made frontstage at the end of the opening of the show in the Henry Miller Theatre in New York. What they were playing was titled, "The World of Carl Sandburg," as you know. There was a standing ovation to me but in the pitch-black beyond the footlights I could not see it. Norman Corwin and I are signing contracts today for the publication next fall of "The World of Carl Sandburg" by Norman Corwin as author. There'll be cheap paperback reprints by Samuel French who publishes for stock and amateurs. If you get a photograph of Bette and me from the Associated Press please get a duplicate for me. I send you these things with no concrete suggestions at all and if nothing comes of them you will never hear no demurs from me. Your book is going to be a nice hayride. I am ready anytime to read proofs or to welcome your good face out here. I am not sure I understand it but long ago I met some mathematician saying, "Make the sign of infinity and pass on."

As ever,
CARL

P. S. On my 75th birthday dinner at Knox College Steichen journeyed from his Umpawaug Farm in Connecticut to be present and to say among other remarks when called on to speak, "On the day that God made Carl He didn't do anything else that day."

June 20, 1961

20th Century Fox
DEAR HARRY:

Please send me four or five copies of the May-June Israelite. I have now read three times the page one piece titled, "The Freedom Riders in Alabama." You are going a little better than ever in your role which I term, "Apostle of Liberty." The book reviews by R.G.* are keen. As I ramble through this current number I get a definite impression it is one of the best you have ever done. You should send a marked copy to Senator Hart of Michigan who has a bill in Congress providing for purchase of a memorial home of Frederick Douglass. I sent him a letter that he can throw into the Congressional Record, saying incidentally that Douglass proves baffling to the White Supremacists. He was a Negro whom Lincoln welcomed at the White House.

A phone call came today from Gwynne Steinbeck saying she has done music to eight poems of mine and that music people who have heard the discs say they are great. She is bringing the discs out here next week and I will hear them and we will discuss them.

Did I send you Sam Marshall's Detroit News story about one angle that I have never met before? A calculation has been made that in order to produce the deaths of six million Jews, the Nazis had to subtract 600,000 men from their armed forces. This, of course, gives an angle on the contribution of the Jews to the destruction of the Nazi armed forces. I have an impression that I mailed to you this Marshall report.

They are elated and jumping with joy at Connemara over a three week visit that they will have from one of the loveliest and

---

* Richard Goldhurst, my son and associate editor.

brightest eighteen year old girls in this country in July, the grand-daughter Karlen Paula. . . . I may have told you that Harcourt Brace will publish, "The World of Carl Sandburg" by Norman Corwin next fall, and it will be fun to see what kind of a race it runs with Carl Sandburg by Harry Golden by God. . . . You may have missed this clipping which shows that you and Ralph McGill is comrades. . . . Do you have a complete list of the high schools and elementary schools named after me? Two elementary schools in the Detroit area have popped up in the last month, and one in Springfield, Ill. On word from you I will send you a complete list. You are free to use if you like the enclosed poem by Charles Hamblett from his book, "A Letter to the Living." . . . At the annual meeting of the Friars last January, a dinner honoring Gary Cooper, I made a five minute speech saying at the end, "I believe we are correct in saying that Gary Cooper is the most beloved illiterate to appear in American history." Then I turned and walked three steps to Gary Cooper and kissed him on the forehead, the first time I have ever done such a thing. Gary, who one time studied cartooning, went to work on a message and a cartoon for me and it was passed on down to where I sat next to Audrey Hepburn. I enclose it for you and howsoever you may wish to use it. But for Christ's sake don't lose it. . . . Do I recall your saying that J. F. Kennedy recited "Cool Tombs" or did he merely mention that he was familiar with it? I had a nice letter from him acknowledging warm appreciation of a two-volume deluxe "Remembrance Rock" I sent him. In my inscription in "Remembrance Rock" I wrote, "I am one of the many who register to your Inaugural Address as an American Classic." He closed his letter, "I have been an admirer of yours for many years and therefore I am extremely pleased to have this inscribed book." . . . As I have told you before, you are always in my prayers.

Faithfully,
CARL

June 26, 1961

DEAR CARL:

I've examined the sundry items you sent me and enjoyed your lengthy letter of June 20 in a thousand ways.

I thought I would return the Gary Cooper item before it gets lost in the jungle of papers here. It is certainly worth saving.

I might very well come out when we each get our set of galleys, although sometimes I think I'd rather not experience that emotion again—of me watching Carl Sandburg read a book about himself which I have written! A fantastic experience, eh wot? Writing about Jesus is a picnic compared to that. Is this not so? Suppose you and George Stevens had to sit there all night (as I did) and watch Him read the stuff. The two of you would take to the hills the first time He looked up from the manuscript.

We will probably give you a long distance call on the 4th of July.

Devotedly,
HARRY

July 28, 1961

20th Century Fox

DEAR HARRY:

I never brought a guitar to Darrow's office and sang. I never met Mrs. Hillman till years after the second and later strike, the strike in 1915. During the fifteen weeks the strike lasted I wrote a story about it every day in the Day Book, with sometimes a front page story. It was on Darrow's return from Los Angeles after his trial and acquittal that we became close thru news stories and an editorial on his announcement that he was for the Allies and against Germany in the first World War. Also he liked my review of his book "Farmington" which the Chicago Daily News book editor had printed as a booklet with a fine photograph of Darrow on the cover. He had occasion once to write me a lead pencil note which ended, "I don't want you to step out of my life," signed merely Darrow. I believe no one ever called him Clarence. He rates for me as being somewhat to Chicago what Diogenes was to Athens. Harry, you may use the foregoing if it can serve, but you are nearly as fantastic as Ben Hecht in having me in Chicago in 1910 and reporting the garment strike and bringing a guitar to Darrow's office and singing for him and Mrs. Hillman.

It is false testimony and borders on fantastic to say: "Sometimes he would go to a convention and not show up for days." I covered five days of a convention of the AF of L in Atlantic City and several other conventions, usually labor, and never failed to show with a story and a byline in Milwaukee and Chicago papers. To show you that I may have a thicker skin than you have, I am willing, if you say so, to go to print with the whole kit and kaboodle as it now stands in cold print on the galley proofs. If what I am writing seems to you overanxious and meticulous, then you fail to understand in the long run I am protecting you as well as myself. I still think there is extraordinary writing and portraiture in the Pack Memorial pieces by James Thurber, Herb Block and Ed Murrow.

333

20th Century Fox

In 1915 came the Amalgamated Clothing Workers fifteen week strike. I wrote a story, long or short, about it every day in the Day Book, with sometimes a front page story. During two weeks Sidney Hillman conducted the strike in bed with flu and I came to his bedside nearly every day and gave him the latest reports that I had. In one way and another I kept in touch with Hillman and his lovely wife, Bessie, and in the 1944 campaign I wrote part of a leaflet widely distributed in Los Angeles. In this leaflet I replied to Hearst's vicious interpretations to the line, "Clear it with Sidney." Like David Dubinsky, Hillman had integrity and constructive abilities all too rare in the world of organized labor.

CARL

Carl shared in the royalties on the book, so his interest was not solely confined to historical accuracy. He was also working side by side with me, a close friend. He knew how onerous writing can be, and he was always hesitant about advising me to throw something out over which I had spent laborious hours. I wrote up all the apocryphal stories about him I came across. I could always tell by Carl's reaction whether they were apocryphal or whether they were true: If Carl simply grunted and handed the story back —out it went. He would always enlarge on the others.

There were two disagreements, and Carl surrendered his prerogatives on both. The first disagreement came over the chapter dealing with his single novel, *Remembrance Rock*.

Carl had made money on the novel, and its publication was attended by appropriately polite reviews. But the novel frankly did not reach the mark he aimed for. I said so:

Remembrance Rock may not be the Great American Novel. It is certainly one of the attempts at the Great American Novel. It took for its subject belief in America, and by doing this, ran the risk of depending upon the image of Sandburg rather than upon its considerable literary merits to gain its audience. As fiction, it ran counter to post-World War II writing. It did not have the cynicism we associate with the usual war-inspired novel. It did not rage against authority, nor express hatred of discipline.

Belief is harder to portray than cynicism, and affirmation more difficult to sound than disillusion. *Remembrance Rock* undeniably had a refreshing vigor in its concentration upon narrative and its ambitious four-part form.

Remembrance Rock makes one remember *Intolerance*, D. W. Griffith's great experiment in film technique. *Intolerance*, too, had a story which encompassed four different narratives. Many have called it the greatest movie ever made. Movie techniques have improved, but after *Intolerance* few new techniques, besides sound, have been introduced. By the same criterion, *Remembrance Rock* is one of the great American novels, just in terms of its sheer ambition. No one is as ambitious as Americans are. In its ambition alone—trying to put America down on paper—*Remembrance Rock* is an accomplishment.

Carl always insisted *Remembrance Rock* was his best prose work. That many dismissed it nettled him. He grunted when he read this. A moment of quiet. Then he said, "Harry, I'm not sure you understand the book."

I explained to Carl that throughout the writing of the biography I had the assistance of my son Richard Goldhurst, that Carl Sandburg himself on more than one occasion had complimented Richard's critical abilities and insights.

"Maybe *he* ought to read the book again," Carl said.

"I am absolutely confident that both Richard and I have read the book enough."

Carl mused. He held the manuscript in his lap. He rose from the rocker, put the manuscript in my hands, and in a bellow said, "Hell, Harry, maybe we ought to have a whole book about *Remembrance Rock*."

The other disagreement I incorporated into the book itself:

Proud words wear hard boots

"How many times do you refer to me as 'a Socialist'?" Carl grumped when I showed him this manuscript. "Hell, you've got me here 'a Socialist' at least a hundred times. Why don't you change a few of them?"

"Carl," I said, "you weren't organizing for the Republican National Committee up there in Wisconsin in 1908, were you?"

"No, I wasn't. I was organizing for the Social Democratic Party but you ought to change a few of those 'a Socialist' anyway."

"What will I change them to?" I asked.

"Make a few of them 'a radical,'" Carl said.

"O.K., Carl, but remember, you're the guy who wrote when you let proud words go, it is not easy to call them back."

In the summer of 1961, Bill Targ, the editor-in-chief at World

Publishing,* sent Carl the copy-edited manuscript to read. When he was finished, Carl had a few remarks to make about stylistic preferences but offered nothing else.

"Whew!" said Bill. "No comment was exactly what I wanted to hear. Because, Harry, if Carl had said, 'Maybe we shouldn't publish the book right now,' you would have had a whale of a job rewriting."

Carl Sandburg was well received. It was sheer joy reading the critiques.

On Sandburg's eighty-fifth birthday, William Jovanovich, the publisher of Harcourt, Brace, gave him a splendid party honoring the publication of *Honey and Salt,* Carl's last book of poems. Justice William O. Douglas was there, Eric Johnston, John Steinbeck, Barbara Tuchman, John Gunther, Marian Anderson, Elia Kazan, Herbert Mitgang, S. L. A. Marshall, and many others, all of them close to Carl.

Carl Sandburg said to me, "Harry, it's a dream come true. I got me a big room, and it's all filled with my friends. Happens once in your life."

We flew back to Charlotte together, and there, in my office, Carl got a chance to read one of the first reviews of *Honey and Salt,* this by Kenneth Rexroth, the poet. Rexroth asked, "Where is the Sandburg who talked of picket lines? Where is the Sandburg who sang of whores?"

Carl put the review down and said, "I am eighty-five years old. I am not going to talk about whores at my age. As far as the union boys are concerned, they are playing the dog races in Miami. The romantic days are over. Now you put that in your *Carolina Israelite.*"

I did.

---

* Now at Putnam's; in fact, this book's editor.

Chapter 29

MY friend Noel Houston always advised the publishers he met that they might get a good book out of Harry Golden. One of these publishers took him seriously. These publishers, in 1957, sent me the railroad fare to come to New York and discuss what I wanted to do. I cut out all the essays Noel had circled in red in the *Israelite* and pasted them into a loose-leaf binder.

When I showed Carl Sandburg Lippincott's letter, he said, "One of the thrills in life is to see everything you ever wrote printed."

In the publisher's offices, I waited outside a conference room while several editors discussed the manuscript. When these fellows admitted me, they promised me a contract on the spot. They had only a few specifications. They thought I should exclude everything from this book that did not pertain to Jews, the Lower East Side, or the immigrants. They wanted, in short, a "Jewish" book. They said, "Leave out the controversy. Leave out Joe McCarthy, the Negro question; leave out those vignettes 'Why I Never Bawl Out a Waitress.' "

I said, "I'll think about it."

I went back to Charlotte and thought about it. I thought and thought. I decided they were dopes. So you see, a publisher no sooner discovered me than unfortunately I discovered integrity.

My disappointment was mitigated by a letter from Ben Zevin, the president of the World Publishing Company in Cleveland and New York. Mr. Zevin was coming to Chapel Hill to see some writers, and he wanted to stop off on his way home and talk to me in Charlotte. Ben is five feet eight inches tall, suave and brilliant, with an infinite degree of taste, as well as a knowledge of every trick of the trade. He had made a great success of World with dictionaries, Bibles, and other books. In Cleveland, World Publishing owned one acre of printing presses which kept turning out every conceivable kind of Bible twenty-four hours a day, seven days a week.

In those days, before World Publishing was purchased by a West Coast conglomerate, it had a lively tradebook division with its headquarters in New York. World published authors such as Art Buchwald, Simone de Beauvoir, Ashley Montagu, MacKinlay Kantor, Lin Yutang, and others, and it had a large children's book department.

When I met Ben Zevin in Charlotte, he said to me, "My son is at Northwestern University. Whenever he comes home, he always asks for the *Carolina Israelite*. I have to dig through all my papers and manuscripts to find him the issues he's missed."

It is one thing to ride in a railroad coach to see some publishers in New York City; it is another to have a publisher come see you. A publisher who comes to see you means BUSINESS.

I told Ben Zevin about the offer I had received from a publisher. I handed over the pasted-up manuscript. Ben Zevin particularly liked the article "Why I Never Bawl Out a Waitress." He said the McCarthy article was first-rate. Integrity, therefore, has its uses. Still, the book needed a great deal of work before Ben Zevin wanted to issue it. The immediate corrections I needed descended from the nature of my writing. I am a journalist, an open-end writer, aiming at filling space rather than accomplishing precision and elegance of phrase. I knew I needed ninety pages of typewritten copy for each issue of the *Israelite*. I sat before a typewriter, always worried about a deadline of sorts, and when I had typed the requisite ninety pages, I went to the printer.

Necessarily, some of my articles needed reduction, some needed expansion; sometimes I was repetitious, sometimes I circled the point like a wary Indian circling the wagon train. I suggested to Ben that I send the manuscript to my son Harry junior, who had just left the Charlotte *Observer* to work for the Detroit *Free Press*. Harry knew editing as only a newspaperman knows it, a fellow who has covered city hall and advanced to the rewrite and then to the city desks. Harry junior is unquestionably one of the best newspaper editors in the business. I felt he could help us get the flavor we wanted for the book—a newspaper flavor, like an editorial page. And indeed, Buddy did all the rearranging and editing, as well as writing the caps for each of the essays.

Ben Zevin was as good as his word. Within a week he sent me a contract. Right after New Year's, 1958, I went to Cleveland with the finished manuscript. Our conferences were short because Buddy had done such a good job; the book was down pat. One of the changes Ben Zevin and Bill Targ wanted was a shortening of the title from *It Could Happen Only in America* to *Only in America*.

Bill Targ congratulated me on the book and said World was going to print 10,000 copies and that the book would be out in July. I promised Ben Zevin and Bill that the copies World didn't sell I would buy back at remaindered prices to offer as premiums to new subscribers. Zevin and Targ thought this was pretty generous of me.

I went back to Charlotte feeling the relaxation a city editor experiences when the presses start their last run: no more worries about fires, rapes, murders, or the visits of the distinguished. Until tomorrow, it's all on the morning paper's time.

A week later I left Charlotte for a lecture tour. Snow, then bitter cold attacked the city, always an inconvenience in the South because winter is usually equable and we taxpayers invest little money in mechanized winter equipment. I was to lecture that Monday night at a temple sisterhood in Passaic, New Jersey.

I was in the middle of a long peroration when I saw a policeman enter the auditorium and proceed down the aisle toward the platform. I thought he was going to ask that a member of the audience move a car blocking traffic. All the policeman did, however, was hand a note to one of the committee chairwomen on the dais. It was for me. I read it when I finished. It said: "Call Charlotte police chief immediately."

Chief Frank Littlejohn told me that the *Carolina Israelite* had been completely destroyed by fire. I called Tom Fesperman, the managing editor of the Charlotte *Observer*, because I knew Tom would have had reporters there to cover the story. Tom said he doubted there was anything left. The building looked like a total loss.

The storm that had swept over the South was now raging in the

339

North. All planes were grounded. One of my hosts volunteered to drive me to Grand Central in New York City. He kept sympathizing with me to a point where his distress equaled mine. I finally had to cheer him and myself up by repeating, "Thank God, the book is at the publisher's."

My terribly gnawing worry was over the subscription list: If it was destroyed, I was destroyed. The *Israelite* was dead. It had taken me fifteen years to build up that list. If it was gone, there was no one to whom to send the paper.

The trains were backed up in the railroad yards. Grand Central was filled with people milling by the thousands trying to get on their way again. I told a trainman my problem. He advised me to get to Washington; it was clear from there down. But he said there wasn't a reservation available for two days. He sighed, "There is nothing I can do."

A young Marine beside me said, "I have a reservation. I'll let you use it to get to Washington." In my agitation I forgot to ask this young man's name. He did a thoroughly agitated older man a great kindness.

Red-eyed Ken Robertson met me. Ken had learned of the fire and rushed to 1229 Elizabeth. He, too, had thought of the subscription list. The police and firemen would not let him into the burning building. Ken then pleaded with them to let him drive the car out of danger. Too risky, they said. Again they held him back. As the building went up in flames which scorched the cold night sky, Ken began to cry. The car, incidentally, survived the fire handily. As the water from the hoses hit the building, it splashed back on the car. The night was so cold it froze immediately, and the next morning the car was still insulated in a huge block of ice.

We pulled up in front of the four charred walls, all that remained of the *Israelite*. The cement cellar was a mass of debris and ashes. Utter devastation is awesome. I was transfixed. Besides the list, which was obviously gone, were file drawer after file drawer of valuable correspondence. Adlai's letters were gone, Carl's, the correspondence with E. Haldeman-Julius. I even had a letter from Einstein which was destroyed in the fire, for I had written him once as a Jewish editor addressing a Jewish scientist and asked him about the theory of relativity. Einstein had replied, "I cannot explain it to you in a letter, but if you come to Princeton, I can play it for you on my violin."

As I stared, Police Chief Littlejohn said, "Harry, we thought it might have been the Klan. It wasn't. It was a faulty flue. It overheated on the cold night."

By this time I had much better control of myself. When a reporter asked me what I was going to do, I replied, "I'll get the paper out if I have to sit on the curb to write it." I added, "The trouble with us philosophers is that we have to worry about keys, money, insurance policies—and mailing lists."

I had faced worse than writing on a curb, which wasn't necessary anyway. Many people came to my aid.

Advertising man Walter Klein said he had an empty office into which I could move right away. My friends the David Wallases said they had a room. When the reporters asked what they could do, I said, "If you'll report the fire and inform your readers the mailing list is gone, that all I need is their name and address, I can recompile everyone." The story of the fire did shortly appear in all the Carolina papers, in the New York *Times,* the Chicago *Tribune,* and many others around the country.

An Episcopal minister spent that afternoon with Ken and me picking up the wet, charred books from the cold ground. The three of us flattened them out in a neighbor's attic, where they could dry. We salvaged 300 out of 2,000.

Other people brought me food. A friend lent me a car.

Ethel Clyde, the heiress of the Clyde Steamship Line, sent me a check for $500 to keep going, and Doris Duke sent me $1,000 with the note, "I read in the *Times* where your books were destroyed. Here's some money to help replace them." Many readers responded to the news story with a letter and a check. One that was typical came from Archibald Henderson, George Bernard Shaw's biographer, who taught at the University of North Carolina:

> Fordell
> 721 E. Franklin Street
> Chapel Hill, North Carolina
> U.S.A.

DEAR HARRY:

You have my all-out, whole-hearted sympathy, for you in your shocking disaster. In 1935 I had a $20,000 fire in my home here; I still keep looking for things that must have "gone up" in that holocaust. I know you are a philosopher with true religion so these qualities will support you through your trials and tribulations.

I particularly deplore the loss of your doubtless much treasured books—and your subscription list.

I enclose check for $10 to apply toward subscription for the future—which may serve as a sort of octogenarian's mite.

All your friends I feel sure will rally to you—if you give the signal that you need a helping hand.

I say to you as Cornstalk shouted to his braves at Point Pleasant all day long, "Be strong!"

Truly,

ARCHIBALD HENDERSON

Another who took out a five-year subscription was the novelist Elick Moll:

DEAR MR. GOLDEN:

Many years ago I gave up reading newspapers. I've saved a great deal of time. I've also missed things, notably your Carolina Israelite which I just heard about. I've read the latest issue and wish not to be defrauded of any in the future by my by-now conditioned reflex to the public prints. Yours is evidently a very private print, deliciously so, and I wish to be a subscriber and Constant Reader. Incidentally, the principal character in my latest TV show (do you ever watch TV? It was called Gentleman From Seventh Avenue) was named Max Golden, which seems to me a singularly happy name and I detect a certain spiritual kinship between you two as well.

I'm glad to have made your acquaintance, belatedly, and look forward with pleasure to your forthcoming monthly visits. (Is it monthly, or bi-monthly?) I look forward also to reading your book. What you say about the writing of a book, and the why of it, is especially pertinent for anyone who has worked in the movies and TV, as I have. I've also got a book coming out in May called Seidman and Son; I've hit with it in a big, not to say fabulous way. It's already been taken by Book of the Month for June and by Readers Digest Condensed Books Summer Edition. It would be hypocritical to deny that the money and general *reclame* have an importance for me but the deep satisfaction is what you and I and all who publish a book or play a piece nicely on the piano or paint a picture experience—I did it. With my little hatchet. I'm not sure it's a worthy feeling, necessarily; certainly we would instantly be cashiered out of a collective society even for mentioning it. But we got it. And I treasure it. I even feel a little smug these days about my friends with the morocco bound volumes of screenplays which they collect. Written by Me, Somebody and Somebody from a book by Somebody, Additional Dialogue by Somebody, Color by Distortion, Inc., Music by Louder Than You Can and played by Gary Cooper—if he lives that long.

Long life and happy writing (and thinking) to you.

ELICK MOLL

Then Chief Frank Littlejohn, who had once captured notorious Roger Touhy after a bank robbery and a 70-mile-an-hour auto chase, set his policemen to sifting carefully through the ashes. They found the blackened, crumbling, ice-coated lists, so hard a man could stand on them. Littlejohn expected to get nothing, but he instructed Lieutenant John Pierczynski of the police laboratories to try. With the fluoroscope and the camera, Pierczynski started to bring the list back to light.

Littlejohn brought me down to the laboratory, and the first name I saw coming through on the blotters was "Sen. Kerr Scott, 452 Senate Office Bldg., Washington, D.C."

"Usually," I said to the papers about Littlejohn, "the police department puts a man out of business. But they're putting me back in. A police lab is for getting clues, but they're making it possible for a Protestant clergyman in Decatur, a schoolteacher in Portland, and a rabbi in Louisville to get a sixteen-page paper from Charlotte."

A month later, I rented a house up the street at 1312 Elizabeth Avenue, where I still have offices.

THE NEXT ISSUE WILL BE A LITTLE LATE, said the story in the Charlotte *Observer*, adding that every issue was always a little late.

Here is the letter I sent to the *Observer* and to the *News* to thank the people of Charlotte:

FROM THE ASHES,
A GOLDEN GLOW

It is with a full heart that I thank you, and through you, the rest of the City of Charlotte for a high-hearted spirit of generosity which followed the fire in my establishment last month.

An unlined flue in a temperature of 8-degrees destroyed my books and my possessions, but has enriched me beyond the wildest dreams of my life. The professional newspapermen across the state

343

and the Christian clergymen throughout the South extended a hand of fellowship such as rarely comes to a man in an entire lifetime. But most of all, the "strangers" from Chantilly, North Charlotte, Second Ward, and Dilworth who called me to say that they held a prayer meeting of thanks that the Charlotte Police Department had restored my subscription lists, of all things!

Such an outpouring of good will and good wishes imposes upon me a tremendous responsibility to justify, to some degree, this line of communication and this fellowship.

A Republican congressman offered to send a letter to all my subscribers; a Democratic senator placed it into the Record, and a note from Mr. Norman Thomas, the Socialist leader and my friend: "I am gratified at the people of Charlotte; my grandparents are buried there; the city has good blood in its veins." To which I say Amen, and thanks from the bottom of my heart.

HARRY GOLDEN
Editor
The Carolina Israelite

344

Chapter 30

Iₙ an article he gave me for the *Israelite* ten years later, Bill Targ reminisced about the day he and I realized that *Only in America* was going to become a best seller. It was publication day, July 27, 1958. After appearing on the Dave Garroway *Today* show that morning, I went to Bill's office, and he was explaining what he thought the book would do. World was pleased and surprised that the United States Army had ordered 902 copies for its post libraries around the country. But, Bill went on, the book trade was unacquainted with my name and reputation and had therefore placed only modest orders.

An office clerk brought in a packet of the first reviews sent over by the clipping service. All of them were favorable, more than favorable, enthusiastic. Then just before noon the phone began to ring. Reorders. Large reorders. Bill Targ's eyes began to widen. After receiving each of these, he would tell me the quantities. With each figure he quoted, a more intense look of disbelief crossed my face.

Bill Targ wrote: "It was some kind of a dream Harry was experiencing—fantasy. But the fact was, the book was an instant sell-out on publication day. Scribner's, Brentano's, Doubleday's, and the wholesalers were out of stock. They had sold out their entire initial orders. We had a best seller, obviously, and a problem. Based on that day's reorders we had to have 25,000 more copies—soon."

Bill is wrong. I was not living in a fantasy. I was fifty-six years old. I felt I was in an actual play. Sudden wealth is a theatrical convention as old as money itself. If I felt like anyone that noon, I felt like Captain Boyle in *Juno and the Paycock*. The inheritance was mine, all mine, but there was a nagging fear that in the third act so many other claimants would appear as to make my claims worthless and reduce me again to poverty.

That noon we went to luncheon at the Oak Room of the Plaza and Richard Rodgers, the composer, stopped at the table and congratulated me on *Only in America*. He told me that all of his friends were reading the book.

I knew this was the once-in-a-lifetime experience every writer hopes for. But I knew—it will never be the same again. I could continue to write books for as long as I wanted—A best seller almost invariably establishes a writer's audience for years—but I would never be as new or as original again. In many ways, I was thankful I was fifty-six years old. If I were twenty-six, I would have a lifetime of trying to reduplicate *Only in America*. At fifty-six, reduplication is not as important, and one does not have that many decades to long for it as fervently.

Every writer who ever lived and finished a book wants it to be a best seller; in the words of Samuel Johnson, if he doesn't write for money, he's a blockhead. *Only in America* sold almost 300,000 copies in the hardback edition. Later it was a great success in the Pocket Books edition. A decade later it still returns substantial royalties. I emphasize "decade later" because I believe, along with Cyril Connolly, that an author should aim at writing a book which a reader can profitably read ten years after it has first been published.

Before *Only in America*, I used to have a continuing acquaintanceship with the fellows in the Charlotte Internal Revenue Service. I used to be $300 in arrears year after year. I always guaranteed to pay off this debt at the rate of $50 a month. Some months I'd miss, not because of any animosity toward the IRS, but because the telephone company got in there first. I could run the *Israelite* for a time without the IRS; I couldn't operate a day without AT&T.

The income-tax fellows were always nice enough about it. They came around and suggested tactfully that if $50 a month was too steep, why not try $25? I used to try $25 a month, and still I missed occasional payments.

One day I gave them each an autographed copy of *Only in America* and handed them a check for $17,000, and I laughed like hell.

I think there are certain reasons why *Only in America* became a popular success. There is humor in the book, much of it understated, and the publisher had the wisdom not to overstate its qualities.

It was a success because it was a "Jewish" book with a difference. A large majority of Jewish writers fall into two camps. There are the apologists who argue in their books that the Jews are the same as everyone else—they play basketball—and there are the historians who blow a few details out of all perspective to prove the Jews are patriots. I won't enumerate the names. Knowing Carl Sandburg meant I had enough of his literary wars to last me a lifetime.

To be sure, I must exempt many Jewish writers from these two categories. Henry Roth's *Call It Sleep*, Saul Bellow's *Seize the Day*, and Bernard Malamud's *The Assistant* are three integral examples of superior literature made from the Jewish experience. There are as well writers who happen to be Jewish but whose central concern is not with the Jewish experience. No one has to know Lionel Trilling is Jewish in order to grasp his insights, nor does anyone have to know S. J. Perelman is Jewish to find him funny.

As for me, I told my audience that the story of the Jew in America began not in 1776 but in 1906. And I told them other things, too. I was really doing it when the others were still wondering how in the world they could lend their efforts to anything that would make a difference.

Last, I believe the book found a large audience because it was a newspaper. The joy of the newspaper is that the reader picks and chooses not only between the advertising and the copy but also which copy is the choicest to read. *Only in America* had the continuity of a newspaper: No one had to read it all the way through in order to learn the news. Many did read it at one sitting; many others spent months reading it.

The book no sooner reached the top of the best-seller list than I thought I would lose it all. As a man with a prison past who wanted to keep it secret, I always knew there was one thing I could not do: run for elective office. *Only in America* taught me there's another thing an ex-convict cannot do if he wants to bury his past: He cannot write a best seller.

Only in America was in full sail on September 18, 1958. It was number one in the *New York Times Book Review*. Nothing makes a publisher and an editor-in-chief happier than a book which is a leading best seller. The book is making money, which is very important, need I say. Equally important is the satisfaction both editor and publisher feel in their judgment. And last, there is very little the publishing company has to do for a best seller—the public does it all. Bill Targ told me he was feeling euphoric that September morning. He expected to have a good luncheon that noon with Ben Zevin, who was coming in from Cleveland, and with me, flying in to appear on a panel show about the race issue.

Bill Targ felt good until he opened his mail.

The first letter said. "Do you know that your author, Harry Golden, is a swindler, a cheat, and an ex-con and jail bird who has victimized widows and orphans?" The letter was unsigned.

It is not a unique experience for a publishing house to receive a hate letter. Some of the correspondents claim the author owes them money; some that the author has fathered her illegitimate child; some letter writers are simply obscene. Cranks. Publishers throw these letters into the wastebasket. Bill did not, however, throw away this letter. It was not obscene. It was not a demand for money past due. It was not the outrage of a woman wronged.*
Bill said he had the distinct, choked-up impression that whoever wrote this unsigned letter was not a crank. Bill read the letter again. He was, he says, sure that the writer knew what he was talking about, that the charge was true.

Bill says he was choked up because he simply could not decide on what he would do with this information. *I'll wait for Ben Zevin,* he thought. *That will give me time to think.* He put the letter under his blotter. Whether this revelation would be ruinous or not he did not know. But he did know that it was going to be a big news story.

Targ was no sooner back at his other tasks than he had a call

---

* All of us—Tiny, Bill Targ, Ben, and I—have always attributed this anonymous letter to a man. It read like a man's letter. Tiny is sure she knows who sent it; so am I—but they are two different men. None of us has ever hazarded a motive. We cannot imagine what it would be.

from Maurice Dolbier, one of the book-page editors at the *Herald Tribune*. Dolbier said he had received a curious anonymous letter that morning and started to read it. Word for word it was the same as the one Targ had received.

Bill said he could not confirm or refute the charges, but he said I was coming in later in the day and we could set it straight then. Would Dolbier wait? If he would wait, Bill promised him the story.

Maurice Dolbier conferred with Irita Van Doren, the literary editor of the *Tribune*, and called back. Irita Van Doren and he and the *Tribune* would wait. But if the letter had been sent to all the tabloids, there was no point in it. If indeed Harry Golden had served a prison sentence, it was no longer book-page but front-page news. Bill asked for a deadline, and the gentlemanly Dolbier gave him one.

When Ben Zevin arrived and read the letter, he said, "There is nothing we can do but wait for Harry. We'll ask him." Since both were expected at an editorial meeting, they detailed Mrs. Eleanor Kask, World Publishing's publicity director, to meet my plane at LaGuardia.

I had revealed my prison record to only three men in the South. One of the first men I told was Josephus Daniels, Woodrow Wilson's Secretary of the Navy. Josephus was then the publisher of the Raleigh *News and Observer*, a Tarheel weighted with honor from a long and vigorous career in and out of government. Josephus came to Charlotte for an appearance under my auspices when I worked for I. D. Blumenthal. If he found out about my prison record after he came, he had every right to accuse me of imposing on his good nature. So one afternoon, in his newspaper office, I told him. Daniels laughed until all his staff heard him. "You were Bishop Cannon's broker?" he kept repeating, and then laughed some more. Josephus Daniels was one of the Methodists and loyal Democrats who had tried to wrest power from the Bishop.

Frank Littlejohn, the chief of police, knew my story and I confided, too, in Hermann Cohen, a Jewish merchant in Charlotte. All these men kept the secret.

Eleanor Kask led me to a taxi, and on the way to New York she put the question to me. She said we were going straight to the offices of World Publishing, where Bill Targ, Ben Zevin, and

Judith Crist of the *Herald Tribune* (she was assigned to write the story) were awaiting me.

I said it was true; I had served a prison sentence from 1929 until 1933. My throat was dry, and I remember Ben and Bill and Eleanor constantly replenishing the Dixie cup with bottled water. It is hard now to re-create this moment, but the thought I remember flashing through me was that this was exactly how Pandora felt when she opened the box.

Miss Crist finished her notes, rose, and said, "I'm sorry, Mr. Golden. I hope you understand."

I said, "I'm a newspaperman. I understand."

Neither Bill, Eleanor, nor Ben Zevin knew what would happen. They kept reassuring me. Bill said World had published books by several men who had gone to jail, that it was nothing new in publishing circles.

"But *they* told you," I said.

"Yes," Bill answered weakly, "they told me. It wasn't news."

These reassurances did not cheer me up at all. I knew I was going to be called a fraud. I was frightened. Before Ben Zevin took me over to the Warwick Hotel, where he maintained a suite, I asked for $10,000 on my *Only in America* account. I was positive that every creditor I had in Charlotte would be on my front stoop tomorrow morning when the story broke. Ben Zevin said not to worry, the money was mine when I wanted it.

I had a lot of time to worry in the Warwick. I called Tiny and said, "The papers know about my prison record." She was quiet a long time, and then she said, "I'll tell the boys." Another worry.

Clara cried. She felt important distributing autographed copies of *Only in America* to business associates and clients. That joy was over.

Max said not to worry about him, worry about myself.

I asked Jake, who was about to leave for a Florida vacation, to look around for a modest hotel or motel I could buy into when the publicity died down.

Next, I called Howard K. Smith at the ABC network and canceled my appearance that night. I had already hurt the civil rights movement enough, I thought. The segregationists were bound to say, "There is one of your leaders who is nothing but an ex-convict."

Last, I called John Kobler at the *Saturday Evening Post*. He had come to Charlotte to write a story about me, soon to appear. I apologized for not telling him of my prison record. John said, "I knew there was something there, a gap. I could sense it, but I couldn't put my finger on it." He thanked me for the courtesy because they were about to put the story into galleys. He was going to make the addition, he said, but the editors were still going to run the story as he wrote it.

Now I had nothing to do but worry. Which I did, pacing back and forth the rest of the evening and night until the *Tribune* hit the stands at around ten.

The story was on the front page:

GOLDEN, BEST SELLER AUTHOR,
REVEALS HIS PRISON PAST
by Judith Crist
1958, N.Y. Herald Tribune Inc.

Twenty-five years of suspense, of "constant fear of success," ended yesterday for Harry L. Golden, author of the nation's top non-fiction best-seller, "Only in America."

They ended with Mr. Golden's disclosure that twenty-five years ago he had served a Federal prison term for using the mails to defraud.

"Do you know what it means to worry about good fortune—do you?" the gray-haired stocky editor asked. "Over the years my wife and I have felt that any day this exposure—the term ex-convict—would come. I asked for nothing, only the right to sit down and write some essays and a book I thought five or six thousand little old ladies would buy. . . ."

Mr. Golden's literary eminence has followed, however, his establishment as one of North Carolina's most influential citizens, since he settled in Charlotte, N.C., in 1940 and began publishing the monthly "Carolina Israelite." A sharp-tongued Yankee newspaper man who has brought the homilies and simplicities of his Lower East Side origins to bear on the complexities and prejudices of Dixie, he has won local and more recently national applause for his warm wit and outspoken stand on controversial issues, including segregation.

Throughout the quarter of a century, there has been nothing to link Mr. Golden with the Harry L. Goldhurst who, on Oct. 16, 1929, pleaded guilty in Federal court in New York to using the mails to defraud, was sentenced to five years in prison, was paroled

351

eighteen months later, had his parole revoked after the late Sen. Carter Glass, of Virginia, protested it, and was released on March 29, 1933, having served the full term with time off for good behavior.

"I have omitted that section of my life in all my writings. I have never lied about it," Mr. Golden, in New York yesterday on business, said. "Over the years I have had to tell a few people. Once I was offered public office. I declined on the ground of my heart condition."

The fifty-six-year-old editor emphasized that he did not wish to make light of his offense, committed in his early twenties. "I conducted a brokerage business in which I failed and filed a petition of bankruptcy. My liabilities, if I may say this, represented 97 per cent paper profits I owed to people with whom I was gambling. I did not realize the full extent of the consequences, that many of these acts were wrong and illegal, and when the full realization of this confronted me, I made sure there would not even be a contest about it. I pleaded guilty. . . ."

It was as Harry L. Golden, the name he finally used, that he sought a new start, clerking in a hotel owned by his brother, doing promotion and selling advertising for two New York newspapers, finally traveling for a concern that specialized in preparing anniversary editions for newspapers.

His travels brought him to Charlotte; he liked the city and decided to stay. Charlotte, North Carolina, and currently the rest of the country have returned his affection.

"Throughout, I was worried about being lucky," Mr. Golden admitted. "The children knew about it, but we never discussed it." His three eldest sons are married, settled on careers, and he has three grandsons. His fourth son, Peter, born in 1937, died last year of muscular dystrophy.

"There was constant ambivalence—to do certain things or not do them, for fear it would come. After all—this prominence—I didn't need it. I made $8,000–$9,000 a year, I have lots of phonograph records, a bit of whiskey, cigars—what did I need big success for? I shuddered every time my publisher talks about money and success. This is an eminence I'm scared the hell of."

But to lay the ghost of the past once and for all, curbing possible rumors and poison-pen innuendo, brings surcease—if not assurance of acceptance, Mr. Golden said. "For the first time in a long time I have withheld nothing. I hope I can go ahead now and finish two books I've wanted to do but kept myself from, one a full autobiography, the other more of my essays."

What will happen to the full lecture schedule ahead of him or the sales of his book as a result of his disclosure is, Mr. Golden conceded, a matter of concern.

"I don't want to be a martyr. I pleaded guilty to something that was wrong. I'd like to be judged on my work and my conduct since. My wife and children feel the way I do. But I can only rely again on the inherent sense of fair play that I've encountered before among my countrymen. It may not have been a coincidence that I called my best-seller 'Only in America.' "

There is something about serious trouble that makes a man sleep, sleep more than he would under happy circumstances. I believe I slept more in the next forty-eight hours than I normally sleep during a whole week. I slept on the plane back to Charlotte, the papers folded in my lap. I just didn't want to wonder what was on the other end.

I was still tired at the Charlotte Airport. Ken Robertson met me, and decent man that he was, he told me the advertising was dummied, the printer was ready, and, lowering his voice, said, "And we had a lot of calls, Harry."

At the office I found Julian Scheer, my good friend. Julian was a columnist then for the Charlotte *News*; now he is the public relations director for the National Aeronautics and Space Administration in Washington, D.C. Julian and I were close; we collaborated on several articles, and we used to boast we were the only poor Jews in Charlotte.

Had he heard the news?

Julian said it came over the ticker around midnight. "But don't worry," he said, "everything will be all right. The calls that are coming through are wonderful."

"You keep taking them," I asked. "I'm going to sleep." Sleep was when I didn't have to think about it.

By the next morning I knew I had weathered the storm—except it wasn't a storm at all. Unanimously the press of North Carolina said in effect: "Harry Golden, you are forgiven. You are a Tarheel. We are proud of you." The New York *Times* editorialized about my past under the caption "The Man Who Was Afraid of Success." *Time* and *Life* magazines both ran stories about me—I almost said about me and "my plight," but I no longer had a plight. I read all of these, of course. I read them because a man who has been in prison never for a moment believes the society really will say, "We'll wash it away." Of all these editorials and

353

stories, the one I wish to reproduce here, the one which seemed the most pertinent and profound, pertinent and profound because its author didn't see my personal story as unique, was that by the philosopher-journalist Max Lerner. It appeared in the Sunday New York *Post*, datelined September 21, under the head "The Secret Places":

It isn't just movie stars and crooners whose private lives harbor skeletons that get revealed in public. The troubles that writers get into are sometimes more disreputable than the ones they write about.

"His sins were scarlet," wrote Hilaire Belloc in an immortal doggerel, "but his books were read." There are two writers currently on the front pages not because of their best-seller books but because of their newly unveiled old sins. They are John McPartland, who wrote a novel called "No Down Payment" about suburban families in California, with its central female an attractive and haughty young wife who gets raped by a hillbilly neighbor and finds that she loved it; and Harry Golden, who put together some tangy columns of his from a one-man magazine into a volume called "Only in America," and found to his surprise that a big audience loved it.

There is little these two men had in common except sudden literary success and the fact that their hidden skeletons came clattering out roughly at the same time. McPartland, who died the other day, had a wedded wife and child he did not acknowledge to the world; while the woman whom he acknowledged as his wife, who had borne him five children, was one to whom he was unmarried. As for Golden, the white light of a best seller has compelled him to lay bare a secret which he wore like a flaming Nessusshirt for years—the fact that he was once convicted and served three and a half years for mail fraud.

I expect a certain malaise among my writing colleagues as they speculate on whose turn it will be to get packed off in the tumbrel next.

* * *

Yet I wonder why all this should strike us as a rarity. Writers are like any other mortals—if anything a bit more complicated in their make-up, with inner agonies out of which (if they are lucky) they can spin ideas or invent fictions that seem to apply to the whole human situation.

Literary history is full of writers whose secrets were well or badly kept. One thinks offhand of Wordsworth's illegitimate French child, of the sexual legends that have clustered around Byron's name (with incest less disputed than some other strains), of Poe's Lolitas, of the menages maintained by a number of French writers, of the double lives of even such eminent Victorians as Dickens and Thackeray and Mill.

Only recently have we learned that the brilliant geologist Clarence King, the intimate of John Hay and Theodore Roosevelt, the man whom Henry Adams called "the most remarkable man of our time," lived an underground life with a beautiful Negro woman, Ada Todd, who bore him five children.

* * *

The remarkable fact about McPartland and Golden was not that they had secrets to keep, but that the secrets remained so long hidden.

Here was Golden, with the tragic prison episode in his life, going into the most exposed of all trades next to politics—personal journalism—and putting out issue after issue of his Carolina Israelite without being spotted. Here was McPartland, with his two menages only 150 miles apart, letting his common-law wife in Monterey get herself chosen as "Monterey Mother of the Year."

We keep chattering incessantly about how small the world has become. But no matter how much it shrinks, there are secret places that every man carries around with him in his heart—and gets away with. The Orwell fantasy about Big Brother who searched out everything in your life and mind was terrifying exactly because it is in these secret places that a man most truly knows himself.

* * *

No, the danger is not that our secrets will be discovered; it is all too easy to get most people to take you at your current face value. The real danger comes at the point when the secret gets too clamant within us, and cries to be spoken.

When you have something that eats you from within, and that you dare not tell the world about, you start by being afraid that it will be revealed and you end by finding it intolerable to live with, and feeling the need to share it.

This tension between the fear and the desire of discovery is one that every anguished man has known. Cops know about this impulse, and DAs; it is one of their most potent weapons, since what they offer their suspect is the relief of ripping the burning shirt from his skin.

* * *

Well, McPartland is dead, and there is only the wrangling over his estate between his multiple broods. As for Golden, who is very much alive, he asks the reporters to tell him whether he is a dead man.

This is what terrifies any writer—the fear that he may not be able to function. The drive to function is the greatest force in any man's life, underlying the drive to survive and to create. For a quarter-century since he left prison, Golden hugged his secret to himself because he wanted to function for what he was, not what he had been. When he became too well known to keep the secret any longer, he had to take the risk of spreading it across the papers, in a gamble that once more he would be allowed to function.

I am all for it. Who dares sit in judgment on a man like this, whose energies have been spent in joyous attack on so many hypocrisies in American life, perhaps because his own split life was yearning to be whole?

There is no question here of repentance, expiation, redemption. You don't become a new man at some point of high resolve. Every day, every moment of his life, a man is renewed because he is washing away the past in the stream of the present. Whatever Harry Golden once was, he is no fake now. He does not have to prove he is a new man.

Adlai Stevenson told the Associated Press reporter, "The story of Harry Golden reminds me of the story of O. Henry who spent three years in prison. I suspect that this experience deepened Harry Golden's understanding, lengthened his vision, and enlarged his heart."

Carl Sandburg said, "The story only ties me closer to him."

Fannie Hurst said, "I couldn't care less."

Do not think the Southern press was in any unanimity over forgiveness. The Charleston (South Carolina) *News and Courier*, among other things, editorialized, "Harry Golden, Charlotte integrationist whose guilty past came to light last week, stands convicted of discrimination. For years he segregated himself from the brotherhood of writers who tell the truth and nothing but the truth." The editors also said:

But it is not essential to literary success to be a jailbird. Even in the light of Mr. Golden's story, we would not recommend that aspiring authors serve their apprenticeship in a cell. With due recognition of Harry Golden's humor, his humanity and his ability to use the English language, we wonder whether an emotional binge over his confession is an influence for the good. It hardly promotes respect for laws of the land other than compulsory mixture of the races.

Said another Southern editor, "Yep, the devil who tempted the late Methodist Bishop James Cannon Jr., to gamble with Methodist money—in worthless stocks and securities back in 1929—has turned his talents from crime to writing." I include this last because it would have even made the Bishop laugh. He, too, in the end had turned from religion to writing.

Many other men extended me a helping hand. Dave Garroway invited me back, and Jack Paar asked me to appear on his late evening program, *The Tonight Show*. Jack Paar even made me a regular on this program. I appeared on it ten or twelve times a year. To Jack Paar I owe an awful lot. He was a great interviewer, one of the best I ever met. His attempt at naïveté was wonderful to behold. On the program one night, he said, "Harry, what is this integration business all about? I understand it not at all." He gave me eight uninterrupted minutes with 20,000,000 viewers.

Right on the heels of the story about my past there came a request from the *Saturday Review* to report on a book. I had never contributed to that prestigious journal before. The book was Marya Mannes' *More in Anger*, and for reasons I cannot remember I was less than complimentary. Four years later I met Marya Mannes at the New York Herald Tribune Forum celebrating Book Week. John Galbraith was also one of the speakers, and he, too, had reviewed *More in Anger* with the same lack of fervor I displayed. Miss Mannes is a strikingly beautiful, gracious, brilliant, and attentive woman. Consequently, Mr. Galbraith and I spent a good part of the afternoon in her company with our eyes downcast, staring at our newly shined shoes.

Over the last decade I have had three or four offers from national magazines to write the story of my jail experience. One of these publications offered a large sum for a three-part serial. I always refused for three reasons: I was ashamed of this episode in my life, terribly ashamed; any man who has a prison record and tries to explain it is bound to attempt mitigation which will make his audience think, *He's innocent like every con thinks he's innocent*; and the last reason was that I believe the people did forgive me, and since they did forgive me, I decided to leave the subject alone.

Not to have detailed the episode in my autobiography, however, would have literally vitiated this book. Having detailed it, I would like to point out the moral. In a letter to George Young of the Los Angeles *Examiner*, William Randolph Hearst wrote:

> I have come to the conclusion that it will be next to impossible to directly pin anything to Bishop Cannon. I am sincere in saying that I consider him to have the best brain in America, no one excepted. He has foreseen and prepared for every attack made upon him. In the Goldhurst affair *there was much news but practically no accomplishment.* His following in the church which he represents was only solidified by it. . . .

The real moral of my story is: *The press taketh away, but the press also giveth back.*

PART V

Chapter 31

O_{nly} *in America* made me a celebrity. Carl Sandburg's definition of a celebrity was a man who eats celery with celerity. Being a celebrity meant that one day and from thereinafter people who did not know and had never met me recognized me. It is flattering to be known in this manner, but there is also a ghostly unreality about it. I feel like a cop out of uniform; without my cap I disorient everyone.

In Philadelphia I either lost or had my wallet stolen. It held a sheaf of credit cards, all of which are necessary to the peripatetic lecturer: an airlines credit card, Diners' Club, American Express, telephone card, the North Carolina National Bank, and one or two more. Whoever stole or found my wallet proceeded immediately to charge items in my name. Soon enough I discovered he charged $13,000 in airline tickets alone. Nor was that the least of his accomplishments. He had also spent a week in a famous hotel in Phoenix, Arizona, on my credit. I say this is an accomplishment because no Jew has ever managed to stay at that particular hotel. Were I in possession of my cards and attempted to register, the hotel would be filled.

Yet our thief enjoyed a glorious stay. He was able to use my name with absolute impunity to the distress of the FBI, the Charlotte city police, and a host of investigators from the credit-card companies. At the same time, no matter where I went, in airline terminals, in taxicabs, in hotel lobbies, there were people who recognized me. They had read one of my books, seen me on a tele-

361

vision panel show, subscribed to the paper, or heard me lecture. But nobody ever looked up when the deadbeat, running amok with charge accounts, presented himself. The truth must be, a celebrity is a face or a presence, not a name or reputation.

Not every writer becomes a celebrity for the simple reason many choose not to. I became a celebrity because my picture appeared in the paper. Once the worst was over, I was not averse to personal publicity. I welcomed the chance to appear on network television shows, like Ed Murrow's *Person to Person,* Dave Garroway's *Today,* and Jack Paar's *The Tonight Show.* Authors interviewed on these shows often enjoyed the reward of increased sales but not invariably.

I reached a point where appearing on Jack Paar's show was not simply aid and benefit to my publisher and myself; I positively enjoyed it. It was a challenge to talk to millions of people in their homes. Frankly, too, Jack Paar brought out the ham in me. There was no reason why he shouldn't. I had spent almost twenty years trying to make a livelihood by dealing with a public of sorts and—lo and behold!—here was the largest, most attentive public in the world. Jack Paar offered everyone an opportunity for expression.

Television is best at reproducing spontaneity. It is no longer a secret that television is not a nursery for great playwrights; most of the scripts are as mechanical as the cameras. Nor will it nurture great actresses and actors. The only real strain on the television director is how to keep the extras from tripping over themselves in the confined space. But television is a natural for the personality, especially the personality speaking off the cuff, unrehearsed.

Jack Paar managed this element of spontaneity by the simple process of interviewing people. He had a certain ease, "effortless communication" as Thoreau called it, and in this century of sputtering inarticulateness, Paar's was a supreme gift. Jack Paar was the first personal journalist on television. He was in effect an editor commenting on the news and human interest stories under his own byline. As often as I appeared on *The Tonight Show,* the more often was I celebrated, to use the word narrowly.

Being a celebrity is like being a member of an exclusive fraternity. Celebrities conduct themselves as though they all were members of the same huge family. When I meet another celebrity,

362

it is as though I were being welcomed back to the family get-together after a long and unexplained absence.

I took to this naturally and unashamedly—and still do. I had been a local celebrity in my hometown for several years. I was always a fixture in Charlotte's St. Patrick's Day Parade. I was a fixture because there are almost no Irishmen in Charlotte. My friend David McConnell, a Scotch-Presbyterian, always wore green on St. Patrick's Day, and all the Jews wore green because everyone wants to be an Irishman on the seventeenth of March. Charlotte is always scrubbing around for a few real Irishmen to lead the parade. More times than not, the city is unsuccessful, and it relies on the more adventurous of its citizens to fill out the parade. I always explained I marched in the absence of my three sons, all of whom are descended from Irish kings.

From his pulpit, a Charlotte rabbi once took me to task for marching in the parade, which happened to fall that year on the Jewish Sabbath. I answered that when the Jews in the city closed their doors on the Sabbath, I would forswear marching in the St. Patrick's Day Parade.

A celebrity has a role he is expected to play, although it is a role he does not have to memorize. It is not hard at all. Being a celebrity has few frustrations, as long as the audience continues to buy books and—remember. There are writers like John Steinbeck or William Faulkner who have an intense concern for their privacy. They want their works recognized, not their faces. I had little choice about my privacy. Once it was invaded, I had just as soon be a celebrity as not.

I couldn't wait to say yes when Ed Murrow asked if CBS could televise my home for his popular *Person to Person* show. I had to say yes anyway, or else the Chamber of Commerce, of whom I am a loyal member, would have cashiered me. Mine was the first and only home in Charlotte CBS visited.

The first thing I did when Murrow asked me if he could come was send the bedspread to the laundry. I didn't tell Ed Murrow that my office was my house, one and the same, indistinguishable. I let them find this out for themselves.

Vernon Cheesemen, the CBS technical expert, said, "One thing I want to make clear is that while we are in your house we all shall conduct ourselves as guests invited to your home. We will furnish our own ashtrays. We will use drop cloths where we set up our equipment. We will have drop cloths at the front entrance. We've been very fortunate in the years of this show. We've handled objects worth thousands of dollars and others with great sentimental value. We've never broken anything." He paused, glanced around at the files, the bed, the desks, and telephones, and reflected aloud, "Course, I don't know how much damage we could do in this house."

So much for being a celebrity. I believe I am more. I am a writer and a journalist, a personal journalist. It was not as a celebrity that I received an invitation from *Life* magazine to brief the editorial staff on the race issue and an invitation from the premier columnist of American journalism, Walter Lippmann, for luncheon at the Metropolitan Club in Washington and from Arthur Hays Sulzberger to meet the New York *Times* editorial staff; it was as a writer.

Being a writer is much better than being a celebrity, but it is much harder. As a celebrity, in one fell swoop on *Person to Person* I entered 30,000 new subscriptions to the *Israelite*. After articles about me appeared in *Life, Time,* the *Saturday Evening Post,* 10,000 more subscriptions came in. As a writer it took me years to collect 17,000 subscribers, and those I had to enter one by one. So being a celebrity is not at all a useless preoccupation.

The correspondence I received was addressed to the writer Harry Golden. I have received more than 500,000 letters from readers in the last decade. There were letters from Protestants in Milwaukee who said, "You are describing my mother," from Catholics in New Haven who said, "The Lower East Side was like our old neighborhood," and from Jewish housewives in Atlanta who said, "You remind me of my uncle who used to read the Yiddish newspaper aloud to us."

Not all the letters were complimentary; not all of them were sane. Many of these letters thrilled me. Immodestly, I quote from one:

March 15th 1965
S. Martino A Mensola
Tel. 600251 Firenze

DEAR MR. GOLDEN,

You are, I suppose, very much used to getting "fan letters" and therefore will not mind getting another from me! An Italo-American friend has sent me "Only in America" for Christmas and I cannot help telling you that few books have given me more pleasure than this one. If only I could have read it to my boss, Bernard Berenson, how he would have loved it. His way of reasoning, his sense of humour were very close to yours. There are many things in your book that he could have said, like "our new breed of knuckleheads" or "the wise guy is a sucker after all." He would have adored the "Vertical Negro Plan" and the "Causerie on Death" and many others. Being myself the daughter of a Southern Italian I was highly amused and surprised to realize how close things like "Buying a suit on the East Side" or "Wishing you long years" are to what still goes on in our southern provinces. There too bargaining is a highly developed art and it is the Saint's day that counts and is celebrated while the birthday remains rather vague. Probably a century old superstition common to all mediterranean lands. B. B. was rich in prophecies about the future of America as "widow land."

I could go on and on about all this and do not want to bore you. So let me just thank you for your book and hope that you will have the time and the strength to write at least eleven thousand more stories.

Sincerely yours,
NICKY MARIANO

(from 1919 to 1959 secretary of Bernard Berenson)

To which I replied:

March 18, 1965

Mme. Nicky Mariano
S. Martino A Mensola
Florence, Italy

DEAR MME. MARIANO:

What has been most rewarding about this career is that so many people I admired from a distance have literally come to my desk here in Charlotte, North Carolina. From Justice Black to John Steinbeck, from Carl Sandburg to Sartre—and now an echo of the most prized of all—Bernard Berenson.

How often I came across your name in his diaries, and he assumed the whole world knew Nicky because I didn't know for a hundred pages that you were a female Nicky. How nonchalantly he mentioned you.

I loved Berenson dearly and when I finally did get to Florence I did not dare intrude. It was less than a year before his passing. But it wasn't till Berenson wrote his diary during the Nazi occupation that I could appreciate that great man. Previously he had written only on art, which was beyond me.

Hitler did it. Berenson would have been the first to say that the literary Humanism he gave to the world was not much of an exchange for the Nazi slaughter, but at least we got that much out of it, as this Jew, turned Catholic, in his old age said, "I am back, back to my fellow scapegoats."

There is an amazing parallel here with Luigi Luzatti, a Jew who wrote the most revered book on St. Francis, and who became Prime Minister of Italy. Luzatti, too, rose in the Parliament to denounce the Russian pogroms of 1905–1906, saying like Berenson, "I have long since left the religion of my mother, but this day I speak—as a Jew again. . . ."

> With high esteem,
> HARRY GOLDEN

Only in America was in print three months when I received a letter from Jerry Lawrence and Robert E. Lee, the playwrights who had written *Inherit the Wind* and *Auntie Mame*. They wanted to make a play out of my book for Broadway. They were polite, gentlemanly, and enthusiastic. They spent a week in Charlotte, prying into everything, asking questions, making notes.

The next time I heard from them was when they sent me the completed play, along with the information that Herman Shumlin would produce and direct it in the fall of 1959. Herman Shumlin is a famous director. One of Mr. Shumlin's greatest successes was Lillian Hellman's *The Little Foxes*. Lawrence and Lee expected that Paul Muni would play the role of Harry Golden.

On my next lecture trip to California, I introduced myself to Paul Muni, who proved to be a generous host. When I left him that afternoon, he said jokingly, "Golden, I can imitate everything about you—except the paunch." Within a few weeks, however, Muni had to withdraw from the play because of serious eye trouble.

Lawrence and Lee and Shumlin next approached Edward G. Robinson, who declined their offer with the explanation, "I'll be damned if I'll play matinees." Finally, they chose Nehemiah Persoff, a young actor, who had recently played Mussolini on a television play.

The first I knew that *Only in America* was in trouble was when I went to Philadelphia the night before its opening there. Herman Shumlin said, "I don't want to open. The play is not ready. We must cast Lee J. Cobb as Golden instead of Persoff. (Mr. Shumlin disliked Nicky Persoff for what reasons I do not know, nor could I fathom. I suspect they were professional rather than personal. Lawrence and Lee and I, however, liked Persoff.) When we put Shumlin's suggestion to a vote, we three carried the day: Open the play.

It did poorly with the Philadelphia critics and with the Philadelphia audience. Again Shumlin begged us not to take the play to New York. By this time I didn't think Lee J. Cobb would make that appreciable a difference. I voted with Lawrence and Lee to take the play to Broadway.

Thus it was that Herman Shumlin and I waited backstage in the Cort Theater on the night of November 19. We heard the audience quiet as the stage manager brought down the lights. There was a moment of breathless silence. Then, "House out. Curtain." Mr. Shumlin raised the curtain, and we could hear the audience applauding the set. As actress Lynn Hamilton spoke the first line, Mr. Shumlin started for the stage door on his way home, his work done. I asked, "Mr. Shumlin, what do you think?"

Mr. Shumlin turned back, stared at the set, and answered, "It's all in the hands of those seven men."

He meant the then seven drama critics of the New York newspapers, also referred to as the Seven Horsemen of the Apocalypse.

These seven men did not like the play. I learned this in Lawrence and Lee's company, hearing the reviews as they telephoned into Bob's apartment that night.

It might seem that the bad reviews which heralded the quick closing of *Only in America* and meant the loss of money to backers, the loss of work to actors, and the loss of prestige and time to authors, producers, and director would result in bitterness. But the opposite was true. I felt close to people connected with the play: to Shepperd Strudwick, who secures tickets for me for every new play in which he appears, to Shannon Bolin, who lives in the Algonquin and who played Tiny, to Shumlin, to Nicky Persoff, and to Lawrence and Lee. Tiny, in fact, is locked in friendship with Jerry Lawrence even more firmly than I. When he was the recipient of an advanced degree from Fairleigh Dickinson University in New Jersey, he insisted she be there to help him celebrate this honor.

367

My own opinion, now that I may indulge in postmortems, is that people would not pay $6.90 to watch a make-believe Harry Golden when for $2 at a Hadassah meeting they can hear the real Harry Golden with luncheon thrown in. In short, there was too much of me in the play, not enough of the times or of Charlotte or of the issue.

Before the production of *Only in America* I was making perhaps twenty appearances a year around the country at $100 to $200 a shot as lecturer. W. Colston Leigh, one of the largest lecture bureaus, approached me. Beatrice Grant, its representative, promised me at least thirty dates a year at at least $1,000 a date. I signed. This money over the years helped support the *Carolina Israelite* when subscriptions began to fall off in the late 1960's. In the first few years I made innumerable speeches at Bonds for Israel rallies, before the national conventions of Jewish fraternal orders, and to thousands of Jewish sisterhood groups.

More and more in recent years, the largest sponsor for lecturers have been the universities. I have lectured to students at the University of Michigan, at UCLA, at the University of Missouri, and at other colleges less prominent, Layne in Pennsylvania, Miles in Birmingham, Alabama, and Pfeiffer in Misenheimer, North Carolina.

Pfeiffer is a Methodist school with 500 students. Just before I went, the faculty and the college administration had integrated, a fact proudly announced. When Pfeiffer listed my lecture, the president of the university told me he received a telegram from one of the school's substantial patrons which read: HARRY GOLDEN IS THE STRAW THAT BROKE THE CAMEL'S BACK.

Integration at Pfeiffer cost the college almost three-quarters of $1,000,000 in canceled pledges from irate alumni and supporters. It cost the college more in inconvenience, for Pfeiffer drew its water from the nearby city of Albemarle. Once Pfeiffer integrated, Albemarle turned off the pipes. The school had to dig its own wells. Pfeiffer thrives today, its confidence, prestige, and integrity intact.

I have spent eight years in a continuing dialogue with college students, answering questions on Little Rock and on Vietnam. I have been cheered and booed, depending on my answers. I have discovered a great truth. The most precious possession we have today is the university. The press is free, but advertisers often influence editors; the clergyman is free, but the layman has usurped the minister's function; the networks are free, but the sponsors write the shows. What makes the university precious is when the professor closes the door at the beginning of the class, he and his students can go at it, uninhibited and undirected. At the University of Florida, where my son Billy is a professor, he asked his class one day, "How many believe in God? Raise your hands." Such a question cannot be asked of the editorial staff, or of the television writer, certainly not of the parishioners. It is not a question anyone ever asks at a business luncheon or for that matter in legislative assembly. It can be asked only in a classroom, and there are other questions just as important which can be asked only in classrooms.

After discussing white racism, the students ask, "What can one man do?" "One man can do a lot," I say. "The next time someone uses the word 'nigger,' put your hand on his wrist and say, 'Please, not in front of me,' and perhaps he will never use the word again in front of anyone. That is something."

I find students generally responsive and fair. In Atlanta, before a college group, I was finishing when a Kluxer rose and shouted, "What's a Jew doing down here trying to change our Southern way of life?"

"I'll tell you what I'm doing down here," I shouted back. "I'm trying to form a Jewish Society for the Preservation of Christian Ethics." These students laughed at him.

Students are not always responsive and fair. The dissidence at Columbia and at Berkeley is not isolated. Indeed not. I felt the dissidence at many schools and universities. It pervades the width and breadth of the land. I attribute this dissidence and dissatisfaction to the ability of the young to *realize* but not *accept* that they are going to live in an unpleasant and inequitable world for the rest of their lives.

When I was a schoolboy and the teacher mentioned France, we thought of Joan of Arc or of Lafayette. When the teacher mentioned England, we thought of Henry VIII and all his wives. Our political life revolved around the precinct chairman, the Tammany Hall man in my case, the sheriff or the county commissioners in Charlotte. But today the new ruler in Indonesia, whose name may be unpronounceable, may do or say something to change the quality of our lives forever. No one is remote. The

369

Prime Minister of Yemen has something to say about our future, and so does the Prime Minister of England. This state of affairs makes life hazardous. Patience and wisdom, not always the virtues of the young, alone accommodate inequity and unpleasantness.

I have lectured before groups other than college students, too. I debated Dr. I. Beverly Lake before a Southern audience in Raleigh, North Carolina. Dr. Lake was a professor of law at Wake Forest University. He is an outspoken segregationist, perhaps the leading segregationist in North Carolina. He has twice run for governor, and after his second campaign he urged his supporters to vote for Dan K. Moore, the conservative Democrat, against Richardson Pryer, the liberal who had won a narrow plurality in the first primary. Lake's decision cost Pryer the election. Today Dr. Lake sits on the State Supreme Court.

On the night we squared off, Dr. Lake, at one point, deplored the fact that integration would mean your sister would marry a Negro.

"Your sister can always say no, can't she?" I retorted, and I believe it was the first time the people who composed this audience ever heard this argument.

When I gave a speech before the Georgia Library Association at Jekyll Island, Georgia, Congresswoman Iris Blitch walked out. She told the press I had offended her deeply with my description of the song "America the Beautiful."

"When he said there was nothing to the song except possibly the last verse," explained Mrs. Blitch, "I felt as a United States Congresswoman I could not stay. I have loved that song all my life."

What I said was that "America the Beautiful" was a song which emphasized "place" while "The Star-Spangled Banner" was an anthem which emphasized idea. I pointed out the wheatfields in Rumania were "more beautiful amber waves of grain," that the Pyrenees were as majestic as "purple mountains" anywhere, and that Brasília was probably the only alabaster city in the world.

As closely as I remember, Mrs. Blitch didn't leave when I voiced these remarks but later, when I prophesied that blood would not run in the streets when the University of Georgia integrated. Anyway, the incident provided a pleasant half hour for the local newsmen.

I was on the stage of the auditorium at Virginia Polytechnic

Institute preparing to debate Republican Senator Strom Thurmond of South Carolina when the college president handed me a note. It said that Martin Luther King had been assassinated in Memphis a half hour before. The president wanted me to make this news known.

Martin Luther King, I told the audience, was the one contemporary who, in attempting to save his people, saved Christianity. This Negro leader had taught us all an important and necessary fact: that Christianity still had its uses. We should be eternally grateful for this lesson.

Strom Thurmond rose and told the people Harry Golden was wrong. Martin Luther King was an agitator.

In the morning, before I left, several of the students had petitioned the dean to lower the American flag to half-mast. The dean said he was sympathetic to this request, but only a federal directive gave him this authority. The students listened to the explanation politely, left the office, climbed the steeple, and lowered the flag themselves. King's loss was a terrible blow to the country, certainly, but leaving that Virginia campus, I could reassure myself that his life was not spent in vain. The flag stayed at half-mast.

All of it wasn't this meaningful. I had accepted an invitation to deliver a lecture before the Emergency Civil Liberties Committee in New York City which I confused with the American Civil Liberties Union of which I am a member. I got many calls that I was going to address a Communist-front organization. Friends warned me. The newspapers warned me, and in the end, I canceled my speech. My place was taken by Senator Stephen Young of Ohio. I was and am ashamed of this. I find it hard to forgive myself for being scared.

Only in America changed my life in some respects but not in the obvious ones. I still have the same friends now I had before its publication. I drink the same amount of bourbon, about three fifths a week: a healthy dollop in the morning, a drink or two before lunch, two in the afternoon, one before dinner, but never anything after sundown. My cigars are the same brand with the exception of 1961, when the Cigar Institute elected me the "Cigar Man of the Year." I was preceded in this post by such men as George Burns and Ernie Kovacs. One of the rewards conferred on the "Cigar Man of the Year" is unending supply of every cigar rolled or manufactured by member firms of the institute. It is not a bad deal. When a Jewish organization elects me "Man of the Year," all I get is a pledge card.

What one expects out of affluence is leisure and ease—precisely what one does not get. After *Only in America* I worked harder than ever before. I worked harder because I was a nonvoluntary spokesman for many people's causes, posts I neither sought nor in which I ever served with distinction.

A good friend of mine, Dr. Holmes Ralston, pastor of a Presbyterian church in Charlotte, banteringly told me it would be well if I became a Christian. And I answered: "No, I cannot do it because the movers of the earth were Jesus, Karl Marx, Sigmund Freud, and Albert Einstein, all Jews, and I cannot give this up."

I was also hailed as a spokesman for the liberals which made them mad since they accused me of never consulting them. When I did consult them, they complained I was a "ritualistic" liberal.

Along with these portfolios, I was the spokesman for the Negroes, which I always denied. Roy Wilkins was a spokesman, and Martin Luther King and Whitney Young. They often made statements contrary to what I believed. We differ in policy, however, not in principle. I was only a spokesman for the *Carolina Israelite,* which I edited and published. By actual count, the *Carolina Israelite* stands third in the number of quotes included in the *Congressional Record*; only the New York *Times* and *Christian Science Monitor* have more.

But the would-be spokesman gets quoted more often than he likes and is constrained to become more responsible. So I also undertook to write a newspaper column for the Bell-McClure Syndicate which appears three times a week in sixty-four papers.

In many respects, getting out a syndicated column is infinitely harder than putting out a personal journal every other month. In the first place, the columnist is not necessarily writing for his own audience but for the general reader. In the second, drumming up a 750-word essay out of your own head three times a week is often an onerous and merciless demand. The subscribers to the *Israelite* often forgave literary indiscretions; why not? They had already paid their money. A newspaper audience does not forgive at all. Cease to interest them, and the managing editor drops you. It happens to all columnists, save Billy Graham, who has never lost a newspaper.

To keep what was now a corporate enterprise going, I hired my son Richard. One of his first duties was to help me prepare the column which started my syndication in February, 1960. The appropriate subject, of course, was Lincoln. We wrote that the moral ambivalence of Americans was nowhere more evident than in the respect they accorded Abraham Lincoln. To a nation of churchgoers, Lincoln professed no creed. To a nation counting romance sacred, Lincoln left a girl at the altar. One of Richard's contributions was: "In a country highly opposed to socialism, we forget that our most respected Republican President once wrote a letter of praise to Karl Marx when *Das Kapital* was published."

The column appeared in the Charlotte *Observer*. One of the officers of the White Citizens Council wrote a letter to the editor asking, "Where is this letter?"

I wanted to answer immediately, so I called Carl Sandburg.

He said, "Harry, I never saw such a letter."

I was a little nettled. I called John Duff, my good friend, who was writing a book on Lincoln. John Duff said he doubted there was such a letter.

More annoyed now than nettled, and a little panicky, I called Richard. He said he didn't know where the letter was, but he definitely remembered a Communist on a soapbox reading it outside the High School of Commerce in New York City in 1941.

I said, "Richard, this is not good enough. The Charlotte paper has an editorial about the letter."

Richard said he'd find it. Two days later, he said, "Maybe I got it wrong. Maybe Marx wrote the letter to Lincoln."

There is nothing like putting your foot in your mouth on your maiden attempt, I thought. And number one son might be right out of a job in a hurry.

I confided this problem to a friend, Hal Seiber, a splendid researcher and then an assistant to a United States Senator. Seiber came up with the answer that afternoon. He found it in the Lincoln Centennial in Washington, D.C. Karl Marx had written to Abraham Lincoln in 1862 asking the President of the United States for an expression to be read at the Working Men's Convention in London. Lincoln did not reply to Karl Marx directly

373

but through the United States Ambassador to the Court of St. James's, Charles Francis Adams. Lincoln directed the ambassador to inform Karl Marx that while he, Lincoln, was sympathetic to the workingman, the President of the United States, as a matter of public policy, made no statements to conventions abroad. Lincoln concluded with a short remark praising *Das Kapital*.

Over the years I have found I didn't need Richard to help me put my foot in my mouth. I could do it all by myself. I wrote up the story of Queen Liliuokalani, Hawaii's last monarch, whom the Americans deposed. In the course of my story, I confused James B. Dole, the pineapple king, with Sanford B. Dole, Hawaii's first governor. More people who knew the difference between the two Doles broke the back of Charlotte postmen. In fact, if as many people knew the last verse of "The Star-Spangled Banner" as knew the difference between the two Doles, I would have to conclude that we are a nation of committed patriots.

My syndicated newspaper columns are usually prepared from four to six weeks in advance. On the day John Glenn thrilled Americans with his successful orbit, my column on the inutility of the eggplant appeared.

I ventured that the mark of the bad cook was a too-fervent devotion to eggplant:

> Bad cooks are crazy about serving eggplant and invent every sort of excuse and plot to make it a main course. Why bad cooks should have lighted on eggplant, I don't know, but I do know they have an utterly strange attraction to this bland and useless vegetable. Eggplant may be a dandy weapon to hurl at Neapolitan tenors who sing flat, but it is no food for a growing boy or growed man, as we say down heah in the South.

John Glenn could still be in space for all the eggplant *aficionados* care.

An avalanche of eggplant recipes inundated my offices. There are eggplant recipes which, should I choose, will enable me to prepare eggplant fritters, eggplant pizzas, eggplant knishes, eggplant appetizers, and a dish I believe is called rat-a-tat-tooey, which is eggplant mixed with unsalted chopped meat.

I had to set up a separate file, still called the eggplant file, to keep this correspondence. I prepared a form letter which said:

374

"Don't worry, dear, he will love you even if you can't boil eggs. Thank you for your letter. I will try to do better."

Of what I have written since *Only in America,* I am proudest of *Mr. Kennedy and the Negroes,* which is used as a textbook in many colleges as a history of the civil rights movement, and *A Little Girl Is Dead,* the story of the Leo Frank case in Georgia. Since Leo Frank was lynched in 1915, there has been a book a decade on the case. *The Leo Frank Case* by young Leonard Dinnerstein succeeded *A Little Girl Is Dead,* and I know another author will succeed Dinnerstein.

There have been critics who absolutely misunderstand me as much as they have misunderstood any author whom they have wounded with their outrageous slings. The criticism I want to answer is that which leaves my written texts and devolves on my personal qualities. I speak specifically here of only three critics: Leslie Fiedler, Norman Mailer, and Philip Roth. Philip Roth complained about my books and dismissed them because they were filled with nostalgia and sentimentality. After reading *Portnoy's Complaint* I understand why I am not Mr. Roth's dish of tea. I respected my father and loved my mother. Judaism gave me an identity; it did not subtract one. And none of these conspired to afflict me with any sexual hang-ups. I was rather sorry to read that the critics are maintaining Mr. Roth brought the Jewish novel to a full cycle. We had a long run from Exodus on. I for one am sorry to see it over. I can only hope that a clever Jewish boy growing up on the West Side, perhaps with college-educated parents who take their responsibility seriously, will one day figure out another method of attack so that the Jew can go on in literature as indeed he goes on in American life.

At the Second Dialogue in Israel, held under the auspices of the American Jewish Congress, Leslie Fiedler, addressing himself to the subject "The Jewish Intellectual and Jewish Identity," unburdened himself about the cultural inconveniences of American life. "I move," said he, "through a country where the secular sanctification of Anne Frank has been utterly astonishing and where the glorification of Harry Golden is utterly appalling."

Why does it have to be me who is what's wrong with America? Can I be as appalling as the Southern California John Birch Society? As the Alabama segregationists? Or, for that matter, as the desecration of the American countryside by superhighways?

Fiedler contributed these same views to *Ramparts,* a Catholic magazine—except in the Catholic essay Anne Frank's deification no longer astonished him since he neglected to mention it. Fiedler was mad at Golden for allowing the public to set him up as a minor prophet.

What appalls me about Leslie Fiedler is that he keeps saying of J. D. Salinger's novel *The Catcher in the Rye* that the name Holden Caulfield "cannily conceals the ethnic origin" of the hero —such origin, of course, being Jewish. He's got to be Jewish, says Fiedler. He comes from the West Side.

This is literary criticism?

Concluding his remarks to the Tel Aviv audience, Fiedler quotes Mailer's poem about me:

> If
> Harry Golden
> is the Gentile's
> Jew
>   can I be-
> come the Golden
> Goy?

From this I take it Norman Mailer doesn't like me, though the only time I ever met him was at the Democratic National Convention in Los Angeles in 1960, when I did him a favor.

Martin Agronsky of NBC said, "Harry, you'd better tell Norman his fly's unzipped," which I hastened to do. Norman zipped his fly, but I could see he put me down as one who would assault nonconformity, for not only was Norman's zipper loose but his pants were rolled up to the knees as though he were going to wade across a swamp, although we were only awaiting the arrival of Jack Kennedy that evening.

Well, no matter. It's probably harder to rhyme Agronsky than Golden.

Chapter 32

On October 28, 1958, a searching police car picked up two Negro boys, James Hanover Thompson, nine, and David "Fuzzy" Simpson, eight, and carried them to the county jail in Monroe, North Carolina. The police held the two boys incommunicado for six days. On November 4 the police notified the boys' mothers—$15-a-week domestic workers—that their sons were to go on trial in a half hour.

The two boys were charged with assault on three white females, aged six and seven. Neither the girls nor their parents ever appeared in the courtroom. Juvenile Court Judge J. Hampton Price presented the girls' testimony, that the defendants had gone into a white neighborhood, climbed down uninvited into a culvert ditch where three white girls were playing, and made a kiss from each of the girls the price for getting out. Two of the girls ran from the ditch, but the third, a seven-year-old, had kissed Hanover Thompson. Judge Price found the boys guilty and committed them to indeterminate terms in reform school.

No one had been permitted to see the boys in jail. Nor, for the first month, was anyone admitted at the reform school. Finally, a reporter and civil rights attorney talked to the boys. The story the boys told was that they had been walking down the street in a white neighborhood and joined a game of cowboys and Indians with a group of white boys. When the game broke up, the Negro youngsters, with one or more white boys, went into the ditch where three little white girls were playing. The white boy suggested a kissing game, and Hanover claimed that both he and the white boys were kissed by one of the little girls. Fuzzy wouldn't play because he was busy inside the culvert "killing granddaddy spiders."

The mother of the white child denied her husband took his shotgun and went looking for the Negro boys. She said that she visited Mrs. Thompson, however, to tell her to "get out." Negro neighbors of the Thompsons and Simpsons stated that white people, one of whom carried a gun, had come looking for the boys' mothers. The mothers were frightened and stayed with neighbors. Until the trial the police told the mothers that the boys were being held without charge for their own protection. That the court appointed no lawyer came as a shock to the families, the NAACP leaders, and the Negro community.

After the trial Mrs. Simpson lost part of her work, and Mrs. Thompson lost all of hers. Both mothers were evicted.

The NAACP petitioned for the release of the boys from reform school on the grounds that they had in no way committed a crime and that they had been denied due process of law.

Juvenile Judge J. Hampton Price of Monroe, who sent the boys to the Morrison Training School for Negroes, said both boys had been on probation at the time of the kissing incident. He called their home life unsuitable and said that they had received no parental supervision.

B. Madison, state commissioner of correction and training, agreed the boys had not committed a crime. They were not convicted of a criminal offense either, he said, and had not, after all, been sentenced to prison. Rather, they had been made wards of the state in their own best interests. He stated that with good behavior, the children would be released when the local welfare department determined that their families would not neglect them and would provide reasonable guidance and home care.

The little white girl's mother, in talking to a reporter, said she learned about the kissing by chance. She was busy and only half listening to the child's rambling talk when, with a shock, she realized it was a little Negro boy who had kissed her daughter. She immediately sat down and elicited the whole story. Lest she do the child any psychological damage, she said, she controlled her voice and uttered no reproaches. Instead, she praised the girl "for having used her head to escape from such a dangerous situation." Then she took the little girl, she said, and thoroughly washed her "sweet little face."

These were the basic details of the Kissing Case which occupied newspaper headlines in the South and in the world for a few months in 1958. The case is a forgotten one now, but I again set forth its history because it portended in microcosm the situation which obtains today. The Kissing Case is a classic example of the inequity of the Negro position. It is as well a perfect illustration of the South's inability to exercise either compassion or justice when an issue involves race. The Kissing Case prompted the first Black Power advocate to make his voice unfortunately heard. And in the long run, the Kissing Case was resolved by the efforts and energies of a few liberal and humane people who were strictly and wholeheartedly bent on redressing injustice done two little boys—the very people who are dismissed today, to whom no one will listen.

The Kissing Case made the headlines because Robert Williams, the Negro head of the Monroe chapter of the NAACP, began exploiting it for his own purposes. This exploitation necessarily made him ignore the plight of Hanover Thompson and Fuzzy Simpson. It was only as long as the two boys remained imprisoned that Williams could keep generating an intense concern in the North, where he successfully held mass rallies at which thousands of dollars were raised. Needless to say, neither the two colored boys nor their mothers received any funds from Williams. Williams was rapidly making these little boys into martyrs, and colored martyrs in the South ultimately become sacrificial victims.

I had known Robert Williams for several years. He was a big, burly man, often bristling with bitterness, outspoken on all occasions. He came to the offices of the *Carolina Israelite* several times to solicit money. These were not large sums, and I was usually able to accommodate the requests. As far as I know, he used the money for political purposes, the purposes he outlined to me and others. Though Williams called me Harry and I called him Robert, I never liked him. I did not feel I was prejudiced in my dislike because Kelly Alexander didn't like Williams either. After all, we reasoned, it is not possible to like everybody on your side. A small NAACP chapter in unsophisticated rural Monroe was worth any amount of money. If Robert Williams flew Castro's flag from his home, well, that was a bee in his bonnet. But when

Williams began saying publicly it was time for Negroes to collect guns, we began to worry—we being people like me, Kelly Alexander, and Dr. Raymond Wheeler of the Southern Regional Council.

In fact, I believe Raymond was in my office when Williams stopped by one day and we suggested perhaps that statement about guns was inflammatory. "This is the worst thing you can do," Raymond argued. "This is what the Southerners are waiting for." Raymond knew. He was a North Carolina boy, born and bred.

Williams told us, "My people want revolution."

It was the first time I heard "my people," the first time I realized we were divided. Fred and Kelly Alexander used to talk about "our people," but they were talking about political precincts and various NAACP chapters. About the overall goals, they always said "we want," meaning liberal whites *and* Negroes. It was not, however, Robert Williams who retained a civil rights lawyer or Robert Williams who recruited an objective reporter to help with the case but Kelly and Fred Alexander and I. Our strategy was to get the boys out of jail on a writ of habeas corpus and then, by arguing for the preservation of their legal rights, keep them out of jail. We hoped to accomplish this before the case drew too much attention. Once the story got into the news, attitudes always harden in the South. Williams beat us to the punch.

There was every reason why decent people should be outraged over the situation, but the outrage also meant the two boys would be forever lost in a tangle of legal explanations and definitions. Certainly interested people would secure their freedom sooner or later, but freedom would mean expensive legal fees and protracted arguing.

Kelly said, "Harry, our best bet is Governor Hodges. The Kissing Case is escalating. It is out of all proportion. Will Hodges talk to you about it?"

Governor Hodges would.

I told the governor that Robert Williams had collected $10,000 the night before in Cleveland, that he was due in Detroit tonight, where he would undoubtedly collect another $10,000. "Why should he get ten thousand dollars over the imprisonment of two boys? Let's get them out of jail," I said.

"I want them out of jail," said Hodges. "But I have a problem. The problem is my constituency." He showed me newspaper clippings from Holland, France, Italy, West Germany, and England. Hodges was an intelligent governor. He did not want this notoriety to continue. He said, "It's bad enough the way it affects the state, but it is even worse in the way it affects Negro families. The court made these two boys wards of the state to protect them. They come from fatherless homes. They have no direction. How can I say the court is wrong?"

"We'll put the homes together again," I suggested.

"This is the only way," Hodges agreed. "If you can guarantee that these two mothers will be established in stable environments, in clean apartments in separate parts of Charlotte, with respectable jobs, I'll let the two boys out tomorrow morning with a governor's fiat. I will inform my constituency that these children have been returned to a decent environment, that they are not running wild at night, that they are going to school." That afternoon Kelly got the mothers jobs, rented two apartments, paying a month's rent on each, and in the morning Luther Hodges was as good as his word and sent Hanover and Fuzzy home. So at one point in the civil rights movement, this was the kind of communication which could exist between intelligent men of goodwill. They could discuss and resolve a problem that beset their community.

Where we once thought the only villains were on the right, now we had them on the left. We had usurped Robert Williams' cause. He was mad about it. He said a great many unpleasant things about me. He was condemning me, but he was also condemning the impulse which motivated liberals, to see black and white both receive equity. In his magazine, the *Crusader,* which he published in Red China, Robert Williams said:

Harry Golden, or Mr. Golden, as he is so fondly called by the "responsible" bourgeoisie nigra leaders, used to be a poverty-stricken champion of integration and the rights of "the colored folks." Harry was a poor liberal Jew of much humor and wit. He amassed a fortune by portraying the black man's arduous and poignant struggle for human rights and dignity as a national light-hearted comic drama. Yes, Mr. Golden the self-styled expert and self-appointed spokesman for quaint and romantic Black America just loved peaceful and nonviolent darkies. As Harry's fortune and bank account changed, so did his view of the romantic souls of black folks. As his stature grew, he was much in demand by southern white gentry as a sort of court jester in easing the beastly racist conscience of the white power-structure.

Well-meaning people, people who were expert in this problem, had visited Robert Williams, had analyzed his tactics, and had concluded that he was as dangerous in his way as a Klansman. Williams was the prototype of Stokely Carmichael. Roy Wilkins believed he was dangerous. Everyone interested in Negro civil rights believed he was dangerous except *Commentary* magazine. *Commentary* magazine concluded that Mr. Williams was right and I was wrong, that Robert Williams was "hard" and I was "soft." But then *Commentary* has a genius for the absolutely wrong statement at the absolutely inopportune time. *Commentary* once concluded that Mrs. Silvercruys, the founder of Minute Women of America, was a typical suburban housewife, a conclusion that must have interested, if not astounded, the actors she had blacklisted. And Norman Podhoretz, *Commentary*'s editor, decided to agonize about his Negro problem at the moment other men were trying to keep the lid on in the cities.

Commentary's conclusion gave Robert Williams the sort of success he needed. A Jewish liberal magazine had disavowed me and had questioned my effectiveness. I was the only man in North Carolina who could have got the two boys out of the reformatory simply and easily. That I had access to the governor, that I could effect liaison between whites and blacks, was too valuable an asset for us embattled partisans to lose. Kelly Alexander came to my defense:

North Carolina State Conference of Branches
National Association for the Advancement of Colored People
Charlotte, N.C.

Office of: Chairman
April 7, 1961

Editor, Commentary
165 East 56th Street
New York, N.Y.

GENTLEMEN:

I was greatly surprised that *Commentary* could be led so far astray in an article on one Robert Williams in the April, 1961 issue by Julian Mayfield. An amazing piece of work. I quote Mr. Mayfield: "I first met Robert Williams at the center of a revolution (in Havana in the summer of 1960) and I am certain that this has colored my attitude toward him. . . . Relations between the Eisenhower administration and the Castro government had deteriorated almost to the breaking point."

We know the nature of some of the broadcasts Mr. Williams has made from Cuba against the United States, which I am sure must have been available to Mr. Mayfield. My purpose, however, is not to question the propriety and decency of such activities. I will leave that to his own conscience.

When a group of white liberals in Charlotte first heard of Robert Williams and his activities in Monroe, Union County (about twenty miles away), they immediately held out a hand of fellowship and cooperation, not only because he was active against segregation but because he was an officer of the NAACP. But they soon had to withdraw their friendship, even before the NAACP found it necessary to remove Williams from his association with us. Dr. Raymond Wheeler of Charlotte and Harry Jones, N.C. Director of the Southern Regional Council, called on Mr. Williams and they reported his statement, in effect: "The time has come to shed some blood."

While we did not attend this meeting, Mr. Williams repeated the same sentence to Harry Golden, to whose publishing office he came several times for assistance. Mr. Golden also cut off all relations with him.

It is precisely the non-violent program of the Negroes of the South that is winning us our battle for first class citizenship. The slightest deviation from this course would set us back another generation. It would lose the movement tremendous support among the white Southerners, much more than appears on the surface. Much, much more.

I was particularly interested in Mr. Mayfield's story about the "Kissing Case." Mr. Mayfield writes, "Without the pressure of world opinion, Williams insists, 'those boys would still be in custody.' "

What an amazing bit of arrogance and what a complete falsehood. Who ever heard of any sovereign state bowing under "pressure of world opinion," and particularly a Southern state? Has this ever happened before?

The NAACP had asked Harry Golden to intercede in this matter for the sake of the children who at that moment were not only in jail, but were being exploited by fund-raisers all over the North.

Mr. Golden had a conference with Governor Luther Hodges (now Secretary of Commerce), and the Governor told him that if we can arrange suitable facilities for these two families in Charlotte and provide some initial support for each of the families, he would order them released. Golden talked with me, the NAACP director of N.C., over the telephone and when I assured him that this will be done for the two mothers and the two boys, the Governor released the children the next morning.

The most amazing story yet to be written out of the South is that over twelve million Negroes, half of them semi-literate, have not made one serious mistake. Their great victory lies in walking India as Gandhi did—to the judge with a writ and the judge says, "You have not yet exhausted all your avenues of relief within your state," and we say; "Yes, your Honor," and start all over again.

And nothing fills a man with so much pride that his life has been useful than the knowledge of participation in this great undertaking.

Sincerely,
KELLY M. ALEXANDER,
Chairman
North Carolina NAACP

Robert Williams later fled to Cuba for keeps after a desperate encounter in Monroe. In August, 1961, Monroe Negroes began demonstrating for an antidiscrimination welfare administration. They staged their demonstrations at segregated swimming pools. Whites became enraged. They harassed these pickets. The Ku Klux Klan took to riding up and down the streets shooting and beating unarmed Negroes. Negroes began seeking out the patrolling cars of the Klansmen.

Into this near-riot situation came a car driven by a couple named Stegall who were unaware of the worsening situation and innocent of any part in it. Negroes mistook their automobile for one of the Klan's. They surrounded it, threatening the elderly occupants.

Robert Williams, aided by Mrs. Mae Mallory, two young colored demonstrators named Harold Reape and Richard Crowder, and a white civil rights worker named John Lowery, rescued the Stegalls and took them into Williams' house for their own safety. An hour and a half later they released the Stegalls.

The state charged these five with kidnapping. Having talked to the lawyers on both sides, I am convinced the charge was unjust

384

and undeserved. A long, sad empirical history informs us, however, that militants often get bum raps. Williams fled to Cuba, which prejudiced the charge against the three young men, all of whom were sentenced to terms of three to five years. Mrs. Mallory fled to New York, then to Michigan, where she tried to fight extradition. She wrote me several letters begging me to help. I had to explain that there was little any of us could do while she was a fugitive, that the only help we could offer was with her trial and, if she were convicted, with pleas for clemency. She was involuntarily returned to North Carolina, stood trial, and was sentenced to a jail term. The jury believed the Stegalls. Under those circumstances our help proved useless.

The strongest allies, the perfect willingness, are too frequently not enough. A strike against the textile mill in Henderson, North Carolina, had gone on for more than a year. It was led by Boyd Payton, a Baptist minister turned union organizer. The North Carolina State Bureau of Investigation, a miniature FBI, with the testimony provided by an *agent provocateur,* convicted Boyd Payton of conspiracy to damage the plant at Henderson.

The conspiracy, so called, perpetrated no crime, nor were these conspirators about to perpetrate a crime. Nevertheless, Boyd Payton was convicted and sentenced to a five-year jail term. Many decent people agitated for Payton's release. Many more petitioned the governor.

Luther Hodges decided he would pardon Payton. Since the governor was leaving office in January, he did not want the pardon construed as a political move. It was no secret that the textile manufacturers who had gone heart and soul for Richard Nixon in 1960 were heart and soul for keeping Boyd Payton in solitary confinement forever. Hodges had secured North Carolina for Jack Kennedy.

Governor Hodges decided to include Boyd Payton among those who would receive Christmas amnesties from the statehouse. To quiet political critics, he asked if the Reverend Billy Graham and Harry Golden would make a special plea for Payton. Billy Graham and I said yes.

We met at my office, a week before Christmas, 1960. Together we agreed we would urge the governor to pardon Payton as a charitable and Christian gesture by the state, that we would not argue the rights of unions, or complain about the cruelty of employers. We would plead only that Payton was a pious man, that he was noted for his devotion to the poor, that he was gentle.

I have always admired Billy Graham since he held the first integrated meeting in Charlotte, an evangelical revival in 1949. Billy told the ministers he would not come if Negroes were segregated, and Billy made it stick. I have no evangelical sympathies, but then Billy Graham does not proselytize.

Billy Graham looks like a big tiger. He is tall, muscular, with a smile bigger than his face. He is as strong as a farm boy, which indeed he once was, but he, too, is gentle and polite. He always shook hands with everyone on the staff of the *Israelite* whenever he stopped by.

On this particular morning, he was accompanied by Mrs. Graham, who is small, trim, vivacious, and pretty. Mrs. Payton, an older woman, also joined us, and we went over the mechanics of our plea. We wanted to be sure there were newspapermen to publicize our appearance and that both of us were in agreement about our approach. We confirmed our appointment.

Then we learned that Boyd Payton, for desperate and unexplained reasons, submitted to a lie detector test which the polygraph expert said he failed. This development was widely reported, and sadly Governor Hodges said in view of the lie detector results he could not grant Payton amnesty. Boyd served several more months until Terry Sanford, the new governor, commuted his sentence the next spring.

I remember the dismay that washed over Billy Graham and me and the pain that was plainly evident in Mrs. Payton's face. Why? Why did he, Boyd, do anything? But then Boyd didn't know of the governor's plan. He was an innocent man, unjustly imprisoned, trying every avenue to win freedom.

I can still feel that dismay, but I can also smile at one of the stories Billy Graham told me that morning while we waited to hear from Hodges. John Kennedy had won election the month before. Billy and I discussed the campaign.

The Reverend Billy Graham is a close friend of Richard Nixon; I believe Billy Graham knew the Nixon family well. He had talked to Richard Nixon before the campaign got under way and had advised Richard Nixon never in any way, by gesture or intimation, to touch on John Kennedy's Catholicism. It may well be that Mr. Nixon had already determined on this strategy; if he hadn't, he certainly heeded Billy Graham's advice.

Early in the campaign, Billy said he had a request from Henry Luce of *Life* magazine. *Life* wanted to print a story by Billy Graham about Richard Nixon, not necessarily an endorsement, but a reminiscence and a description of the man. Billy agreed.

The precinct politicos in North Carolina learned the date for which the article was scheduled. The Asheville democratic chairman called Billy, and Billy explained why he had written the piece. Someone from the governor's office called next. Billy said he explained again. Finally, one of the Senators from North Carolina called and said the Kennedys had recruited Reinhold Niebuhr of Union Theological Seminary in New York City to describe John F. Kennedy, the whole man, for *Life* magazine.

Billy said he began to wonder had he done the right thing. He told me he asked God, "If You don't want that article in *Life* magazine, Lord, please take it out."

Sure enough, there was an explosion in the Congo, and Henry Luce telephoned to say *Life* had postponed the Nixon article one week.

Billy Graham informed Henry Luce that *Life* had postponed the article forever.

"Wait a minute," argued Mr. Luce.

"God took the article out of *Life* this week and He doesn't want it in next week," insisted the Reverend Dr. Graham.

Henry Luce said, "Wait a minute—"

But not even Henry Luce of *Time, Life,* and *Fortune* could countermand His will.

We failed with Payton, and Williams got the better of us, but there were successes, too. The sit-ins started in North Carolina. The first sit-in, of course, was in Oklahoma City in 1944. It was disbanded by the police and did not become epidemic. The sit-ins of 1961 did. From Charlotte the sit-ins spread all over the South and invariably ended by merchants granting the demands of the demonstrators for integrated services in the downtown stores.

At first, the sit-ins caused no stir in Charlotte. The students from Johnson C. Smith planned and executed the demonstrations, sitting in the Walgreen's Drugstore on Main and Tryon, parading before Ivey's, circling Belk's. Charlotte took it all in stride. Nobody ran downtown to gape or jostle, just the usual shoppers who were amused and often sympathetic. The police maintained law and order. There were no arrests. Some of the white kids, the usual delinquents, poured ketchup on the colored boys at the counters, they taunted and tried to provoke the demonstrators, but there was no violence.

The demonstrators were led by Charlie Jones, a senior at Johnson C. Smith. He was an attractive young man, with beautiful white teeth and a light skin. He was dressed impeccably, stood erect, and for all the world looked like an Ivy Leaguer. He came to the *Israelite* on the morning of the second day somewhat disturbed. Several of the colored ministers had cornered him the night before and prophesied he couldn't keep the demonstration going, that he was hurting the cause of the Negro and the town. These ministers did not confuse as much as they saddened young Mr. Jones. For all his sophistication, he was still a Southern boy brought up to respect his ministers. He had helped precipitate a crucial situation, and here were the voices of authority telling him to call it off while his fellow students kept telling him to go forward. Charlie asked how he was to resolve this.

Julian Scheer of the Charlotte *News* was in the office, and he said, "Uncle Tom's talking to you, Charlie. You keep the sit-ins going."

I asked, "Charlie, how did you come up with this idea?"

Charlie said, "When different peoples live in close propinquity—"

"Can it, Charlie," said Julian. "What made you do it?"

"We heard the boys in Greensboro were going to do it," Charlie answered.

"That's more like it," said Julian. "That's a real good reason."

The Uncle Toms are those ministers whose churches have been built and supported by rich members of the white Establishment, the ministers whose ministries are dependent upon white sponsorship. The Uncle Toms were not Charlie Jones' only moral dilemma.

I was gone that Saturday, but Richard was in the office when Charlie paid us another call. Now the white merchants had reached him. They told him there were little old ladies from South Carolina who were afraid to come to Charlotte for fear of violence. They complained the boys from Johnson C. Smith were victimizing them, they loved Negroes really, they were all for integration, but what could they do about the Southern way of life? Similar sentiments had appeared editorially in many newspapers. Charlie Jones wanted to explain the motives of the demonstrators. He had chosen to write a letter to the New York *Times.*

In it he admitted that being a victim of circumstances was indeed a sad affair, as no one better than colored boys knew. But he also pointed out that in both English and American law and custom "no room at the inn" is an inadmissible excuse. The innkeeper makes room, and so storekeepers have no right to choose to whom to sell, no matter how other customers complain.

Richard saw that there was nothing he could add to the letter, so he simply helped Charlie send it over the wire to the *Times,* where it did appear the next Sunday, March, 1961.

But the sit-ins were still several weeks from realizing their goals. There was no slackening of their effort. Julian Scheer, for several years one of the best columnists in the South, complained that he would make more than $1,000 that month as a stringer for *Time,* the *Christian Science Monitor,* and the Chicago *Sun-Times,* reporting on the sit-ins, not one word of which would appear in a Charlotte newspaper. Not one word did. Nor did my newspaper columns appear when I wrote about the sit-ins. However, as soon as the sit-ins started, *Life* magazine asked me for a report which hurriedly I sent off:

> For southern Negroes, dime-store sandwiches were always better "out the back door." Since most of the kitchen help in the southern chain stores is colored, they made the back-door sandwiches of monumental proportions. But the Negro no longer wants them. The law has urged him into the very center of American middle-class society, the public school. Having gained this, the Negro now wants to sit down at the counter. The lettuce there may be wilted and the egg salad watery, but the Negro knows his posture will mark him a first-class citizen.
>
> For the visible difference between master and slave is that though they work together, fight together, even starve together, when the master sits, the slave must stand. The insistence that the Negro remain vertical is the last vestige of the ante-bellum agrarian South.
>
> The segregationist will stand himself before he lets the Negro sit. But the segregationist is dying. The current wave of sit-downs began in North Carolina. In this area—and apparently elsewhere in

the South—the reaction of the white people has been significant. Most of them do not seem to care what is going on at the dime stores. The whites can see the Negro demonstrators: clean-cut, quiet students. The students appear to be without leadership, with a hastily selected spokesman whenever one is needed, and they cause the police no trouble. Most Southerners know these are the Negro students who should have attended integrated high schools. This knowledge shames them.

In contrast, the white hecklers, yelling "Remember Little Rock" as they did in Chattanooga, wear black leather jackets, skinny tight Levis, are constantly combing their ducktail haircuts and walk about with their Mighty Mouse comic books rolled into a back pocket. They stand and grin, spit on the sidewalk, race by and backfire their cars, and jeer.

Among white Southerners there is considerable built-in sympathy for the Negro students. White store patrons occasionally pass by and whisper, "We're with you," or "Stick it out." The southern white woman cannot help but understand. She knows shopping is a gruelling all-day excursion. She knows what it means to sit down, kick off her shoes and buy the kids a Coke or an orangeade.

The storekeeper, too, knows what it means. The Negro in most large southern cities represents from 20% to 30% of the retail purchasing power. The students seeking service at lunch counters seem to have memorized the statistics. They say: "We are welcomed with open arms at counters one, two, three, four and five but denied service at six because it happens to be selling food and drink."

But as a matter of fact two classes of Negroes have been sitting at these same counters for many years. The first is the "to go" Negro. If he orders something "to go," it is presumed by all and sundry that a white man has sent him. Then we have the most preferred of all Negroes, the "white-coat-black-leather bowtie" Negro who sits even while whites are standing. The white-coat Negro, whose uniform identifies him as the white man's servant, does not even have to say "to go." He gives his order and the counterman automatically asks: "How does he want it, with mustard or mayonnaise?" The rest of the Negro population has had to go to the back door. But the back-door sandwich so good to eat is now too humiliating to buy.

During the past 25 years the Negro has assimilated the values of the society around him and he wants "in." His quiet persistence follows the pattern established in the Montgomery, Ala. bus strike of several years ago. In Montgomery the failure of the community leadership to sense the deep meaning and the strength of the protest brought tension, strife and substantial economic loss to that city. Today's southern leaders would be extremely naive if they failed to realize the serious nature of the newest demonstrations.

These protests will not go away until peaceful and honorable solutions are found to end the imposed inferiority of nearly 30% of the southern population. The Negro students are amused at the whites' standard rationalization: "The Negroes here were very happy until the NAACP came along." In some of the larger southern cities the local Negro community has actually been prodding the NAACP to take more vigorous legal action. The Negro adults, moreover, are almost 100% behind the lunch counter protests. Throughout the South every Negro community knows what is at stake. They have always known. A few years ago when various southern governors hinted that public school integration would cost thousands of Negro teachers their jobs, convention after convention of Negro teachers still voted overwhelmingly for speedy integration. . . .

Because of all of this the Negro now commands the battle. He not only possesses two powerful weapons, but he also knows how to use them with maximum effect. The first weapon is the economic buying power of the emerging Negro middle class. The Negro has been encouraged to use this power, particularly in the purchase of luxury goods, by the southern merchant. The Southerner gave the Negro his second weapon as well. It is the ultimate weapon—Christianity—and the Negro is using it.

What should have been an easy victory for the students from Johnson C. Smith was instead a long struggle, made so by the intransigence of George M. Ivey.

When I first came to Charlotte, North Carolina, almost thirty years ago, one of the citizens who made my life easier was George M. Ivey. On more than one occasion Mr. Ivey lent me money to keep my newspaper going. On many other occasions he paid my telephone bill.

He was my idea of the aristocratic Southerner, courteous, always erect, and always disciplined. He was also the chairman of the board of the multimillion-dollar complex that is Ivey's Stores, the main branch of which is in Charlotte, and other stores all over the Carolinas and in Florida.

He represented the old South, and a great many things happened to George M. and his stores in the last two decades.

When George came back from the war in 1918, his father, J. B. Ivey, who founded the first store, told him, "I need a wrapper in the basement." The next day, still in his uniform, George M. began his career in retailing in a basement which admitted no light or air.

A militant and pious churchman, George M. Ivey installed meditation rooms in the stores, and on Sunday the drapes were drawn over the windows, and as president of the corporation, he instructed all his employees never to transact or plan business detail on the day of rest.

The sit-ins annoyed him because the boys concentrated on his store. George Ivey did not understand integration. Pious as he was, Ivey point-blank told his good friend Billy Graham, "I will not discuss integration with you or anyone." George M. Ivey was concerned about how long the demonstrations would last. He asked my advice, worrying all the while that his customers from South Carolina wouldn't like the colored pickets. He said he might let the colored boys use the snack bar in the basement, but he would never desegregate his Tulip Room on the roof.

"You should desegregate your Tulip Room right away," I suggested. "Very few people, let alone colored college boys, have six dollars for one of the Tulip Room lunches."

All the stores in Charlotte with snack bars or restaurants were picketed by students of Johnson C. Smith University. (Norman Thomas's grandfather, Dr. Stephen A. Mattoon, was the first president of this Negro university.) Dr. and Mrs. Mattoon are buried on the grounds of Johnson C. Smith University, which now boasts a student body whose members come from all over the world. The sit-ins lasted for several weeks, and there were few instances of disorder except for the constant heckling by whites. The students sat at the snack bars with their books and did their homework while the waitresses stood around waiting for word from management to serve them—a word that never came. White boys standing behind the Negro female students poured ketchup in their hair and harassed them in many other ways, but the students remained unmoved.

George M. Ivey began to weaken in his stand and made his decision at the beginning of the third week of the protest.

When finally Ivey's integrated, everybody followed suit, thus ending the Charlotte sit-ins.

Three years later Mayor Stan Brookshire, along with several

wealthy businessmen, invited twenty of the Negro leaders of Charlotte to lunch. Each of the white men took several guests to one of the posh Charlotte restaurants, and integration on that level became a *fait accompli* one noontime. The desperate and vicious joke about taking a nigger to lunch is not without its profound implications. "Taking a nigger to lunch" would do much for the folks who populate what Dr. Sterling W. Brown, the president of the National Conference of Christians and Jews, calls the "third society," the whites and blacks who believe integration is not only feasible but desirable, the people who do not want separate schools, separate states, separate existences.

Lunch, of course, will not do everything. As recently as 1965, Kelly Alexander sued the Charlotte Chamber of Commerce, the sponsoring agent of the Shrine Bowl Football Game in Charlotte, which pits the high school all-stars from North Carolina against the all-stars from South Carolina. The Shrine Bowl commissioners overlooked a colored fullback from Charlotte who had scored more points than Red Grange and for whose favor several colleges sent recruiters.

Kelly's suit threatened to cancel or postpone the Shrine Bowl Game, than which there is nothing dearer to the ardent Charlotte sports fan. That night segregationists or football fans placed a bomb under Kelly's house, one under Fred's house, and one under the political leader of Charlotte's Negroes Reginald Hawkins' house. The bombs blew away the porches, but no one was hurt, and no one was deterred.

The court refused to cancel the game, but it warned the Chamber of Commerce that it would not tolerate discrimination in any city-owned facility in the future.

When the Freedom Riders came South in 1962 and 1963, 1312 Elizabeth Avenue was a stopping point for many of the young who were hitchhiking or busing to Albany, Georgia, or Selma, Alabama, or St. Augustine, Florida. I gave them money and dinner and let them sleep on the floor. Two rabbis came by on their way to meet the Freedom Riders in Albany, and we sat around and talked all night, and they slept on the floor, too.

The last happy moment of the civil rights movement was the March on Washington in 1963. The original idea belonged to A. Philip Randolph, who wanted to march on Washington in 1944.

Franklin D. Roosevelt dissuaded him because of the war. This time Martin Luther King, James Farmer, Bayard Rustin, and Roy Wilkins said, "Let's go." The March on Washington was in the planning stage for six months. I heard from Martin Luther King in a letter saying, "I count on you."

I took a plane to Washington. Although there were many who came from Charlotte, I was the only white man to go. I stayed at the Mayflower Hotel with Norman Thomas. In the morning, we went to a grouping place, and there I met Harold Stassen and Tom Wicker of the New York *Times*, who walked along with me and Norman Thomas on the march. I was asked to go on radio. The Voice of America wanted me to describe the significance of the march, which I did.

On that morning—a jubilee morning, I thought—the legal lynchings had not yet claimed the lives of civil rights workers like the Reverend James J. Reeb or Viola Liuzzo. Black militancy was still in the ground. No city had been razed by rioters. The March on Washington in 1963 was the high-water mark of liberalism. Not until we finish this fight will we know another day with the stirring excitement of Martin Luther King, Jr.'s speech "I Have a Dream" and the esthetic thrill of hearing Joan Baez lead 250,000 people in singing "We Shall Overcome."

Segregation, caste, dies hard. Not until 1968, when the Kerner Report was published, more technically the *Report of the National Advisory Commission on Civil Disorders,* did America face the fact that the majority of its citizens are covertly racist. The Kerner Report is probably Lyndon B. Johnson's true contribution to the country, not because the Kerner Report said anything new—it did not—but because for the first time the leaders of the country said it. Governor Otto Kerner is a leader, and Mayor John Lindsay, and Senators Fred Harris and Edward Brooke, and Congressmen James Corman and William McCulloch, and executive Charles B. Thornton and Police Chief Herbert Jenkins, and Steelworkers president I. W. Abel, and Roy Wilkins and Kentucky Commerce Commissioner Katherine Peden.

Others had always said we are inequitous and racist. I had said it. But I was not a leader. Just how important the Kerner Report is was illustrated in the Presidential election of 1968, when none of the candidates mentioned it, though "law and order" was one of the key issues. One day, however, they will teach the Kerner Report in the schools.

I sent the following letter on August 18, 1967:

Mr. Ralph Featherstone, Director
Student Nonviolent Coordinating Committee
1971½ Auburn Ave., N.E.
Atlanta, Georgia

DEAR SIR:

I hereby resign from the Student Nonviolent Coordinating Committtee and withdraw my support. Your recent newsletter which follows the pro-Arab, pro-Soviet, and racist lines with heavy overtones of anti-Semitism was a disgrace. You have thus joined the American Nazi Party and the Ku Klux Klan.

Criticizing American Jews as well as Israelis, your newsletter links the Negro cause with that of the Arabs.

Negroes have been victims of racism for too long to indulge in group stereotype and racial hate themselves. The cartoons in your newsletter were particularly coarse and obscene, and your anti-Semitism comes with ill grace from an organization for which Schwerner and Goodman, two Jewish boys, along with the Negro Chaney, were murdered in 1964 while doing field work for your organization in Philadelphia, Mississippi.

I also charge that your organization has made a mockery of nonviolence and you have done the Negro struggle for equality in America a grave injustice.

Yours truly,
HARRY GOLDEN

The curious response my published letter elicited came from the segregationists and the members of the White Citizens Council. They confessed both to me and in the letters to the editor that while they were ignorant of whatever it was SNCC worked for, it had to be good if Harry Golden quit the organization.

Negro anti-Semitism does not worry me. I have said as much in a recent letter to the New York *Times*, dated October 24, 1968:

TO THE EDITOR:

I read Mr. Kovach's Oct. 23 article on Negro anti-Semitism in The Times, and I would say, after all, why should we segregate anti-Semites? Is there really a difference between white and colored anti-Semites?

Are there different ways of dealing with anti-Semites? And why should we be surprised that there are Negro anti-Semites?

More, of course, is involved than the fear of property deterioration, sloppy neighborhoods or interracial marriage. Negro anti-Semitism is a symptom of the dilemma of the American middle-class or near-middle-class. Again, wealth or middle-class status is no longer the goal in itself. Instead, these classes are afflicted with the fear of displacement.

Negro anti-Semitism takes into consideration all the Negroes' own resentment. Anyone who has ever succeeded loses his first "friend." It is much easier to believe that one has pulled himself up by his own bootstraps.

And the Jew was indeed the Negro's first friend, almost from the day the Negro was allowed a friend. The Jew was the first white man to grant the newly liberated Negro some degree of humanity. In the most rigid days of segregation Jewish peddlers began to sell the Negroes on credit and the Jew was the first white man to sell a Negro an insurance policy. But when most of the Christian-owned stores warned Negroes: "Don't touch unless you buy," the Jewish merchant allowed the Negro to try on the dress or the suit or the hat.

Elderly Negro women have told me that when the Jew "collector man" came around she insisted that the children see the book with their name on the account sheet, "Mr. and Mrs. Isaac Jones." These were the days in the Southern Christian society when if the Negroes purchased even a plug of tobacco it was put on the account sheet of the farmer or landowner for whom he worked.

There is no doubt there are Negro anti-Semites, and that as the Negroes escape the margins of society there will probably be many more Negro anti-Semites. And as Negroes enter the open society they may find the Jew a terrible burden. As his "first friend," the Jew must forever remain identified with the Negro status of racial inferiority. Fellowship with the Jew will prove no bargain for the Negro. The Jew knew him "when."

Basically, however, Negro anti-Semitism is peripheral to the whole subject, the main issue. Whether some Negroes are or are not anti-Semites bears not at all upon whether the Negroes achieve first-class citizenship and that their children are uninhibited and unimpeded by segregation and discrimination.

The Negro lawyers who have walked in and out of the American courtroom during these last twenty years have made the Constitution of the United States a living document. The struggle has convinced Americans and continues to convince them every day that the Constitution means just what it says. Thus we Jews have achieved a great victory, without even being exposed to the firing line.

Basically, however, a Negro anti-Semite is about as convincing as a Jewish white supremacist.

HARRY GOLDEN

Perhaps this book is my swan song. After all, I am a man nearing seventy. Sandburg told me he used to pray while writing *Abraham Lincoln: The War Years.* His prayers went, "God, if You let me finish this book, I will go willingly." If God would let me write one more book, I could only wish it was a report of the final triumph of civil rights in America.

As my father said, however, "There is always something we want to see how it works out."

Chapter 33

STEPPING from the El Al plane onto the soil of Israel in late summer, 1959, I felt I was stepping not into the Jewish past or the Jewish history, but into the Jewish present. I had wanted to step into this present since the 1930's.

George Mulcahey was one of my partners when I sold advertising space on the New York *Daily Mirror*. Every time Mulcahey would take a drink, he would hold the glass aloft and declare, "Someday I'm going to Ireland to kiss the Blarney Stone." Mulcahey had a deep sense of belonging because he was Irish. His sense of belonging made me envious. What made me a Zionist was that I wanted this same sense of belonging. So I used to echo Mulcahey's promise with my own. I would say, "And someday I am going to Palestine to see the Tomb of Rachel." And now I could behold this tomb, carved out of solid rock.

There is little in Israel really to impress the eye. A small country with a few mountain ranges of moderate size, an arid triangle to the south, plains and valleys yielding fair produce, Israel is comparable in size to the state of Massachusetts. It has a population of 2,500,000. Its economic mainstay is agriculture, and much of this, particularly in the south, is practiced with great difficulty on recalcitrant nonsoil. Mineral wealth is negligible, and raw materials must be imported in great quantities.

Yet this little strip of ground, with its limited physical assets, has been the focus of the world's attention for 3,000 years. It is the matrix for the great religions of the West, a holy place alike to Jews and Christians, and to Moslem Arabs, who trace their lineage through Ishmael, the nomadic son of Abraham. Israel is the human story in miniature, a microcosm; it summarizes within its shifting boundaries man's striving for freedom and his irrepressible quest for a homeland.

Israel has emerged from the cocoon of history. Israel has no fewer than 1,000 clinics, 400 hospitals, 500 mother-and-child health centers. For the population of 2,500,000 there are some 5,000 doctors, 1 doctor for every 420 inhabitants, by far the highest ratio in the world. For the Arabs in Israel this means the highest life expectancy in the Arabic-speaking world. Israel is free from the ravaging epidemics of its neighbors—malaria, typhus, typhoid, tuberculosis. An elaborate network of adequate facilities has kept the Jewish population in remarkably good health. The nation's youth, most of them toughened by army service, are in demonstrably better physical condition than the great majority of American teen-agers. This in Israel, a Middle Eastern country heretofore an area filled with peoples to whom death is never premature. The Syrian child no longer bothers to wave the flies from his face. The Jordanian child has never brushed his teeth. More Egyptian children die in birth than live. Surrounded by semi-invalidism, the Jewish republic is more than an outpost of democracy on the rim of Asia. It is precisely for its health that Israel becomes important not only to the stability of the Middle East, but to the world.

The trouble spots of the world are the underdeveloped areas: the Congo, Nigeria, the Far East, the American slum. Call them, as does our State Department, "underdevelopia," we know that these are the areas which can throw this globe into a convulsion. The solution for calming these trouble spots is simple enough: Teach the populations therein to develop their own resources, but implementing this is indeed difficult.

Israel no longer belongs in underdevelopia. It has a self-sustaining economy. It is the only underdeveloped country that has managed this within a generation. To be sure, it managed it with large amounts of aid, but some of the other underdeveloped countries have had larger transfusions of American dollars and Soviet rubles and have managed nothing yet.

Twenty-five years ago it was impossible to imagine there could be an Israel in the Middle East. Today it is impossible to imagine

399

what the Middle East would be without Israel. That is another way of estimating Israel's importance to the world. None of us has to estimate Israel's importance to Jews.

There is no doubt Israel owes a great deal to American Jews. American Jews planted the trees that now floriate on the steep and rocky hillsides. The America Hadassahs, ORT's, all the fraternal organizations, helped found the hospitals and the welfare clinics. The United Jewish Appeal has funneled millions of dollars into the Israeli economy, all of them charitably donated. The real question is: How much more do American Jews owe Israel? American Jews can never repay Israel for what the Israelis have given them. What Israel has given the American Jews is what it gave me, a sense of belonging. Israel has removed the enigma of homelessness that plagued all Jews in all times and places. For the first time American Jews can use the four words without hesitation: "I am a Jew."

Every Jew realizes Israel saved his brethren. After World War II, Europe with the exception of Russia, England, and France was a continent of refugees. Among these were the homeless, disenfranchised, hopeless Jews, the remnants of the Nazi Holocaust which claimed 6,000,000 of them. The healthy members of the world community have stringent laws dictating who may and who may not immigrate. In Australia, in America, in Canada, no one with trachoma may immigrate. No one the object of charity may immigrate. These are minimum requirements sensible enough, necessary enough. But Israel established a new concept in human relations. "Bring us the stretcher cases first," they said. "Bring us the blind, the lame, the halt, the wretched, the poor. The healthy can come later." The minimum requirement to immigrate into Israel is the declaration "I am a Jew." The immigrant needs no papers, no testimonials, no affidavits, signed by rabbis, no religious test. Here, for the first time, immigrants may come into a country where they are not punctured with needles or forced to display their teeth.

Israel takes as bona fide from anyone the statement "I am a Jew." This policy, which is humane, is also practical. It has worked. To this day Israel provides the only answer for the homeless Jews of Europe.

Israel is an anomaly among modern nations. It is the one coun-

400

try whose exodus is not from the farms to the cities, but from the cities to the farms, or rather to the kibbutzim.

Eleanor Roosevelt said that the kibbutz was the greatest example of man's freedom. Living there means living on the principle of all for one and one for all. A kibbutz is a farm, by American standards modest, although kibbutzim vary in size. Some are 100 acres, some 200, some 300; perhaps a few are larger. A kibbutz is equipped with the apparatus of any modern farm—tractors, milking machines, cows, aluminum silos, and homes, little cottages, for the residents. When a family has another child, it moves into a larger cottage. When a son goes out to Tel Aviv to become a journalist, the parents move into a smaller cottage.

A kibbutz is completely organized, everyone assigned a job. The majority of the men and women farm. A kibbutz has a carpenter, its own teachers, doctors, nurses, and a board of governors. Many of the kibbutzim have established the beginnings of a winter industry when the farming season is over. For example, in Ein Hashofet, a kibbutz near the Lebanese border, the farmers sell bolts and nails, manufactured in the winter, to Bulgaria and Turkey. Another kibbutz I saw reconditions motors. The kibbutz has an all-volunteer fire department. It needs no police. So far none of them has juvenile delinquents, probably because of the age-old Jewish injunction *Klal Israel*—the delinquency of one hurts all.

The kibbutz is now an integral part of the character of Israel in the same way a Pittsburgh steel factory or a Ford Motor plant is part of the character of America. The kibbutz exemplifies the direction the country has elected, probably a direction irreversible.

Moshe Barzalai, a friend of mine in Ein Hashofet, told me he came there from Brooklyn in the 1930's. The one thing he gave up, he says, was his chance to become a millionaire. He exchanged this opportunity for total security. In return for his work, he gets his eyeglasses, his clothes, his housing, education for his children, two weeks' vacation, and his own library for the rest of his life. Moshe was pretty sure back in Brooklyn he wasn't going to become the millionaire. He was driving a cab, and from where he sat, behind that steering wheel, it looked as if he would always be driving a cab. Today he chops the beaks off chickens lest they peck one another to death. He is an expert egg candler. He is also a good soldier, belonging to the citizen army of Israel, the army

401

which has won three wars in the last twenty years against the Arab forces.

But the Israelis come in all shapes and sizes. In the same kibbutz I met one of those hardy Israeli women soldiers. She carried a flashlight and a Sten gun, and around her shoulders was strung a bandolier. She looked positively intrepid. She was a patriotic, loyal citizen, unafraid of the hazards of the border, and what she wanted to do most of all was marry an American millionaire, as all Israeli girls want to do.

Teddy Kollek, now the mayor of Jerusalem, then the executive secretary to Prime Minister David Ben-Gurion, prepared an itinerary for me on my first trip. Teddy knew America and Americans well because he had spent the years during the first Arab-Israeli war in New York buying munitions and airplanes. It was Teddy Kollek who, after the six-day war with the Arabs in 1967, dared and succeeded in making Jerusalem one city for Arab and Jew when the cease-fire was arranged.

I traveled all of Israel from Beersheba to Eilat.

In Nazareth I visited the Arab community and met there Dr. Petty, a Baptist minister from North Carolina. Dr. Petty showed me the carpentry shop where it is reputed Joseph, the husband of the Virgin, worked at his trade. As Dr. Petty and I exited into the square, a big bus drew to a stop filled with American Haddassies. One of them shouted, "There's Harry Golden," and I had to pose for snapshots with a dozen different matrons who forgot all about Joseph's carpentry shop.

In Tel Aviv I got into a long conversation with a cabdriver, Bajalel Katz. Bajalel told me of his trials and tribulations as a young student in Germany and Austria. Everyone made fun of his name. He complained to his father. The father said, "Your name is Bajalel. Bajalel you will live; Bajalel you will die." His fellow students gave him no rest. When the family moved from Germany to Austria, the situation moved with him. So desperate was Bajalel as a young boy he once gave a teacher another name. He said his first name was Heinz. When his ruse was uncovered by a report card, the father went after him. "Bajalel you will live; Bajalel you will die. It's your name."

"Then I came to Israel," said Katz. "When the immigration official asked me my name, I said, 'Bajalel Katz.' The fellow never looked up. I knew I was home."

402

I walked through Mea Shearim, an enclave in Jerusalem housing the ultra-Orthodox. I saw a sign warning WOMEN OF JERUSALEM, COVER YOUR ARMS WHEN YOU ENTER.

In a *shenk* (saloon) I bought everybody a drink and got into an argument with an old fellow who insisted no one vote in the coming election. A vote would acknowledge the political existence of Israel. The people of Mea Shearim await only the Messiah. I asked, "How do you know Ben-Gurion isn't the Messiah?"

"Because," said this old fellow, "he didn't come on a white donkey as it is prophesied in the Book."

Teddy Kollek introduced me to Ben-Gurion, who invited me to dinner. The Prime Minister lived in a suburban home in Jerusalem, and only the presence of an Israeli soldier on guard distinguished it as the house of a high government official. When I presented myself, I was admitted by Paula Ben-Gurion, noted for her ability to speak her own mind. She saw me and said sadly, "You're too fat." She said it three times that evening, the last time when we sat down to a dinner of Wiener schnitzel.

I was not the only one to feel the bite of Paula Ben-Gurion's acerbic tongue. Preparing for a party, she found herself short of milk. She ran outside and said to the soldier guarding the home, "Run and get me milk."

"I cannot leave my post," said the man. "I'm here to guard the Prime Minister."

She grabbed the rifle from him and said, "I'll guard the Prime Minister. You get the milk."

Dr. A. Frank, whom I met at the Hadassah Hospital, lived near the Ben-Gurions. His wife walked their child to the nearby school. One cold morning Paula Ben-Gurion ran from her home and accosted mother and son on the sidewalk. "Is this the way you care for a child?" asked Mrs. Ben-Gurion. She wrapped a scarf around the little boy's neck. "That's the way an Israeli should go to school," she thundered.

David Ben-Gurion was a genial man, responsive and intelligent. But he could harangue the new visitor, and he did harangue me. He told me all the Jews from the United States should prepare immediately to emigrate to Israel.

"But they're American citizens," I said.

"They are not Americans," the Prime Minister argued; "they are Jews. Israel needs them."

"You're absolutely right," I agreed. "But sometimes it's hard leaving the land of your fathers. It's all the fault of Moses. He should have turned left, instead of right, and then the Israelis would have the oil and the Arabs would have the sand and the Americans could stay home."

Ben-Gurion was deeply interested in the race issue in the South because he was afraid it might be duplicated in Israel with the black Jews who came from the Atlas Mountains in Africa. And to a degree, prejudice does exist against these black Jews from Algeria and Tunis, though it is not as intense as it is here. Israelis, however, worry as hard as Mississippians about mixed marriages. I told Ben-Gurion the liberals in America agitated for education to remedy bigotry and abolish the caste system and the Israeli liberals should agitate no less.

President Yizhak Ben-Zvi also worried about this problem. We discussed it. I told the president I had visited the Yemenite colonies in Israel. The Yemenite Jews from the Arabian Peninsula are small, dark-complexioned, and are probably the best silversmiths in the world. The Yemenite Jews lived on that peninsula for 2,000 years, isolated from the world.

"It is very probable," I told Ben-Zvi, "that Jesus, who was a Jew, looked like a Yemenite Jew."

"There is only one thing wrong with your theory," said Ben-Zvi, a world-renowned archeologist and anthropologist. "What is wrong with your theory is that the goyim who came to that isolated peninsula also looked like Yemenite Jews."

Yael Dayan introduced me to her father, the famous General Moshe Dayan. I had met Yael some years before, when she came to Charlotte to speak at a Bonds for Israel rally.

This young lady, in her early twenties then, showed me several chapters of a novel in English which she was writing. I sent these chapters on to Bill Targ at World Publishing; World contracted for the book. Her book was called *New Face in the Mirror*, and it recounted the experiences of a young girl in the Israeli Army.

While the book sold well in the United States, it created a scandal in Israel. Among other things, Yael noted how the army girls often slept promiscuously with the soldiers. My publisher in Israel is Steimatzky, and his daughter Miriam confided in me, "We in the army hate Yael for writing the book. But we are really jealous of her. She is in Athens, London, and New York. She is an authoress while some of us are still walking guard."

The night Yael introduced me to her father, I met a trim man, five feet nine inches tall, who looked the typical British soldier. General Dayan, too, is an archeologist, and his home is filled with artifacts dug from the Judaean Hills. Moshe Dayan can name the date of every piece of pottery on his shelves.

I asked General Dayan about Israel's future *vis-à-vis* the Arabs, and he said, "As long as we can get American money, French Mystères, and Israeli boys, we will have no trouble with the Arabs."

Moshe Sharett, later the Prime Minister of Israel, invited me on this visit to accompany him on his political campaigning. He was running for a seat in the Israeli Knesset (Parliament). In fact, I trailed along with all of them during the election—Levi Eshkol, Ben-Gurion, Moshe Dayan, finding them like the Tammany sachems I knew as a boy. They promised everybody good times and prosperity and peace. The only difference is the Israelis make these promises without neckties.

"No necktie" is *de rigueur* in Israel. As I left with Moshe Sharett one morning, he turned and said, "Golden, you'd better put on a necktie; otherwise you'll find yourself in the Knesset."

Ambassador Ogden Reid, now a New York Congressman, told me he, too, had made the same mistake. He went to an Israel function one evening *sans* necktie only to find all the Israelis showed up in dinner jackets and black tie. Knowing when and where to put on a necktie is the test of understanding Israel, as knowing all the variant meanings of the word "just" is the test of understanding English.

It was to Mea Shearim I repaired again when *Life* magazine sent me to Israel to cover the trial of Adolf Eichmann. I spoke there to the chief rabbi of the enclave, Avram Bloom, whom I found seated at a center table, surrounded by nine of his colleagues, other rabbis. I asked Rabbi Bloom what he thought of Eichmann, and he answered, "We are not interested in the accused or the accuser. All we are interested in is the Messiah."

During the course of the trial, I stayed at the King David Hotel in Jerusalem. Coincidentally, I was staying at the same hotel in which Robert Servatius, the German lawyer who served as Eichmann's counsel, had accommodations. Every morning, when I walked under the canopy to await the limousine, I noticed a crowd, all of whom stared curiously at me. What I realized toward the end was that these folks confused me with Servatius, who was, to say the least, as portly and corpulent and wore the same eyeglasses as I. A pointless irony perhaps, but an irony for all that.

The article I submitted, which appeared in the April 21, 1961, issue of *Life*, has been anthologized more than any other piece I have written save "Buying a Suit on the Lower East Side." Consequently, I have no wish to reproduce all of it here. But I want to quote several of its salient paragraphs:

> When Gideon Hausner, the Israeli attorney general, began "I stand before you, judges of Israel," I felt a sudden chill. A quick glance around the courtroom convinced me most of the five hundred journalists and writers shared my experience.
>
> What Mr. Hausner told us when he said, "I stand before you, judges of Israel," was that we were witnessing one of the great dramas of history. Precisely because that opening phrase was spoken in Jerusalem, the Holy City, to which mankind looks for its earliest beginning, the phrase was spoken as part of the unbroken thread of history. We were sitting only a few miles from the fortress Betar which fell to the legions of the Roman Emperor Hadrian in the year 135 A.D. . . .
>
> What was most remarkable about Adolf Eichmann, sitting in his booth of bullet proof glass, was that he was so ordinary looking. He might have been a waiter, a window cleaner perhaps, or an insurance agent. But the defendant's very drabness was an advantage for the Israelis. A man of overwhelming personality, such as the late Hermann Goering, might have intruded himself upon the story, and the Israelis were intent upon telling the story. It is part of their four thousand year history. More than that, it is a religious obligation: "And thou shalt tell it to thy son."
>
> Yet despite his ordinary appearance, this Adolf Eichmann was really a stranger, a stranger to the human race, who had come among us as the central figure in the greatest of all murder trials. . . .
>
> The Prime Minister himself expressed the opinion which seemed to be the general atmosphere surrounding the Eichmann trial. "Our concern is not one of vengeance but only of documenting an era in which genocide became a policy of a political state." And on this basis the Israelis were willing to shoulder all the risks in-

volved in the attempt to bring this ordinary-looking man to justice for the most incredible crime in history. . . .

The article caught me up in many a dialogue in Charlotte. I had a public discussion with one of the eminent jurists of North Carolina, the Honorable Donald Phillips. Judge Phillips said the whole Eichmann trial was a farce, that the defendant had been kidnapped illegally, and that he should not be hanged.

Banteringly, I said to Judge Phillips that in the condemned cells of the prison in our state capital was a Negro named Mellot Faust who was awaiting execution in the gas chamber.

Faust was found guilty of shooting and killing a white policeman during a street corner brawl. Faust wrested the policeman's revolver from him, and when the policeman tried to wrest it back, Faust shot and killed him. He turned himself over to the authorities the next day. Having talked to Faust, I was willing to testify he was a mental incompetent. He told me he expected to attend a fish fry a few minutes after his execution. I told Judge Phillips that regarding his concern for Eichmann, if he prevented the execution of Mellot Faust, I would write to Ben-Gurion asking the Israeli Prime Minister not to hang Eichmann. Eichmann for Faust—that was a fair trade. I was only joking, of course. I had no influence with Ben-Gurion. But I hope that I made a point. Israel executed Eichmann and North Carolina executed Mellot Faust.

It is my belief that at least one of the reasons for the concern over Eichmann's execution was based on the universal reservoir of anti-Semitism. It is true that the democratic process in the English-speaking countries has kept the anti-Semite within the bonds of law. But this latent anti-Semitism has been shocked by the prospect of the Jews themselves hanging an anti-Semite, executing a man who in his turn murdered Jews. It is bewildering because it had never happened before.

What made me proud of Israel was not that it executed Eichmann. I am not sure an execution takes courage. What makes me proud, what should make all Jews proud of Israel, is that it is the one place in the world (outside New York City) where a Jewish prostitute can be arrested by a Jewish cop and sentenced by a Jewish judge, a situation which to my mind is the essence of day-to-day civilization.

When a Jewish traffic cop in Israel signals a car to the curb, the inhabitants are invariably surprised. Is it possible, they ask, arresting a Jew in Israel? They tell the policeman their long sad history. They tell him about the uprooting of their native community, about the terror of the concentration camps, about the demeaning and hopeless life they led as DP's, about the struggle to arrive safely in Israel. The cop listens. When the offending motorist is through, the policeman says gently, "Here is your ticket. Everything you told me, tell the judge, too."

If Israel resembles anyplace else, it resembles the American West at the turn of the century. Chief Justice Earl Warren of the United States Supreme Court said in an interview on his visit, "This country is very much like California in the time of my father."

In all, I have been to Israel five times. On four of those trips I stopped off at London. I was in London in 1959, the year of the bicentennial of the birth of William Wilberforce, the English evangelist who abolished the slave trade by convincing Parliament it was a religious and Christian problem, not a political or economic issue.

I had written about Wilberforce in the *Israelite*, once pointing out why he had succeeded where Tom Paine had failed: Paine wrote polemics; Wilberforce prayed. So I bought a wreath of flowers from a green shop, as the English call it, and took a cab to Westminster Abbey. The guard showed me Wilberforce's crypt. My wreath was signed HARRY GOLDEN, CHARLOTTE, NORTH CAROLINA. I laid it between two other wreaths, one from Ghana and another from Nigeria.

London is the one city where an American, disembarking from a plane or arriving from a steamship, feels immediately at home. When I went to the British Museum, I sat in the chair Karl Marx had occupied all the time he was writing *Das Kapital*. Marx was one of the first, if not the first, philosopher-economists to use primary references. The British Museum gave him all the files and information he asked for.

Near Marx's chair is the chair Isaac D'Israeli, the father of the Prime Minister, Benjamin Disraeli, occupied for several decades. Isaac D'Israeli went to the British Museum every morning much as other men daily go to work. From that chair, Isaac D'Israeli produced some excellent books, the best of which is *Curiosities of Literature*, a compendium of arcane facts about writers and writing. I reread it once a year, and it aways provided me with more articles than I care to count for the pages of my paper.

Walking about London, I followed Samuel Johnson's advice: Stick to the alleys of the city. These small streets are filled with excellent restaurants and interesting people.

The Jews in London, I found, worry about the same problems the Jews in Teaneck, New Jersey, worry about. Isaac Wolfson, a Jewish financier, had bought Harrod's, a famous department store like Lord & Taylor's. "Wolfson shouldn't have bought that store," some Jews told me. "Harrod's was high British."

Lord Boothby, who had served in Anthony Eden's Cabinet, told me at dinner that when the Israelis, British, and French had almost reached Suez, Nasser had a plane revved up on a Cairo landing strip filled with money, pointed toward Switzerland. Only Eisenhower saved Egypt for Nasser.

A delightful host, Boothby also told me the story about the circumcision of Ariel, the statue which graces the top of the BBC Building. When the statue was unveiled, the length of the penis shocked and maybe dismayed many. Led by Lord Reith, the many complained. The BBC convened a board of pediatricians whose duty it was to determine how long an eight-year-old boy's penis should be. Ultimately, the sculptor chiseled away.

On one of my visits, during December, 1961, I stopped at the town house of a good friend in the Marble Arch section. My host has a delightful sense of humor, and he gets the point. As we passed through his great hall, he stopped at a large oaken table on which were arranged hundreds of Christmas cards. He nudged me and wickedly whispered, "Let's you and I riffle through these and see if we can find one from a Christian."

I have visited Germany three times, the first visit again on an assignment from *Life*, this time to write an article about Germany and the Jews. The truth about Germany, I saw, was that it was no longer a culture but only an economy. I wrote:

On the Lower East Side of New York, where I grew up, the old men in the synagogue always complained about children underfoot. The little boys stepped on everyone's toes as they squeezed back and forth through the pews, they disturbed prayers as they ran up and down the aisles, and the shoulders of the elders hunched as the children slammed the doors.

The synagogues of Germany today are strangely quiet. The Jews of Germany now are mostly old people, a small spiritless community, a dwindling remnant of the six hundred thousand who were once a vital force in the nation. They are reviled by a few, fiercely protected by some, ignored by most. Dozens of young students all across West Germany told me they had never even met a Jew.

If they are ever going to meet one, they may have to move fast. Before too many years pass, the newspapers may run a picture under the headline, "The Last Jew in Germany. . . ."

Stanley Kramer, the movie producer, invited me on a junket to Berlin to see the premiere of his motion picture *Judgment at Nuremburg*. Aboard the airplane were columnists Bob Considine, Earl Wilson, and Art Buchwald. Spencer Tracy and Judy Garland were with us, and she kissed me when we met saying, "Mr. Golden, you have a little bit of God in you."

I replied, "God made us all in His own image?"

On the way over, may I say the whiskey spilled? My seat companion was that estimable actor Mr. Richard Widmark. Mr. Widmark is a steadfast and undiscouraged milk drinker. I know of no one else who could go into the Crazy Horse Café in Paris and order milk with every expectation it would soon be served.

Mr. Widmark likes milk well enough to have invented several ploys to counteract the laughter drinking milk often occasions. In our jet plane, when the stewardess came down the aisle asking everyone what he would like to drink, Mr. Widmark stuck to his guns. The passengers said, "Bourbon," "Martini," or "Scotch."

"Milk, please," said Mr. Widmark.

The stewardess repeated, "Milk?"

Mr. Widmark bent over as though in pain and said, "Upset stomach."

The stewardess brought him the milk; when she served him, her lip quivered with pity.

"All over the world," Widmark said to me, "I have to go through that 'upset stomach' business to drink my milk in peace."

By the Berlin Wall, I answered the questions put me by my interviewer, Mike Wallace of ABC. He asked what I thought about the Communists and their motive in building the wall.

I told him I didn't think the wall was built out of any recognizable human fears but out of the imagined fears of a desperate superstate. "Yesterday morning," I said, "I talked to two rabbis in

410

East Berlin, both of whom are Communists. The one thing they wanted to know was: 'Is Judy Garland a Jewish girl?' There is some curiosity the wall does not stop."

From covering the Eichmann trial, I went to Korea in 1961, having accepted an invitation from Agnes Crawford, chief librarian at the Pentagon, to visit that outpost as a guest of the United States Eighth Army and speak to the men in each of the installations during National Library Week.

I made twenty speeches in Korea, visiting every Eighth Army area from Pusan to Panmunjom. In the demilitarized zone the Communists up on the hill kept binoculars trained on our party. Our officers told me that they watch every bit of activity on our side. Even the visit of a Library Week lecturer is important.

At each installation I was the house guest of the commanding officer. Since I was traveling light, General Francis T. Pachler of the Seventh Infantry Division lent me a bathrobe and slippers. The next day General John A. Seitz took off his red (artillery) scarf to send to my second son, Harry junior, who was once in charge of three 155-mm. guns.

Brigadier General and Mrs. Walter A. Huntsberry invited me to their home for a pleasant evening.

I visited with General and Mrs. Guy S. Meloy and discussed philosophy with General Carl Darnell far into the night.

Korea is a hardship tour of duty, and the officers and men serve their thirteen months without their wives and families, except those who must deal with their Korean opposite numbers, both military and political. At this level there must be an exchange of the social amenities in order to make any headway at all. Thus, out of fifty-three top American military and political officers I met, only eight, including the commander in chief, had their families with them. But the eight wives I met confirmed a suspicion I have had for some years—that Army officers do marry the handsomest women in America.

My escort was Major Joseph D'Amico, an Italian from Milwaukee, who entered the Army as a private and won his commission in the field. He belongs to the Seventh Infantry Division, which he described to me (at least a million times) as being "In War Invincible, in Peace Prepared." Every time I seemed to be impressed with an Army command, Joe curled up his lip—"Wait till you get to my outfit." His outfit reckons time in terms of service

411

in Korea. Thus, the masthead of the division newspaper *Bayonet* proclaims: "5,097 days in Korea," etc.

When the United States asks a man to do a chore, they give him a rating so that he will receive the privileges which will make him as comfortable as possible. I was rated GS-16—a simulated brigadier general. My escort, Major D'Amico, never left my side, but this was solely for my personal welfare. He never intruded when privates and sergeants asked to speak to me alone. It was a little embarrassing when we arrived at the various living quarters, and particularly at the Sanno Hotel in Tokyo. Being a "brigadier general," I was given a suite of two or three rooms, with a servant to press my clothes and run errands, while this battle-scarred veteran, Joe D'Amico, had to be content with a small room and do many things for himself.

The Army feels that you are still in its "service" until you return to your home base. Thus, I was a brigadier general until the moment I entered 1312 Elizabeth Avenue, Charlotte, North Carolina. I often wonder if I had continued to percolate around without touching home base whether I would still have this rating.

Major D'Amico's superior and the man directly in charge of my visit was Colonel William W. Rossing, special service officer, whom the Koreans call Papa. He is a tough soldier, but a kinder man you'll rarely meet. Colonel Rossing has a magnificent head of white hair, but I do not recommend that you engage him in a wrestling match or a footrace.

The most impressive aspect of my visit was working with the corps of librarians headed by Miss Dorothy Goddard. In some areas, and particularly with the front-line combat divisions, you will find an American woman in charge of a small library, often alone, or perhaps with another girl in the Red Cross or Family Service. Their facilities, I assure you, are not up to the standard of the Waldorf-Astoria. In some places there are no inside rest rooms, and the six-month seasons of humidity and dust are not pleasant. Yet I have rarely seen a group of more dedicated people, devoted to an idea of getting books to the men and providing a library in each sector where the men can gather to read books, hold discussions, and listen to the latest recordings from the States.

After each of my speeches I went to the library for a question-and-answer period. Nearly always one soldier would whisper, "Don't let the brass kid you too much." Without revealing the man's identity I always tried to draw him out during the question period. But on one occasion I had to be direct.

In one of my speeches I said that no segment of the American society is as "colorblind" as the Eighth Army in Korea. There are Negro helicopter pilots and Negro officers sitting in their proper places at the dinner tables. The Pacific *Stars and Stripes* faithfully reported each of my speeches. The day after this particular speech, a boy handed me a clipping of it across which he had written "Crap." I showed this to a dozen other soldiers, including a Negro captain and three Negro privates. They said there was no basis for what the fellow had written. During that day's question-and-answer period I told the assembled men about the clipping which had been handed me and said that I genuinely wanted to know if I was wrong in my estimate. The man who gave me the clipping spoke up, and all credit to him. He admitted what he had done but explained that he did not refer to the "integration" problem; he objected rather to the fact that some GI's call the Koreans Gooks. Well, that was an entirely different matter and one which I had not discussed at all because I knew nothing about it. I have to give credit to that soldier because he walked over to a Negro private, put his arm around him, and said, "I did not mean this kind of integration."

Other messages were handed to me, but of a less controversial nature, such as the one from Sergeant Rothblat, "Tell Max Asnas of the Stage [the celebrated delicatessen on New York's Seventh Avenue] to send me a salami—tell him I was his bookie for a while." (Max complied immediately with two salamis.)

I was told at the farewell banquet at the Officers' Club in Seoul that it was the first social event attended by the commander in chief, General Carter B. Magruder. I told the officers and civilians at the dinner that it was embarrassing to have such a fuss made over me by men who had been in battle.

General Magruder in his reply said that he could understand my embarrassment, but he added, "Perhaps we think that you too have been useful."

Chapter 34

I first met the Kennedys in Boston where I delivered an address on behalf of the National Association for Retarded Children in 1957. Eunice Shriver was the recipient on that occasion of the committee's annual award. My selection as a speaker by the program committee was not accidental. I had written often about retarded children in the *Israelite*, and I was the father of one.

I said that 90 percent of all retarded children are educable, and it is to this task that we who are interested must direct ourselves.

After the dinner a Boston politician named Mr. Ward introduced me to Senator John Kenendy, Robert Kennedy, and Mrs. Joseph Kennedy. I had met Mrs. Shriver earlier. I also met Richard Cardinal Cushing and a host of other proper and improper Bostonians.

Jack Kennedy had contended for the Vice Presidential nomination at the 1956 convention, only to lose it to Estes Kefauver. As we discussed this recent political history, it crossed my mind that John Kennedy still wanted the Vice Presidential nomination in 1960, and that the way to secure the Vice Presidential nomination was to pretend to want the Presidency.

When the Senator began to make more noise than most Vice Presidential aspirants, I wondered if he really thought the Democrats would nominate him. I had several chances to editorialize on this development in the *Israelite*. The first of these editorials appeared in early 1959:

414

Senator Kennedy wants to be President and he is running hard for it. His one liability—or better, his one supposed liability (which may well be his strength)—is that he is a member of an American minority. Senator Kennedy is a Roman Catholic.

Politicians, reputable citizens, and pillars of the community will tell you there is a taboo against running Catholics for Presidents. Look at Al Smith. He lost the 1928 election because he was a Catholic. This is not self-pity on the part of our Catholics. The fine historian Edmund A. Moore of the University of Connecticut who wrote *A Catholic Runs for President* concluded that ". . . although the defeat of Smith was caused by a combination of forces and factors, his religion played a large, though not wholly calculable part."

Remembering what happened to Al Smith, Senator Kennedy recently gave *Look* magazine an exclusive interview in which he tried to explain his position as an aspirant for the Presidential nomination and as a Catholic. Senator Kennedy said, "Whatever one's religion in his private life may be, for the office holder nothing takes precedence over his oath to uphold the Constitution and all of its parts—including the First Amendment and the strict separation of Church and State."

This seemed reasonable enough. But it stirred up a hornet's nest. Neither the Protestants nor the Jews nor the Seventh Day Adventists opposed the statement, but instead the Roman Catholics. Catholic publications throughout the country accused the statement of everything.

The *Ave Maria,* which is published at Notre Dame, Ind., said, "Something does indeed take precedence over the obligation to uphold the Constitution—namely conscience. And this applies no matter what the religion of the office holder. No man may rightfully act against his conscience. To relegate conscience to private life is dangerous because it leads to secularism."

Editor Hoyt of the Kansas City-St. Joseph *Register* said: "It seems a bitter thing that a Catholic politician of the stature of Senator Kennedy should have to be reminded by non-Catholics that his ultimate loyalty is not to the state but to God."

And the St. Louis *Review,* which is the weekly paper of the St. Louis archdiocese, accused Kennedy of putting his religion in his back pocket and said, "He was encouraging the Catholic baiter by suggesting that the Constitution and Catholicism are at odds."

The Catholic publications then saw Kennedy as variously providing aid and comfort to anti-Catholics and issuing an invitation to secularism in private life.

But I think Jack Kennedy said the right thing, not only as a citizen, but as a Catholic. If any Catholic thinks Kennedy can run for President without discussing his Catholicism, I can only say, "Get thee to a nunnery."

Re-read the arguments proposed by the publications I have listed. Eight years ago in the furor of cleaning up the Communists, Marxists, and Trotskyites the Catholic press argued that the Communists, the Marxists and the Trotskyites should be barred from public office, teaching school, and performing on the silver screen, the TV tube, and the air waves because they did not owe *ultimate* loyalty to the Constitution. If the Catholics were right then, how can they be right now?

Moreover, Mr. Kennedy is speaking practically, not theoretically. I am quite sure if God spoke to him personally while he were President and said, "I've just told the Pope there's something wrong with the 21st Amendment; now I'm telling you, and I'm going to tell Bishop Oxnam and Abba Hillel Silver this afternoon," I am sure Mr. Kennedy would do his best to make God happy, no matter how he had to violate the Constitution. But God, in His Infinite Wisdom did not see fit to talk to any of our Presidents, let alone aspiring nominees.

I concluded the essay by wondering why *Look* hadn't interviewed Richard Nixon about *his* beliefs. Mr. Nixon is a Quaker, and pacifism is a cornerstone of the Quaker religion.

Curiously, the only Catholic who thanked me for my efforts was Senator John Kennedy. In a short note he said he had read the article with interest.

When I finally was convinced that Senator Kennedy indeed wanted to be President, though I was sure he couldn't be nominated, I wrote:

If America elects a President who is of the Roman Catholic faith at this moment in world history, it will be worth the equivalent of fifty cobalt bombs in our ideological war against the Soviet Union. That part of the world which we call "neutral" or "uncommitted" may not have been able to decipher our foreign policy in recent years, and they may not have shown adequate appreciation for our military and financial aid, but they will know our democracy still has a tremendous vitality because at our most critical hour, a member of a minority religious group was able to win the highest political office in America.

. . . The arguments we will hear in such a campaign will be to the effect that religious belief has no standing in logic or constitu-

416

tional principle, yet the religious argument could be decisive against Kennedy in states where the margin will be close. There may be some who will insist, "I wouldn't vote for a Catholic for President," but on close examination you will find they voted for Hoover, Landon, Dewey, and Eisenhower. . . .

In April, 1959, I had a letter from Meyer Feldman, Senator Kennedy's legislative assistant. Feldman invited me to meet the Senator the next time I was in Washington.

The reason the Senator wanted to see me was to discuss politics in the South, particularly how the race issue and religion would affect those politics.

I told Senator Kennedy, "The Baptists in the South are interested in one thing—the separation of church and state. They will not take federal money for their hospitals because they think the receipt of that money abridges the separation. If you win the nomination, you will not have trouble with the Baptists since you, too, are concerned with maintaining the separation of church and state."

Kennedy was exceptionally well informed on the race issue. He confided that he was disappointed at Eisenhower's slow reaction to the Supreme Court decisions. There was a need to do something, he said, to lance the festering sore, and Eisenhower somehow thought the sore would cure itself. He said the Civil Rights Division of the Justice Department had two attorneys. "There should be forty-two attorneys," he said.

Our discussion lasted two hours. It is my guess he held many such discussions with other men around the country from whom he thought he could learn something. Principally, that is what he wanted to do—learn. I am sure of this because when I introduced myself, I told him that editorially and financially and every way possible I would be supporting Adlai Stevenson for the nomination in 1960. Kennedy answered that Stevenson was a good candidate.

A month later I met Bobby Kennedy when he and I were both guests on Jack Paar's show. In the course of his interview, Bobby told Jack Paar that Dave Beck was a thief and that Jimmy Hoffa was a bigger thief. Jack Paar leaned back in his chair and asked, "Is there a libel lawyer in the house?"

I came on after Bobby; as they say in show business, he is a tough act to follow. My comment on the Kennedy brothers was absolutely prophetic. I said, "I would like to have a parlay on Jack and Bobby Kennedy in the next decade." Certainly I would have collected.

Behind the stage was a small room, enveloped with velvet curtains where Paar's guests awaited their turn. When *The Tonight Show* concluded, Bobby was still there. He started a conversation with me. Then he said, "Let's get something to eat."

"Where shall we go?" I asked.

"Do you know where I'd like to go?" he asked. "I'd like to go to Lindy's. I've never been there."

The reason for his waiting was obvious. He wanted a Jew to take him to Lindy's.

I explained all the exquisite delights of the Jewish cuisine. Bobby heard me out and opted for a steak and two glasses of milk while I made do with the boiled beef flanken and two glasses of bourbon. As long as I knew him, I never saw Bobby Kennedy take a drink. He asked me a lot of questions about the *Carolina Israelite*. Was it profitable? Where did I get the materials? How did I manage it?

In my turn, I asked him about Jimmy Hoffa. Bobby put down his knife and fork, looked at me, and said, "In a Senate committee hearing I asked Jimmy Hoffa why he had lent a Minneapolis company which had locked out union members three hundred thousand dollars of union funds. Jimmy Hoffa told us one thing had nothing to do with another, that the union had made a good business deal, that it had secured a mortgage on the company's building. Mr. Golden, Jimmy Hoffa is an evil man."

I was glad I wasn't Jimmy Hoffa. There was no cynicism or skepticism in Bobby. John Kennedy knew men were not always honest and not always trustworthy; Bobby was a Puritan. Corruption outraged him, as heresy outraged Cotton Mather.

I went on to Chicago to speak at an editor's convention. I had invited John Kennedy to hear me if he were in the city. He wrote me:

John F. Kennedy
Massachusetts

Committees:
Foreign Relations
Labor and Public Welfare
Joint Economic Committee
United States Senate
Washington, D.C.
July 29, 1959

Mr. Harry Golden, Editor
The Carolina Israelite
1312 Elizabeth Avenue
P.O. Box 2505
Charlotte, North Carolina

DEAR MR. GOLDEN:

I hope you will forgive me for not replying to your letter of July 21 earlier, but it did not reach my desk until it was too late for me to make the trip to Chicago. I particularly regret the fact that there was no one there to represent the Kennedy family, so that those assembled could know of our admiration for you. I have a sister and a brother-in-law in Chicago who could have been pressed into service in such a cause.

Your generous comments about the Kennedys are very much appreciated. I noticed that you injected your personal opinion about Bob and me into the discussion following Bob's appearance on the Jack Paar show. Both of us are grateful for your support.

With every good wish,

Sincerely,
JOHN F. KENNEDY

JFK/md

Early in 1960, of course, John Kennedy declared for the Democratic nomination. It was Adlai Stevenson who surprised me with the news that the nomination was within Kennedy's reach. Stevenson told me he wanted to run again but that he expected a tough fight for the nomination. Herbert Lehman and Eleanor Roosevelt, however, kept prodding him, insisting the party would turn to him for the 1960 campaign.

"Your support from the Northeastern states," I said, "will be enough to overcome Stuart Symington."

Stevenson shook his head. "It will not be Stuart Symington," he said. "It will be either John Kennedy or Lyndon Johnson."

419

"Well, Kennedy has a great problem as a Catholic, and Johnson has a great problem as a Southerner."

"Those are the only two reasons why I think it can be me," Stevenson said.

But by late spring Stevenson had given up on his chances. I was in Chicago and stopped by his office to give him some speeches I had written. Stevenson read them through, laid them on his desk, and put his hands over them. He said, "I am not going to make it, Harry."

"Who else can make it?" I asked.

"John Kennedy," Stevenson said. "He won the nomination in the primaries. Kennedy will probably win the nomination on the first ballot."

"Estes Kefauver won all the primaries and didn't get the nomination," I offered.

Stevenson shrugged. "This time it's different. If it is not Kennedy, it will be Johnson. Sure as shooting"—he smiled—"it will not be me."

There was something in Adlai's manner as he told me that made me know he believed this in the roots of his soul. After a moment's silence, I asked, "Governor, why are you persevering then?"

Stevenson rose and pulled out a huge file drawer. I saw hundreds of folders inside marked "Herbert Lehman," "Eleanor Roosevelt," "Harry Truman," and the names of many famous liberals. Stevenson pointed to these folders and said, "This is why I am persevering. Because I cannot let them down."

I realized Adlai Stevenson was his own victim. He was captive of a cult his own presence had brought into being, and now he could not convince the cult he had no more magic. The cult is for the backwoods, not for the hard and realistic center stage of politics. I left Stevenson that afternoon with more admiration for him than ever.

I covered the convention for the Bell-McClure Syndicate, and I was in Los Angeles a few days early. On the Saturday before the convention convened, I went over to interview Jack Kennedy in one of the hotel suites his staff had rented. I talked with him alone. When he asked if I was still for Stevenson, I said, "As a reporter and a citizen, I hope Adlai Stevenson wins."

Kennedy asked, "If I win, how will you feel?"

I said, "I will go all out for the Democratic nominee."

John Kennedy said, "If I win, I will need all the help I can get from people who are not themselves Catholics. I will need them to clarify the issue of the separation of church and state."

Stevenson was a delegate from Illinois, and consequently he was on the floor of the convention. I talked to him frequently. I heard Newton Minow, his law partner, urge him constantly to come out for Jack Kennedy. Stevenson said he preferred not to do it, remembering, I suppose, all those people who had worked so hard for him over the last eight years.

When Kennedy won on the first ballot, Newton Minow said sadly, "You made a big mistake."

Stevenson shrugged.

Julian Scheer, the Charlotte *News* columnist, and I both knew Bobby Kennedy. We went up to his hotel room in the Los Angeles Ambassador the next morning. We wanted to ask who the Vice Presidential nominee would be. Bobby admitted us, and when we got in the room, we found the only other occupant was Ted Kennedy, now the United States Senator from Massachusetts.

"It will be Lyndon B. Johnson," whispered Bobby to our question. Since Robert Kennedy and I were casual friends and since Julian was slated for an administration job if Kennedy won, I think Bobby felt free to express himself with us. But he was quite matter-of-fact about Lyndon Johnson. If he did not jump for joy over Lyndon's selection, let it be understood Robert Kennedy rarely jumped for joy over anything.

"Was anyone else considered?" I asked.

"Scoop Jackson and Symington," he said. "But not really." He told us the formal announcement would only come from John F. Kennedy that afternoon.

Julian and I stuck pretty close to Robert Kennedy all day. We were joined by other newsmen from time to time. Since we knew the secret they all were seeking, everything he said had greater significance to us than to our colleagues. When the future Attorney General went to Jack Kennedy's suite, we did not, of course, follow him inside, but we knew something was going on. There was an adjoining suite and it was from the discussion in there that the newspapers first built up the story of dissension over Lyndon B. Johnson's nomination.

In this adjoining suite were Mayor Richard Daley of Chicago, Mayor Robert Wagner of New York, and other Democratic leaders from around the country. It was they who objected to Lyndon B. Johnson because they were afraid that Texas would not help the ticket in the big cities. Daley did most of the talking. Jack Kennedy asked his brother to report this to Lyndon Johnson. If there was a floor fight, was Johnson prepared to go all out?

Johnson said he would fight for the Vice Presidency. With that, Jack Kennedy made his announcement. It was now 3 P.M., and Julian and I had not missed a single heartbeat since 11 A.M.

After two or three conversations with Governor LeRoy Collins of Florida and a request from the Democratic national campaign headquarters, I agreed to make personal appearances in behalf of John F. Kennedy's candidacy. I was to give five speeches in Michigan and twenty in California, at meetings prearranged by the national campaign committee. I was to deliver lectures to Jewish and Negro audiences.

In the beginning of the campaign John F. Kennedy did not have Negro support. There was no reason for Negroes to support him. As a Congressman and a Senator he had not been conspicuously or even particularly active in civil rights legislation.

During the campaign of 1960, however, he telephoned Mrs. Martin Luther King when her husband, the religious leader of the protest movement of the Southern Negro, was given a four-month prison sentence technically for not having a Georgia driver's license. Perhaps Mr. Kennedy's call was dictated by a humane concern for the welfare of Dr. King, but the opposition nevertheless interpreted his telephone call politically, and it is also true that Mr. Kennedy made political capital on it. Thus the careers of Martin Luther King and John F. Kennedy coincided in decisive fashion during the 1960 Presidential campaign.

Senator John F. Kennedy and Vice President Richard M. Nixon, as had Presidential candidates before them, thought of the Negro in terms of a momentary political advantage. Each planned a gambit for white and Negro votes. It was a political gamble for both Kennedy and Nixon. Robert Kennedy's first reaction to the news of Dr. Martin Luther King's sentence was: "Four months for a traffic violation?"

The Kennedy commitment on behalf of the victimized Dr. King may have been shrewd politics, but the Kennedys had no way of knowing that this momentary intervention by its very nature had to become an absolute policy. Nor did Mr. Nixon realize

422

that his decision not to intervene on that particular day would end all hopes of his participation in the social revolution of the American Negro.

I digress because I was in a position to see Negroes realizing John F. Kennedy really was concerned over their welfare. From lukewarm receptions I progressed to thunderous applause in Michigan. Since I was delivering the same speech, in the same manner, it was not my own improvement that won me cheers, it was that an ethnic bloc of the electorate had found a champion.

In California I was joined by Carl Sandburg, whom the national campaign committee had also impressed into John F. Kennedy's very own lecture bureau. The audience was usually Jewish. Hugh O'Brian or Shelley Winters would introduce me, and I would go through Kennedy's record as a Congressman and Senator, and then I would cite the promises that could only be realized with his election. It was not hard to arouse these crowds. When the audience was at a fever pitch, I would say, "Folks, I have a bonus for you—Carl Sandburg."

Carl would shuffle from the wings onto the stage, shake hands with me, turn to the audience, and say in his measured tones, "We are just a couple of North Carolina boys plugging for a Boston Irishman."

We met Kennedy once in California. That meeting was brief. Kennedy wanted to know what kind of reception were we getting and what did we think. I told him excitedly, "You are going to win." Carl nodded his head and said slowly, "You are the next President."

With Kennedy's inauguration, the race issue passed from protest into demonstration. There were the Freedom Riders, the sit-ins, and the marches. As the Negroes became more militant, the South became more intransigent. The police in the South unleashed dogs on the demonstrators; they battered them with hoses; they tortured them with cattle prods.

Kennedy had the prescience that things were boiling up, that the explosion was nearing. His intuition was right. Things did explode with the Court order to the University of Mississippi to admit James Meredith. The Kennedys tried everything to see that Meredith's registration was peaceful. Robert Kennedy even called one of the most famous football heroes of the nation, a Southerner and a graduate of the University of Mississippi, Charlie Conerly, the quarterback of the New York professional football Giants. Bobby asked for a statement, not praising integration, merely urging compliance with the law to save the honor of beloved Ole Miss. Conerly, who played on a team which numbered many Negroes, thought it over for three days. Sadly he gave the Attorney General his answer, "I cannot do it."

With the riot at Oxford, Kennedy began to anticipate the need for civil rights legislation. I believe he must have asked several editors and writers for their opinion on the race issue, sentiments he could use when the time came.

I sent him a lengthy memorandum which I gave first to Ed Murrow. Murrow wrote me: "The Kennedy Declaration sings out loud and clear. I passed it on and the transmission was tinged with envy. Would that I could write so well."

The memorandum is too long to quote in its entirety, but these are its salient points:

The Constitution of the United States of America charges me, the President, to take care that the laws be faithfully executed. It confers great powers upon the President that this be done. The President can veto bills passed by the Congress, he can reconvene the Congress when he thinks necessary, he can dispatch troops anywhere in the world, he can even, as Abraham Lincoln did, suspend the writ of habeas corpus.

What the Constitution does not provide for is the easy and quick resolution of a crisis which involves Americans against Americans—the white race against the Negroes. The Constitution does not make this provision because read rightly the Constitution presumes not only upon the conscience and the justice of the President but upon the conscience and the justice of the American people.

In truth all documents, no matter how revered or how aged, are meaningless unless just citizens and just officers of the government read them in good conscience. All documents are meaningless, all charters and declarations are meaningless, all constitutions are meaningless if people do not know right from wrong. . . .

Neither the President nor any of his cabinet members nor any federal officials can change the hearts of men. The individual alone, abetted by his belief in God, can change his heart. But the President and the officers of the government can say, "Obey the law." The Judaic-Christian civilization strives and still strives for an equality of love. The President and the government cannot expect to succeed where these religious concepts sometimes fail. All the President can do is pledge the efforts of his office. To that end I so pledge.

I therefore direct the executive branch of this government that:

1. No citizen shall hereafter be denied appointment to and employment and promotion in any federal agency solely because of his race, color, creed, or ethnic origin;

2. No person employed by or serving in any federal agency or in any federal government or in any federal employment under federal supervision or support shall be separated from other persons similarly employed or in separate service solely because of race, color, creed or ethnic origin;

3. No person shall be denied access to service in any agency in any manner supported by federal funds, grants-in-aid, loans, licenses, or insurance on the base of race, color, creed or ethnic origins; nor shall a person be denied complete freedom from access or use of facilities of transportation and trade in all interstate activities and commerce;

4. No federal funds or other forms of federal assistance shall be made available to any state or local government or private institution or agency or facilities which exclude or segregate any citizens on the basis of race, creed, or color or ethnic origin;

5. No federal contract shall be entered into in any state, private, firm or institution which refuses employment and promotion opportunities to any citizen because of his race, creed, color, or ethnic origin.

To implement this code I direct every federal agency to review its present policies, to develop procedures, and to make assignments from among its personnel to see that this Declaration is executed not only throughout the agency but also in all programs which are supervised by the agencies, although administered by local or state government or private institutions or organizations.

Further, I hereby establish a Civil Rights Declaration Commission to coordinate and supervise the efforts of the respective agencies in implementation of this Declaration.

I've heard it said that this is an action long awaited of us by many of the nations of the world; I believe this Declaration on behalf of the American people once and for all to do away with the barrier of a man's color and creed, as a true measure of his worth will win us friends.

Emerson wrote: "Your manners are always under examination and by committees little suspected but are awarding or denying you very high prizes when you least think of it."

I'm sure our example will continue to help men everywhere who struggle for their freedom.

But what the rest of the world sees and hears us do is not as important as what we see and hear ourselves do, and this is not as important as what God sees and hears us do, for it is He who hath made us and not we ourselves.

Ralph McGill suggested much the same in his memorandum, and I am sure many other writers also urged these policies. All of them were incorporated by John Kennedy in his Fair Housing and Equal Employment Directives, which were issued during the second year of his Presidency.

When ex-Governor George Wallace stood in the door to block the Court-ordered registration of two Negroes in the University of Alabama, John Kennedy, on June 11, 1963, over national television and radio, proposed a new civil rights bill. When he concluded his address, I determined on writing a book about the New Frontier administration which I would call *Mr. Kennedy and the Negroes.*

This book would be an attempt to assess how successfully Mr. Kennedy had played politics as an emancipator or civil rights President. Whether he was a civil rights President because of political expediency, or because he could not avoid being a civil rights President, or because he believed in this cause with all his intellectual fervor and being—all this is irrelevant. He remains the civil rights President.

What impressed itself quite clearly in the three years of Mr. Kennedy's Presidency was that his politics had come to include a total commitment to the social revolution of the American Negro.

I had conceived the idea the winter before when I was invited to the centennial celebration of the Emancipation Proclamation at the White House. I did not talk to the President about this project then mostly because I was involved in writing *A Little Girl Is Dead.* In fact, all I did talk to him about on that occasion was the exercise then in vogue of marching 50 miles like the Marines.

I said, "I hope you're not going to ask me to walk fifty miles, Mr. President."

Kennedy laughed and said, "That whole idea was Pierre Salinger's. The White House is getting hundreds of letters from doctors all over the country asking, Why are we trying to kill the American constituency?"

426

But on that occasion I did speak tentatively to Arthur Schlesinger, Jr., about the book. I said I would probably need the President's help, and Schlesinger said I was pretty sure to have it.

So that June I broached the idea to Kennedy himself. Kennedy promised his help. All he demurred about was the title. "There's a fine book, *Mr. Lincoln and the Negroes*," he said. "Don't you think *Mr. Kennedy and the Negroes* is presumptuous?"

I said, "You deserve it. You are the second emancipator President. You and Robert Kennedy have smashed the legal remnants of segregation in the South."

What seems obvious to me now but did not then was that John F. Kennedy had a certain affinity for writers. Carl Sandburg and I had campaigned for him in California, so if we had due bills, we could call them in. But I think Kennedy liked reporters and journalists and writers. The novelist Norman Mailer says what impressed him most with Kennedy when he met Kennedy was not that Kennedy discussed his books but that he discussed *The Deer Park* which Mailer confesses was not well received.

My guess is that Kennedy liked writers because he was not in awe of them. He himself could have been a writer, and perhaps a great one, perhaps not, but at any rate a reputable one. A man who had written a book which won the acclaim of *Profiles in Courage* would never hunger for expression since he had achieved it brilliantly. But a man will not write about politics when he can run for office.

The President wrote a directive to Lee White, his civil rights assistant, asking him to be sure I had access to any information I wanted. Robert Kennedy turned me over to John Doar, one of Burke Marshall's assistants in the Justice Department.

Lee White got me all the past and proposed legislation. He showed me the correspondence from segregationist governors, as well as the reports of telephone conversations the President had conducted with governors like George Wallace and Ross Barnett. Governor Barnett kept thanking the President for all the good work he was doing for the chicken farmers and in the next breath offered to send James Meredith to the best school up North.

John Doar gave me all the materials of the technical workings of the Justice Department. It was Doar who showed me the directive Kennedy sent to the Justice Department with the handwritten injunction: "Get the road maps and go."

This injunction was prompted by Senator James O. Eastland's warning. The President and Attorney General had decided to correct voting inequities in the South. Eastland said, "Whatever the Supreme Court decides is not the law of the land, but the law of the case. So you will have to sue us for every registrar, every Negro, and every county in the South."

"Get the road maps and go," was John Kennedy's answer.

Without Lee White, John Doar, Burke Marshall, and Bobby Kennedy, I could not possibly have written the book. One federal action becomes in time a mountain of transcripts which would fill a library room. The case of the *United States v. Louisiana,* to cite one example, ran to something like 400 volumes. But John Doar and Bobby Kennedy summarized the history of the case for me in fifty pages. I, in turn, made a shorter summary. I was able to tell my readers how the Justice Department lawyers went into Louisiana and approached hundreds upon hundreds of Negro shacks, asking the occupants, "When did you register? When did you *try* to register? When did you vote? When did you *try* to vote? What happened?" These lawyers also asked, "What school did you go to?" The Justice Department lawyers next questioned hundreds of one-mule white farmers, asking them the same questions.

The gravamen of the Justice Department's charge was that the deficiency in education was ignored in the case of the white registrant and overvalued in the case of the colored registrant. The registrars of Louisiana were discriminating. Judge J. Minor Wisdom ruled in favor of the Justice Department. He directed the registrars to cease discriminatory practices, insisting "a wall of separation must come down."

There were many other cases and histories which the hardworking Doar and Marshall provided. I stayed in Washington but three weeks, and I had all the basic research when I went home. During that three weeks I saw John Kennedy three times. He always knew what I was after. One morning he told me that two of his close friends in the Senate had just left the White House. They were Senators George Smathers of Florida and Richard Russell of Georgia. They were opposed to the Civil Rights Bill and had come to ask him why the Negroes were so special. They argued that the Irish came to America without a dime, had suffered the advertisements which stated "No Irish Need Apply," and now one of them without special legislation was the President. The

Jews had come, had suffered in the sweatshops, and they, too, without special legislation had become governors, Cabinet members, and Senators. The Slavs, the Poles, the Hungarians were equally disadvantaged. Now they sent their sons to Cornell. Why, these two Senators asked, did the Negroes need special legislation?

"Do you know what I told them?" Kennedy said.

I knew it would be good.

"I told them," he said, "that you are forgetting one thing in your recital—color. This man, unlike the Irishman, cannot change his name to hide his origin. He cannot move away to achieve anonymity. No one will let him forget he is a black man. That is why he must have legislation every step of the way, and I mean to give it to him while I am in the White House."

The last time I saw Kennedy was the morning before I returned to Charlotte. I was waiting in the anteroom for my interview when John Kenneth Galbraith exited from the President's office. Galbraith looked at me and shouted, "That's the best thing you've ever written."

In the President's office, Kennedy rose behind his desk, pointed that characteristic finger, and also shouted, "That's the best thing you've ever written."

Both were referring to the one-sentence lead editorial which had appeared in the *Carolina Israelite* three days before. I said of Barry Goldwater's increasing popularity among Republicans, "I always knew the first Jewish President would be an Episcopalian." One of the columnists on the New York *Times* had picked it up and quoted it and it was in the *Times'* pages that Kennedy and Galbraith read it. I did not realize it then—flushed with my own cleverness—it was a good memory to have of my last meeting with the thirty-fifth President.

To prepare the book, I had Richard for the historical research and some of the writing, but for the material from the Justice Department I had to call on my good friend J. Spencer Bell, of the United States Court of Appeals for the Fourth Circuit.

Spencer gave so willingly of his time that I was embarrassed. It was Spencer who gave me real insight into the workings of the Supreme Court. Spencer told me that in writing about the Supreme Court ruling of 1954 which ruled segregation in the public schools unconstitutional, I must not pay heed to the critics who held this ruling was not legal but sociological. "Everyone forgets," said Spencer, "that *Plessy v. Ferguson,* which established the principle of separate but equal, was also a sociological decision."

Homer Plessy, one-eighth Negro and seven-eighths white, was arrested in Louisiana when he refused to ride in the colored coach of a railroad train as required by the Louisiana statutes. He claimed that the Jim Crow statutes violated the Thirteenth and Fourteenth Amendments and named as defendant Judge Ferguson of Louisiana, assigned to conduct Plessy's criminal trial. Plessy lost in the Louisiana courts, and the Supreme Court affirmed their rulings. Plessy had argued that state-enforced segregation stamped Negroes with a badge of inferiority. The High Court disagreed. The Court argued that segregation did not deprive the Negro of any basic rights as a citizen except through his own choice. With separate but equal facilities it is harder and harder to see how a man can be a citizen under separate but equal justice. For the Supreme Court in its *Plessy v. Ferguson* decision was commanding Negroes to be inferior citizens of their states and to that extent rejecting them as full citizens of the United States. It is manifestly impossible to imagine how, in any operative sense, a man can be a citizen without fellow citizens once in a while associating with him.

This reasoning was Spencer's. "At least," concluded Spencer, "point out that the Warren Court quoted reputable authorities. They quoted Gunnar Mrydal. The Court in eighteen ninety-six quoted nobody. They were making sociological judgments pure and simple and bad sociological judgments at that."

Like Judge John J. Parker, Spencer believed segregation did not come down from heaven; it came down from law. And law can change. Once upon a time we executed pickpockets. Some states now do not execute murderers.

I learned of John Kennedy's assassination driving back from the post office, where I had just sent Bill Targ the first five chapters of the Kennedy book. When I was able to concentrate on this work again, it was I who began to worry about the title. I did not want my readers to think I was publishing another assassination account. I did not want *Mr. Kennedy and the Negroes* lost among the spate of books recounting the glamor of John Kennedy's administration. World Publishing said I had written a good book, and a good book deserves a good title.

I think the book had a far greater success than its sales indicated. In hardback it sold 30,000 copies. But the State Department has reprinted it in softback in eleven languages. It was included in the kit every delegate to the Democratic National Convention received in 1964. It is still in print.

One of the congratulatory messages I received upon its publication was from John Kennedy's widow:

January 19, 1965

DEAR MR. GOLDEN:

I do want to thank you for sending me the bound edition of "Mr. Kennedy and the Negroes," and I know this book will be of great significance to many people throughout the country.

You were kind to remember me and your book will certainly be a most important edition to the Kennedy Library.

With best wishes,

Sincerely,
JACQUELINE KENNEDY

Mr. Harry Golden
c/o The Carolina Israelite
P.O. Box 2505
Charlotte 1, North Carolina

Which proves I am one of the few writers in the world to get on the good side of Jackie Kennedy. While I never brought up the subject of William Manchester and *his* book, *The Death of a President,* to Robert Kennedy, he brought it up to me. With that passionate pilgrim stare, he said, "Manchester kept telling us he didn't want any money, insisted he didn't want the money. And he sold that book to *Look* magazine for six hundred and twenty-five thousand dollars." I had the feeling another Jimmy Hoffa was on the loose. If there was a fault in Bobby, it was that: Disagreement made you enemies, and all his enemies were Jimmy Hoffas.

The next time Bobby mentioned William Manchester and the money, I said, "When I wrote *Mr. Kennedy and the Negroes,* I took no vow of poverty." Bobby repeated his charge as though he hadn't heard me. By this time I was confident William Manchester could take care of himself, so I left the subject alone.

I was pretty close to Bobby Kennedy, at least as close as an older man and an editor can be to a younger man who could become the political leader of the free world. We became close friends when he asked me to help him in his campaign for the

Senate seat in New York. If I wanted to talk it over, he suggested meeting him in his home in Washington, Hickory Hill.

When I presented myself at the door, I was questioned on my name and identity by one of his children. I said, "I'm Harry Golden." The little girl ran through the house shouting, "Daddy! Daddy! Mr. Goldwater is here."

Bobby Kennedy and I had been in almost constant communication for three years about the civil rights struggle. I had no idea of participating in a campaign in New York. The carpetbag issue was hot enough without a Tarheel intruding. But Bobby was terribly worried about the "Jewish vote" in New York. He told me, "The vast majority are Democrats; if the Democrats vote for me, I'm in—but I do not believe I can overcome wholesale defections."

Senator Kenneth Keating had refused to endorse Barry Goldwater, his party's Presidential candidate, and made no attack on the national administration, which was politic, considering those dozen or more "Johnson and Keating" committees in the Jewish districts.

Abe Feinberg, the philanthropist; Max Schuster, the publisher; and David Dubinsky, the labor leader, said the Democrats needed all the help they could get. So I volunteered, on one condition: There must be no remuneration, and I was to pay my own expenses.

As one who had worked in the civil rights movement for more than twenty years, I was fascinated by the work of Attorney General Robert Kennedy. What made the new Attorney General so effective was that until he assumed his Cabinet post, he had no idea of the dimensions the social revolution of the American Negro had assumed. As Attorney General, Robert Kennedy encountered wrongs he could hardly believe existed in our time. Whenever he had to talk with Governors Ross Barnett and George Wallace or Southern peace officers or sheriffs, Bobby kept asking, "But don't you know this is wrong?"

I had every reason for supporting Robert Kennedy for Senator. I sent a personal letter to my 6,000 subscribers in New York State. Soon my bookkeeper sent me clusters of little red cards: "These people refuse to renew because of your support of Robert Kennedy." I received 100 more angry letters from civic leaders and rabbis, some of them my devoted personal friends. "How ungrateful can you be working against this wonderful man, Kenneth

Keating, our best friend in Washington, the most effective friend of Israel?" they said.

I discussed all this with Bobby at breakfast one morning at the Hotel Carlyle. This young Irishman sounded like a rabbinical student who had just spent a year listening to Horace Kallen and Maurice Samuel.

"I can understand it," Kennedy said. "There's still a deep scar for what the church did to the Jews—it goes back to the Middle Ages. My brother was up against the same thing, but Jack's advantage in New York was that his opponent was Nixon and the Jews could not take Nixon. My opponent, on the other hand, is a man greatly admired and, from what I have seen, greatly beloved by the Jewish people. Furthermore, the Jews, since the days of the Cossacks, look with suspicion on the investigator, and that's all I've ever really been so far, an investigator and a cop."

On another occasion I asked him why his candidacy aroused such opposition from intellectuals like Baldwin, Vidal, Mailer, I. F. Stone, and other people who have been in the forefront of the civil rights movement. Bobby replied: "There's only one explanation I can give—many intellectuals resented Jack right up to the time he was taken from us. They have transferred that resentment to a more acceptable target—me. Maybe I'm wrong but that's all I can make of it . . . fellows like Alexander Bickel, knowledgeable men, have pointed to the Jimmy Hoffa thing, and I suspect that's where the 'ruthless' comes in. What they conveniently forget is that the Morals Board of the AFL-CIO drummed Hoffa out of the organized labor on less than half of what our Senate committee and later the Department of Justice uncovered."

When I asked him a question about his father, Bobby said, "I think the cynics have deliberately withheld the fact that my father tipped the balance in favor of lend-lease before the Senate Foreign Relations Committee. The America Firsters thereafter called him worse names than any the liberals have ever had for him." I never brought up Joseph Kennedy again. Bobby had that old-fashioned devotion young sons used to have for their fathers.

Once the campaign really got under way, I made several trips to New York to tape radio broadcasts (three in Yiddish and six in English, of all things) and to appear on a television program, all sponsored by Bobby. On October 21, I canceled several lectures to go to New York to speak to Jewish audiences. The Lib-

433

eral Party and David Dubinsky provided a limousine, and Walter Kirschenbaum, in his off-hours as an official in the License Bureau, volunteered as chauffeur.

Kennedy's plurality was amazing. Bobby ran less than 15 percent behind President Johnson in those districts which had given us so much concern.

If the election had been held on October 15, Senator Keating would have swept these New York City districts.

But the Senator made a mistake during the last two weeks of the campaign. Bobby Kennedy and his supporters were quick to take advantage of it. By October 24 it was clear that Keating had overplayed the Israel issue. The Jews had become embarrassed by this pleading to their special interest. I communicated this to Bobby. Paul Screvane, president of the New York City Council and a Kennedy adviser, had also sensed it. He said, "Let's keep our fingers crossed." On October 29 at P.S. 95 in the Bronx, before a a large audience of working people, I tried it out. I did not mention the words "Jew," "Israel," or "Nasser," but spoke only of Kennedy's hope to help liberalize the immigration laws and support a strong federal aid to education bill. The response was gratifying. We were on our way.

Senator Keating went right on, and some of his supporters now compounded the blunder. The Citizens for Keating Headquarters at 521 Fifth Avenue distributed a poster, NASSER FOR KENNEDY, which they quickly withdrew for another version, NASSER AGAINST KEATING. Herbert Brownell, Keating's manager, told a reporter, "It's factual." Knowing of the growing embarrassment of the Jewish voters, we literally jumped for joy. It had its effect also on the non-Jewish voters: "Why is he always talking about Nasser?" asked the Irish, the Italians, the Puerto Ricans, and the plain ordinary Protestants.

At an outdoor rally sponsored by the members of the International Ladies Garment Workers Union everybody spoke for Bobby Kennedy, including Dubinsky, Bob Wagner, and Hubert Humphrey, who held up the NASSER FOR KENNEDY circular and shouted, "If you see any of these circulars, here's what to do with them," and Senator Humphrey tore it up in a million pieces and threw it into the air. The next day the *Jewish Day-Morning Journal* and the *Jewish Daily Forward* came out for Bobby Kennedy. There was still a hurdle—the Keating challenges to Bobby for a debate.

434

Luckily Bobby Kennedy's liaison in these negotiations was this same fascinating Italian, Paul Screvane. The idea was not to debate on television but to lose as little ground as possible in the denial. Bobby Kennedy and Paul Screvane pulled it off. This was wise, as the California campaign between Salinger and Murphy proved. A highly aware Pierre Salinger debated on TV with an opponent who had spent forty years of his life before the cameras.

Bobby Kennedy said, "Why enter a fight where the most you can do is break even? Mr. Keating looks like everybody's grandfather; he's a beautiful man. On TV he will read what the New York *Times* and the *Reporter* said about him, and then this ruthless young Irishman will talk about the amendments Mr. Keating voted on, and where will this get me? Let's get him on radio." Keating challenged these tactics. But the main test was yet to come. He bought one hour of prime television time on NBC and dared Kennedy to appear.

It was a serious moment in the campaign, and Bobby called for a full discussion. He was in Great Neck, resting after a strenuous day. There were ten of us at headquarters, each with a telephone receiver. Kennedy talked to each of us three times—asking an opinion on whether to go. Soon Ed Guthman, the press officer, shouted, "It's now the hawks and doves. Let's see how it turns out." The leading hawks turned out to be Arthur Schlesinger and I, who argued, "This is it, Bobby, you must go this time." The doves were led by Paul Screvane, who kept repeating two words—"absolutely no." When it came around to me the second time, I repeated, "This is one time you must go, Bobby."

Kennedy said, "Harry, you've got white hair, you debate Keating." When it got around for the third time to Schlesinger, who repeated the argument, Bobby said, "Art, that's why I'm the candidate and not you."

Screvane and Bobby prevailed. The former Attorney General finally said, "No, let's get the helicopter and go make a speech someplace—on Long Island maybe. What I lose because I don't go is nothing compared with what I will lose if I go. Let's keep trying to get the fellow on the radio."

Luck was on our side. Four days before the election Barry Gray, who conducts a popular radio program in New York, invited Bobby for a midnight interview. Amazingly, Senator Keating took the bait, demanding equal time. We came well prepared. Seated around Bobby were five assistants with ideas, clippings, and speeches. Senator Keating read what the New York *Times*, the *Reporter*, and the *Nation* said about him, and Bobby asked, "Do you think it's something *special* for a New York Senator to be for civil rights and for all those other liberal measures? I'd like to enumerate now your votes when you were a conservative Congressman representing a conservative constituency."

It was a devastating argument, embarrassingly so, for most of us, including Bobby, were genuinely sorry that our opponent Keating was really such a nice man.

In each of my speeches there was always one question asked about how ruthless Bobby Kennedy was. After several experiments, I found the answer: "His wife and children don't think he's ruthless."

After Bobby was elected, I saw him several times, usually for lunch in the Senate Dining Room. He was often accompanied by Senator Birch Bayh, who was perhaps his closest friend. As often as we met, we discussed the civil rights and the race issues. I remember Bobby saying, "If I were a Negro, I'd riot, too."

"How would you quell the riots?" I asked.

"Jobs, education, housing—more legislation," Bobby said.

Birch Bayh often assented.

When the critics of the Warren Report started publishing their polemics and critiques, Bobby said to me, "The family is satisfied it is just this one man." I never heard Bobby Kennedy refer to Lee Harvey Oswald by name. He called him "that fellow" or "that man."

What led me to dismiss the Warren Report critics was that Robert Kennedy, at the time of the assassination one of the most powerful men in the United States, would certainly have pursued the conspirators given a single trace of their existence. Ted Kennedy, a Senator, who loved his brother as dearly as Robert, would have turned over every stone in the world to find an accomplice had he believed Oswald had one. In addition to these two men, neither J. Edgar Hoover nor the President of the United States saw any reason to disagree with the findings of the Warren Commission.

"I am going to declare for the nomination," Bobby told me over the phone.

"I am not surprised," I said. "I had a hunch you might."

"I'll need you," he said.

"I'm your man."

I do not think that it was Eugene McCarthy's primary victory in New Hampshire that determined Bobby. I incline to think it was the Tet offensive waged by the Vietcong which convinced him the war was lost, that power alone would not win. As a matter of fact the Vietnamese have spent 2,000 years in internecine warfare. The Japanese could not solidify Vietnam, and the Japanese generals realized that their great land army was being wasted. The French could not win with better equipment and more men. We, in our turn, even with helicopters, are coming to realize that soldiers and matériel are at a disadvantage against bandits who know the terrain.

But I did not lend my services to Bobby because I disapproved of the war. I wanted to help make him the President because I thought he was the one man who could bridge the growing distance between white and black Americans, between poor and rich citizens.

California was the key primary. Winning would not guarantee him the nomination, he said, but it would go a long way toward it; losing that primary would close out his chances.

The Kennedy staff set up a series of speeches for me to deliver between San Diego and San Francisco. I spoke to either Jews or Negroes. I always argued the man to unite white and black was Robert Kennedy. More, I said, he was a sure winner. From the beginning I found tremendous support for his candidacy.

Traveling with his staff, I realized Bobby Kennedy's political skill. In every town, large or small, Kennedy collected Spanish-American and Mexican workers. He and his staff taught them to pore over the phone books, calling friends and relatives.

Bobby Kennedy was as diligent as a Tammany Hall sachem in canvassing California precincts. The Tammany Hall leader recruited canvassers and gave each of them a five-cent school notebook and assigned each of them certain blocks of the precincts. They were to call on every family, write down their name and address, and ask certain questions. Of the Jews, they asked about schools and children: "Does your son expect to go to college?" Of the Poles and Italians, about jobs: "Does your husband like his job?"

"Why do you ask these questions?" the Poles, the Jews, and the

Italians asked. The answer: "Big John Mahoney, our candidate for Congress, is interested in you. *He* wants to know."

In California, Bobby's canvassers asked these questions of the Negroes and the Mexican-Americans: "Bobby Kennedy, running for President of the United States, is interested in you. He wants to know."

Bobby told them, "Bring back these notebooks filled with names and addresses and the story about jobs and schools."

They scheduled buses to transport potential voters to the registrars. When Bobby Kennedy left a town, he left it with a political apparatus. This apparatus had not been set up before because setting them up takes time and money—and knowledge. But I am positive that Alan Cranston's Senate victory over Max Rafferty in California is in no small way due to the organizations Bobby Kennedy set up five months before. Elections are won or lost to the degree a politician can organize voters. In a few short months Bobby Kennedy made political sophisticates out of vineyard workers and laborers, itinerants and the unemployed, the people who had never before realized the weight of their political leverage.

I finished the last of the scheduled speeches two nights before the primary election. Bobby Kennedy and I went to Kanter's, a Jewish restaurant in Los Angeles. Lots of Jews came over to the table and shook hands with us.

"I am sure I am going to win," Bobby told me. "And I'm going to chase Hubert Humphrey up and down America. And what's more, Eugene McCarthy will help me."

I caught a plane to Atlanta, and winging through the night, I remembered that it was in a Jewish restaurant—Lindy's—that Bobby and I had first become friendly.

I learned of the shooting in the early morning as I was preparing to go to New York. At the Algonquin Hotel in New York that noon, the reporter Jimmy Breslin called and said, "The Senator does not have a chance. He is going to die."

A terrible loneliness washed over me. That loneliness did not afflict only those who knew and loved Robert Kennedy; it afflicted millions of sensitive Americans. When President John F. Kennedy was murdered in Dallas, I remember the rage that consumed me. But we are living, as the Reverend Ralph Abernathy says, in a decade of assassination, and the rage has passed into aching loneliness and often despair.

We despair because assassination has become a nervous impulse in American life. The disaffected walk our streets, crouch in hotel kitchens, lever high-powered rifles through rooming-house windows.

Why we harbor the murderously disaffected is best answered by the psychiatrists and sociologists. The disaffected are usually the poor and the impotent, and they shoot the rich and the strong. The disaffected who so change our life may be deranged and deluded, but almost always they are propelled by some political motivation. Sirhan Sirhan, brooding over the Arab defeat, did not kill an Israeli minister, which is how a Jordanian patriot might react; he killed one of Israel's advocates, which did nothing for his purpose but brought tumult and destruction upon ours. The disaffected have turned homicidal. The superfluous have turned dangerous. The loneliness descends finally in the realization that this peril has no meaning.

The Kennedy family sent me a telegram which noted the pew I was to occupy in St. Patrick's Cathedral and the number of the car I was to board on the train. I did not go to Robert Kennedy's funeral, however. That Saturday I went to Memphis, where my son Billy was getting married. They expected me. It was where I belonged.

Epilogue

FINISHED, finished at last with the book I had delayed writing for so long. I always wanted to wait with this book, not because I was modest or humble, but because I wanted to see how things would turn out. I was waiting for that event or series of events that would not only climax the work but lend it scope and significance, make every word and sentence and paragraph instantly meaningful and dramatic. But in the end, I had to forsake my personal apocalypse. What made me commence this book was the realization that I was no different from any other man; I was growing old; I was mortal.

In December, 1966, I went to Charlotte Memorial Hospital for an emergency gallbladder operation. My dear friend Dr. Raymond Wheeler made a midnight diagnosis of this condition. Then my friend Anita Brown called Dr. Paul Sanger, who rushed to the hospital with his colleague, Dr. Harry Daugherty. These three doctors spent two nights sleeping in the hospital, fortunately for me because after the operation, I stopped breathing. The doctors performed a tracheotomy. For four days I lay in a deep coma in the intensive care unit. Drs. Wheeler, Langer, and Daugherty saved my life.

When I came out of it and, in fact, still underwent an additional operation for gallstones, I thought, *What a prosaic way to die.* An infected gallbladder is an unromantic killer, but it would make me as dead as the next man. That infected gallbladder could have proved the most ruthless of all censors. Not to have written the book I wanted would have been sheer negligence. I wanted the people who are important to me to know how I saw things, felt them, what I thought some sixty-odd years was all about. I had been spared for this.

In the beginning, I thought I would write a story about a newsboy who sold papers outside the Little Hungary Restaurant on East Houston Street and who grew up to publish his own newspaper in a city miles and years removed from his imagination. But then I realized it wasn't my newspaper or me which was important; it was the miles and the years. The problem, as Paul Sanger once put it, "How to traverse those miles and years, that's what you're after, isn't it, Harry?"

Dr. Paul Sanger parked his big Lincoln in front of my house every night at 6 P.M. and came inside and we spent an hour talking. Paul Sanger used to sit on the couch, sometimes with a bourbon, sometimes not, and say, "Start talking," as though I were his mentor.

The truth is I learned more from him than he did from me. Many of the things I've written have been filled with insights and conclusions about health and medicine that could only have come from one of the premier doctors of the country. Paul had helped develop one of the machines which made open-heart surgery possible, and he traveled all over the world teaching other doctors how to operate it. He was a great humanitarian, deeply concerned with the welfare of the world and with its people. Paul Sanger brought to philosophy and politics the same thought that he brought to science and to medicine: "There is no pain on earth like the pain of a new idea."

Dr. Sanger died of cancer in Houston, Texas. He was a brave man to the end, but still the scientist, trusting that if anything could be done, science would do it. I had wanted very much for him to see how I traversed those miles and years we talked about.

I had one friend less. Even as I write this epilogue, I learned three good friends died within a month of one another: Ralph McGill, publisher of the Atlanta *Constitution;* Bill Baggs, editor of the Miami *News;* and John Steinbeck, Nobel Prize-winning author. An old man has fewer and fewer friends each year. The longer I waited, therefore, the fewer there would be of those friends to read over and try to understand what I thought I was all about.

I wanted to describe the tremendous history an individual sees in a single lifetime. When my father was a little boy, Bismarck had not yet become the political master of Europe. In fact, my father was fourteen years old when the French were beaten at Sedan and Bismarck crowned the first William Kaiser of a unified Germany.

I remembered the *Verein* doctor who worked in the days before specialized medicine and lacked the wonderful remedies and specialized skills doctors command today. These doctors were hired by the Jewish fraternal orders and societies, called *Vereins* which charged their members 50 cents every three months.

These wonderful men, the *Verein* doctors, climbed four or five flights of tenement stairs countless times a day. When they discovered tuberculosis in the chest of a sweatshop worker, they knew they could not advise him to go to a warmer and drier climate. This man had a wife and four children in the house and couldn't afford to lose one day's wages. What could the doctor do for him? Often only prescribe cough medicine and tell the workingman to rest as much as possible after work, and once in a while the *Verein* doctor would write on the prescription slip, "Join the Cloakmakers' Union."

The *Verein* doctor is no more. But while I lay unconscious in the intensive care unit, a colored sharecropper recuperated beside me, his therapies and medication and care supported by Medicare, which will one day try to save all of us from the ravages of illness—rich or poor, successes or failures.

That a colored sharecropper left the hospital on the same day I did is, for me, part of the American dream, an idea with no parallel in history. Each of us can jot down a version of the American dream, and I suspect each version would have validty. Essentially, the dream is the opportunity to enter the open society on the basis of character, talent, and willingness to participate, to be involved in the common welfare and security.

This idea is uniquely American. Even in sister democracies we find that the economic and social classes are still stratified to a considerable degree. The apprentice to a tailor will become a tailor. The boy who throws the peanuts at the cricket game will grow up to be the foreman of the boys who throw the peanuts at the cricket game. But in the American dream that boy can become the center fielder.

This privilege is not handed us on a silver platter. There are many heartaches and many struggles, because this American dream needs to be guarded night and day, guarded from those who believe history goes in a straight line and who say, as they have said at many critical moments, "Let us stop the process; let us digest our gains; let us do it later, gradually maybe."

We have another such crisis today. Yet the racial crisis that invades the American conscience today invades it at a time when it must be united and ready for the most crucial struggle of its history. Even in President Jefferson's day, with continents remote from one another and with communication primitive, the author of the Declaration of Independence realized that we must have "a decent respect to the opinions of mankind."

It was wanting to say this, among other things, that lent urgency to my efforts. No, I realized, I couldn't wait to see how things turned out. I couldn't afford to. Now was the right time. The only time is now.

Index

447